EARLY CHILDHOOD EDUCATION

EARLY CHILDHOOD EDUCATION

An International Encyclopedia

Volume 3
O–Z

Edited by
Rebecca S. New and Moncrieff Cochran

PRAEGER

Westport, Connecticut
London

Library of Congress Cataloging-in-Publication Data

Early childhood education [four volumes] : an international encyclopedia / edited by Rebecca
S. New and Moncrieff Cochran.

    p. cm.

    Includes bibliographical references and index.

    ISBN 0-313-33100-6 (set : alk. paper)—ISBN 0-313-33101-4 (vol 1 : alk. paper)—
    ISBN 0-313-33102-2 (vol 2 : alk. paper)—ISBN 0-313-33103-0 (vol 3 : alk. paper)—
    ISBN 0-313-34143-5 (vol 4 : alk. paper)

    1. Early childhood education—Encyclopedias.   I. New, Rebecca Staples.   II. Cochran,
    Moncrieff.

  LB1139.23.E272   2007

  372.2103—dc22   2006035011

British Library Cataloguing in Publication Data is available.

Library of Congress Catalog Card Number: 2006035011
ISBN: 0-313-33100-6 (set)
      0-313-33101-4 (vol. 1)
      0-313-33102-2 (vol. 2)
      0-313-33103-0 (vol. 3)
      0-313-34143-5 (vol. 4)

First published in 2007

Praeger Publishers, 88 Post Road West, Westport, CT 06881
An imprint of Greenwood Publishing Group, Inc.
www.praeger.com

Printed in the United States of America

The paper used in this book complies with the
Permanent Paper Standard issued by the National
Information Standards Organization (Z39.48-1984).

10 9 8 7 6 5 4 3 2 1

Contents

O

Obesity

The World Health Organisation has identified obesity as the most visible pre-
ventable health condition related to illness and premature death worldwide. Many
experts in the fields of child health and nutrition have identified childhood obesity
as a critical health issue for this millennium. The dramatic growth of childhood
obesity both internationally and within the United States parallels the increase
in the prevalence of adult obesity. The prevalence of overweight in the United
States among two- to five-year-old children has doubled during the past thirty
years. High prevalence rates (some studies suggest as many as 28%) of obesity
in low-income preschool children are especially alarming. This epidemic appears
to be the result of many interrelated factors associated with the American culture, including increased serving sizes, increased availability of junk food, unhealthy school lunches, inadequate school physical education, scarcity of safe
playgrounds, busy parents and increasing **television**, video game, and computer
usage. While researchers were initially concerned that overweight and obesity in
childhood would lead to health-related problems and disabilities in adulthood, it
is now clear that there are significant health risks associated with obesity in children. Associated health risks during childhood include elevated blood pressure,
orthopedic impairments such as hip and joint pain, liver disease, and diabetes. In
fact, it appears that there are few organ systems that are not adversely affected
by obesity in childhood, and the consequences begin during childhood.

The significant impact of childhood obesity is not limited, however, to physical, orthopedic, and skeletal problems. "The most widespread consequences
of childhood obesity are psychosocial. Obese children become targets of early
and systematic discrimination" (Dietz, 1998, p. 518). Widespread harassment of
overweight children and weight stereotyping has been shown to begin as early
as nursery school and continue throughout childhood. This rejection as well as
discrimination from their peers causes young children with obesity to have poor
self-esteem and may lead to depression and withdrawal, decreased physical activity, and increased emotion-induced eating. A vicious cycle is often created in

which children who are overweight or obese avoid **play**, particularly active play situations, fearing embarrassment, thus avoiding the very type of physical activity that would increase caloric expenditure and reduce or limit weight gain. Instead, such children are more often engaged in solitary and sedentary activity.

To change the behaviors of young children, interventions with schools and parents are critical. Indeed, respectful and ongoing relationships with **families** may be the most important component in the success of obesity prevention programs for preschoolers for multiple reasons. Parents influence the dietary behaviors of their children by acting as role models and teaching their children about food. The ways in which parents offer food to their children, or their child feeding practices, also influence the subsequent eating behaviors of their children. For example, child feeding practices such as pressuring children to eat healthy foods or restricting them from eating less healthy foods, have been associated with increased preferences for the restricted foods, increased dietary intake, decreased self-regulation of food intake, and increased body weight in children. Parents also play a role in the development of the activity patterns of their children by acting as role models, being physically active with their children, and encouraging or discouraging activity. When both parents are active, a child is almost six times more likely to be active than if neither parent is active (Moore et al., 1991).

Early childhood educators serve a critical role in educating the child as well as the family regarding the necessity of a healthy lifestyle. In addition, it is critical for early childhood educators to create a supportive environment for children of all sizes and shapes. By focusing on health as opposed to weight, early childhood educators create an environment in which all children feel safe to be physically active and to eat healthy. Early childhood educators can create school environments that involve developmentally appropriate physical activity, including opportunities for play and a physical education curriculum, familiarity with basic **nutrition,** and acceptance of body diversity. Within the context of the early childhood **curriculum,** young children can be taught how to garden, how to do basic food preparation, how to actively play, and how to communicate positively with one another. Early childhood educators can also educate parents on topics that facilitate a healthy lifestyle such as goal setting, time management, stress management, communication, and appropriate reward systems. Parents should be encouraged to eat as a family as this is associated with better nutrition and stronger communication. Parents and early childhood educators should also minimize the use of food as a reward or strategy for **behavior management,** as this may encourage a preference for that food as well as an unhealthy association between emotional needs and foods. Finally, early childhood educators and parents should examine their own behaviors as they serve as role models to children.

The increasing rates of obesity in our youngest children necessitate a collaborative effort between early childhood professionals and family members to instill healthy behaviors in children at a young age. The focus on healthy behaviors such as nutrition and physical activity, along with **self-esteem,** are the cornerstones of obesity prevention. Prevention is the most effective way to affect the prevalence of obesity and requires immediate action. *See also* Curriculum, Physical Development; Developmentally Appropriate Practice(s); Parents and Parent Involvement; Peers and Friends.

Further Readings: Birch, L. L., D. W. Marlin, and J. Rotter (1984). Eating as the "means" activity in a contingency: Effects on young children's food preferences. *Child Development* 55, 431–439; Dietz, W. H. (1998). Health consequences of obesity in youth: Childhood predictors of adult disease. *Pediatrics* 101(3 Pt 2), 518–525; Hood, E. (2005). Sharing solutions for childhood obesity. *Environmental Health Perspectives* 113(8), A520–A522; Huettig, C. Adapted Physical Education, Project Inspire. Available online at www.twu.edu/inspire. Huettig, C., S. S. Rich, J. Engelbrecht, C. Sanborn, E. V. Essery, N. DiMarco, et al. (2006). Growing with EASE: Eating, activity, and self-esteem. *Young Children, Journal of the National Association for the Education of Young Children* 61(3), 26–30. Moore, L. L., D. A. Lombardi, M. J. White, J. L. Campbell, S. A. Oliveria, R. C. Ellison (1991). Influence of parents' physical activity levels on activity levels of young children. *Journal of Pediatrics* 118(2), 215–219; Stolley, M. R., M. L. Fitzgibbon, A. Dyer, L. Van Horn, C. K. Kaufer, L. Schiffer (2003). Hip-Hop to Health Jr., an obesity prevention program for minority preschool children: Baseline characteristics of participants. *Prev Med* 36(3), 320–329; World Health Organisation (2003). Information sheet. Obesity and overweight. Geneva, Switzerland: WHO. Available online at www.who.int/dietphysicalactivity/media/en/gsfs_obesity.pdf.

Shannon S. Rich, Charlotte Sanborn, Nancy DiMarco, and Eve Essery

OECD. *See* Organisation for Economic Co-operation and Development

OMEP. *See* World Organization for Early Childhood Education

Open Education

The term *open education* began to be widely used among preschool and elementary school educators in the United States toward the end of the 1960s, and generally referred to a set of practices exemplified in the infant schools (children from five to seven years old) in Great Britain, where it was most often referred to as "the integrated day."

Problems of Definition

The practices alluded to by the term *open education* are difficult to define, although the literature attempting to do so is quite extensive. The formulation of an operational definition is not only difficult, but was strongly resisted by adherents at the time fearing the development of orthodoxies, doctrines, and rigidities. One widely cited definition is "a set of shared attitudes and convictions about the nature of childhood, learning and schooling" (attributed to Charles Silberman, Flurry, 1972, p. 102). The British Infant Schools were brought to the attention of Americans in a series of three articles by Joseph Featherstone that appeared in the monthly publication *The New Republic* in 1967 and later republished in a book titled *Schools Where Children Learn*. Many American educators referred to the practices encompassed by "open education" as "British Infant School," some used labels such as "activity-centered," "humanistic," "child-centered," and "progressive" education. Agreement upon which of these many terms best conveyed the desired connotations of open education was not achieved before the movement itself faded away.

An overview of the many reports and discussions of practices associated with the open education movement suggests that the term mainly served to distinguish it from the formal or closed conventional teacher-centered practices most typical of elementary education at the time. In much of the literature on open education, a strong theme is the quality of relationships among the children and between children and their teachers and the way this quality influences the climate or openness of the classroom. The relationships attributed to open classrooms were characterized by honesty, respect, warmth, trust, and humaneness.

Another source of difficulty encountered in establishing a reliable definition is the great variety of forms in which open education was implemented in the United States. Some classes were organized for mixed age groups, some were open throughout the whole day, and others only partially; still others used the term *open* to describe large spaces shared by several different classes, typically of the same age/grade level. No idea or single version of the open classroom was advocated, endorsed, or adopted by any professional group or association.

The literature on the open education movement that accumulated during the early 1970s clearly indicates that it was stimulated by the impressive developments in British infant education during the 1950s and 1960s and was given strong support in the so-called Plowden Report (Central Advisory Council for Education, 1967).

General Features of Open Education

A review of the literature focused on open education suggests that it varies from formal teacher-centered education on the following six major dimensions: the use of space and time; sources, type, and content of children's activities; and the teacher–child relationship:

1. Use of Space. In varying degrees, the use of space and the movement of children, materials and equipment within it, were less routinized, fixed, or invariable in the open than in the traditional formal classrooms. In open informal classrooms, the movement of children also included locations outside of the classrooms and the school itself more frequently than in the formal classrooms.
2. Activities of the Children. In varying degrees, the range of encouraged and permitted activities was wider, less confined or fixed, and more open-ended in open than in formal classrooms. Activities in open–informal classes transcended the classroom itself.
3. Source of Activity Selection. The more open or informal the classroom, the more likely that the children's activities were pursuits, extensions, or elaborations of their own spontaneous interests, rather than activities selected solely by the teachers or a prescribed curriculum or set of standards.
4. Content and Topics. In varying degrees, the range of topics or content to which the children's attention and energy were guided was wider, and more open-ended than in formal teacher-centered classrooms. Content went beyond classroom, and included field studies now referred to as investigations or projects in which children study first-hand and in depth phenomena in their own environments.
5. Time. In varying degrees, the assignment of time for specified categories of classroom activities was more flexible in open and informal than in teacher-centered classrooms.

6. Teacher–Child Relationships.
   a) In the open classrooms, teacher–child interactions were likely to be initiated as often by the children as they were by the teachers.
   b) In the open classroom, the teacher was more likely to work with individual children than with large groups or all children in the class at one time. The more open the classroom the less often the teacher addressed the whole class as an instructional unit.
   c) In the open informal classroom, the teacher was more likely to be seen giving suggestions, guidance, encouragement, information, directions, feedback, clarification, and/or posing questions, (primarily during individual teacher–child encounters).
   d) In the open classroom, the teacher's response to undesirable behavior was likely to be to offer the child an interpretation of his actions in terms of the classroom group's life and its moral as well as functional implications. The teacher was unlikely to ignore the behavior or to exact punishment.
   e) In the open–informal classroom, teachers were likely to emphasize appropriately high standards of work as in the formal traditional classroom.

In much of the literature concerning open education, there is strong emphasis on achieving an open "climate." The specific cues by which observers judge a classroom climate are not clear. They appear to be related to the wide variety of activities to be seen; the "project-oriented" organization of the room, the active involvement of children with each other and the teacher's constant guidance, and to the encouragement and stimulation of individual and small group work.

The characteristics of open classrooms as outlined earlier could enable teachers to be more responsive to individual children's learning needs and interests. The management of time, space, and materials could provide for the individual and collaborative work that enabled children to be engaged in different activities in the same classroom. The classroom organization could indeed be flexible but was also inevitably complex. Unfortunately, teachers frequently tended to underestimate the demands of this way of teaching; such tendencies to oversimplify these demands led to ineffective educational practice. In turn, critics of open classroom practices were able to show examples of poor teaching where teachers had misunderstood the nature of the challenges and complexity of this way of working with children.

Open education gained in popularity as a set of ideals and practices during the 1960s and early 1970s. This coincided with the social optimism accompanying the civil rights movement, the establishment of the nationwide program for young children called **Project Head Start**, and the promises of increased prosperity and equality of educational opportunity. In the 1960s, there was generally a high level of confidence in national institutions, educational, financial, business, and political. However, the open education movement was relatively short-lived and at least three main factors contributed to its demise by the late 1970s: problems with accountability, teacher education, and research.

The lack of clarity in the descriptions of open classroom management and the nature of the demands on the teacher made open education practices less amenable to control and oversight by school administrators. The different ways in which the ideals of open education were exemplified and the practices were implemented made the training of teachers more difficult for those providing courses to prepare teachers to teach this way. The variations in practice also defied any scientific research and evaluation that might have supported its continuation.

In the social context of education at the time, there was general suspicion that teachers were not taking full responsibility for actively teaching children what they should know and do. It is noteworthy in relation to public perceptions of education that schools operate within and reflect the wider society of which they are a microcosm. Societies are moved by successive waves of social, political, and national optimism and pessimism. Within the United States and the United Kingdom as well, the decline and disappearance of open education coincided with a political shift to the right, a perceived decline in educational standards, a disillusionment with the power of education to improve economic prosperity, and a move away from seeing the role of education as primarily concerned with the development of children as individuals.

In the 1980s, national opinion polls marked a considerable loss of confidence in institutions both public and private including education (Tyack and Cuban, 1995). Public confidence in the nation's schools declined sharply with repeated calls for increased accountability, an emphasis on higher achievement, and "back to basics." Confidence in schools was further undermined by the report of a policy commission on education entitled *A Nation at Risk*. The report blamed the perceived national educational and economic decline on falling standards in school achievement.

Although it was influential only for a few years in the 1960s and early '70s, the open education movement left its mark on a generation of teachers and schools. Many of the same ideals are echoed in recent educational developments in early childhood education influenced by the popularity of practice in the schools of **Reggio Emilia**, the emergent and creative **curriculum**, inquiry-based and **project approaches** at the beginning of the twenty-first century. However, challenging the demands of its implementation, as a set of educational practices, open education belongs to an enduring tradition of progressive educational ideals that remain as a backdrop to American educational innovation.

Further Readings: Central Advisory Council for Education (1967). *Children and their primary schools (Plowden Report)*. 2 vols. London: Her Majesty's Stationery Office; Flurry, Ruth C. (1972). Open education. "What is it?" In Ewald B. Nyquist and Gene R. Hawkes, eds., *Open education. A sourcebook for parents and teachers*. New York: Bantam Books, pp. 102–108; National Commission on Excellence in Education (1983). *A nation at risk: The imperative for education reform;* Tyack, D. and L. Cuban (1995). *Tinkering towards utopia: A century of school reform*. Cambridge, MA: Harvard University Press.

Lilian G. Katz and Sylvia Chard

Organisation for Economic Co-Operation and Development (OECD)

The Organisation for Economic Co-operation and Development (OECD) is an intergovernmental organization of thirty member countries, each committed to democratic government and the market economy. The OECD grew out of the Organisation for European Economic Cooperation (OEEC). Under the Marshall

Plan, the OEEC administered aid from the United States and Canada to support the reconstruction of Europe after World War II. Founded in 1961 and located in Paris, the OECD provides a forum in which governments of advanced industrialized nations can compare their experiences, discuss the problems they share, and seek solutions that can then be applied within their own national contexts (Sullivan, 1997). The OECD increasingly uses its expertise to serve developing countries and emerging markets around the world. Funded by its member countries, the OECD compiles extensive statistics and regularly conducts policy analyses in fields including economics, education, labor, and social affairs.

Education has been an integral part of the OECD's work for many years. Recent activities include country reviews of education systems as well as "thematic reviews" of tertiary education, school-to-work transitions, adult learning, and financing lifelong learning. The OECD publishes annually *Education at a Glance*, a volume of comparative education indicators, and *Education Policy Analysis,* analyses of current education policy issues. The OECD also runs the Programme for International Student Assessment (PISA), an achievement study in more than forty countries. More recently, the OECD's prolific education work has expanded to include the early years of children's lives.

Improving the quality of, and access to, early childhood education and care (ECEC) has become a major policy priority in OECD member countries. In 1998, the OECD launched a thematic review of ECEC policy with the goal of strengthening the foundation of lifelong learning. Taking a broader and more holistic approach than previous cross-national studies, the review provided a comparative analysis of major policy developments and issues in twelve OECD countries— Australia, Belgium, the Czech Republic, Denmark, Finland, Italy, the Netherlands, Norway, Portugal, Sweden, the United Kingdom, and the United States. Since the completion of the first phase of the review in 2001, eight additional countries have been reviewed: Austria, Canada, France, Germany, Hungary, Ireland, Korea, and Mexico. Country-focused background reports and policy analyses are available at http://www.oecd.org/edu/earlychildhood. In addition, the study's comparative report, *Starting Strong: Early Childhood Education and Care* (OECD, 2001) analyzes recent policy developments, highlights innovative approaches, and proposes policy options that can be adapted to different national contexts.

As an international organization, the OECD complements the role of ministries, research institutions, and think tanks by documenting recent developments in the ECEC field and providing a comparative framework with which to analyze current policies. Highlighting innovative policies and practices of other nations also may challenge national decision makers to see their own policies in a new light and consider fresh alternatives. Perhaps most important, OECD activities have brought together policy makers, practitioners, researchers, and advocates from member countries to exchange diverse perspectives on how to improve the care and education of young children. These national and international policy discussions have fuelled important ECEC reforms that will need to be monitored and evaluated in the coming years.

Further Readings: Neuman, M. J., and J. Bennett (2001). Starting strong: Policy implications for early childhood education and care in the U.S. *Phi Delta Kappan* 83(3), 246–254; Organisation for Economic Co-operation and Development [OECD]. 1996.

Making Lifelong Learning a Reality for All. Paris: OECD; OECD (2001). Starting strong: Early childhood education and care. Paris: OECD; Sullivan, Scott (1997). From war to wealth: 50 years of innovation. Paris: OECD; OECD reports and related publications. Available online at http://www.oecd.org/edu/earlychildhood.

John Bennet and Michelle J. Neuman

Osborn, D. Keith (1927–1994)

Dr. D. Keith Osborn was a pioneer in the field of early childhood education in the United States. Osborn earned his bachelor's degree at Emory University, a master's degree in early childhood education at the State University of Iowa, and a doctoral degree at Wayne State University. At the time of his teaching in 1950, Osborn was one of only a few male faculty members in the field of early childhood education.

In 1965, he was the Chairman of the Division of Community Services at the Merrill-Palmer Institute in Detroit, Michigan, where he served for 16 years. In February 1965, he became the Chief Educational Consultant to Project **Head Start** and later a member of the Head Start Planning Committee (Califano, 1997). Concerning the "War on Poverty," the Johnson administration called for "special programs devised for four- and five-year-olds, which will improve the child's opportunities and achievements" (Hymes, 1979, p. 32). Project Head Start emerged as the answer to that call.

Designed as a comprehensive program to be implemented in the summer of 1965, Osborn was called on for his expertise in early childhood education. Specifically, he and his colleagues on the planning committee for Head Start initiated trends such as reduced class sizes for young children, on-site support consultants, and university preparation programs for teachers of young children that have had a long-lasting influence on the field of early childhood education. Osborn was especially instrumental in the initial training of teachers in Head Start as well as the design of high quality early childhood classrooms that support the development of the whole child. Training in early childhood education, as advanced by Professor Osborn, was important from the assistant in the classroom to the university faculty member. Osborn's initial writings on the outcomes of Head Start (archived at the Merrill-Palmer Institute) noted the importance of continuity of high-quality educational environments once children left Head Start. These assertions supported the need for research on programming for young children, including Head Start, to validate the efforts and best practices of early childhood educators.

Osborn, in a printed interview, highlighted his beliefs about the contributions that he made to Head Start that included a focus on the whole child, helping teachers see the importance of including parents, and mechanisms for regional training support. Such support exists to this day in the training and technical staff offices for Head Start and **Early Head Start** in the ten regions of the United States.

Osborn's professional contributions also include service on the planning committee for the Children's Television Workshop, the President's Council on Early Childhood Education, and the President's Council on Television. His work on these committees influenced his research on television violence and young children's perceptions of television. Osborn advocated for changes from the television industry as well as the role that families play in moderating their children's television viewing. His work with early childhood educators focused on practical and developmentally appropriate teaching strategies, including books from the 1950s to the 1970s on cognitive activities, creative activities, and classroom management.

Osborn served as vice president for the **Association for Childhood Education International** (ACEI) from 1959 to 1961. He was a professor of education and child development at the University of Georgia for twenty-six years. Osborn's written work carefully accounted for the history of early childhood education and child development and its influence on current and future practice. In his text, *Early Childhood Education in Historical Perspective*, Professor Osborn chronicled the influences on early childhood education in the United States. His work extended to examining educational experiences for underrepresented groups. Osborn's scholarly record included more than 600 presentations to professional groups and over 100 publications. *See also* National Head State Association.

Further Readings: Califano, J. A. (1997). Head start, a retrospective view: The founders. In E. Zigler and J. Valentine, eds., *Project Head Start: A legacy of the war on poverty*. 2nd ed. Alexandria, VA: The National Head Start Association; Hymes, J. L. (1979). The early days of Project Head Start. *Early childhood education, living history interviews*. Berkeley, CA: Hacienda Press; Osborn, D. K. (1991). *Early childhood education in historical perspective*. Athens, GA: Daye Press, Inc.

Stacey Neuharth-Pritchett, Charlotte Wallinga, and Boyoung Park

Owen, Grace (1873–1965)

Grace Owen was honorary secretary of Britain's Nursery School Association from 1923 to 1933. Owen was a pivotal figure at the City of Manchester Training College for nursery school teachers and ran the Manchester nursery school in the 1920s. When Abigail Adams **Eliot** visited the school in 1921, she described Owen as "scientific and 'broad-minded'" (Beatty, 1995). Owen was a graduate of Teachers College and sister-in-law of psychologist James McKeen Cattell. She was instrumental in the creation of a "federation" of the Child Study Association, the Educational Guild, the Educational Handiwork Association, the Froebel Society, and the Nursery School Association in 1925. Owen also played a key role in designing the Nursery School Association's "Suggested Scheme of Training" for teachers.

In her classic book on *Nursery School Education* (1920), Owen notes that "nearly half of English three and four-year-olds were being perched miserably on wooden benches, chanting the alphabet" (TES Web site) in schools which "laid a deplorable emphasis on definite instruction given to rows of children seated in galleries, kept in order by strict . . . discipline" (Owen, p. 11–12). In opposing these practices, Owen was committed to the notion that "careless gaiety and bubbling fun are true evidences of the untrammeled spirit, and where these are absent, there is something wrong" (p. 24). She lauded the Education Act of 1918 as evidence that "the country as a whole has ... perceived that all schemes of national reconstruction ... are based on shifting sand if the young life of the nation is not sound, healthy and well-developed during the first critical years" (p. 15). Owen was optimistic that the Act's proposed Nursery School would not be "hampered by the traditions of past generations" and thus "free to work out its own salvation" (p. 15).

Nursery schools were to be "included in every housing scheme" (p. 14) and open to all children over the age of two. Owen believed these should "secure ... freedom from nervous strain, and happy occupation for all children" (p. 13), counteracting the effects of "Narrow streets and hard pavements, ill built houses and drab and meager home conditions" (p. 23). Other benefits of the nursery included "grown-up friends who have plenty of time to play with [the children], answer their questions, and wait for them while they slowly learn to perform all the little duties of their daily lives," since "The intelligent child has more bodily and mental activity between the ages of two and six than can be easily satisfied by the very busy people with whom he lives, most of whom do not understand what he does, or wants to know, is at all important" (p. 20).

The nursery school Owen envisioned included "a garden ... because it is for the child an infinite source of ideas of life, growth, form and colour ... it calls out his early sympathies" (p. 23) and a "sunny aspect." Owen specified further details of this nursery school, such that "time-tables are abolished" (p. 17) and "the numbers of children ... in a single Nursery School is strictly limited by the need for individual care and an intimate personal relationship between the children and the mother of the group" (p. 21).

Owen pointed to other virtues of the nursery school experience: "The daily habits that have to be learned ... are not nearly so difficult and irksome when others are sharing the experience ... much that is a real trial when done at home is accomplished with enthusiasm when it is part of the Nursery School routine" (p. 20). And "the growing instinct of self-assertion—healthy in itself—is kept in due check by the absorbing interest of living with other children, and the necessity for the spirit of give-and-take which it involves" (p. 21). In addition, "Generous impulses ... and habits of considerate action can be encouraged and these will surely have their effective influence on that future day when the real fight with selfish impulses must take place" (p. 24).

Owen further asserted "instruction in the Nursery School ... has no place. No reading, writing, no number lessons should on any account be required—no object-lessons ... should be allowed, for the time for these things has not yet come. Up to the age of six the child is usually fully occupied in mind and body with learning from actual experience ... he is experimenting with his limbs, sense, hands, in a thousand ways. But should he show spontaneously a great desire to learn to write or read, he should not be thwarted ... yet no special encouragement should be given—for the energy thus used is diverted from direct experience" (p. 25).

Testing and standard assessments were also emphatically forbidden in Owen's nursery school. "All test of progress should be rigidly excluded.... The Nursery School has nothing to do with standard results as known in the elementary school" (p. 25). Rather, learning is evident through children's "healthy growth of body, increase of physical control and power of sustained attention, multiplying interests, and happy freedom in creative activity" (p. 25). With reference to the training of nursery school personnel, Owen (1920) asserts, "the teacher may or may not be specially trained" (p. 17).

Although Owen recognized that "the right conditions and equipment ... will bring an increase in expenditure per head so far considered sufficient for young children ... it is the time to throw aside half measure, and spend ungrudgingly in an unsparing effort to put the feet of the children of the coming generations firmly on life's path. May public opinion not be found wanting!" (p. 16). *See also* Child Study Movement; Froebel, Friedrich.

Further Readings: Beatty, Barbara (1995). *Preschool education in America: The culture of young children from the colonial era to present.* New Haven, CT: Yale University Press; Owen, Grace, ed. (1920). *Nursery school education.* New York: E.P. Dutton and Company.

Web Site: TES Web site at http://www.tes.co.uk/section/story/?section=Archive&sub_section=Friday&story_id=305019&Type=0.

Gay Wilgus

Owen, Robert (1771–1858)

Robert Owen, industrialist, philosopher, and social and educational reformer, was also the creator of what can be considered the first employment-related early childhood care program in the Western world. But Owen's "Infant School" was far more than a care program for the children of working parents, it was allied with a broader undertaking, the New Institution for the Formation of Character (1816), both located in New Lanark, Scotland.

Owen was born in Newton, Montgomeryshire, Wales, in 1771. By the age of seventeen he was employed in the drapery trade in Manchester, a city that would become the epicenter of the English Industrial Revolution. By 1799, Owen and two partners were in a position to purchase the textile mills of David Dale in New Lanark. Dale (Owen's future father-in-law) and Owen were both progressive in their views as employers, with particular interests in the welfare of children.

In the early 1810s, Owen visited Johann **Pestalozzi** at Yverdun, as had many other progressive thinkers and educators—indeed, Friedrich **Froebel** lived in Yverdun from 1807 to 1809 (Pence, 1980). By 1812, Owen's ideas regarding education and development had begun to take form and were presented in his first public speech in 1812, which was followed by his first publication in 1813, *The First Essay on the Principle of the Formation of Character*. At the core of his thought was the environmentalist belief that "the constitution of every infant, except in case of organic disease, is capable of being formed or matured, either into a very inferior, or a very superior being according to the qualities of the external circumstances allowed to influence that constitution from birth" (Owen, 1842, p. 1).

Owen's *First Essay* was followed by three others (1813–1814) and collectively they comprise his *A New View of Society* (1816). In that book, Owen takes issue with the excesses of capitalism and the failure of the Church to play an appropriate and effective role in stemming such excesses.

Owen called on society and, in particular, those in positions of wealth and influence, to address the need for social change. New Lanark became his own experiment in ways in which the "constitutions" of individuals might be improved for the betterment of all. Owen's New Institution for the Formation of Character included as part of its structure an Infant School, which accepted children from the age of eighteen months. There were approximately eighty children enrolled in the Infant School in 1816, with both a male and a female teacher.

Owen did not believe that children of such a young age should receive formal instruction.

> "The children were not to be annoyed with books, but were taught the uses and nature of qualities of the common things around them by familiar conversation, when the children's curiosity was excited so as to induce them to ask questions respecting them." (Rusk, p. 134)

The Infant School teachers were trained that "they were on no account ever to beat any one of the children or to threaten them in any manner." Owen's son, Robert Dale Owen, who later taught in the New Institution, confirmed that "all rewards and punishments, whatever, except such as Nature herself has provided . . . are sedulously excluded as being equally unjust in themselves and prejudiced in their effects" (Salmon and Hindshaw, p. 25).

Owen's Infant School was the first of what became a broader movement in the 1820s in the United Kingdom, in North America, and more broadly. Owen's pedagogical approach was, however, not adopted by all such programs, many of which followed a more restrictive, instructive monitorial model. Owen was himself a part of the "internationalization" of the Infant Schools process, establishing an Infant School in the utopian community he helped found and fund at New Harmony, Indiana, in 1825.

Further Readings: Pence, A. R. (1980). Preschool programs of the nineteenth century: Towards a history of preschool child care in America. Unpublished doctoral dissertation, University of Oregon, Eugene. Rusk, R. R. (1933). *A history of infant education.* London: University of London Press; Salmon, D., and W. Hindshaw (1904). *Infant schools, their history and theory.* London: Longmans Green and Co.

Alan Pence

P

Parental Substance Abuse

Adult behavior can have a profound effect on child development and behavior. Data from the Adverse Childhood Experiences Study (ACE) suggests strongly that children are affected in a variety of ways by exposure to such adult risk factors as mental illness, especially depression, alcohol and/or drug abuse, and domestic violence. These adult risk factors have been linked to their child's behavior, including childhood depression and other child mental health concerns, risk-taking behavior impacting school and peer relations, and self-regulatory behavior problems. The probable co-morbidity of these adult risk factors suggests that children are likely to grow up in homes with multiple risk factors, for example, living with a depressed mother who uses drugs to self-medicate her painful affect or growing up in a family where alcohol use exacerbates an abusive relationship between the parents. The ACE data indicate a *correlation rather than causation* between adult risk factors and child behavior, providing evidence that each child's genetic makeup, **temperament,** and environmental factors impact outcomes for individual children.

Children of parents who abuse substances are themselves at double jeopardy for becoming addicts; they may have a biological predisposition for use of substances, especially alcohol, and they are more at risk for experiencing physical and/or sexual abuse as young children. These two forces— the biological and the environmental—often predict a child's risk for their own substance abuse as a way of dealing with the trauma of their early maltreatment. This vicious cycle of parental substance abuse increasing the risk for physical and/or **sexual abuse** in childhood creates generational patterns of addiction in families. Thus identifying and intervening early in the lives of children experiencing such a significant adult risk factor as substance abuse is critical to individual child development.

Addiction

Addiction has been described as a chronic, progressive, and potentially fatal disease with characteristic signs and symptoms. Addiction does not reflect amoral behavior or a lack of willpower—it is a characteristic of the disease that most addicts cannot stop their substance use without treatment, regardless of their desire for sobriety. The hallmarks of addiction are a loss of control over substance use and continued use despite negative consequences. These three aspects of addiction—chronic use, loss of control, and use despite negative consequences define addiction and answer many of the questions posed by providers and early childhood professionals. Why did she continue to use during her pregnancy? Why did she spend the food money on drugs? Why are her children so angry and out of control now that she is out of detox?

Many adults use drugs and alcohol to mediate their own painful affect in the face of the guilt, shame, and/or rage in their lives. And their children feel powerless to protect their parent(s), shame about having to make excuses for their parent's behavior, or anger at the lack of consistent care giving and nurturing that all children need. A significant proportion of adults engaged in substance abuse report having been sexually abused as children. To numb their own pain, these children begin to use drugs that then increase their shame and feelings of self-loathing and guilt. And so the cycle continues.

The Impact of Substance Use on Child Development

This cycle of substance abuse and trauma directly affects children's daily lives. Children live with the unpredictability and chaos of parents who cycle through binges and crashes. They learn to take the emotional temperature of the house—*who is using, who is sleeping in the house, who is angry.* They live with the effects of their parents' emotional numbing that leaves little energy left for nurturing and protecting children. They often feel isolated, alone, and confused by the inconsistent care from various caregivers who may frequent the house or from well-meaning relatives who often enable the parents' drug use. They may experience several out of home placements while their parents struggle with their addictions. This recurring theme of emotional unavailability and abandonment is a potent one for children living with parents who abuse substances.

Children also live with family secrets of shame, guilt, and fear. People with addictions become preoccupied with getting and taking drugs to the exclusion of all other needs and responsibilities, including taking care of themselves and parenting their children. They don't provide adequate food, they are unable to organize themselves to get children ready for **child care**, and they cannot help their children negotiate the daily events in their lives. While some children withdraw in the face of these negative experiences, others express their concerns with rage and aggression. They learn the don'ts: don't trust adults, don't talk about what's going on at home, and don't feel anything about their experiences. To cope with this pain and the unpredictability of their lives, many children themselves turn to drugs as a way of overcoming their sense of powerlessness, low self-esteem, and social failure. Adult children of alcoholics report missing out on childhood because they assumed the role of caring for their parents or younger siblings. Living with a parent who is addicted poses significant challenges to the development of trust, attachment, autonomy, and modulation of effect for children.

Trust and attachment. The role of parental **attachment** figures is to provide consistency, security, and limits for children while helping them develop internalized, integrated constructs for the self in relation to others. But children who are struggling with issues of trust rising from their sense of abandonment, loss, inconsistency, and lack of appropriate boundaries within their families create disordered models for attachment. They either connect indiscriminately to anyone who will pay attention to them ("any warm body will do") or they reject all attempts by adults to nurture and set limits for them. Without experiencing a deep-felt sense of trust within a primary relationship, they internalize a model of mistrust that makes it difficult to connect to other adults who might support them such as teachers or foster parents.

Autonomy and self-esteem. Parents struggling with their own addictions are often unable to help their children successfully resolve such salient issues of family development as attachment, autonomy, individuation, and eventual independence. They place unreasonable demands on their children, leaving them with feelings of self-doubt and failure. The children believe that if they were only good/smart/pretty enough, everything would be better. The family secrets they carry make it hard for them to connect to other caregiving adults outside the family, worrying that their secrets might be betrayed, or worse, that they themselves are part of the secret. They struggle to be autonomous, but worry about balancing their own self-care with their caregiving responsibilities to their parents and younger siblings. They have very low **self-esteem,** and, as with most self-fulfilling prophecies, act out against or withdraw from the very people who might help them—their teachers, counselors, pediatricians.

Modulation of affect. Although adults use substances to break down their inhibitions or to feel better about themselves, the main effect of continued alcohol or drug use is to numb feelings, leaving people unable to identify their feelings or to match their feelings to appropriate social situations such as frightening or sad events. As parents, they have an extremely difficult time identifying or labeling emotions for their children, modeling appropriate feeling states, or helping their children deal with emotions in a socially acceptable way. Thus children of addicts are often emotionally volatile and labile, unable to modulate their own feelings of sadness, anger, or fear. Their ability to maintain their attention, focus on the tasks at hand, and follow rules can be challenged by their internal disorganization, arousal states, and such environmental influences as excess noise and the movement of other children, or emotionally laden sounds such as police sirens.

Prenatal exposure. Much is still unknown about the effects of prenatal cocaine exposure. Research on prenatal marijuana and tobacco exposure suggests that, even if no drug effects are found between the ages of six months and six years, the increasing cognitive demands and social expectations of school or puberty may unmask a series of risks from exposure not previously identified. Cumulative environmental risk and protective factors may also exacerbate or moderate negative cognitive and behavioral outcomes as children mature. Among children aged

582 PARENTAL SUBSTANCE ABUSE

six years or younger, there is no convincing evidence that prenatal cocaine exposure is associated with developmental toxic effects that are different in severity,
scope, or kind from the sequelae of multiple other risk factors. Many findings
once thought to be specific effects of in utero cocaine exposure are correlated
with other factors, including prenatal exposure to tobacco, marijuana, or alcohol,
and the quality of the child's environment.

Long-term studies using sophisticated assessment techniques indicate that prenatally exposed children may have subtle but significant impairments in their
ability to regulate emotions and focus and sustain attention on a task. These neurobehavioral deficits may place these children on a developmental pathway that
leads to poor school performance and other adverse consequences over time.
Thus the impact of addiction on children might best be understood as an environmental effect, focusing more attention on inadequate/poor parenting, poverty,
institutional racism, stress, community violence, and a chaotic, disorganized life
style. These factors alone, independent of drug exposure, can lead to poor developmental outcomes for young children. And when these developmental outcomes
are confounded by prenatal substance exposure, children are at much higher risk
for experiencing the double jeopardy of substance exposure and poverty. Prenatal
exposure may impact their ability to modulate their affect; the chaotic postnatal
environment then exacerbates that inability by neglecting to provide kids with
appropriate boundaries, predictable routines, or the comfort of familiar adults.

Breaking the Cycle: Interventions

Parental substance abuse intensifies the already well-recognized environmental
hazards of poverty, violence, homelessness, depression, inadequate or abusive
parenting, and multiple short-term foster placements. The best way to help children is not only to address their particular behavior or developmental problems
but also to intervene to change the environmental influences that negatively affect the child. In other words, the best way to help a child is to help the parent
recover. Supporting the development of a young child living with a substance-
abusing parent requires a two-generational model of care by considering adult risk
behavior as a critical component in addressing the development and behavior of
children.

Intervention approaches for young children with language delays, attachment
disorders, regulatory concerns, attention disturbances, and motor problems have
been well documented in the early intervention literature and are very effective for
children impacted by parental substance abuse. But the challenge for providers is
to understand the child's behavior within the context of the family's relationships
and their ability to function. Providers must think carefully about the environment
in which the child lives before deciding on an intervention approach. For children
of addicted parents, their behavior may have much less to do with the early
intervention or classroom environment than with the internal neurobehavioral
mechanisms that control affect, attention, and arousal. Providers cannot plan
strategies for a "disruptive" child without considering the family factors. Providers
need training and ongoing supervision to be able to ask hard questions about
family history and child-rearing practices in culturally sensitive ways. For example,

providers might ask a parent "Who does your child remind you of? Do you think you (or his father) acted like this in preschool?" The answers to these questions provide significant insight into how the family sees the child, their expectations for her/his behavior, and issues that might be impacting the child at home.

The Role of Children in Their Parent's Recovery

The birth of a baby can present substance abusing parents with a wide open window of opportunity. Children can be a powerful motivating force for parents to examine their behavior, to have the strength needed to enter treatment, to consider a different life for themselves and their family. A new baby can also precipitate a crisis that forces family members to confront the substance abusing parent. Family-focused interventions for addicted parents and their young children require a delicate balancing act in which providers must consider both the adult's needs and those of the child. Treatment that focuses exclusively on the adult or the child ignores the power of the parent–child dyad and the advantages that can come from changing the family system.

The challenge in providing family-focused interventions is literally to get the parent's attention and to develop a therapeutic relationship with them. The ability to form these alliances is based on the severity of the parent's addiction, their level of denial, potential for relapse, and the presence of concomitant psychiatric concerns. These problems also interfere with the ability of the provider to model behavior, give information, and help the parents support their baby's self-regulation, developmental skills, and emotional health. Yet, there are many advantages to family-focused interventions for parents struggling with addiction. At the onset of drug treatment, the parent–child relationship can sustain the parent through the difficult early detoxification and rehabilitation period. Providers can use the baby's behavior as a vehicle to reach the parent and begin to establish a therapeutic relationship with her around her concerns for her child. Infants demonstrate a wealth of behaviors that indicate their feelings, their connection to the people around them, and their development. By smiling exclusively for her father or no longer crying when his mother picks him up, infants use these preferential signals to indicate to the parent how central he/she is to the child ("when he sees you, his whole face lights up"). Second, children provide a powerful basis for examining a parent's life decisions and choices. Simply asking why a particular name was chosen for the baby gives enormous insight into the life experiences and family history. ("She's named for my grandma who raised me after my mom left; he's named for his father in prison"). As they talk about their children, parents narrate their own lives, offering providers a chance to empathize with traumatic events, to correct misconceptions, and to support the parent's vision for the future.

And while children can be a significant source of pride and self-esteem for parents, they can also be triggers for anger, repressed memories, relapse, or depression. Teaching parents basic child development can help them understand that when their child cries for them when they leave, the child is not spoiled, but missing the person who is so central in his life—his parent. Issues of abandonment are often pivotal in the lives of addicts. By helping them to see their role in supporting their child's growing independence, providers can help them to place new meaning on events in their own lives, on how they understand and interact with their children, and on how they respond to their own losses, anger, and pain. Finally, children offer addicted parents hope for a future in which they can attain sobriety and maintain their family; in other words, a better life for themselves and their children.

Further Readings: Brooks, C. S., B. Zuckerman, A. Bamforth, J. Cole, and M. Kaplan-Sanoff (1994). Clinical issues related substance-involved mothers and their infants. *Infant Mental Health Journal* 15(2), 202-217; Feletti, V., R. Anda, D. Nordenberg, D. F. Williamson, A. M. Spitz, V. Edwards, M. P. Koss, and J. S. (1998). The relationship of adult health status to childhood abuse and household Dysfunction. *American Journal of Preventive Medicine* 14, 245-258; Frank, D. A., M. Augustyn, W. Knight, T. Pell, and B. Zuckerman (2001). Growth, development, and behavior in early childhood following prenatal cocaine exposure: A systematic review. *JAMA* 285(12), 1613-1625; M. Kaplan-Sanoff, B. Zuckerman, and S. Parker (1991). Poverty and early childhood development: What do we know and what should we do? *Infants and Young Children*; Sameroff, A., R. Seifer, R. Barocas, M. Zax, and S. Greenspan (1987). Intelligence quotient scores for 4 year old children: Social environmental risk factors. *Pediatrics* 79, 343-350; Shonkoff, J., and D. Phillips (2000). *Neurons to neighborhoods: The science of early child development*. Washington, DC: National Academy of Sciences.

Margot Kaplan-Sanoff

Parenting Education

Parenting education refers to the process of increasing adult knowledge and skills about the development of parents and of children so as to enhance child-rearing practices and strengthen the parent–child relationship. It works on the assumption that parents can change and become better parents, and that parenting styles and practices can be modified to benefit children, parents, and families. The goals of parenting education are multiple, including improving parenting skills, the prevention of **child abuse and neglect**, the promotion of children's health and school **readiness**, and the personal growth of parents. Because research shows that racial and socioeconomic differences in parenting practices impact differences in children's **cognitive development**, parenting education is also proposed as a strategy to address the achievement gap.

The many parenting books, magazines, television shows, and Internet sites indicate the strong interest parents have for information and support. A national survey of American adults conducted in 2000 reported that one third of adults felt very unprepared and another third only "somewhat prepared" for parenthood (DYG, Inc., 2000). In addition, the survey revealed significant gaps among parents and other adults in their knowledge of the development of children newborn to age six. Better educated parents and those with higher incomes are more knowledgeable of current child development theories than those who are less well educated and have lower incomes; and fathers are less well informed than mothers. Although most parents turn to other family members for information and support on parenting, parenting education is typically available through community-based programs.

Parenting education in the United States has a long history that can be traced back to the seventeenth century. During the colonial period, much of the available practical advice on infant and child care focused on the moral and religious upbringing of children. The next two hundred years witnessed an increase in the number of American authors publishing parenting education materials; a shift to content that was both developmental and spiritual in nature; and the creation of mothers' groups as a mode of conveying information and advice.

With the growth of industrialization and immigration in the late nineteenth and early twentieth centuries, social reformers became concerned about child-rearing and "mothering," particularly in poor families. Their efforts took various forms, including visits to families by social workers and the development of settlement houses that offered multiple services to immigrant families. This period also saw the establishment of various parent education organizations, including the National Congress of Mothers in 1897 (today called the PTA). Mass media outlets began to carry materials for parents including publications like *Good Housekeeping* and *Ladies Home Journal* (Schlossman, 1976). In the 1960s War on Poverty, a new wave of parenting education programs flourished. By the mid-1970s, a number of individuals and groups initiated programs with many of the characteristics associated with contemporary family support and parenting education. These characteristics include a goal-oriented framework for parenting education, sustained and comprehensive support to young families, referrals to other services, child development services, and a climate that engages parents to share and explore child-rearing beliefs and practices.

As was the case with historical attempts to change parenting practices, con-temporary parenting education and support programs rest on the assumptions that early childhood is a critical period in the development and that the home is a critical context in which development takes place. By providing parents of young children with information about and support for child rearing, programs increasingly reject the notion of *parens patriae*—that either the state or the family alone are accountable for children—and embrace the idea that fostering children's development is the mutual responsibility of the family, the state, and the broader community.

Studies of the family and child development confirm the need for parenting education and support. For example, it is widely recognized that warm, recipro-cal parent–child relationships foster children's cognitive development and social competence. Hart and Risley (1995), for example, found that parenting from birth to age three is especially critical to children's language development and their future academic performance. However, of great concern to policy makers are findings from such research about the impact of poverty on parenting and child outcomes. By having parents who talked to them more often, children from pro-fessional families showed dramatically greater rates of vocabulary growth and also richer forms of language use and interaction than children from welfare families. The implication of studies such as these is that, by the time poor children enter preschool, they are already disadvantaged compared with their middle-class peers.

The timing of **poverty** in children's lives appears as one important dimension with long-lasting effects—and significant implications for parenting education. Being poor during the preschool years correlates with low rates of high school completion, as compared with poverty during the childhood and adolescent years. The home environment in particular mediates the effects of poverty on children. Income instability and the chronic stresses of poverty are associated with maternal depression, which, in turn, is related to more punitive and less nurturing parenting behaviors, and, subsequently, preschool children's lower levels of cognitive development and increased behavioral problems (McLoyd, 1995). In response to these findings, it has been suggested that parenting education focus on reading to children and providing them with stimulating learning experiences in order to improve children's cognitive development; to reduce children's behavioral problems, parenting programs should focus on parenting skills and improving parents' psychological well-being; and to promote children's healthy development in multiple domains, comprehensive social supports be offered to families (Yeung, Linver and Brooks-Gunn, 2002).

Certain community factors may counteract the negative outcomes of poverty and other life stressors. Parents' social networks buffer negative parenting as friends, neighbors and kin provide emotional, informational and parenting support as well as role modeling. Parents who receive more emotional support and have a heterogeneous social network exhibit more warmth and responsiveness, offer a more stimulating cognitive home environment and feel more effective as parents than their counterparts with fewer and more homogenous social networks. Children who overcome adversity come from families that are caring and supportive, maintain high expectations, and provide opportunities for meaningful participation in the family (Benard, 1991). For parents to create these environments families must exist in supportive communities. The notion that "it takes a village to raise a child" situates parenting education in a broader ecological framework of community-based support and social service system change.

Models

Parenting education is best represented as a series of overlapping approaches and strategies. Programs might range from intensive interventions focused on highly specific objectives over several months to multiyear initiatives that provide a range of services over a longer period of time. Cultural characteristics such as family communication styles, routines, and parenting practices also carry implications for parenting programs. Parenting programs are charged with the task of aligning with family cultural styles and material circumstances, while simultaneously conveying middle-class practices that are associated with children's cognitive and socioemotional development. To do this effectively, programs define their own underlying values as well as build on the characteristics, constraints and opportunities of specific groups including immigrant populations, parents of children with special needs and fathers.

Parenting education programs can be classified into three general models: those that provide parenting and other supports solely to parents; those that provide services to parents through their involvement in educational services offered to their children; and those that unite these two components. A large part of what we know about parent education programs comes from evaluations of intervention programs based on each of these models.

Parenting support models rely on professional or paraprofessional staff to provide information and support about parenting and child development. Meetings may take place within the home environment (home visiting) or in other settings. In this model the focus is on helping parents fulfill their role as parents and educators of their children.

Parent involvement models are usually center-based and primarily provide an educational curriculum to preschoolers or infants and toddlers. Recognizing the sustained effects of parent involvement in early education, these programs include parent support groups, offer parenting classes and conduct parent meetings. Often the content of this model focuses on children's educational development.

The "two-generation" approach combines services for parents with child-focused curricula. Some of these programs provide integrated and comprehensive services for poor families. They combine work experiences and job training, social services, parenting education and child care.

Evaluation

Are parenting education and support programs effective? Several evaluations point to mixed and conditional results. Evaluations of six major home visiting programs point to some benefits in parenting and the lack of large and consistent benefits in child development. Most of these programs, however, struggled to implement services according to the program design and to engage families. Failure to deliver the intended number of home visits and substantial attrition rates likely affected program outcomes (Gomby, Culross, and Behrman, 1999). Home visiting in poor families is also more likely to help those who are well-functioning rather than those with severe, multiple problems (Larner et al., 1992).

Head Start is the most well-known example of the parent involvement model. Quasi-experimental studies reveal short and long-term effects on cognitive ability and school performance. However, the specific impact of Head Start's family involvement and parenting education programs is less well studied. Another example of the parent involvement model, the Chicago Child-Parent Center (CPC), is a comprehensive preschool program for low-income children in Chicago. Results of a longitudinal study showed that children who participated in CPC had more years of completed education, and that parent involvement was the most important program predictor of children's early and later school related outcomes (Clements, Reynolds, and Hickey, 2004).

Two-generation programs tend to be the most successful in promoting long-term developmental gains for children from low-income families (Yoshikawa, 1995). Early Head Start, one example of this approach, provides parent education and educational child care, and is implemented in center-based and home-based settings. A longitudinal randomized evaluation finds positive child outcomes in cognitive, language, and social emotional development. Early Head Start parents showed increased support for children's language development and learning and had lower rates of punitive discipline practices (Raikes, Love and Chazan-Cohen, 2004).

Although much research has focused on outcome evaluation, it is equally important to understand program characteristics and the process by which an intervention brings about its various outcomes. A synthesis of process evaluations of various home visiting programs found variation in program success by who delivered the services (e.g., professional vs. paraprofessional staff) and the connections between those workers and the families they visit. In the Early Head Start evaluation, experimental effects were greatest in the sites rated with the highest level of implementation (Love et al. 2002).

Conclusion

Parenting education assumes that parents can and should change the ways they rear their children. While parenting is malleable it is also very difficult to change. Although the outcomes of parenting education and support programs tend to be modest, stronger outcomes are observed with programs are characterized by previously described best practices (McCartney and Dearing 2002). This finding provides good reason for society to invest in well-designed programs and to fund them at levels that ensure quality implementation. Changing parenting is also complex and value-laden, and influenced by social and cultural contexts that lie beyond the purview of parenting education programs. This suggests the need of a comprehensive national family policy of which parenting education is an important part. Such a policy would encompass workplace changes to meet the needs of parents of young children, parental leave policies, parenting education, quality early childhood education, and affordable health care. For all those concerned about healthy parenting and child well-being, the road ahead lies in building the political will to effect this policy transformation. *See also* Parents and Parent Involvement; Peers and Friends.

Further Readings: Clements, M. A., A. J. Reynolds, and E. Hickey (2004). Site-level predictors of children's school and social competence in the Chicago Child-Parent Centers. *Early Childhood Research Quarterly* 19, 273–296; DYG, Inc. (2000). What grown-ups understand about child development: A national benchmark study. Washington, DC: Zero to Three. Available online at http://www.zerotothree.org; Gomby, D. S., P. L. Culross, and R. E. Behrman (1999). Home visiting: Analysis and recommendations. *The Future of Children: Home Visiting: Recent Program Evaluation* 9(1), 4–26; Hart, B., and T. R. Risely (1995) *Meaningful differences in the everyday experience of young American children.* Baltimore: Paul H. Brookes Publishing Company; Larner, M., R. Halpern, and O. Harkavy, eds. (1992). *Fair start for children: lessons learned from seven demonstration projects.* New Haven, CT: Yale University Press; Love, J. M., E. Eliason-Kinker, C. M. Ross, P. Z. Schochet, J. Brooks-Gunn, and D. Paulsell (2002). *Making a difference in the lives of infants and toddlers and their families: The impacts of Early Head Start.* Washington, DC: U.S. Department of Health and Human Services, Commissioners Office of Research and Evaluation, Administration or Children Youth and Families; McCartney, K., and E. Dearing (2002). Evaluating effect sizes in the policy arena. *The Evaluation Exchange: Family Support* 8(1), 4,7. Cambridge, MA: Harvard Family Research Project; McLoyd, V. C. (1995); Poverty, parenting and policy: Meeting the support needs of poor parents. In H. E. Fitzgerald, B. M. Lester, and B. S. Zuckerman, eds., *Children of poverty: Research, health, and policy issues.* New York: Garland Publishing, Inc., pp. 269–303; Raikes, H., J. Love, and R. Chazan-Cohen (2004). Infant-toddler intervention on the road to school readiness: Lessons from Early Head Start. *The Evaluation exchange: Early childhood programs and evaluation issue.* Vol. 10. Cambridge, MA: Harvard Family Research Project, pp. 22–23; Schlossman, S. L. (1976). Before home start: Notes toward a history of parent education in America, 1897–1929. *Harvard Educational Review* 46(3), 436–466; Yeung, W. J., M. R.

Linver, and J. Brooks-Gunn (2002). How money matters for young children's development: Parental investment and family processes. *Child Development* 73, 1861–1879; Yoshikawa, H. (1995). Long-term effects of early childhood programs on social outcomes and delinquency. *The Future of Children: Long-Term Outcomes of Early Childhood Programs* 5(3), 51–75.

M. Elena Lopez and Margaret Caspe

Parents and Parent Involvement

Parents provide children with the care they need to survive and become culturally competent. **Attachment**, the emotional tie between a child and caregiver, is universal, but the goals and patterns of child-rearing vary both between and within cultures. The parental role may be carried out by someone other than the biological parent (i.e., adoptive or grandparent). **Developmentally appropriate practice** calls for effective partnerships between early childhood educators and parents.

Parenting

Human evolution has resulted in behavioral systems in both children and their caregivers that prepare children for life in their particular culture. Newborns arrive with the capacity to cry when they feel discomfort, attend alertly to a human face, and root and suckle on a breast to get nourishment. These capacities in babies are universal and seem to be designed to engage responsive care from an adult. As they grow older, children further rely on parents to engage them in learning language, solving problems, and relating to others. Parents typically provide this care and guidance based upon cultural models. They respond to the baby's cries, nourish them, and guide them in learning skills in accordance with implicit cultural goals for child-rearing. In all cultures, parents are typically the primary caregivers for young children. But there is considerable variation in how these caregiving activities are carried out and how they are shared between parents and with other members of the society—older children, extended family, professional caregivers. For example, among the Kung San in South Africa, babies are in constant contact with their mothers and feed frequently. Conversely, Dutch mothers tend to establish a strict feeding schedule very early in a child's life. And many American parents let their babies sleep in separate rooms. Middle-class American mothers talk with their young children about everyday events, asking questions that they already know the answers to. Economically disadvantaged American Appalachian mothers ask questions of their children that they need the answers to. Language is used to tell stories rather than engage in school-like discourse.

The variation in parental behavior is based upon implicit cultural goals and environmental demands. For example, the constant contact of Kung San infants with their mothers not only protects them from the various threats in their environment but also prepares them for close, interdependent relationships necessary in a small social group that share limited resources. Reflecting different cultural goals, parenting practices that encourage sleeping in separate rooms and didactic conversation among middle-class American **families** prepare children for independence and success in school (LeVine, 1988).

Although based primarily in culture, parenting style and capacity are also related to specific familial and societal forces. Socioeconomic status, religious beliefs, substance abuse, migration and immigration, war, disability, and other factors influence how parents care for their children. Two parents may share the parenting role, or fathers may take primary caregiving roles for children's care. Extended family involvement may be constant and expected or parents may be entirely disconnected from relatives.

There is no singular script or prescription for how to be a good parent. Children born with various characteristics, economic and social factors, and changing cultural values as well as individual parental dispositions all conspire against singular guidance about childrearing. Parents, whether in traditional societies or postindustrial societies, have always looked to others for guidance. In traditional societies such sources included extended family and community leaders. Increasingly they look to other sources—media (television and magazines), the books of experts, pediatricians, and early childhood educators (Small, 1998).

Parent Involvement

Early childhood educators require children and their parents to adapt to the policies and practices of their programs, but when early childhood educators work with a child, they are also joining a system of care around that child. Urie **Bronfenbrenner** (1979, 1986) maintained that it is in the best interest of the child for the various people—parents and others who care for children—to do so consistently. The child grows and learns best when these caregivers communicate with each other and share similar child-rearing patterns and goals. The focus of this partnership is the well-being of the child, but often there are disagreements between parents and other caregivers. Differing implicit and culturally based beliefs about child-rearing and the meaning of children's behavior are both natural and inevitable. This may require substantive communication and negotiation. Furthermore, parents may have ambivalent feelings about leaving children in the care of others for a variety of reasons, including the need to maintain an adequate income. Exchanges between parents and others who care for their children may be charged with deep emotions.

The role of early childhood educators is to protect, care for, and support the cognitive, physical, and social–emotional development of young children. To do this well, they must work in alliance with parents. The goal of healthy development of young children is best met when the primary influence on that development is effective. As the primary source for that development is the child's parents, the early childhood educator's role must include supporting the competence and well-being of parents (Shpancer, 2000). Many early childhood programs, such as **Head Start** and **Early Head Start,** have **parenting education** as a central program component. Close relationships with parents and other family members is a hallmark of early childhood programs in Italy (New and Mallory, 2005).

Contemporary theories of child development as well as recent research supports the premise that forming and sustaining effective and authentic partnerships with parents is the foundation of high quality early childhood education (Turnbull,

Turbiville, and Turnbull, 2000). Practices that support such partnerships may include the following:

- transition into the program that allows for forming strong relationships between parents, teachers, and children together;
- regular and ongoing teacher–parent communication about the children's health, behavior, and progress;
- honest, timely, and open communication about developmental or behavioral concerns;
- parental participation in decision making about caregiving practices, curriculum, and overall program policy;
- parental participation in program activities (e.g., volunteering in the classroom, field trips, sharing particular skills);
- opportunities, as appropriate, for teachers to visit children's homes;
- attention to family culture in program planning;
- specific activities that encourage the participation of fathers;
- referral and collaboration with programs that address family support needs such as housing, substance abuse counseling, and health care; and
- parent meetings and support groups.

Effective teacher–parent alliances have benefits for children and parents as well as for the continual development of early childhood educators. Parents, as the primary force in the development of children, are essential partners with early childhood educators not only because they provide information about their children but also because they bring a rich and complex cultural understanding to the care of children. When teachers learn from parents they deepen their view of childhood and the care of children.

Further Readings: Brazelton, T. B. (1992). *Touchpoints: The essential reference.* New York: Perseus Books; Bronfenbrenner, U. (1979). Contexts of childrearing: Problems and prospects. *American Psychologist 34,* 844–850; Bronfenbrenner, U. (1986). Ecology of the family as a context for human development: Research perspectives. *Developmental Psychology 22,* 723–742; Goodnow, Jacqueline J., and W. Andrew Collins (1990). *Development according to parents: The nature, sources, and consequences of parents' ideas.* Hillsdale, NJ: Erlbaum. Harkness, Sara, and Super Charles, eds. (1996); *Parents' cultural belief systems.* New York: Guilford Press. LeVine, R. A. (1988); Human parental care: Universal goals, cultural strategies, individual behavior. In R. A. LeVine, P. M. Miller, and M. M. West, eds., *Parental behavior in diverse societies.* San Francisco: Jossey-Bass, pp. 3–12; New, R., and B. Mallory (2005). Children as catalysts for adult relations: New partnerships in home-school-community relations in Italian early childhood education. In O. Saracho and B. Spodek, eds., *Contemporary perspectives in early childhood education: Families and communities.* Greenwich, CT: Information Age Publishing, pp. 163–179; Shpancer, N. (2000). The home-daycare link: Mapping children's new world order. *Early Childhood Research Quarterly 17,* 374–392; Small, M. (1998). *Our Babies, ourselves: How biology and culture shape the way we parent.* New York: Anchor Books; Turnbull, A., V. Turbiville, and H. R. Turnbull (2000). Evolution of family-professional relationships: Collective empowerment for the 21st century. In J. Shonkoff and S. Meisels, eds., *Handbook of early childhood intervention.* 2nd ed. New York: Cambridge University Press, pp. 630–650.

John Hornstein

Parker, Francis W. (1837–1902)

To the general public, progressive education is often associated with John **Dewey** and no one else. However, Dewey was neither the first nor the last educator to embrace and develop the principles that define a progressive approach. In fact, Dewey owed much to one of the unsung heroes in the progressive education movement. That hero was Francis W. Parker. Dewey once referred to Parker as "the father of progressive education" (Cremin, 1961).

Parker was a practitioner, not a writer or theorist, which is why he remains relatively unsung. Born in New Hampshire in 1837 and widely traveled in Europe where he studied the latest innovations in education, Parker took over a failing Quincy, Massachusetts school system in 1873. As superintendent of the Quincy schools, Parker led a reform to place children's observing, describing, and understanding at the center of the curriculum. Everything was aimed at making learning meaningful for children and at making school a community with a warm and friendly, even home-like atmosphere.

The results were immediate and positive. The Quincy children thrived in Parkers' schools, and soon educators were referring to "the Quincy system." Parker, himself, downplayed his innovations calling them simply a matter of common sense.

Parker went on to become principal of the Cook County Normal School of Chicago. At the Normal school, he developed his approach further and even gave lectures and produced essays on his approach. However, his lectures and writings were few and did not have a lasting effect. The main and lasting effect came when two parents enrolled their children in the practice school.

In 1894 and 1895, Professor and Mrs. John Dewey had a thorough look at Parker's school as their two children thrived in the school's younger grades. Then, in 1896, they established their own "Laboratory School," with Parker and his school clearly in mind. It is, then, not too much to say that Dewey's writings on education, though rooted in his training as a philosopher, were equally rooted in Francis Parker's progressive approach and his school.

Further Readings: Cremin, L. (1961). *The transformation of the school: Progressivism in American education, 1976-1957.* New York: Alfred A. Knopf.

W. George Scarlett

Parten, Mildred (1902–)

Mildred Parten received a Ph.D. in sociology from the University of Minnesota in 1929. Best known for her work related to children's play, her landmark study, which was based on her doctoral dissertation, was published in 1932. In this work, Parten describes categories of children's social play, defined as occurring when children play in groups. Consistent with new understandings emerging from the **Child Study movement,** she identified an age-related progression in the types of social play that characterized early childhood.

Parten identified six categories of play that ranged, in her view, from the least to the most developmentally complex. The first category of social play she labeled as *unoccupied behavior* and is actually not play, but an observation of others' play. A child participating in unoccupied behavior will generally be seen moving about the classroom from one area to another, but not getting involved in any particular activity. He may be seen standing around, following the teacher, or sitting in one spot glancing around the room.

The second category of social play Parten identified, in which the child is an *onlooker*, is closely related to unoccupied behavior. As an onlooker, the child observes a group of children playing, but does not overtly enter into the play activity with them. He may talk to the children whom he is observing, ask questions, or give suggestions and stays within speaking distance of the group playing so that he can see and hear the play that is taking place.

Parten identified a third category of social play as *solitary play* or playing alone. A child participating in solitary play will play by herself and independently from other children with toys that are different from those being used around her. The child pursues her own play without reference to the activities of others.

The fourth category, which is closely related to solitary play, is identified as *parallel play*. While participating in parallel play, the child continues to play independently, but the activity she chooses brings her within close proximity of other children. She plays with toys that are similar, perhaps using them in similar ways, but does not interact in the play themes of the children nearby. In other words, she plays beside the other children, but not with the other children.

The fifth category, *associative play*, is the first in which the child plays with other children. When participating in associative play, the child interacts and shares materials with other children, but does not engage in a common activity with those around him.

The final category, identified as *cooperative play*, is the most social form of play and involves children playing together in a shared activity. The group is organized with a goal, such as creating a product, playing games, or participating in a dramatic play scenario. Various group members fulfill different roles and those roles complement each other and allow the play to continue in an organized and methodical manner.

Parten's research suggested that, as children grow and mature, they tend to progress through these categories, and their play becomes more complex with age. She noted, further, that earlier types of social play do not disappear entirely and may be revisited occasionally, even as the child becomes capable of more complex levels of social play. Although more recent perspectives on children's play challenge this linear progression—noting, for example, that solitary play may entail high levels of creativity and critical thinking—few early childhood professionals or researchers discuss or study children's play without recognition of the insights provided by Mildred Parten.

Further Readings: Feeney, S., D. Christensen, and E. Moravcik (2006). *Who am I in the lives of children?* 7th ed. Upper Saddle River, NJ: Merrill Prentice Hall. Parten, Mildred B. (1932). Social participation among pre-school children. *The Journal of Abnormal and Social Psychology* 27, 243–269; Sluss, Dorothy J. (2005). *Supporting play: Birth through age eight.* Clifton Park, NY: Thomson Delmar Learning.

Angie Baum

Pavlov, Ivan Petrovich (1849–1936)

Ivan Pavlov, a Nobel Prize-winning Russian scientist, discovered, while studying the digestive processes of dogs, that reflexive behavior can be controlled, or "conditioned," by external events. Pavlov showed how a previously neutral stimulus (the sound of a metronome) could elicit an involuntary response (salivation) if it was repeatedly paired with a stimulus that produced the reflex naturally (food). Pavlov termed this phenomenon *classical conditioning*. A brilliant methodologist, Pavlov's research laid the groundwork for American academics, most notably Edward **Thorndike**, John B. **Watson,** and B.F. Skinner, to formulate and establish a purely objective science of learning, known as *behaviorism*.

Pavlov, the first child of a poor family, was born on September 14, 1849, at Ryazan in central Russia. Peter Dmitrievich Pavlov, his father and also the village priest, urged young Ivan toward theology, but Pavlov's love of natural science led him instead to the lifelong study of physiology. Pavlov's education began in the church schools of Ryazan but continued until he obtained an advanced degree and a fellowship award from the Academy of Medical Surgery. His early research, carried out at the clinic of S.P. Botkin, focused on the nervous system. In 1890, Pavlov became the director of the Department of Physiology at the Institute of Experimental Medicine in St. Petersburg. Here he remained for 45 years, building the Institute into an influential center of physiological research.

Conditioned Reflexes (1927), which was published in English, established Pavlov's reputation in the West and won widespread acclaim. The recognition that accompanied winning the Nobel Prize in 1904 may have protected Pavlov from persecution during and after the Russian Revolution. A government decree signed by Lenin in 1921 recognized Pavlov's service to the working class; the Communist Party and the Soviet government provided well for Pavlov and his collaborators. The Soviet Union established itself as an international center for the study of physiology by 1935, a position secured in part because of Ivan Pavlov's contributions. Pavlov remained actively involved in research until his death at age 87.

Pavlov is sometimes credited with starting the behavioristic revolution in psychology, which saw an abrupt shift toward studying only what was directly observable. An American psychologist, John B. Watson, is more appropriately recognized as the founder of radical behaviorism. Watson applied Pavlov's methods to the study of children, successfully demonstrating that fear could be learned and then extinguished in a child by classical conditioning. Watson advanced a theoretical position that weighted environment much more heavily than heredity in the nature-nurture debate—a point of view related to social improvement. It was perhaps inevitable that Watson would soon be criticizing the nation's mothers for failing to provide healthy conditions for their children's growth.

Educators too felt the impact of behaviorism. At Teachers College in New York City, colleagues Edward Thorndike and Patty Smith **Hill** emphasized the importance of habit formation during the early years. Experimentation with children now involved stimulus-response psychology—educators sought to define desirable behavior and condition children to produce it.

In more recent times, B.F. Skinner's theory of operant conditioning described how reinforcement can be used to modify behavior, a principle that soon infiltrated early childhood education. Using praise, token systems, or behavioral charts with the intention of altering children's behavior are all practices that derive from reinforcement theory.

Behavioristic practices are firmly established in many American schools, particularly in special education. Whether these contemporary applications should be associated with the work of Ivan Pavlov, however, is open to debate.

Further Readings: Babkin, B. P. (1949). *Pavlov.* Chicago: University of Chicago Press. Frolov, Y. P. (1937). *Pavlov and his school.* London: K. Paul, Trench, Trubner, and Company. Pavlov, I. P. (1927). *Conditioned reflexes: An investigation of the physiological activity of the cerebral cortex.* Translated by G. V. Anrep, London: Oxford University Press. Windholz, George (1997). Ivan P. Pavlov: An overview of his life and psychological work. *American Psychologist*, 52(9), 941–946.

Ann C. Benjamin

PCER. *See* Preschool Curriculum Evaluation Research Program

Peabody, Elizabeth Palmer (1804–1894)

Elizabeth Palmer Peabody was an American Transcendentalist, member of the Common School Movement, lecturer in the Concord School of Philosophy, and the leader of the campaign to establish kindergartens during the nineteenth century. Peabody opened the first English-speaking kindergarten in the United States in Boston in 1860. Her 1863 *Guide to the Kindergarten and Moral Culture of Infancy*, coauthored with her sister, Mary Tyler Peabody Mann, was widely considered the most authoritative work on the theory and practice of the kindergarten during the 1860s and 1870s.

The eldest of six children, Elizabeth Palmer Peabody was born in Billerica, Massachusetts, in 1804 and grew up in Salem, Massachusetts. Her father, Dr. Nathaniel Peabody, was a teacher at Philips Andover Academy, who later studied medicine and dentistry at Harvard. Her mother, Elizabeth Palmer Peabody, was the headmistress of a girl's boarding school. Elizabeth received her education at her mother's school and proved to be an exceptionally gifted student. At the age of sixteen, she became her mother's assistant, went on to teach in Maine and Massachusetts, and later studied Greek with Ralph Waldo Emerson and history and philosophy with William Ellery Channing.

In 1825, Peabody and her sister Mary founded the Beacon Hill School in Boston, where they developed a curriculum designed to capture the child's imagination through the study of literature, the arts, dramatic play, and creative writing. Based on her work at the school, Peabody authored a series of textbooks and guides for teachers in which she advocated an education of loving nurturance, example, and exploration. Bronson Alcott admired the series and asked her to join him at his experimental Temple School in Concord in 1834. Peabody published a favorable description of Alcott's innovations in *Record of a School* in 1835. The following year, a public controversy erupted over Alcott's classroom discussions of sex and the gospels. Although Peabody defended him, their collaboration ended in 1837.

Peabody returned to Boston and turned her attention to social and educational reform. She opened a bookstore to promote transcendentalist literature and make foreign-language texts (many of which she translated herself) more widely available, hosted literary discussions with radical Margaret Fuller, lent support to abolitionist and suffragist causes, and became editor of the *Dial*. She and Mary Peabody, later the wife of Horace Mann, became active in the Common School Movement. In 1859, Peabody read an article on the educational theory of Friedrich **Froebel** and the German **Kindergarten** and recognized a striking resemblance to her own philosophy of early childhood education. She immediately began to urge common schoolers to add kindergarten to their reform agenda. In 1860, she and Mary Mann opened a kindergarten in Boston. The publication of their *Guide to the Kindergarten* in 1863 initiated the national Kindergarten Movement. Elizabeth Palmer Peabody became its acknowledged leader.

During the late 1860s, Peabody toured German schools and recruited Froebel's students to work in model kindergartens in Boston, New York City, Washington, D.C., and Los Angeles. She formed a national network of kindergarten teachers, lectured throughout the country, founded and edited the *Kindergarten Messenger*, and served as president of the American Froebel Union. She was appointed to the National Education Association's Kindergarten Committee and in 1876 organized a kindergarten demonstration class for the American Centennial Exposition in Philadelphia. Although her health began to fail in her later years, Peabody continued to work for the cause of kindergarten well into her eighties. She died in 1894.

Further Readings: Peabody, Elizabeth Palmer, and Mary Tyler Mann (1863). *Guide to the kindergarten and moral culture of infancy*. Boston: T. O. H. P. Burnham. Peabody, Elizabeth Palmer (1886). *Lectures in the training schools for kindergartners*. Boston: D.C. Heath and Company. Ronda, Bruce A. (1999). *Elizabeth Palmer Peabody: A reformer on her own terms*. Cambridge, MA: Harvard University Press.

Susan Douglas Franzosa

Pedagogy

Pedagogy is typically defined as the art and science of teaching. The term dates back hundreds of years to the Greek word "pedagogue." Originally, a pedagogue was a servant (often a slave) who attended to a young boy's ancillary educational needs such as carrying books and accompanying him to school (Monroe 1913). The word is now synonymous with "teaching," the art and science of educating others through enacting pedagogy of some form. Pedagogy therefore is not synonymous with the term **curriculum,** or what children should know and be taught. Pedagogy encompasses the psychological, cultural, political, and socioemotional processes of teaching young children.

Teaching young children is a dynamic process that demands not only that a teacher have a fully realized vision of the goals and content present in a curriculum but also a theoretical understanding of how best to assist students to learn. In addition, he or she must develop and become expert in using a repertoire of strategies to respond effectively to both an individual student's learning and those of subgroups and the class as a whole. In other words, pedagogy is a teacher's tool kit that encompasses his or her professional philosophy about teaching, learning and the purposes of early education, a knowledge base that informs these beliefs, as well as a range of methods for putting these views into action (Katz 1995). This toolkit is developed through professional preparation opportunities as well as teachers' individual experiences of schooling.

At the same time what kinds of tools a teacher chooses to use on any given day is also shaped by the contexts in which they work. For example, a teacher in a **Head Start** program enacts a different kind of pedagogy than a public school teacher because of the differing curriculum goals, training opportunities, standards, and assessment procedures of their sponsoring agency. Teachers' pedagogy is also influenced by whether they work in an urban, suburban, or rural setting and the socioeconomic and demographic backgrounds of the families they serve. Families and administrators hold particular assumptions about what it means to be a teacher, and those assumptions mediate how a teacher operates in the classroom.

Similarly, pedagogy is not limited to the classroom and school context but is also influenced by the evolution of differing ideas that over time change the ways teaching young children is defined and described. For example, the questioning of the research base underpinning the original guidelines for **developmentally appropriate practice** (DAP) (e.g., Mallory and New 1994) as well as wider dissemination of the theories of Lev **Vygotsky** led to a revised set of guidelines that address issues of culture and context (Bredekamp and Copple 1997). In addition, decisions about which research, theories and knowledges are used to inform pedagogy are also the product of politics. In the 1960s, the launching of Sputnik and a concern that students in the United States were not performing well in math and science contributed to a backlash against Dewey's experience-based education and an increased focus on academic skills (Krogh and Slentz 2001).

Thus, early childhood pedagogy is not simply an interpersonal interaction between teacher and students but the outcome of a set of relationships between the individual understandings and biographies of teachers, the contexts in which they act, as well as sociocultural and political forces operating at the macro level of society (Luke 1996). Even when teachers subscribe to a particular form of pedagogy (e.g., constructivist), their moment-to-moment encounters with children are shaped by a number of competing forces. As a consequence, despite the field claiming to have a core set of pedagogical practices (e.g., DAP), there is much diversity in early childhood pedagogy. Some of these pedagogies include child-centered education, play, the use of materials and structuring of the environment to facilitate problem solving and inquiry, democratic pedagogy, critical pedagogy, and direct instruction.

In early childhood, pedagogy is not a widely used term, perhaps because the research base of the field has focused less on teachers and teaching and more on the application of child development knowledge (Genishi, Ryan, Ochsner, and Yarnall 2001). However, early education in the twenty-first century is one characterized by both increasing standardization and diversity. Sophisticated forms of technology and globalization have lead to a diversity of student populations and family structures that has never before been experienced. At the same time the current emphasis across the Western world to harness early education as a means of ensuring ongoing productivity is resulting in increasing standardization. Given these circumstances, it is quite probable that much more attention will need to be given to teachers and pedagogy to learn how to respond effectively to young children in these changed and changing times.

Further Readings: Bredekamp, Sue, and Carol Copple, eds. (1997). *Developmentally appropriate practice in early childhood programs.* Rev. ed. Washington DC: National Association for the Education of Young Children. Edwards, C. P. (2002). Three approaches from Europe: Waldorf, Montessori, and Reggio Emilia. *Early Childhood Research and Practice* [Online], 4(1). Genishi, Celia, Sharon Ryan, Mindy Ochsner, and Mary Yarnall (2001). Teaching in early childhood education: Understanding practices through research and theory. In Virginia Richardson, ed., *Handbook of research on teaching.* 4th ed. Washington DC: American Educational Research Association, pp. 1175–1210; Katz, L. (1995). *Talks with teachers of young children.* Norwood, NJ: Ablex Publishing Corporation; Krogh, S. L., and K. L. Slentz (2001). *Early childhood education, yesterday, today and tomorrow.* Mahwah, NJ: Lawrence Erlbaum Associates. Luke, C. (1996). Introduction. In Carmen Luke, ed., *Feminisms and pedagogies of everyday life.* Albany: State University of New York Press, pp. 1–27; Mallory, B., and R. S. New, eds. (1994). *Diversity and developmentally appropriate practices: challenges for early childhood education.* New York: Teachers College Press. Monroe, P. (1913). *A cyclopedia of education.* New York: Macmillan.

Sharon Ryan and Amy Hornbeck

Pedagogy, Activity-Based/Experiential

Activity-based, experiential pedagogy asserts that effective learning in early childhood (and sometimes beyond) requires opportunities for children to engage in activities on their own initiative for extended periods of time. The immediate, active interplay with objects and their inherent concepts, or consideration of people's roles and their various relationships to one another, allows children to begin to develop an authentic understanding of how they work. The underlying theories of this form of pedagogy posit that children are not passive recipients of knowledge transmitted from their environment, but active participants in their own development as they interpret, construct, and transform their experiences, taking learning into their own hands both literally and figuratively. Many current educational philosophies in the United States and Europe make use of these theories in their rationale for child-directed, play-based experiences at school, including the approaches of Maria **Montessori** (1962), **Waldorf** (Oldfield, 2001), **Reggio Emilia**, the Creative Curriculum, **High/Scope**, and Koplow's therapeutic curriculum (1996).

The roots of activity-based, experiential pedagogy go back to the early 1800s, when German educator Friedrich **Froebel** (1782–1852) created the first **kindergarten** program, a carefully planned and monitored environment where young children could freely use thoughtfully selected materials that Froebel called gifts.

These gifts, also known as occupations, included geometric shapes made of wood and metal, yarn and cloth, paper, pencils, and scissors. Froebel believed that **play** is the heart of the learning process, utilizing children's "channeling of spontaneous energies into orderly behavior" (Gutek, 1991). He conceived of the classroom as a place to experience happiness and fulfillment at an early age and to develop a sense of self, benefiting both the individual and society as the child grew toward adulthood.

Soon after Froebel, the new field of psychology provided a plethora of theories supporting activity-based, experiential learning, including the work of Sigmund **Freud**, Erik **Erikson**, Jean **Piaget**, and Lev **Vygotsky**. Central to their concepts of ego development (Freud), identity formation (Erikson), equilibration (Piaget), and the zone of proximal development (Vygotsky) is the premise that children are active agents in their own individual development.

In the United States, John **Dewey** (1859–1952) articulated a philosophy of experience-based learning as a dialectic between students and mentors. He believed that learning began when a student encountered experiences where there was doubt, uncertainty, and questioning. Dewey considered the human mind, from the youngest age onward, to have the capacity for seeking answers through self-initiated, trial-and-error inquiry, facilitated by a teacher or mentor figure. He implemented his educational philosophy in developing the Laboratory School at the University of Chicago.

American psychologist and educator Jerome **Bruner** (born 1915) extended Dewey's ideas to their more contemporary expression—namely, the role of play in early education. Bruner describes play as an approach to action, rather than as a particular form of activity. The important characteristic of the mental approach to experiences during play is its nonliteral, not-for-real premise. In play with objects and during pretending, children engage in hypothetical thinking: "What if I be the auntie and you be the policeman and my dog is sick . . ." Children work through ideas to their logical conclusions and then rewrite the script, switching roles and trying out different possibilities. Play is critical to development, Bruner argues, because through it children refine their skills in symbolic thinking and in using symbols, particularly language, as they establish a sense of meaningful connection to the ideas and experiences around them (1977).

American early childhood educator Vivian Paley has provided some of the richest descriptions in the professional literature of young children's learning through **play as storytelling**. Her many books (c.f., 1981) describe the implementation of play-based experiential learning in contemporary early childhood classrooms. Paley's work expands our understanding of experience-based activity as pedagogy and, in particular, the teacher's role. As Paley has grown in her understanding of children's play, she has revised her understanding of the teacher's role in relation to children's learning:

> There was a time when I believed it was my task to show the children how to solve their problems. I wrote: I do not ask you to stop thinking about play. Our contract [between teacher and children] read more like this: If you will keep trying to explain yourselves, I will keep showing you how to think about the problems you need to solve.

After a few years, the contract needed to be rewritten: Let me study your play and figure out how play helps you solve your problems. Play contains your questions, and I must know what questions you are asking before mine will be useful.

Even this is not accurate enough. Today I would add: Put your play into formal narratives, and I will help you and your classmates listen to one another. In this way, you will build a literature of images and themes, of beginnings and endings, of references and allusions. You must invent your own literature if you are to connect your ideas to the ideas of others. (1990, p. 18)

Paley explores how child-initiated activities in the classroom are opportunities for learning not just because children interact with objects and people, but because there is a teacher present who can prepare the environment for such learning, observe, and at times interact with children during their activities. For experiential activity to be a form of pedagogy, a teacher is necessary: a teacher who is conscious of what can be gained from the experiences and can guide children toward those benefits (McNamee, 2005).

American educator Judith Lindfors delineates some of the early childhood teacher's roles as *providing, learning, observing,* and *responding* (1987). Her description of these roles provides a blueprint for implementing activity-based, experiential learning. As provider, the teacher ensures that there is space, materials, and time for children to engage in self-initiated activities. The teacher also provides a safe environment for children's experimentation and exploration, including psychological support through acknowledgment of their choices. She provides questions and suggestions to spur, challenge, and extend their thinking about the objects, ideas, or people they are considering.

Lindfors' "teacher as learner" (as opposed to "teacher as knower") emphasizes the importance of uncovering children's own interests and questions and following their thought processes. Listening is an essential skill to fulfill this role. As a learner, the teacher is continually challenged to rethink and refine her pedagogical approach.

Listening is closely related to observing—both yield rich insights about children's paths of inquiry. When teachers observe, they seek to "read children's behavior" (Lindfors 1987, p. 302) and find meaning in their actions and comments. The teacher as observer is viewing and interpreting the learning situation from the child's point of view. Having observed, she is in a stronger position to assume the role of responder.

Responding often begins with a statement reflecting back to the children what the teacher is seeing—details about their choice of activity, their arrangement and use of materials, their affect while working. Teachers look for openings to ask questions, to find out if the child wants to think out loud or wants help with some aspect of the activity. It is a delicate balance between responding and intruding, but the boundaries are usually discussed and negotiated on an ongoing basis as part of the discourse patterns in classrooms where children customarily take initiative for learning. Responding as a teacher also includes commenting on children's efforts in a way that provides emotional and intellectual validation for what they are trying to achieve and expands the possibilities inherent in their activity. Lindfors writes, "Now the response is to help, now to meet the child's idea with a new idea, now to suggest, now to encourage, now to partner—always sensitive to the particular child at the particular moment" (1987, p. 306).

Activity-based, experiential learning does not mean that children can do anything they choose at any time. Likewise, for the teacher to carry out the role of pedagogical leader in this approach requires discipline and training. Lindfors argues that the role mirrors what family and community members do, intuitively and unconsciously, in the language-learning process outside of schools. The principles of adult guidance in out-of-school environments are similar to the role of the teacher in the experience-based classroom, where the knowing, judging teacher is replaced by the listening, learning teacher (1987).

American psychologist Barbara Rogoff looks at experiential learning beyond the classroom (2003). Focusing primarily on non-Western cultures, where teaching and learning are often embedded in activities in which younger members of the family and community participate alongside more mature and experienced members, she highlights the social and cultural dynamics that shape learning in and out of school. These dynamics usually involve fluctuating relationships of control, active work, talk, and experimenting as tasks get done, and learning likewise—learning that is both intentional as well as a by-product of the apprenticeships children have with elders in their families, communities and schools. Like Rogoff, American psychologist Michael Cole takes a sociocultural approach to the study of human development and education (1999) in a wide range of school and community settings. The work of Rogoff, Cole and their colleagues is helping to illuminate the broader principles of activity-based, experiential pedagogy that cross school, home, and community environments and provide the foundation for optimizing learning in each of these settings.

Further Readings: Bruner, J. (1977). Introduction. In B. Tizard and D. Harvey, eds. *Biology and Play.* London: Heinemann Medical Books. Cole, M. (1996). *Cultural psychology: A once and future discipline.* Cambridge, MA: The Belknap Press of Harvard University Press. Erikson, E. (1950). *Childhood and society.* 2nd ed. New York: W.W. Norton. Gutek, G. (1991). Cultural foundations of education: a biographical introduction. New York: MacMillan Publishing Company. Koplow, L., ed. (1996). *Unsmiling faces: How preschools can heal.* New York: Teachers College Press. Lindfors, J. (1987). *Children's language and learning.* 2nd ed. Englewood Cliffs, NJ: Prentice-Hall, Inc. McNamee, G. D. (2005). The one who gathers children: The work of Vivian Gussin Paley and current debates about how we educate young children. *Journal of Early Childhood Teacher Education* 25, 275–296. Montessori, M. (1962). *The discovery of the child.* Wheaton, IL: Theosophical Press. Oldfield, L. (2001). Free to learn: Introducing Steiner Waldorf early childhood education. Gloucestershire: Hawthorn Press. Paley, V. G. (1981). *Wally's stories.* Cambridge, MA: Harvard University Press. Rogoff, B. (2003). *The cultural nature of human development.* New York: Oxford University Press. Weikart, D. P., L. Rogers, Adcock, C., and D. McClelland (1971). *The cognitively oriented curriculum: a framework for preschool teachers.* Washington, DC: NAEYC.

Gillian D. McNamee

Pedagogy, Child-Centered

A child-centered pedagogy places learners in the foreground of the educative process. It is their purposes, interests, and needs that guide curriculum formation. The belief that the most appropriate education for young children should be child-centered has its roots in the progressive education movement that emerged in the late eighteenth century. Influenced by the naturalistic ideas of Jean-Jacques **Rousseau**, Johann **Pestalozzi**, and Friedrich **Froebel** that opposed traditional school approaches and reflecting wider social currents that embraced the ideal of progress through science and reason, progressive educators believed that "a natural educational methodology could free man by advancing him along the path to a better world" (Gutek, 1972, p. 386). At the turn of the 20th century, American progressive educators began a quest to change the school curriculum from a focus on the intellect trained through recitation and teacher direction, to one that emphasized beginning with the child and encouraging development of problem solving and social skills through direct experience with the environment. By educating for understanding and cooperation, progressive educators claimed that the next generation would have the intellectual tools to create and maintain a democratic, free, and open society. The progressive zeal for education as the means for improving society impacted all arenas of education, including the world of the young child in **kindergarten**.

It was the rigid interpretation of the Froebelian curriculum implemented in kindergartens across the United States that came under the attack of the progressives in early education. Seeking to replace intuitive and philosophical ways of knowing about young children, the progressives advocated for a scientific knowledge base and practices built on psychological principles (Silin, 1987). During this period of ferment, the child study movement emerged as a unique field of inquiry. Employing questionnaires and scientific observation of children's behavior, G. Stanley **Hall** argued for the direct study of the child in naturalistic settings as the basis for educational decision making. Around the same time, John **Dewey** proposed a science of education based on a pragmatic philosophy of experience. Children's interests and purposes were to be used to develop educational experiences that engaged students in problem solving and learning the skills for participating in a democracy. While both of these theoretical approaches suggested that kindergarten curriculum begins with the child, others like Edward Lee **Thorndike** argued for kindergarten teachers to "stimulate the formation of acceptable habits in children and to inhibit inappropriate ones" (Weber, 1969, p. 54).

Over the first three decades of the 20th century, progressive kindergarten educators experimented with the challenge of replacing the inflexible sequence of the Froebelian gifts (manipulative activities) and occupations (handwork projects) as the organizers of the curriculum with other experiences and materials that were based on these new educational theories. Although diversity abounded both in the theoretical rationales and the practices labeled progressive, Weber (1969) argues that by 1925, most reconstructed kindergarten programs were characterized by similar features: (a) using children's play as the natural medium for learning, (b) basing curriculum on knowledge of young children's development and interests, (c) a concern for proper health, (d) a work-play period, and (e) similar materials such as blocks, dolls, etc.

Although the progressive movement lost its dominant hold on the kindergarten curriculum during the ensuing decades, its child-centered approaches have continued through the field's increasing use of child development knowledge as the primary source for decisions regarding methods and programs (Silin, 1987). The theories and research drawn from developmental psychology have generated different approaches to the practice of child-centered education (e.g., the **Bank Street** Approach, **Developmentally Appropriate Practice** (DAP), **High/Scope** Curriculum, the **Project Approach**) but all of these versions are united by similar themes.

The first of these themes is autonomy. Children are viewed as individuals with their own desires, interests, and needs who require freedom from adult authority to explore ideas independently (Burman, 1994). Tied to developing children's autonomy, therefore, is the opportunity for student choice in the curriculum. Children are assumed to know when they are ready to learn and to be able to make appropriate choices about their learning. Through exercising their freedom to choose, children develop independence, self-control, and responsibility. Third is the validation of children's natural need to play as pedagogy. Play is intrinsically tied to children's interests; therefore, child-centered educators argue that play fosters persistence and competence because children find learning meaningful (Burman, 1994). Fourth, rather than compartmentalizing knowledge, in a child-centered pedagogy, knowledge is integrated. Children learn through experience in the physical and social worlds with teachers assisting them to connect ideas encountered during play to broader disciplines and frameworks of ideas. Thus, the final theme is the construct of the teacher as a facilitator and supporter of children's learning. Rather than instructing children, teachers structure the environment, selecting activities and offering suggestions or questions that will allow children to continue to explore and build on their learning (Burman, 1994). In contrast to the oppressive practices of transmission educational approaches, advocates for a child-centered education argue that the emphasis on personal choice and freedom from adult authority in a developmentally appropriate curriculum responds to individual differences and ensures educational success for all.

Despite the widespread endorsement of child-centered pedagogy in the field, political and intellectual forces have begun to disrupt what is meant by this term. Using critical theories to deconstruct the values and methods of developmental psychology, and developmentally appropriate practice, some scholars question whether teachers can enact individually and culturally appropriate practices when most of the studies underpinning accepted views of children's development have been conducted with homogenous populations (white, middle-class) (New 1994). For these scholars, child-centered pedagogy cannot be grounded by child development knowledge alone, but must be informed by a range of knowledges that enable teachers to respond to diversity and the ways in which childhood is changing (Ryan and Grieshaber 2004). Paradoxically, at the same time as this debate is taking place, there is also increasing standardization of the early childhood curriculum as evidenced by the imposition of academic standards for preschool (Roskos and Neuman. 2005), the increasing expectation that teachers use empirically validated curriculum models, and the implementation of a national curriculum in some countries (e.g., Great Britain). Therefore, similar to the ferment that took place at the beginning of the twentieth century, the aims and methods of child-centered pedagogy are once again being contested. How child-centered pedagogies are re-envisioned for the twenty-first century remains unclear. What is clear, however, is that because of globalization, to be child-centered will require teachers to respond to ever-increasingly diverse student populations, changing family structures, and an expansion in the kinds of knowledge and experiences children bring with them to early childhood programs.

Further Readings: Burman, Erica (1994). *Deconstructing developmental psychology.* London: Routledge. Gutek, Gerald L. (1972). *A history of the western educational experience.* New York: Random House. Neuman, Susan, B., and Kathleen Roskos (2005). The state of prekindergarten standards. *Early Childhood Research Quarterly* 20(2), 125–145; New, Rebecca (1994). Culture, child development, and developmentally appropriate practices: Teachers as collaborative researchers. In Bruce Mallory and Rebecca New, eds., *Diversity and developmentally appropriate practices: Challenges for early childhood education.* New York: Teachers College Press, pp. 65–83; Ryan, Sharon, and Susan J. Grieshaber. (2004). It's more than child development: Critical theories, research, and teaching young children. *Young Children* 59, 44–52; Silin, Jonathan (1987). The early childhood educator's knowledge base: A reconsideration. In Lillian Katz, ed. *Current topics in early childhood education.* Vol. 7. Norwood, NJ: Ablex, pp. 17–31; Weber, Evelyn (1969). *The kindergarten.* New York: Teachers College Press. Williams, Leslie R. (1992). Determining the curriculum. In Carol Seefeldt, ed., *The early childhood curriculum: A review of current research.* New York: Teachers College Press, pp. 1–15.

Sharon Ryan

Pedagogy, Play-Based

Play has been the cornerstone of high quality early childhood pedagogy in Western society since the early days of the field almost two hundred years ago (Klugman and Smilansky, 1990). All of the major theorists, from Friedrich **Froebel** to Jean **Piaget,** locate play as the primary developmental task of preschoolers. However, while almost everyone places play at the center of their curriculum, there has never been consensus about what play is or why it is a valuable activity for young children. Depending on what theory you subscribe to, play can be organized as a highly structured activity that is primarily designed to teach particular skills, or as a completely exploratory activity free from any adult interference. Current understandings of play are reflected in several examples of a play-based early childhood pedagogy that puts this theory into practice.

In the last several decades the work of the Russian psychologist Lev **Vygotsky** has emerged as one of the most influential theories in the creation of educational programs for young children. Vygotsky's work on **culture**, learning, and development has had a major impact on what is considered **developmentally appropriate practice** and has helped shape many of the more recent **curriculum** and programs for young children. However, while his name has become well known, there has been only limited attention paid to Vygotsky's ideas about play and this limited focus has affected our ability to make full use of Vygotsky's work to develop pedagogies that are creative, developmental and true to the improvisational nature of children's play.

For Vygotsky (1978), play is not just an outward expression of a child's developmental level; it is an activity that leads development. Play allows children to function on the outer edge of their zone of proximal development, to be ahead of where they are. Vygotsky believed that development does not happen inside the child, but that it comes into existence socially. He created the concept of the zone of proximal development (ZPD) to give expression to the relationship between what the child can do independently and what the child can do in collaboration with others (Newman and Holzman, 1993). Vygotsky argued that if we only focus on what the child can do independently then we only see what has already developed and we miss what is developing. He pointed out that children are able to do many more things within a supportive social context than they can do alone.

Over the years there have been many interpretations of the ZPD. Some psychologists and educators have focused on the instrumental value of the ZPD as a teaching technique for helping an individual child do what is a little beyond her or his independent skill level by being supported by an adult or a more skilled peer. However, another way to understand the ZPD is as a creative, improvisational activity. The ZPD is the activity of people creating environments where children (and adults) can take risks, make mistakes, and support each other to do what they do not yet know how to do. It is by participating in creating environments where learning can occur that children learn (Newman and Holzman, 1993; Wink, 2001).

Vygotsky talked about the creation of zones of proximal development in many different situations—babies learning to speak, the instructional environment of formal schooling, and, for the purposes of this article, in the play activities of preschool-age children. According to Vygotsky in the following excerpt, it is in play that children are able to do what they do not yet know how to do:

> play creates a zone of proximal development for the child. In play a child always behaves beyond his average age, above his daily behavior; in play it is as though he were a head taller than himself. (Vygotsky, 1978, p. 102)

What makes play a ZPD? Why are children able to perform "a head taller than" themselves when they play? Vygotsky took pains to point out that a distinguishing feature of all play is that it involves the creation of an imaginary situation. Whether it is a game of chess or baseball or an imaginary play scenario about being Princesses fighting a dragon, all play involves creating, and working within, an imaginary situation.

In addition, Vygotsky also pointed out that all play has rules. This may not be immediately apparent when we picture the seemingly chaotic play of preschool-age children, but Vygotsky was talking about a particular kind of rules—rules that are in the service of, and help to create, the imaginary situation. For Vygotsky, it is the relationship between the imaginary situation and the rules that are created that makes the play of young children a ZPD.

This is not an easy concept to grasp, so let's take for example a group of four-year olds playing at being princesses. This is clearly an imaginary situation—no one is really a princess—but what kind of rules are there? They are not the same as the rules of chess or Monopoly where the rules have been established by other people long before the game starts. When playing at being princesses the children have to create the rules for the play as they go along. While they may be influenced by what they have seen of princesses on TV or in fairy tales, the children have to figure out how they are going to play at being princesses together at the same time that they are playing at being princesses. Among other things they have to decide who is going to be a Princess, what other characters there will be, how the characters will behave, what their relationships are going to be like, how long they are going to play, etc. But they don't do this before they play at being princesses, they create these rules in the process of creating the princesses play. The rules are inseparable from the playing of the game—determining these things is what brings the play situation into existence. In this situation the rules are both the tool for creating the imaginary situation and they are the imaginary situation itself.

From this perspective, the play of young children is a zone of proximal development because it is in playing that children are most actively involved in creating the activity. In play children do not conform or adapt to a preexistent reality, they create an imaginary situation and the rules for performing in that imaginary situation at the same time (Newman and Holzman, 1993). The children, as both the creator and the follower of the rules, can perform in ways that are in advance of what they can do in other situations (Vygotsky, 1978). Many educators and psychologists have pointed out that it is this feature of play—the fact that the players themselves create it—that makes play such a great way for children to learn and develop.

Examples of Playful Pedagogies

The remainder of this entry is devoted to two examples of early childhood pedagogy that I believe exemplify this Vygotskian understanding of play and the zone of proximal development.

Playworlds. The Playworlds project was first created in Finland by Gunilla Lundqvist (1995) and has been further developed by Penti Haikkarainin (2004). Playworlds has taken place in preschools and elementary schools in Japan, Finland, and the United States. In the Playworlds project (Baumer, Ferholt and Lecusay, 2005; Rainio, 2005), children and adults cocreate an imaginary world using children's literature, fables and folk tales as the starting point. Each day for an extended period of time the classroom (or part of the classroom) is transformed into a fictional world where the adults take on the roles of the characters in the book and the children help shape the performances as both characters and commentators. Through this collaboration children are supported to continue being creative even as they make the transition from free play to organized school activities.

> The idea is that in playworlds two seemingly different worlds, of play and school, of children and adults meet in an institutional context and develop a new form of improvised and dramatized learning activity. (Rainio, 2005)

Improvisational Play Intervention

Barbara O'Neill (2004) is an early childhood special education teacher who works as a SEIT (Special Education Itinerant Teacher) in New York City. Her job is to work in general education preschools with children who have been diagnosed as having a learning or developmental disability. She has developed an approach to play intervention that is based on the similarities between the fantasy play of young children and the performance art of improv comedians. In both activities the participants create unscripted scenes or stories using their collective imaginations.

Most of the children that O'Neill works with have trouble participating in fantasy play with other children. Traditional play intervention programs address this "deficit" by teaching the children isolated play skills, coaching them through interactions with other children or teaching the typically developing children how play with special needs children. O'Neill has developed an approach where she teaches mixed groupings of children the games and activities that adult improv comedians play—she creates a preschool improv ensemble with both special needs and typically developing children.

In improv anything any performer says or does is considered an offer and the job of the improv troupe is to make use of all offers by using them to create the scene. As O'Neill (2004) says, "This includes the good, the bad, the weird and the interesting. (p. 5)" In the improv play groups O'Neill and the children make use of all the offers the children make—even something as simple as a head shake, a hand gesture, or a single inaudible word are usable in the improv games. While O'Neill may have to be the one to make use of these offers in the beginning, over time the ensemble develops in their ability to include everyone. As the ensemble develops, the children learn that they are players, and from a Vygotskian perspective, they are able to perform ahead of where they are.

> I think the biggest thing that I want children to have is to start to see themselves as performers and creators. These are children who at the age of 4 already have lowered expectations for who they will become. So I really want to help the kids I work with to understand that they constantly have different choices they can make and don't have to react the way they are supposed to react, the way they usually react. (O'Neill, 2005)

Conclusion

In both the Playworlds and the Improvisational Play Interventions children and adults create imaginary situations together and in doing so the children are able to stretch and do things they would not otherwise be able to do. They are just two examples of the infinite ways play can be a central part of developmentally appropriate and innovative pedagogy for young children.

Further Readings: Baumer, S., B. Ferholt, and R. Lecusay (2006). Promoting narrative competence through adult-child joint pretense: Lessons from the Scandinavian educational practice of playworld. *Cognitive Development*, 20(4) 576-590. Hakkarainen, P. (2004). Narrative learning in the fifth dimension. *Critical Social Studies* 2004(1), 1-20;

Klugman, E., and S. Smilansky (1990). *Children's play and learning: Perspectives and policy implications.* New York: TC Press. Lundqvist, G. (1995). *The aesthetics of play: A didactic study of play and culture in preschools.* Uppsala, Sweden: Uppsala Studies in Education. O'Neill, B. (2004). *Improvisational play interventions: A SEIT teacher chronicles the development of a play group.* Unpublished manuscript. New York: Teachers College, Columbia University. Newman, F., and L. Holzman (1993). *Lev Vygostsky: Revolutionary scientist.* London: Routledge. Rainio, P. (2005). *Emergence of a playworld. The formation of subjects of learning in interaction between children and adults.* Working Papers 32. Helsinki, Finland: Center for Activity Theory and Developmental Work Research. Sawyer, K. (1997). *Pretend play as improvisation: Conversation in the preschool classroom.* New York: Lawrence Erlbaum Associates. Van Hoorn, J., P. Nourot, B. Scales, and K. Alward (2003). *Play at the center of the curriculum.* 3rd ed. Upper Saddle River, NJ: Merrill Prentice Hall. Vygotsky, L. (1978). *Mind in society.* Cambridge, MA: Harvard University Press. Wink, J. (2001). *A vision of Vygotsky.* New York: Putney.

Carrie Lobman

Pedagogy, Social Justice/Equity

Social justice/equity pedagogy is a multifaceted approach to teaching and learning that seeks to identify, resist, and transform various forms of oppression (race, class, gender, sexual orientation, etc.) in schools and society. Social justice/equity pedagogy is based on two premises about the relationship between schools and society. First, schools have both a social responsibility and obligation to produce citizens who are able to participate meaningfully and substantively within an ever-changing, technological, multicultural and global democracy. Second, what occurs daily in classrooms between teachers and students both *shapes* and *is shaped* by social, cultural, historical, and current political contexts. As such, social justice/equity pedagogy serves as an education reform effort that is rooted in the everyday classroom interactions between students, teachers, parents, and administrators. The ultimate and additional goal of social justice/equity pedagogy is to ignite social reform and change within other institutions throughout society. Within this framework, the purpose of teaching and education is more than achieving traditional academic and social outcomes. Rather, the ultimate purpose of teaching (and education) is to identify and scrutinize current inequitable practices within schools and society while simultaneously creating socially just, democratic, and liberatory alternatives for tomorrow's society. Furthermore, educators pursuant of this approach labor to employ a pedagogical praxis that is as follows:

- **Critical/reflective:** Students are encouraged and taught to closely interrogate all knowledge for various forms of bias. Students learn to ask critical questions such as, "Who benefits and who suffers?" "Was that fair or unfair?" "Whose knowledge is this?" "What perspective(s) is/are missing?" Social justice/equity educators approach and present no information or knowledge as objective, value-free, and uncontested truth. In contrast, teachers acknowledge that all knowledge presented in school contexts is subjective and engage students in activities that encourage them to critically analyze and problematize the curriculum. In addition, to help students develop an understanding that no particular form of knowledge is more significant than any other form or source of knowledge, teachers encourage and include critiques of real-life events, situations, movies, structures, among others. Through these processes of critical analysis and reflection, students ultimately develop a sense of critical consciousness needed to identify and combat oppression within their localized school contexts and the larger society. Young children are especially eager to discuss their interpretations of what is fair.

- **Culturally Relevant and Responsive:** Social justice/equity teachers do not see student's native/home culture as an impediment to school success as was traditionally the case with the most deficit-oriented models of school reform; instead, they use students' home culture as an important and useful tool in helping students develop and acquire school knowledge, skills, and dispositions. Teachers construct lessons in ways that learning will be meaningful and relevant to cultural and lived experiences of the students involved. In this process, students are not required to shed their home or native cultures while working to acquire the school culture. Instead, socially just/equitable educators work to maintain and build upon students' home/native cultures while aiding students in acquiring the skills, dispositions, language, and knowledge base necessary to be successful in school settings and beyond. Teachers frame curriculum and teaching around issues that are naturally important to the students' everyday needs and interests. In this sense, teachers create a **curriculum** that is tentative and ever-emergent based on what interests, questions, and or challenges students are involved in from moment to moment. It is important to note that this does not mean that socially just/equitable teachers don't adhere to specific and rigorous standards in their teaching. What this does mean is that, compared to other pedagogical strategies frequently used in settings with a significant population of students of color (e.g., direct instruction, teaching to the test), students' interests and needs are used as the basis by which curricula content is taught. Finally, a core theme in culturally relevant and responsive teaching is the notion of education as a project of social activism and social justice. Teachers not only encourage students to 'trouble' oppressive structures in society, but they also make spaces for them to work toward developing solutions to these problems. The teacher's role, within this tenet, is to provide support, encouragement, insight, and resources for children to take social action toward resisting and eradicating many of these troubling structures. Moreover, teachers work to help students connect with their current acts toward social change and historical legacies of social justice. In early childhood setting with young children, this sort of endeavor resonates with principles of an antibias multicultural curriculum.
- **Multicultural and Antioppressive:** In an attempt to address the changing demographics in public schools, socially just teachers use action-oriented measures in identifying, combating, and deconstructing injustice within localized learning contexts. First, teachers labor to identify, resist, and transform deep-seated and overarching oppressive pedagogical structures (i.e., tracking, ability grouping, etc.) within their immediate classroom and school contexts. Next, teachers work to transform the curriculum to become more inclusive and respectful of the histories, knowledges, and ways of seeing and knowing that their students bring to school. Lastly, teachers work to incorporate multiple and culture/race-specific pedagogical strategies for teaching and assessment. In this sense, teachers work to construct pedagogical

practices that are both equitable (fair in terms of the needs of the individual student) and equal (fair in terms of what is accessible/available to all students).

- **Active/participatory:** Socially just/equitable teachers believe that learning is a social process that requires active participation and engagement in learning activities. Therefore, as contrasted with more traditional and passive models of teaching and learning, where students are perceived as empty receptacles awaiting deposits of knowledge from teachers, social justice/equity pedagogy encourages teachers to create learning opportunities in which students can actively construct/create their own meanings. In this sense, learning is a matter of doing or being and not simply recitation or memorization. Therefore, teachers frequently use teaching strategies, for example, role playing, mock trials, and voting—a strategy that young children can learn to understand and utilize in their own democratic decision making.

- **Democratic:** Socially just/equitable educators work to create classroom environments that are democratic in nature. That is, at its core, teachers work to create classroom settings where students are encouraged to challenge, question, and solve problems collectively and collaboratively. Students are urged to think about and make decisions in terms of "what is best" for the majority or group and the individual students within the class. Social justice/equity educators believe that democracy is a concept that students must experience in order to understand it. They frequently utilize pedagogical strategies like inquiry and experimentation to convey themes and concepts related to social justice/equity. The social studies curriculum for young children emphasizes similar goals.

- **Caring/Loving/Passionate:** Social justice/equity teachers work to create classroom and learning environments in which students feel cared about and in which care for others in the classroom and the world is promoted.

- **Academic Achievement:** Social justice/equity pedagogy not only strives to aid students in making social changes in tomorrow's society, but it also works to teach students how to be successful within the current society. Through its use of critical and activist curriculum and teaching experiences, social justice/equity pedagogy aims to inspire higher levels of academic performance than more traditional forms of teaching and assessment. The basic premise is that when students write, discuss, reflect, and think about "real" ideas, content, and issues, they are more likely to exhibit higher levels of engagement, motivation, investment, and ultimately achievement than when students are disengaged and disconnected from the content being taught. *See also* Curriculum, Emergent; Curriculum, Social Studies; Multicultural and Antibias Education.

Further Readings: Banks, Cherry A. McGee, and James A. Banks (1995). Equity pedagogy: An essential component of multicultural education. *Theory into Practice* 34, 152–158. Bigelow, B., B. Harvey, S. Karp, and L. Miller (2001). *Rethinking our classrooms: Teaching for equity and justice.* Burlington, VT: Rethinking Schools. Dewey, J. (1966). *Democracy and education.* New York: Free Press. Freire, P. (1997). *Pedagogy of the oppressed.* New York: Continuum. Gay, Geneva (2002). Preparing for culturally responsive teaching. *Journal of Teacher Education* 53(2), 106–116. Ladson-Billings, G. (1994). *Dreamkeepers: Successful teachers of African-American children.* San Francisco: Jossey-Bass. Noddings, N. (2003). C*aring: A feminine approach to ethics and moral education.* Berkeley: University of California Press. Vygotsky, S. L. (1978). *Mind in society.* Cambridge, MA: Harvard University Press.

Terry Husband and Adrienne Dixon

Peer Culture

The concept of "peer culture" has been researched and elaborated over the past two decades by Sociologist William Corsaro and his students, and by colleagues who have been inspired by him. In his original work, Corsaro (1985) immersed himself in a preschool classroom for a contextualized, situated, and extended look at the life world of three- and four-year-olds as they play and interact with each other—on their own terms, for their own purposes, and with their own rhythms. What resulted from this long-term fieldwork was a landmark theoretical contribution, a description of children's group life as peer culture. Corsaro defines peer culture as "a stable set of activities or routines, artifacts, values or concerns that kids produce and share in interaction with each other" (2003, p. 37). Corsaro takes an interpretive view of culture as public, collective, and performative, in contrast to traditional work that defines culture as internalized, shared values and norms guiding behavior and affecting individual development, which are transmitted across generations. In introducing this interpretive cultural lens to the study of childhood, Corsaro extends and reinterprets the meanings of children's group life, friendships, and peer involvements, previously the topics of such classic work as Opie and Opie's (1959) study of the game play of British children and Konner's (1981) study of infant behavior and juveniles among the Kung San.

Corsaro's contributions have helped us gain a fuller understanding of the meanings and nature of children's play, of the social dynamics (which they must negotiate), and of the complex accomplishment of group life. Taking a cross-cultural, comparative perspective in early educational settings in the United States and Italy, Corsaro's research reveals much about children's affiliation with each other as a process of social construction and face-to-face negotiation; the production and sharing of local peer cultures in American and Italian contexts; the relationships between children's peer culture constructions and their conceptions of and reactions to adult rules and constraints; children's rejection and exclusion of others as they protect fragile "interactive space" and; children's appropriation of wider popular cultures resources (e.g., myths, folklore, television and movies, literature) into peer culture themes and texts. Taken in total, Corsaro's contribution has been the construction of a theory of childhood socialization as a process of interpretive reproduction, rather than a process of social transmission.

Building on Corsaro's peer culture theory, one team of early childhood researchers used a series of linked analyses to examine classroom processes for understanding friendship and peer culture life within the context of becoming a student (summarized in Kantor and Fernie, 2003). Different aspects of these mutually informing analyses were used to demonstrate how the value and meanings of particular artifacts are locally constructed and, thus, become mediators of children's peer culture play; how affiliation, inclusion, and exclusion are created and managed to serve local peer culture dynamics rather than in reaction to individuals' personality attributes; how children and teachers position themselves (in relationship to others) in ways that are more complex than simple labels such as "peer," "leader," and "teacher" connote; how the learning of literacy is embedded within school and peer cultures; how participation in school events such as circle time and small group develops over time and is situated within the larger and particular school and peer cultures; and how multiple aspects of children's subject identities are constructed in play, peer interactions, and school events.

Other researchers have explored similar phenomena without necessarily using the term *peer culture*. For example, Vivian Paley writes of the social worlds of children at play in her many volumes written over the length of her career. In such classics as *Superheroes in the Doll Corner* (1984) Paley interprets classroom dynamics from children's perspectives and explores the meanings of their social dynamics. Similarly, Dyson's links between writing and what she calls the "unofficial world of the classroom" (Dyson, 1997) and Gutierrez and collegues' (1997) exploration of what they call the "third space" in classroom life evokes images and concerns similar to Corsaro's peer culture notion.

The growing body of work on children's peer cultures makes an important contribution to a set of enduring questions explored by scores of child development and early childhood researchers and teachers. What is the value and the various outcomes of children's play? How does children's play change over time? What are the long-term benefits of children's play? What are children's successful and unsuccessful strategies for interacting with their peers? What contributes to leadership and popularity in socially successful children and conversely, what contributes to peer rejection, isolation, or unpopularity in children who are unsuccessful at such an early age? How do we provide supports and intervention for children who are less successful in social interaction and play? Taken together, these earlier studies have provided us with descriptions of the developmental trajectory (i.e., stages) of children's play, the relationship between child development and adult endpoints, and a perspective (i.e., sociometrics) on various social statuses and their behavioral characteristics and long-term consequences. This larger and important research tradition has given us important guidance to support children at play.

But research that answers these questions reflects adult perspectives, theories and concerns. To fully understand the nature and meanings of children's play, we also need to take into account children's perspectives, a view of the group as well as the individual, and children's views of the social worlds they create. Sociologist William Corsaro knew this and entered children's worlds to see what he would find there. *See also* Peers and Friends.

Further Readings: Corsaro, W. A. (1985). *Friendship and peer culture in the early years.* Norwood, NJ: Ablex. Corsaro, W. A. (1996). Transitions in early childhood: The promise of comparative, longitudinal, ethnography. In R. Jessor, A. Colby, and R. Shweder, eds., *Ethnography and human development.* Chicago: University of Chicago Press, pp. 419–457; Corsaro, W. A. (2003). *"We're friends, right?": Inside kids' culture.* Washington, DC: Joseph Henry Press. Corsaro, W. A. (2004). *The sociology of childhood.* Thousand Oaks, CA: Pine Forge Press; Dyson, A. H. (1997). *Writing superheroes: Contemporary childhood, popular culture, and classroom literacy.* New York: Teachers College Press; Gutierrez, K., D. Baquedano-Lopez, P. Turner, and G. Myrna (1997). Putting language back into language arts: When the radical middle meets the third space. *Language Arts* 74(5), 368–378; Kantor, R., and D. Fernie, eds. (2003). Early childhood classroom processes. Cresskill, NJ: Hampton Press. Konner M. J. (1981). Evolution of human behavior development. In R. H. Munroe, R. L. Munroe, and J. M. Whiting, eds., *Handbook of cross-cultural human development.* New York: Garland STPM Press, pp. 3–52; Opie, I., and P. Opie (1959).

The lore and language of school children. Oxford: Oxford University Press. Paley, V. G. (1984). *Boys and girls: Superheroes in the doll corner.* Chicago: University of Chicago Press. Ramsey, P. (1991). *Making friends in school: Promoting peer relationships in early childhood.* New York: Teachers College Press. Rizzo, T. (1989). *Friendship development among children in school.* Norwood, NJ: Ablex.

Rebecca Kantor and David Fernie

Peers and Friends

Sometime during the second year, young children usually experience large increases in the amount of time they spend interacting with their peers or age mates. As young children's social interactions with peers outside of the family group increases, so does the importance of these relations in shaping their lives and development. This entry will describe some theories or concepts that help us understand peer interactions and explain the types of social interactions and relationships that young children experience. It will also discuss the characteristics and skills of children that affect peer interactions and describe possible short- and long-term consequences of these relations.

Underlying Theories and Concepts

One contemporary framework that is particularly useful in considering children's relations with peers is the *child-by-environment perspective* (e.g., Ladd 2003). This approach tells us that children come to social settings with different sets of traits and skills that help determine the kinds of peer interactions they experience. This approach also suggests that aspects of a particular social setting itself (e.g., a preschool classroom) will likewise have effects on children's interactions and adjustment. Peer social interactions thus become a "two-way street," with children bringing characteristics or social skills to a context, and the peers (and others) in that setting responding and affecting the social relations and the adjustment a child experiences in that setting. Adults interested in understanding young children's peer relations should look closely at the characteristics of the child *and* those of the peer environment, and view them as parts of an interacting system. Efforts to improve children's peer relations or social adjustment may also need to target specific aspects of both the child and peer environment in order to be successful.

Another important idea that shapes our understanding of young children's peer relationships comes from **attachment** theory. This theory suggests that children form peer relationships using a model of the self and others based on their early caregiver relationships (see the section Parenting and Family). Cognitive theorists Jean **Piaget** and Lev **Vygotsky** also suggested that peer interactions play a role in **cognitive development** and problem solving. In their models, conflict (Piaget) and cooperation (Vygotsky) with peers support cognitive development and more advanced thinking and reasoning. Research has supported the idea that children working with peers often display more advanced problem-solving ability than they can when working alone.

The Peer Environment: Interactions and Relationships

In any setting where children are with peers there is a range in the degree of social contact. At one end of the range there are minimal interactions where children seldom communicate with peers or coordinate their activities, for example, short-term interactions with peers they don't know. At the other end of the range are relationships that involve repeated and frequent interactions, intimacy, communication, and cooperation; elaborate pretend games of house or school are examples of this. The degree of cooperation, communication, and interaction that young children are capable of with peers also increases dramatically across early childhood as communication skills, cognitive development, and emotional control improve. Given these different types of relations, it follows that there are likely to be different effects on children participating in them—some of these possible outcomes are discussed below.

Play with peers. Mildred **Parten** (1933), a pioneer in studying children's peer relations, suggested that preschoolers' social interactions emerge in a sequence that begins with *nonsocial activity*, where toddlers watch others without interaction or engage in solitary, individual play near one another. This is followed by limited interactions in *parallel play*, where children play near each other while doing similar activities but do not try to influence the **play** of others or cooperate. Next comes the more complex and demanding interactions of *associative play*, where children play separately but interact verbally, exchange toys and ideas, and comment on each other's behavior. Finally, the most complex and demanding play interactions to emerge in older toddlers are labeled *cooperative play*, where children play make-believe games and coordinate intricate pretend roles and activity. While Parten's categories have been elaborated upon, the order that she suggested remains accurate, although we now know that even older children still spend a significant proportion of their time in solitary or parallel play. Only certain kinds of solitary activity, such as high proportions of aimless or unoccupied activity, or a high degree of repetitive motor action, suggest developmental delay or adjustment problems.

Friendships. As children's social abilities develop and their peer interactions increase, they begin to have peers with whom they develop more intimate dyadic relationships, or friendships. While some psychologists argue that younger toddlers may not actually maintain friendships in the sense that school-aged children do, it is clear that even two-year-olds interact more and prefer familiar peers and playmates with whom they have positive relationships. Older toddlers and preschoolers are usually capable of describing their friends and friendships in a way that makes it clear they value and enjoy these one-on-one relationships. Young children's friendships also often involve conflict as well (often more conflict occurs within friendships than with peers who are not friends). Children vary widely in their ability to maintain and repair relationships in the face of conflict, and the degree of conflict present in a friendship also helps define the quality of that relationship. By early childhood most children participate in at least a few close friendships, but relationships vary in quality, with some friendships characterized by high levels of conflict and stress. Within larger groups of children, there are also networks of dyads that form small groups within classrooms or peer settings, with some children being more socially connected across the different groups, while others are more isolated.

Group relations. As children interact in larger groups (e.g., in preschool classrooms), there are social relations at the group level that are important as well. Researchers have labeled some of these relations as peer acceptance or popularity—this reflects how well liked a child is, in general, by their peer group. Acceptance is not the intimate and dyadic relationship of friendship, but a picture of how well accepted the child is as a playmate. This type of relationship provides children with different social resources than friendships, and it may be more important as an indicator of how easily a child is able to get peer support for completing academic tasks or gain access to peer groups, play materials, or playground equipment.

Children also tend to form dominance hierarchies in their peer groups. This ordering of children according to their power and status often determines which children prevail in conflicts within the group (e.g., over toys or playground equipment). Established dominance hierarchies, though they are formed using verbal or physical conflict, often serve to reduce the level of aggression in groups as children become aware of their roles and the roles of others in the hierarchy.

Child Characteristics: What's Important for Developing Peer Interactions and Relationships?

Traits, behaviors, and peers. An important characteristic in young children's ability to enter into peer relations is their behavior. For example, peers quickly notice which of their age mates tend to more aggressive or withdrawn. Both of these characteristics have a negative impact on children's friendships and the degree to which they are liked ordisliked by peers (i.e., accepted vs. rejected). Aggressive children, in particular, are frequently avoided by peers and tend to have lower-quality friendships, with more conflict and less trust or intimacy. Aggression and social withdrawal are both associated with early temperamental characteristics that children display—infants with difficult or active **temperaments** may be more aggressive as toddlers or preschoolers, whereas more inhibited infants tend to be more withdrawn.

Emotional control also appears to be an early ability that supports better peer relations. Toddlers who are highly emotional and have less emotional control, even if they are sociable, often have a more difficult time entering into positive social interactions and maintaining relationships. Preschoolers who are better able to regulate their emotions tend to be more socially competent, have more friends, and are more popular as playmates. While children's tendencies to be more aggressive or withdrawn have strong connections to their genetic makeup and are likely inherited from their parents, the early social environment is also important in shaping their skills and later relations with peers.

Parenting and family. Attachment theory tells us that children's later social relationships are based on an internal model of themselves that they form in their early caregiver interactions. Infants and toddlers with caregivers that give them reliable, sensitive, warm, and caring support tend to become more securely attached. These children trust caregivers and form a more positive caregiver–child bond—those children who receive less consistent or sensitive care are more likely to be insecurely attached. Securely attached children tend to be more socially competent and skilled in interactions with peers and adults and are also more likely to have greater social self-competence. These characteristics, in turn, help children more confidently explore new surroundings and social settings. Research also demonstrates that securely attached toddlers do better navigating the social challenges of preschool and the daily demands of getting along with others.

Parents also directly teach children social skills and/or coach peer behaviors. For example, parents who actively arrange and encourage peer play opportunities for young children tend to have children who are socially well adjusted. How parents oversee these play interactions is also important: parents who are either too intrusive or who don't monitor peer interactions closely enough tend to have preschoolers who are less socially well adjusted later on. Appropriate parental or adult monitoring (including that of teachers) that allows children as much responsibility in their interactions as they may safely handle on their own is helpful for children as they learn to interact with peers independently.

This support for child autonomy, in the context of a warm and supportive relationship and consistent standards for age-appropriate behavior, also helps foster positive peer interactions. Parents who use more authoritarian or coercive practices tend to have children who are more aggressive and more likely to be rejected by peers. In many cultures and communities, teachers also fulfill similar roles to parents as they support positive peer interactions. Warm relationships with teachers, especially those that support appropriate levels of autonomy, also help foster more socially skilled and well-adjusted preschoolers.

Across cultures. As we consider parent and teacher roles in peer relations, it becomes apparent that there is likely to be a lot of variation in parent influence on children's peer relations across cultural settings and communities. As cultural values vary, so too do parent and teacher support for different kinds of relationships or social skills. On one hand, there is remarkable agreement among cross-cultural studies (e.g., in China and in Canada) that positive and supportive relations with parents are linked to having well-adjusted children. Parents in China, however, are more likely to value group cohesion and may encourage their children to be more cautious, dependent, and self-restrained. In their culture, shy and quiet children are more likely to be labeled as good children—these beliefs are not typically found in the same degree in North American or European families. Similarly, Chinese parents may socialize their children to be more behaviorally inhibited than North American children—this may be an adaptive trait for Chinese toddlers (e.g., Chen, Hasting, and Rubin, 1998). In addition to social behaviors, the particular kinds of relationships that are valued may also differ. Chinese parents are more likely to value cooperative and less conflictual relationships than North American parents (this is not to say that relationships of North American children are less adaptive—only that they often include more conflict). Psychologists believe that this is related to cultural values of individualism/autonomy versus group identity/collectivism—Western cultures such as those typical of North America typically place a higher value on individualism, while other cultures value collectivist ideals more highly.

This evidence suggests that the social skills and peer relations that are "best" in a culture or community are likely to vary along with cultural norms. It seems clear that an accurate understanding of peer relations and their effects on adjustment must look at the cultural norms and practices in the community of interest.

Outcomes: What Are Some of the Long-Term Effects of Peer Relations?

The interaction of child characteristics with the peer context clearly makes up an important part of young children's lives. Accordingly, we can also describe some important outcomes that have consistently been linked to early peer relations. While it is a difficult job to tease out the effects of the relations from those of the child's individual behavior, some outcomes have shown up consistently and over long enough periods for us to describe here. Whether the peer context is a source of support or stress, it is likely to impact children's futures in a number of ways.

Academic and cognitive effects. Children who have a history of being rejected by peers are more likely than accepted children to have long-term adjustment problems, especially in academic settings. This may be especially true for those with longer histories of rejection. Young children who begin preschool or **kindergarten** with peer relationship problems and especially those who have long-term peer problems, are often less engaged in the classroom or achieve lower grades later on. These problems can extend to truancy, school drop-out, and delinquency in adolescence. Children who have no friends or have only a few friendships of poor quality are also more likely to have academic adjustment problems, as well as social and emotional difficulties.

Social and psychological adjustment. Rejected children also often have long-term psychological problems such as increased aggression, substance abuse, internalizing problems, and attention problems. More accepted children typically have better long-term adjustment patterns. Children who have quality friendships *and* view their relationships positively also appear to be better adjusted psychologically and see their friendships as a source of social and emotional support. In kindergarten classrooms, for example, children with friends were happier at school, viewed classmates as more supportive, and had more positive attitudes about school. Children with no close friendships (as opposed to even one or two), in particular, appear especially at risk for more negative attitudes and later adjustment problems.

In sum, children's peer relations in early childhood take different forms and serve different functions as children develop. It is clear that children, their families, and their schools all have important characteristics that affect the quality and adjustment outcomes of peer relations. Children's temperament and family environment impact the skills and behaviors that they bring to peer contexts. The interactions and relationships in those contexts, in turn, shape later adjustment. The social characteristics and behaviors children display with peers in early childhood are important in shaping the peer relations that occur. Understanding more about children's peer interactions and how the processes they experience in these relations might affect later adjustment are central to any understanding of young children's welfare and development. *See also* Culture; Parents and Parent Involvement; Peer Culture; Preschool/Prekindergarten Programs.

Further Readings: Buhs, E. S., and G. W. Ladd (2001). Peer rejection in kindergarten as an antecedent of young children's school adjustment: An examination of mediating processes. *Developmental Psychology* 37, 550–560; Chen, X., P. D. Hastings, and K. H. Rubin (1998). Child-rearing attitudes and behavioral inhibition in Chinese and Canadian toddlers: A cross-cultural study. *Developmental Psychology* 34, 677–686; Coie, J. D. (2004). The impact of negative social experiences on the development of antisocial behavior. In J. B. Kupersmidt and K. A. Dodge, eds., *Children's peer relations: From development to intervention*. Washington, DC: American Psychological Association, pp. 243–267; Ladd, G. W. (2003). Probing the adaptive significance of children's behavior and relationships in the school context: A child by environment perspective. *Advances in Child Behavior and Development* 31, 43–104; Rubin, K. H., W. Bukowski, and J. Parker (1998). Peer interactions, relationships and groups. In W. Damon, series ed. and N. Eisenberg, vol. ed., *Handbook of child psychology*. 5th ed. New York: Wiley, pp. 619–700; Parten, M. (1933). Social play among preschool children. *Journal of Abnormal and social Psychology* 28, 136–147.

Eric S. Buhs and Melanie S. Rudy

Pestalozzi, Johann (1746–1827)

Johann Heinrich Pestalozzi, often referred to as one of the most influential modern educators, was born in Zurich, Switzerland, in 1746. Johann's father died when he was only five, but his mother and sister managed to raise the young boy and send him off to school when he was nine. Although he was not a particularly good student, he always felt that education was the ultimate answer to the problems of society.

Originally, Pestalozzi studied theology at the University of Zurich and planned to become a preacher, but due to his shyness, he soon turned to the study of law. While studying, Pestalozzi became greatly impressed by the writings of Jean Jacques **Rousseau** and aspired to put these theories into practice. In 1767, Pestalozzi visited an experimental farm in the canton of Bern where he learned many experimental methods of farming and was impressed by the farmer's interest in the welfare of his workers. In 1768, Pestalozzi secured a loan and bought a farm nearby, which he called "Neuhof." In 1769, he met and married Anna Schulthess, a well-to-do, well-educated woman who ultimately shared Pestalozzi's successes and failures for the next fifty years. When the agricultural experiment failed, he turned his farm into an educational experiment for poor villagers. In 1774, Pestalozzi assembled a group of social castoffs at Neuhof and set them to work in his spinning mill. He also taught them some industrial skills in hopes of bettering their position. When this endeavor turned into a financial disaster, he turned toward education as a way to elevate these citizens from their poverty.

In 1781, Pestalozzi published his famous novel *Leonard and Gertrude*. This book described many of Pestalozzi's ideas about education and social justice. Pestalozzi was later asked by the village of Stanz to set up a school for the many children who had been orphaned by the recent wars. Although his school lasted only a short year, Pestalozzi next moved to the Castle of Burgdorf to open another school. While at Burgdorf, he wrote a systematic treatise on Education entitled "How Gertrude Teaches Her Children." In 1805, he moved his school to its final location in Yverdon. Students and teachers traveled from many nations to experience this "new" educational system, and returned home to improve their own schools. Here, Pestalozzi labored with his ideals of education and appropriate treatment of young children. In 1815, his wife died, and in 1825, the school at Yverdon closed because of dissension among Pestalozzi's teachers. In 1827, Pestalozzi died, alone and destitute.

Pestalozzi's lessons proceeded from the concrete to the abstract, from simple to complex. Classrooms were child-centered, where children learned from doing activities rather than being told about experiences. Children would first observe activities and interact with materials, and then they would express their impressions of the objects as they perceived them, and finally they would form their own understanding of the experiences. Pestalozzi stressed that early education needed to emphasize experiences, not book learning. Through concrete experiences, the child moves into abstract understandings of the world around it.

Pestalozzi's methods look quite familiar to students in our own school of the twenty-first century, but these methods were quite new in Pestalozzi's day. Pestalozzi felt that all children should be educated equally, regardless of gender or economic conditions. His approach to early childhood education stemmed from his love for children and his conviction that each child held the promise of individual potential. He further believed that educators should not intrude upon that natural development and that instruction reflecting the needs of the individual rather than the group as a whole.

Further Readings: Lascarides, V. C., and B. F. Hinitz (2000). Johann Pestalozzi. In *History of early childhood education* (pp. 53–62). New York: Falmer Press; Monroe, W. S. (1969). The history of the Pestalozzian movement in the United States. New York: Arno Press. Pestalozzi, J. H. (1898). *How Gertrude teaches her children.* Syracuse, NY: C.W. Bardeen. Silber, K. (1973). *Pestalozzi: The man and his work.* New York: Schocken Books.

Martha Latorre

Philanthropy and Young Children

It has been argued that organized philanthropy remains one of the least known and most pervasive of financial networks throughout the United States, as it operates with remarkable freedom. Waldemar Nielson summarizes philanthropy as follows:

> As a group, they are institutions like no others, operating in their own unique degree of abstraction from external imposed rules. They are private, and yet their activities cut across a broad spectrum of public concerns and public issues. They are not only important power centers in American life not controlled by market forces, electoral constituencies, bodies of members, or even formally established canons of conduct, all of which give them their extraordinary flexibility and potential influence. Yet they remain little known and even less understood, shrouded in mystery, inspiring in some the highest hopes and expectations and in others dark fears and resentments. By some they are seen as the Hope of the Future, our Secret Weapon for progress; by others as our Fifth Column; and by still others as our invisible Fourth Branch of Government. (quoted in Watson, 1993, p. 1)

Although early education receives only a small portion of foundation assets, private foundations have played a significant role in supporting in early childhood education, in increasing opportunities for young children and in advancing the early childhood profession in the United States of America. Two major themes have characterized foundation giving in the field: private foundation funding has (1) sparked innovation and experimentation and (2) elevated attention to systems change. In spite of these contributions, enduring and emerging concerns remain about the impact of philanthropy on the field of early care and education.

Foundations Promote Innovation and Experimentation

Private philanthropy has been a major source of support for many innovations in early childhood education. These innovations were critical as early educators worked to develop evidence about the effectiveness and impact of their work, and to build public will for improved early care and educational policies and practices. Innovative projects and model programs, as well as experimentation with replication strategies, have been the cornerstone of the work done by early childhood specialty foundations such as the A.L. Mailman Foundation and the Foundation for Child Development. Larger, comprehensive national foundations such as Ford, Kellogg, and Mott have also played significant roles at different points in time. Together, these efforts have sponsored new approaches, leveraged strategic opportunities and advanced critical issues that have informed the early care and education field.

To illustrate the range of projects that have been funded, a few examples follow:

• The Harris Foundation, established in 1946, helped establish the Erikson Institute in 1966 to train teachers for **Head Start**. In 1986, Harris also helped to initiate a public–private partnership, the Beethoven experiment, which brought prenatal care and exemplary early childhood practice to mothers-to-be in the Robert Taylor Homes in Chicago. Beethoven's ultimate goal was to insure that these children would be "ready for school" when they entered **kindergarten**. The Beethoven Project tested critical early learning theories in a real-life community-based setting, drawing national attention to successful **early interventions** in the very first years of life.

- In 1958, the **National Association for the Education of Young Children** (NAEYC) national office was established partly as a result of gifts from the Elizabeth McCormick Memorial Fund. In 1984, the **accreditation** system was field tested in four sites with the support of several small foundations.

In the 1990s, what is now The Early Childhood Equity Alliance was launched by the Kellogg Foundation with later support from the A. L. Mailman Family Foundation, the Peppercorn Foundation, Bernard Van Leer Foundation, and others. The Alliance nurtures and connects people engaged in racial and social justice education and action with and for young children, families, and communities.

Foundations Work to Achieve Systems Change

In addition to their support of "silo" projects, foundations have also supported efforts to leverage public funding for young children and to support systems change. This work is particularly noteworthy when one considers the fact that many philanthropic organizations were founded without any specific charitable purpose in mind. Rockefeller and Carnegie were rare among philanthropists because they wanted to leverage their gifts by influencing patterns of government spending. Perhaps only a small number of foundations had in mind what Neilssen calls "scientific philanthropy"—getting at the root causes of social ills rather than merely ameliorating the symptoms (see Watson, 1993).

Nevertheless, foundations can be credited with drawing attention to neglected areas of child development and boosting activity in important areas through strategic grant making. A few examples include the following:

- In the 1970s when the Edna McConnell Clark Foundation established its interest in child welfare, its support of this work through several national organizations is credited with promoting change. In the 1990s, the W.K. Kellogg's "Families for Kids" imitative, along with work of the Dave Thomas Foundation, combined program, media, evaluation and advocacy tools to help create a movement for federal and state policy changes affecting the movement of foster children into permanent homes.
- The Caroline and Sigmund Schott Foundation played a pivotal role in establishing the nonprofit organization that led a state-wide effort to achieve universal preschool in the state of Massachusetts.
- The Foundation for Child Development has played a leadership role in research and dissemination of information.

Policy change has also been promoted by foundations' support of many important commissions and committees addressing children's issues. The 1991 report of the bipartisan National Commission on Children is credited with forcing social conservatives to acknowledge the need for economic supports for children (Schmitt, 2004). Similarly The Carnegie Task Force on Meeting the Needs of Young Children issued the influential report "Starting Points: Meeting the Needs of Young Children" in 1994.

Recognizing the limitations of work being done by individual funders, several collaborative efforts by grant makers have been established to foster strategic thinking and sharing.

- Grantmakers for Children, Youth and Families was established in 1985 as an affinity group of the Council on Foundations. Today, representatives from more than 500 private, corporate, community and family foundations participate in its activities.

- To better target interest in young children among those funders deeply committed to early childhood, in 1994 an informal group of staff from five foundations came together to create the Early Childhood Funders Collaborative. Today ECFC membership includes about 30 foundations who seek to increase the visibility and importance of quality in early childhood care and education and to increase private and public investment. This affiliation of individuals, often drawn from the early childhood profession, is deeply immersed in supporting early childhood education for the long haul. By 1995 it was decided to form a funding pool to support major leadership initiatives. Two such initiatives had been funded by 2004.
- With respect to specific funding issues, groups of foundations often come together to address specific concerns. For example, today The Packard Foundation, the Joyce Foundation, the Schumann Fund for New Jersey and the McCormick Tribune Foundation are collaborating with the Pew Charitable Trusts around universal preschool issues.

Limits of Philanthropy

Major issues are associated with foundation funding in the field of early care and education. Chief among them are the following seven concerns.

1. **Foundations constrain the advancement of work in the early education field because of their short term funding cycles.** Most foundation grant commitments are for a term of one to three years. This funding pattern may not allow for the development of strong institutions that can plan for and sustain long-term change.
2. **Foundation funding strategies are typically project focused and categorical.** By establishing their priorities in interest areas (i.e., in housing, health, education), foundation funding has, in many ways, mirrored the federal program structure. Single issue organizations may be favored in this context. This structure, however, does not reflect the interrelationships among these categories in children's lives. Further, the project focus of most funding has the consequence of offering relatively little support and few resources to support strategic planning, capacity-building or fund raising activities. Moreover, "projects" are often ill equipped to address the structural and root causes of child well-being such as poverty; to focus on critical activities such as constituency building; or to create a coherent vision for social change compared to reactive activity reflecting social trends.
3. **Foundations may have unrealistic outcomes and accountability requirements for grantees.** Categorical project funding is often tied to the expectation that grantees will produce specific outcomes within a certain timeframe. In turn, grantees have often complained that these outcomes reflect unrealistic expectations about what can be produced in return for relatively small amounts of money and time.
4. **Foundations have been a financial base of child advocacy organizations.** Many early education or multiissue child advocacy programs receive a majority of their support from private dollars. This "good news" is accompanied by a major shortcoming: while foundations have played a vital role in sustaining child advocacy groups, these groups are, in turn, very dependent on foundation funding, finding it difficult to develop a diverse funding base or to develop hard revenue sources on which to rely. As a result, important initiatives, such as the Early Childhood Equity Alliance, operate under difficult financial circumstances. Many other initiatives, such as the

Ecumenical Child Care organization, found it difficult to consistently sustain their level of organizational activity due to fiscal challenges.

5. **Foundations are not inclined to invest in advocacy activities and social change.** Progressive foundations woefully underfund public intellectuals, policy thinkers and policy work, relative to more conservative organizations. This is argued to have a limiting impact on the capacity of children's organizations to disseminate information, engage in strategic media work, interact with policy makers and coordinate research and advocacy. Although there are certainly exceptions to this tendency, evidence shows that few foundations seem willing to fund advocacy activities (Covington, 2001). Rather, foundation funding has largely focused on funding discrete projects or programs not connected to the more fundamental economic and policy questions of the early childhood profession or the well-being of young children themselves.

6. **There is an increasing tendency for foundations to design and direct their own initiatives.** A major trend in philanthropy is that foundations are increasing designing and directing their own initiatives, and working through grantees to achieve those goals. In this way, foundations may have undue influence on foundation-dependent organizations who grumble about being the "implementers" of foundation-directed initiatives. Further, with a rapid growth of new foundations, one finds heightened interest in "venture philanthropy"—new donors, exemplified by persons such as such as Bill Gates, seek a more engaged and directed approached to philanthropy. These venture philanthropists show a renewed focus on building partnerships, exit strategies, accountability measures and building networks. Grantees may find that they have to structure their work around the funding initiatives of the foundations.

7. **Grantees often feel that the unequal partnerships with foundations effectively limit the vision for the field of early care and education.** The "unequal partnership" is evidenced by many factors, including a lack of feedback about negative funding decisions. Thus, dialog and discussion and learning do not always occur, sometimes fostering a mutual lack of candor as foundations influence choices of strategic issues, strategies and methods.

Conclusion

According to Watson,

Traditional philanthropy operates according to self-defined goals of charity for the poor and the promotion of high culture. Charity is extremely gratifying for those who engage in it, as evidenced by the symbolic link between arts and its patrons. But what makes traditional grantmaking easy—gratification—is precisely what makes empowerment as a strategy for grantmaking so difficult. Building capacity among powerless people requires the creation of alternative sites of decision making, validation, and power. In the abstract, these issues may not seem to be troubling, but in the real world, they frequently involve choices between well-run institutions that are known and loved, and weak, emerging organizations about which foundation boards and staff have little knowledge and with which have even less contact. Empowerment is threatening because it is messy. When people have the capacity to act for themselves, they frequently do—and not necessarily in ways that people who have acted for them anticipate or welcome. (Watson, 1993, p. 8)

However important and strategic foundation giving may be, it is important to remember that private giving is dwarfed by state spending. Ultimate growth in early education services is tied to how well those public resources can be leveraged. *See also* Advocacy and Leadership in Early childhood Education; Preschool/Prekindergarter Programs.

Further Readings: Convington, Sally (1997). *Moving a public policy agenda: The strategic philanthropy of conservative foundations.* Washington, DC: National Committee for Responsive Philanthropy. Dowie, Mark (2001). *American foundations: An investigative history.* Cambridge, MA: MIT Press. Foster, Catherine Crystal, and Anjali Srivastava (1996). *Forging the links: How advocates connect kids and public benefits.* Washington, DC: National Committee for Responsive Philanthropy. Jenkins, Craig J. (1998). A channeling social protest: Foundation patronage of contemporary social movements. In Walter W. Powell and Elisabeth S. Clemens, eds., *Private action and the public good.* New Haven, CT: Yale University Press, pp. 206–216. Johnson, Robert Matthews (1998). *The first charity: How philanthropy can contribute to democracy in America.* Cabin John, MD: Seven Locks Press. Lakoff, George (1996). *Moral politics: What conservatives know that liberals don't.* Chicago: Chicago University Press. Mitchell, Ann, and Rima Shore (1998). Next steps toward quality in early care and education: A report commissioned by the Early Childhood Funders Collaborative. Neilsen, Waldemar A. (1985). *The golden donors: A new anatomy of the great foundations.* New York: E.P. Dutton. Schmitt, M. (2004). Kid's Aren't Us. *The American Prospect Online.* Takanishi, Ruby (1998). Children in poverty: Reflections on the roles of philanthropy and public policy. In Charles Clotfelter and Thomas Ehrlich, eds., *The future of philanthropy in a changing America.* Vol. 2. The Ninety-Third American Assembly, April 23–26. Los Angeles, CA: The Getty Center. Watson, B. C. (1993). Minorities and marginality in American foundations. Association of Black Foundation Executives. Weiss, Heather B., and M. Elena Lopez (1998). *New strategies in foundation grantmaking for children and youth.* Cambridge, MA: Harvard Family Research Project.

Valora Washington

Physical Education. *See* Curriculum, Physical Development

Piaget, Jean (1896–1980)

Jean Piaget is often believed to have been a Swiss psychologist, but psychology for him was only a means of studying epistemological questions scientifically. For centuries, epistemologists had debated questions such as "How do we know what we think we know?" and Piaget insisted that these questions should be answered scientifically rather than by philosophical speculation. His doctorate from the University of Neuchatel (1918) was in natural sciences with a dissertation on the mollusks of Valais. This training in zoology led him to study knowledge from a perspective that encompassed all animals' adaptation to their environment. This perspective is what took him to psychology, to try to explain the development of human knowledge by looking for parallels with children's process of acquiring knowledge.

As Piaget said in *Piaget on Piaget* (1977), his theory is almost always misunderstood. "Some think I am an empiricist. . . . Others think I am a neo-maturationist or even an innatist. . . . But I am a constructivist," he said. (The term *constructivism*, too, later led to confusion because there are many kinds of constructivisms.)

Piaget's opposition to empiricism is especially important for early childhood education, which has long been dominated by empiricist thinking. Empiricists believe, in essence, that human beings acquire knowledge by internalizing it directly from the external world through the senses. As a constructivist, Piaget proved that human beings create their own knowledge from the inside, constantly modifying it by interacting with people and objects. Human knowledge is organized through a logico-mathematical framework that takes many years for each individual to construct, he said, and human beings see in the environment only what their own logico-mathematical organization enables them to see. This theory was sketched in *The Construction of Reality in the Child* (1937/1954) and elaborated in more than sixty books.

Piaget was acutely aware that science only describes and explains phenomena. He was careful to say that the application of science to practical problems like education was beyond the scope of his work. By thus limiting his concerns to the description and explanation of knowledge, he gave to educators a scientific foundation for their art. Just as medicine is an art based on scientific explanations of illnesses, he said, education must become an art based on a scientific explanation of how children learn (Piaget, 1948/1973). By limiting his work to the description and explanation of knowledge, he also enabled educators to understand the scientific revolution his theory brought to behaviorism. Just as the heliocentric theory revolutionized the geocentric theory by extending the scope of the old theory and turning it upside down, Piaget's constructivism extended the scope of behaviorism and turned it upside down. As a biologist, he said that all animals (including human beings) adapt to reward and punishment, but human beings are much more complicated than lower animals.

Part of Piaget's constructivism concerns children's moral development (Piaget, 1932). He made a distinction between the morality of heteronomy and the morality of autonomy. The former is the morality of obedience to ready-made rules and people in authority taught through reward and punishment–a morality compatible with behaviorism. The morality of autonomy, on the other hand, is the morality of each individual making his or her own decisions by taking relevant factors into account. Piaget showed with evidence that all children begin by being heteronomous but that some are raised to become increasingly autonomous. When asked why it was bad to lie, for example, young, heteronomous children replied, "Because you get punished," and when Piaget asked if it would be all right to lie if one were not punished, these children answered "Yes." More autonomous children replied, on the other hand, that lying is bad because people wouldn't be able to believe each other if they lied. Piaget was not an educator, but he explained how some adults foster the development of autonomy in children. His theory thus has much to offer for the advancement of education.

Further Readings: Piaget, Jean (1932). *The moral judgment of the child*. London: Kegan Paul. Piaget, Jean. (1952). Jean Piaget. In Edwin G. Boring, Herbert S. Longfeld, Heinz Werner, and R. M. Yerkes, eds., *A history of psychology in autobiography*. Vol. IV. Worcester, MA: Clark University Press, pp. 237–256; Piaget, Jean (1954). *The construction of reality in the child*. New York: Basic Books. Originally published 1937; Piaget, Jean. (1971). *Biology and knowledge*. Chicago: University of Chicago Press; Originally published 1967. Piaget, Jean. (1973). *To understand is to invent*. New York: Viking.

Originally published 1948. Piaget, Jean (1977). *Piaget on Piaget.* New Haven, CT: Yale University Media Design Studio. Piaget, Jean, and Barbel Inhelder (1969). *The psychology of the child.* New York: Basic Books. Originally published 1966.

Constance Kamii

PITC. *See* Program for Infant Toddler Caregivers

Play

Play is both a noun and a verb. When describing the activity of children, it is more aptly defined as *playing*—a state of being that children experience and make happen. Even when children are playing, they often go in and out of the play scene, demonstrating the metacognitive activity associated with this complex behavior. In spite of a wealth of lay and professional literature on this topic, there remains a great deal of ambiguity about the nature and significance of play in children's lives and as it might contribute to their learning and development.

One response to this ambiguity has been to develop criteria for determining what is and is not play. Some guidelines have proven difficult to interpret, such as the requirement that play be *intrinsically motivated* (Smith & Vollstedt, 1985). Others, such as the view that play produces *positive affect* or is *flexible, voluntary, egalitarian,* and (typically) *nonliteral* (i.e., based on pretense), distinguish play from other activities much of the time but not always (Sutton-Smith & Kelly-Byrne, 1984). These varying criteria reflect the challenge that this seemingly natural behavior presents to those who wish to better understand and support children's play. They are also the results of diverse theoretical interpretations of this human activity.

Theories of Play in Early Childhood Practice

Contemporary interpretations of play within the context of early childhood education are drawn from diverse theoretical interpretations of play, including its course of development and its role in the child's development. Evidence of the following theories of play can be found in many U.S. early childhood education settings.

Psychoanalytic theory and play. Those from within the psychoanalytic tradition established by **Sigmund Freud** have long been interested in helping children whose problems stem from difficulty in managing feelings. They have shown how helpful it is to focus on children's abilities to express and cope with feelings, not just because feelings such as anger and love are powerful but also because feelings produce powerful *intrapsychic conflicts.* The analytically minded also focus on feelings of helplessness, believing that children can become overwhelmed by their smallness and their feelings of helplessness. They need help to gain a healthy sense of being in control.

This focus on problems associated with feelings has a great deal to do with children's play. Theorists working out of the psychoanalytic tradition have shown how play can reveal children's struggles with conflicting feelings. **Play therapy** has a well-respected tradition for helping children to use play to master their feelings and sense of helplessness—as when young children are helped to recover from a painful hospital experience by helping them, in play, to take on the role of doctor—giving needles, bad-tasting medicine, and so forth. The view is that through such play, children can regain a sense of being in control. Teachers such as Vivian Paley understand that **play as storytelling**, and especially superhero play, is one way in which children acknowledge fears, test imaginary strengths and capabilities, and cope with their feelings of helplessness.

Cognitive–developmental theory and play. Cognitive–developmental approaches focus on explaining development in terms of structural changes that define different *stages*. The great Swiss psychologist **Jean Piaget** identified three broad stages of play's development: a stage dominated by nonsymbolic *practice games* (e.g., repeatedly jumping off a step), followed by a stage dominated by make-believe and *symbolic games*, followed by a stage dominated by *games with rules* (Piaget, 1962). These stages describe the form or structure of play, not its themes or content.

Piaget saw play as serving the important function of *consolidating* thinking skills as well as, knowledge and information that children have recently acquired. A simple example of teachers' uses of this principle can be found in their responses to young children's interest in construction machinery—diggers, bulldozers, steamrollers—and the process of repairing roads and putting up buildings. If given appropriate play materials (toy diggers, bulldozers, steamrollers) and opportunities to play, young children will build their own ditches and bridges, using play to consolidate what they have learned through observing outside the classroom. The presence of sand and water tables in the early childhood classroom and the postponement of games with rules until at least the primary grades give further evidence of the influence of Piaget's stage-based interpretation of play on contemporary practice.

Lev Vygotsky, a Russian psychologist and educator, is another well-known cognitive–developmental theorist whose work has served as the foundation of **socio-cultural theory**. As an educator as well as a psychologist, Vygotsky was interested in how children learn and how learning contributes to development. Vygotsky emphasized the way parents and teachers help children develop by working within their *zone of proximal development,* that psychological "space" just beyond children's comfort zone where they are used to functioning but not so far beyond that they cannot stretch and grow with the support of more competent others.

In the case of play, Vygotsky saw young children using their play as a self-made zone of proximal development, a boot-strapping operation to help them *free thought from perception* (as when they imagine what is not immediately in front of them). Vygotsky regarded play as a *leading source* of children's **cognitive development** (Vygotsky, 1976). Teachers who create time and space for children to engage in complex collaborative and constructive play are influenced by this view of play as it both challenges and supports children's learning.

Contemporary interpretations of children's learning reflect two major shifts in how cognitive development is conceived, the first of which is a move away from a linear model of progress from cognition as fantasy-based to thinking that is entirely determined by logic (Harris, 2000). Piaget's view was that children outgrow make-believe by becoming more logical, when, for example, they give up make-believe play for games with rules. Contemporary scholars argue that imagination continues to develop well into adulthood, as evidenced by imagination in older children's and adolescents' play (Singer & Singer, 1990).

The other shift has been toward appreciating the interface among culture, play, and cognitive development—a relationship Vygotsky identified that anthropologists and cultural psychologists have documented in communities around the world. Decades of studies in diverse cultures demonstrate a variety of ways in which the sociocultural context supports children's development. In many cultures work, not play, is the principal domain where children are supported to think and develop, and these children acquire the skills, dispositions, and understandings that are associated with healthy development. In some settings those qualities typically assigned to play seem to characterize other forms of child activity. For example, observers of **Reggio Emilia** classrooms who see children deeply engaged in long-term *progettazione* are often challenged to distinguish between children hard at work and children absorbed in play. In the classroom and on the playground, children's imagination, intelligence, friendships, and exuberance characterize their joint activities.

Socio-cultural and ecological theories and play. As indicated, children's engagement with the material and social worlds occurs within multiple and nested contexts (home, neighborhood, etc.) that deeply affect whether and how children play. Theories that explain play in terms of contextual influences are often referred to collectively as *cultural–ecological theories.*

With respect to play, culture can be found in the smallest details—in an offhand reference to a television show during doll-play, in the particular materials chosen for building a play house, in the preference for one type of play over another, in whether or not parents encourage children to play, and in whether certain kinds of play are considered good or bad. Much can be learned about cultural influences on play from surface matters, details that can be observed and measured. There are now numerous studies on the interface between **play and gender** stereotypes.

Socio-cultural theory also points to other types of influences, including underlying assumptions, values, and worldviews as reflected in cultural routines and social relations. For example, some cultures value and support patterns of relationship that are *interdependent.* Within such a context, a child's development will be measured in terms of the child's capacity to successfully participate in collaborative activities that emphasize the family or the community rather than the individual. In these cultures, harmony among group members is prized and play in such a context is less likely to feature competition. In contrast, cultures that are categorized as *individualistic* will emphasize autonomous behavior and a capacity for individual achievement. Play in such a context is more likely to feature, for example, individual ownership of toys as well as competition. Early childhood educators are increasingly aware of the extent to which children bring cultural values, including those regarding gender and **race**, into their play spaces and activities.

Such cultural features are associated not only with how children play, but with how play is supported and encouraged. In the dominant North American culture, most assume that play is good, even essential, for children; and that adults should be actively involved in supporting and at times coaching children's play. Another common assumption is that children's age-mates are natural and appropriate play partners. These assumptions are also culturally embedded. That is, members of diverse cultures hold different beliefs about the nature and value of children's play (New, 1994).

Evolutionary and comparative theories and play. Evolutionary theories have been particularly important in developing the rhetoric of progress. **Jerome Bruner** (1972) argued that play is a major precursor to the emergence of language and symbolic behavior in higher primates and humans, noting that old-world monkeys play less than later-evolving new-world monkeys, who seem to use play to imitate and practice important skills.

The study of play among nonhuman animals has also contributed enormously to the development of play theory. Comparative studies have dispelled a number of common misconceptions about play, including the belief that play is principally a form of practice for the future. For example, the "galumphing" movement characterizing play fighting among juvenile baboons exists side by side with remarkably agile movements carried out when fighting is for real; the one does not lead to the other though.

Perhaps what is most important about the research having to do with evolution and nonhuman animals is that it has bolstered the argument for studying children's play. Play, it turns out, is ubiquitous. It connects not only different groups within the human species but different animal species as well. When we play with a family pet or observe a colt cavorting, we feel this connection. Paradoxically, then, by studying the diverse ways that different species play, evolutionary and comparative theorists have fostered a sense of unity among all animal species.

Play Rhetorics and Controversies

Play theorist Brian Sutton-Smith has proposed we focus on *play rhetorics* as a means of conceptualizing the nature and functions of play (Sutton-Smith, 1995). He suggests that there are several rhetorics of children's play, each emphasizing some presumed general function. One in particular has been embraced by many in the field of early childhood education: the *rhetoric of progress*. Within this particular rhetoric, play is discussed as being good for children's physical, emotional, cognitive, and social development. Educators talk about play preparing children for the future. In spite of continuing controversies regarding evidence (or the lack of it) that might support this interpretation, that play promotes progress has been the dominant rhetoric among scholars as well as among parents, educators, and ordinary people in industrialized cultures such as the United States.

Insufficient evidence for making claims about play's positive functions isn't the only shortcoming of the rhetoric of progress. Critics suggest that the rhetoric of progress can lead to the idealization of play and to overlooking its darker, harmful side. A view of play as "'good for children'" can also mean that adults are unprepared for times when they need to stop or prevent some forms of play—such as when some children find it "'fun'" to bully. This idealization of play may also be used to justify taking control of children's play to enhance its beneficial properties, based on the belief that, if play is essential for children's future, it shouldn't be left to children to choose how to play.

While researchers debate the merits and meanings of their studies on children's play, many believe that play need not be justified on the grounds that it prepares children for the future. Rather, it is a vital and challenging activity that helps children thrive in the present. But even this last statement is itself based upon a rhetoric.

Development of Play

A developmental perspective on play provides a way of evaluating children's play and whether and how it is maturing over time. In particular, a developmental perspective focuses on the degree to which play becomes more complex and organized, more sophisticated and subtle, and more flexible and self-aware. For example, a parent may notice a child shifting from "feeding" her doll to having her doll "feed" another doll. This change from using a doll figure as a passive agent only to using a doll figure as an active agent demonstrates the child's developing capacity to decenter and coordinate perspectives and roles. In this example, development is defined by changes in the play's structure, not by changes in its content. The content is the same, feeding a baby. This distinction between *structure* and *content* is crucial to understanding how play develops and how children develop as well.

Understanding how play develops also requires understanding development within differing play *media*. For example, play with dolls has a different developmental trajectory than does play with wooden blocks. Doll play develops to the extent that children come to use dolls to enact narratives and create story worlds. Block play develops to the extent that children come to use blocks to build three-dimensional constructions with specific contours and specific spaces. In doll play, then, children demonstrate and elaborate upon their understandings of the social and relational world. In block play, children extend their capacities to plan, design, and create, to think about objects and space. In developing their play within any given medium, children usually begin by first exploring the properties and potentials of the medium itself. Only after spending time exploring do children normally use a play medium for symbolic or representational purposes (Scarlett et al., 2004).

Play within the Early Childhood Classroom

In most U.S. early childhood classrooms, a variety of play forms and materials are typically present: small manipulative toys and games in the form of puzzles, connecting blocks, and pattern-making materials; an area designated as "'housekeeping,'" where children's make-believe or pretend play is expected to take place; and an area set aside for constructive play—space that may take up as much as one-fourth of the room, or may be limited to a small corner. In addition to classroom areas dedicated to play, some early childhood programs have outdoor areas adjacent to the classroom, while others have access to larger playgrounds shared with other groups of children. These spaces and materials reflect financial resources, time allocation, and pedagogical perspectives on what and how children should learn—including understandings and views of the role of play in early childhood education.

Two forms of play have received particular attention by early childhood educators: socio-dramatic play and constructive play—though often the two occur together. Both socio-dramatic and constructive play appear to make particular contributions to children's early development.

Make-believe play. Early childhood has often been described as the golden age of make-believe. Vygotsky suggests that the capacity and motivation for rich and imaginative make-believe play comes, in part, from the young child's basic predicament. On the one hand, the young child can symbolize not only what is directly in front of her but also wishes and fantasies. On the other hand, she has so many wishes that cannot be satisfied—to drive a car, to control her parents—that play serves as a valuable means of acting upon these wishes. Furthermore, make-believe play also allows children to explore topics they find fascinating—whether it's dinosaurs, space travel, or music videos. Psycho-analytic theories suggest that children also use make-believe play to manage their anxieties. Capturing the monster, rocking the baby, and escaping the enemy are examples of play responses to real and imagined fears.

Make-believe play has long been recognized as a supportive context for language, social, and cognitive development. Recent observations stress the contributions of make-believe play for developing narrative as a *framework for thinking* (Singer & Singer, 1990). The distinction here is between *paradigmatic* and *narrative frameworks* for thinking. Paradigmatic frameworks organize thinking around propositions, distinctions, and logic. They are used in conversations where explanation and argument are what matter most. Narrative frameworks organize thinking around events and characters. They are used in conversations where describing real and imagined dramas is what matters most. Each framework has its place in the ongoing need to understand and know reality.

Make-believe play also supports children's emotional development and capacity for self-regulation. Not only do children learn to moderate their behaviors to stay within the play-script; make-believe play supports emotional development by helping children express emotions and impulses symbolically. When young children engage in joint pretend play, they learn to coordinate their own perspectives with those of others. The challenge of "'staying with the story'" serves as a powerful incentive for children to integrate and coordinate their own interests and desires with those of others; and to learn how to negotiate multiple points of view.

Constructive play. Among U.S. educators and parents, there is a selective bias toward supporting the sort of play in which a child is trying to construct something, such as a fort made with blocks (Forman, 1998). Certainly, educators understand that make-believe play is not the only sort of play that supports children's development and their relationships with one another. When young children play alongside each other, whether while feeding dolls or building block towers, they pay attention to and imitate each other and, as observed decades ago by **Mildred Parten** (1932), soon enough join together in more complex and collaborative play activity. Play thus supports not only developmental, but social aims. Children learn to share materials and space with peers, and to make and keep friends. Constructive play often creates such a context for children's social and emotional development. Even make-believe or dramatic play becomes constructive play when children construct the setting and props to support their full-blown story.

Much of the research on constructive play has focused on its contributions to children's cognitive development. As children consider how best to construct a drawbridge or a roof that will be stable, they engage in hypothesis generating and problem solving that provides insights into their cognitive processes. As children's constructions become more structurally complex with age, they increasingly utilize symbols to represent components that might have previously been left to chance. Thus the object and its referent serve as windows into children's thinking about the world. As children observe and compare their efforts, they seek ways to describe their structures, benefiting linguistically as well as intellectually by reflecting on and analyzing their efforts.

In settings where children's play is valued, there are a variety of forms of support that make a difference in what and how children play. Adults support play's development, not just in broad ways such as by helping children feel secure and confident, but also in more focused ways such as by suggesting extensions of play—"Is the baby hungry?"—and by helping children fit Lego bricks together. Physical settings support play's development by offering conditions and materials to play with, whether it's a lake and beach to play at skipping rocks, a jungle gym to play at climbing and swinging, or a shelf of blocks to play at building a fort. Children support each other's play and development, especially by extending or suggesting new lines of play. Children support their own development through their active engagement and problem solving. The **teachers' role** in supporting play is now receiving particular attention among early childhood educators.

Conclusion

In spite of the fact that a bulk of the early childhood professional literature extols the virtues of play in the classroom, recent policy initiatives, including **No Child Left Behind,** have left teachers faced with the challenge of trying to incorporate play into a classroom that is now subject to heightened academic expectations. As some scholars attempt to reconceptualize play as an ethical and moral dimension of childhood, others are giving increased attention to the many ways in which play can be used to support children's early preacademic skills and understandings. Recent play scholarship highlights its improvisational nature and suggests that the capacity to engage in sustained pretend play is foundational to the development of creativity, conversational competence, and literacy (Sawyer, 1997). As the controversy continues about the nature and role of play in the early childhood classroom, there is consensus about play's central importance to children themselves. Play's fascination—to children and to the adults who observe them-ensures that it will continue to be a topic of study in our efforts to better understand and utilize play as it enhances children's lives, their learning and development.

Further Readings: Bruner, J. (1972). The nature and uses of immaturity. *American Psychologist* 27, 687-708; Fromberg, Doris (1999). A review of research on play. In C. Seefeldt (Ed.), *The early childhood curriculum: Current findings in theory and practice*, pp. 27-53. New York: Teachers College Press; Harris, P. (2000). *The work of the imagination*. Malden, MA: Blackwell Publishers; New, R. (1994). Child's play—una cosa naturale: An italian perspective. In J. Ropnarine, E. Johnson, and F. Hooper (Eds.), *Children's play in diverse cultures*. Albany, N.Y.: State University of New York Press, pp. 123-145; Parten, M. (1932). Social participation among preschool children. *Journal of Abnormal and Social Psychology* 27, 243-369. Piaget, J. (1962). *Play, dreams, and imitation*. New York: Wiley. Sawyer, K. (1997); *Pretend play as improvisation: Conversation in the preschool classroom*. Mahwah, N.J.: Erlbaum; Scarlett, W. G., Naudeau, S., Salonius-Pasternak, D., and Ponte, I. (2004). *Children's play*. Thousand Oaks, CA: Sage; Singer, D., and Singer, J. (1990). *The house of make-believe: Children's play and the developing imagination*. Cambridge, MA: Harvard University Press; Smith, P., and Vollstedt, R. (1985). On defining play: An empirical study of the relationship between play and various play criteria. *Child Development* 56, 1042-1050; Sutton-Smith, B. (1995). Does play prepare the future? In J. Goldstein (Ed.), *Toys, play, and child development*. New York: Cambridge University Press; Sutton-Smith, B., and Kelly-Byrne, D. (1984). The idealization of play. In P. Smith (Ed.), *Play in animals and humans*. Oxford, UK: Basil Blackwell. Vygotsky, L. (1976). Play and its role in the mental development of the child. In J. Bruner, A. Jolly and K. Sylva (Eds.), *Play—its role in development and evolution*. New York: Basic Books, Inc; Fromberg, D. (1999). A review of research on play. In C. Seefeldt (Ed.), *The early childhood curriculum: Current findings in theory and practice*. New York: Teachers College Press, pp. 27-53.

W. George Scarlett and Rebecca S. New

Play and Gender

Gender is an organizing schema for many social interactions and is constructed through multiple social contexts, including children's planned and spontaneous play with one another. Play is a central force in the lives of most young children and serves to both reflect and promote their cognitive, communication, social-emotional and sensory-motor development. As part of children's social–emotional growth, play provides the context for children to explore their notions of identity, including their gender formation. Gender is an important part of the "sense of self" they are creating in their interactions with the world (Cherland 1994). As they develop their identity, they perform behaviors associated with their sex and their gender and the managing of social activities to proclaim membership in a particular gender.

The following scenario depicts typical stereotypes of gender differences, in this instance in play, as girls engage in homemaking and fashion themes and other more sedentary small muscle activities while boys engage in more competitive, rough and tumble, and construction activities. Gender preferences for sex-stereotypic activities and toys begin to appear for children as young as 2 years old (Garvey 2000). Play provides one of the earliest domains both at home and in school where gendered narratives and activities are shaped and take on personal meanings for identity formation.

> A 4-year-old girl, Ginny, plays in the housekeeping center. Ginny pretends to be the mommy. She assigns Audrey, another 4-year-old, the role of the baby, and to Peter the roles of a Daddy and a plumber. Peter only stays in this scenario for a very short time and then runs off to join a group of boys in the block area.

Young children become gendered persons as they negotiate with each other in a participation structure of differentiated roles, rights, obligations, intentions and actions within a classroom (Fernie, Davies, Kantor, and McMurray 1993). They enact these activities through their choice of clothes, materials and other props, the roles they assume, negotiate and attribute to others, and the peers they exclude or include within their play (Corsaro 1985). Their play becomes a safe haven to try on new roles, experiment with identity, negotiate what fits, vent feelings, and even choose their own endings. Pretend play, the most open-ended of all activities, allows children to try out possibilities without suffering the penalties that otherwise might accompany such actions.

Gender differences are universal, but their particular features appear to be shaped by culture and environment. The example of rough and tumble play illustrates this dual principle, as a type of play evident not only primarily with boys in the United States but also among the boys in Mistecans of Mexican and the Taira of Okinawa. However, the girls of the Pilaga Indians and the Kung of Botswana also engage in rough and tumble play (Garvey 2000).

There have been many theories attributed to better understanding gender differences and the role of early childhood educators in fostering children's identity formation. Some theories propose a type of sponge model in which children learn about their gender through their experiences with their social institutions such as families, media, and educators. From this perspective, children become a product of their society's values. This image of identity formation ignores the fact that children do not receive one message from these institutions about their identity but potentially many different messages from many different sources. Furthermore, it fails to explain why children accept or reject dominant understandings and how they make their choices between alternative and dominant understandings.

Contributions from a poststructuralist framework expand on these modernist theories by understanding identity formation as a complex interaction between a person's gender, race, class and sexuality. Children are born into a social world with preexisting social structures and meanings. The relationships they have between individuals and social institutions are fluid, interdependent and, mutually constructing. Identity formation is a process in which the child actively constructs meaning through reading and interpreting experiences, but is not free to construct any meanings or any identities they want (McNaughton 2000). According to Walkerdine (1981) and Harre and Davies (2000) children develop their identities by forming their subjectivity (i.e., ways of knowing) about themselves in their world. Identities are not fixed but are rather formed first and then tailored over time through social interactions with cultural resources and activities. Children develop their sense of self by how they position themselves through their discourse in relationship to others. Through children's use of language with their peers and adults they discover the power of being accepted, rejected and how to negotiate particular membership groups. These types of dialogues help children to distinguish themselves from others.

Parents, teachers, and peers all have roles in reinforcing or challenging children's sex-typed play behaviors. Gender-fair practices and encouragement to try out different roles in play activities must be a conscious effort made by caregivers and early childhood professionals, given the considerable implications for social development and the formation of identity. Many in the field now believe that children need space to experiment with and challenge gender boundaries. From this perspective, the role of the educator becomes one of engaging children in conversations about different voices and perspectives on the world in order for them to learn there are multiple ways of being masculine and feminine. This interpretation of the role of children's play in their early learning and development places it squarely in the category of "controversial topics" to be carefully explored with children, their families, and others in the field of early childhood education. *See also* Gender and Gender Stereotyping in Early Childhood Education; Play as Storytelling.

Further Readings: Cherland, Meredith R. (1994). Untangling gender: Children, fiction and useful theory. *The New Advocate* 7(4), 253-264; Corsaro, W. (1985). *Friendship and peer culture in the early years*. Norwood, NJ: Ablex; Davies, Bronwyn, and Ron Harre (2000). Positioning: The discursive production of selves. In Bronwyn Davies, ed., *A body of writing, 1990-1999*. Walnut Creek, CA: AltaMira Press, pp. 87-106; Fernie, David E., Bronwyn Davies, Rebecca Kantor, and Paula McMurray (1993). Becoming a person in the preschool: Creating integrated gender, school culture, and peer culture positionings. *Qualitative Studies in Education* 6(2), 95-110; Garvey, Catherine (1990). *Play*. Cambridge, MA: Harvard University Press; MacNaughton, Glenda (2000). *Rethinking gender in early childhood education*. Thousand Oaks, CA: Sage Publications; Walkerdine, Valerie (1981). Sex, power and pedagogy. *Screen* 38, 14-24.

Lori Grine and Laurie Katz

Play as Storytelling

Young children tell stories as naturally as they run and climb, making up dramatic scenes and playing them out with no instruction. A preschooler in the doll corner stirring a pot and setting the table has begun a story in which Mama will be a central figure. To enter the story and make it a social event, someone need only curl up in a crib and whine, "Ma-ma, Ma-ma," or put on high heels and announce, "I'm the big sister. The baby is hungry." Another child might throw on a cape and run in shouting, "A monster is coming! I'll save you!" Alternatively, he could put on a vest and tie and say, "I'm home!," prepared to call the doctor if the baby is sick or become a hunter if the wolf is heard in the forest.

The process is familiar and seldom given the honorific of storytelling. Yet it is fair to say that this self-imposed task of thinking up character, plot and dialogue, the common occupation of children everywhere, is the essence of storytelling. Even before "Once upon a time" or "happily ever after" the stories are there, preparing the foundation for all the narratives to come, laying out the binary verities of gain and loss, safety and danger, friendship and loneliness, power and vulnerability, family and stranger, in repetitive tableaus that move from nursery to outer space to dark forest at the mere mention of a code word or character.

Children would seem to be born storytellers, knowing how to place every thought and feeling into story form. If they worry about being lost, they can become the rescuers who search: "Me and Josh losted our baby," says Angela, shoving a doll under a pile of dressups. Later, with a slight change of perspective, she moves a step up the narrative ladder. "The mommy and daddy goed hunting for their little baby," she dictates to the teacher. "It's under a mushroom someplace."

Finding the baby does not end the play or the story, and should a naughty kitten happen by, a meowing loudly, the plot continues. "Bad kitty, you waked the baby," soon to be followed by a reverse application of empathy, "Come here, little kitty, hurry up and lock the door, sister, there's a noise!"

It is play, of course, but it is also story in action, just as storytelling is play put into narrative form. Sam, age four, has never "done" stories before. That is, he has not dictated a story to a teacher for the purpose of having his classmates act it out. When I enter his Head Start classroom, he is playing alone in the doll corner, swinging a man's tie around his head in large arcs. "Fire, fire!" he shouts. Seeing me, he adds, "Old person on fire!"

"That sounds like a fireman story," I say. "If you tell me what you are playing, I'll write it down and later we'll act it out with the other children." Sam looks interested. "I'm the fire truck," he says. "Then the house is on fire. And the older person, and a cat. I put it out and I go home."

Soon Sam's story will fulfill its destiny, from play to a facsimile on paper to the theatrical version on a pretend stage, and later, to a continuation in the block area. When the children are seated around the rug, I read aloud Sam's script, the roles are handed out, and the actors perform their parts with nearly the same spontaneity as in play. After the story is acted out, everyone understands what it means to have a story to tell. The newly defined "storytellers" dictate brief scenes about lost puppies, princesses walking to the playground, Batman in flight, big brothers playing with little brothers, and a mommy who "bumped into a car crash." One might think the children have been telling and dramatizing stories all along and, in a way they have, since it is so much like play.

In the world of fantasy play and storytelling, children intuitively become the characters that represent their feelings, then work out a plot in which to encase the logical actions. Whether storyteller, story player, or story observer, it is the most compelling activity of the early years. Pretending to be someone else, they find the common threads that connect them to people and ideas, materials and motives, as they turn private thoughts into public events.

"In play," the Russian psychologist Lev Vygotsky tells us, "a child is above his average age, above his daily behavior; in play it is as though he were a head taller than himself." Vygotsky might well have been describing play as storytelling. Two sisters walking along who suddenly tell each other, "Pretend we are sisters going for a walk," have become storytellers, free to imagine new relationships and responses, parts of new dramas that create their own ceremonies. The roles are assigned and, for the duration of the plot, events will be governed by an evolving set of rules that reflect the children's own language, logic, and lore.

Play and its core of storytelling are the primary realities in the preschool and kindergarten. You listen to my story and I'll listen to yours and we will build communal narratives, a growing network of commonly held phrases and images, feelings and perceptions, set inside the known and unknown.

"Sh-sh! The baby is crying under a mushroom."

"I'm the good fairy to take her to the ball."

"When she's older, you mean. We didn't finish babies yet. And the dad isn't the prince yet."

"And the superhero is coming too, don't forget."

In half a dozen lines of spontaneous dialogue, these emerging storytellers examine the present and future modes of their craft; the ever-changing scenes are theirs to envision, using the characters of their own choosing. There is an urgency in the children's desire to organize themselves into a drama, and they know it is up to them to provide the substance and structure that brings each episode to the point where a new set of details can be arranged. It is a process in which the premises are continually reviewed and the participants are emboldened to reach further into new lines of thinking. In the art of making up and acting out stories, children create their own entry into the community of learners.

Further Readings: Paley, Vivian (1990). *The boy who would be a helicopter*. Cambridge, MA: Harvard University Press; Paley, Vivian (2004). *A child's work: The importance of fantasy play*. Chicago: University of Chicago Press.

Vivian Paley

Play and the Teacher's Role

What do teachers do while children play? Do they sit or stand or watch? Get out equipment and toys? Sweep up leaves? Take a break? Play with materials with children? Take photos? Help settle disputes? "Free play" in early childhood settings usually means lots of choices of things for children to do. Teachers also make decisions about different ways of behaving and responding to children's play.

When children are playing, most early childhood professionals watch and listen, whether attending to one child's play or to a small social group's play, because they are interested in what young children are able to do, how they express themselves to each other, and how they make sense of their daily lives, dreams, and fantasies. When children are healthy and feel safe, play's the thing children choose to do. Play is intentional: the child is agent of her own actions; she controls the context and the plot. Play is natural for children and most do it competently. With plenty of time and support for playing, children learn new play skills—they become master players. Better than adults, children understand play and they use play to understand. Some suggest that play is the lens through which children understand the world around them. Play is also developmental in that children play differently and for different reasons at different times in their lives. During the period of early childhood, and especially when children are two, three, four, five, or six years old, play is the mode through which they learn, represent their ideas, encounter events in the natural world, and practice solving complex social and practical problems. Research makes explicit the type of learning that takes place during children's play as contrasted to what is not learned when children perceive the context as "work" (Wing, 1995).

Play as Context and Reflection of Children's Development

Before the child can read, she or he is a master of sign systems in play.

With his arms outstretched and fingers touching to fashion a circle, Dennis runs across the yard to a large cardboard box where two friends are waiting. His gesture is at first meaningless ... but Dennis's friends can read it—they know he is a ninja turtle bringing pizza home. (Reynolds and Jones, 1997, p. 35)

Play is also where young imaginations are stimulated and talk flourishes.

Playing Dr. Jones, Aretha has a clipboard and pencil. She asks a group of girls "what is your last name?" Luanda responds "Dulce Cricket." Aretha: "Dulce Christmas?" Luanda: "My name is Ca-gu-a. Aretha: "My name is Dr. Jones." Luanda: "Hi Dr. Jones. My name is Ca-goo – I – ca." (Ibid., 60)

Close observation of children's play stimulates teachers' thinking and makes clear that there are many types and purposes of play. William Corsaro's research traces a direct link between children's play activity as contributing to and shaping the life of the community (Corsaro, 2005). Vivian Paley's writing (1986) shows, in vivid stories from her classroom, what a teacher can learn about children and their peer cultures; as well as what teachers can do to scaffold play by observing and asking questions to which she "does not know the answer." Scholars who have dedicated their research to studying children's play convey a variety of perspectives about the meanings of play. Today, most early childhood educators believe that play—and particularly fantasy play—gives children access to unlimited possibilities for action and meaning making.

Watching children at play and talking about it afterwards is not only a means to learn about children's development. It is also a strategy some teachers use to remain alert to their own roles in supporting play and interpreting the multiple possible meanings and value of play for young children. Systematic observations of preschool children's play that included a focus on what adults do while children play revealed that the art of teaching is like the art of play—there are multiple choices for action, and a teacher can know the consequences of his or her action through reflection (Jones and Reynolds, 1992). By asking questions such as "Has my intervention sustained the play?" "Has it interrupted the child's play? If so, how?" teachers can learn to respect the child's right to play and to respond to the unlimited possibilities of children's preoccupations. Renewed attention to the importance of teachers' observations seems to reinforce previous research findings that learning through play is indirectly affected by various teaching practices. This research does not necessarily point to a direct relationship such that teacher action → child learning. Rather, the indirect effect is that teacher support of good play → child learning by engaging in good play; the child's mental construction is the result of activity and meaning making which happens through play.

Multiple roles for teachers

Effective teaching in early childhood settings cultivates children's potential by inventing child-friendly play opportunities. In support of play, adults may act in one or more roles: stage manager, mediator, player, scribe, assessor and communicator, and planner.

Stage manager is an essential role. In an orderly, well-provisioned environment with plenty of time and space for play, most children will be able to initiate and sustain their own play. Teacher-as-stage manager considers the following: Are there program practices that interfere with good play? Should play spaces be closed in the early morning or evening? Are there rules that limit where children can use certain materials? Outside, do children have opportunities for gross motor play, construction play, and also pretend play?

Mediator uses problem-solving strategies to sustain rather than interrupt play. Teacher-as-mediator does not focus on rule enforcement such as "inside voices" or "only three in the doll corner." The content of the play matters to the teacher, and he or she mediates to sustain the play, not interrupt it—"Jerry, tell Mariana why you're so upset. Mariana, tell Jerry why you're so upset. And then we can talk about how you want to solve the problem."

Not all teachers are comfortable with the role of *player*. To effectively play with children the teacher listens to children's play scripts and builds on them without taking over. Adults often coopt children's agendas by using play to teach concepts. "Is your car going down? Is it going down the freeway ramp? Is it going fast? How many cars do you have? Is your car going up again? Ebony, can you answer my question?" (Jones and Reynolds, 1992, p. 52). In contrast, when genuinely sharing children's curiosity and emotions, the *player* teacher effectively uses power to flow with their agenda for play. A teacher wanting to effectively co-play can ask herself "What is the name of this play from the children's perspectives?"

> Bobby, on his hands and knees, is crawling around on the floor pretending to be a lion.
> Teacher: So now you're the lion. Lion, don't eat me!
> The lion growls forcefully at a child playing nurse who is delivering prescriptions, small pieces of scrap paper on which she has written her name. She says, "Stop Lion!"
> The lion chases somebody into another part of the room. The teacher brings the lion back. To two girls she says, "Let's be gentle with our lion. Baby lion, please don't eat somebody."
> The teacher shows the girls how to pat the lion on the head.
> Lion: I'm a big lion now.
> The lion crawls across the floor to a bed. There he curls up and says to the nurse:

"Get me better."
The nurse gets her medical bag. She pulls out a stethoscope and listens to the lion's
   heart. She announces, "He's sick." (Reynolds, 1993)

One teaching perspective on this child's play might be "Bobby is annoying everybody today. He needs time away from the group to calm down." Instead, the
teacher in the above scene effectively integrated Bobby's lion play script with
neighboring hospital play. Perhaps she recognized that a lion's roar might soften
in the company of a caring nurse.

Scribe combines naturally with *player* when the teacher scribes words children dictate but cannot yet write themselves. "Will you write "popsicles" on my
shopping list?" In this way teacher-as-scribe supports children's early literacy and
number learning through play. Children recognize the power of written words;
a child-dictated teacher-scribed sign "Don't knock over this hospital! Sammie and
Rachel" is enough of a stimulus to caution others about moving around the blocks
area.

The teacher as *assessor and communicator* documents children's play through
sketches, children's words, photos, and taking notes. Representing children's
play in panels, storytelling, and online documentation are some of the many ways
teachers can share the concepts and content of children's play. Teachers may
also discover that documenting play is a powerful way to communicate play's
meaning to parents.

Of all the roles for teachers in supporting and using children's play to promote
further learning and development, the role of *planner* is likely most essential to
supporting children's play. Observations of play generate possibilities for curriculum, and in the role of *planner* a teacher makes decisions about time, opportunities, and materials as they support or hinder children's play. Teachers can decide
to make changes in the physical environment, add props, discuss possibilities for
a field trip that builds on children's information, or focus on a shared interest as
project work by a small group. As children assume roles and invent play scenarios
with an imagined plot and story, they engage in hypothetical thinking. When
children use materials, ideas, logic, symbols, and possibilities for action flexibly
and spontaneously, they are playing to *get smart*, practicing initiative, divergent
thinking, curiosity, problem solving, and critical thinking. "It is through play with
materials and relationships, invention of classification systems, and solving problems in dialogue with others that young children develop the basic skills they will
need to become effective contributors to the health of a changing world" (Jones,
2003, p 34).

Teachers who are committed to complex, sustained, and interactive dramatic
play for the children in their care need opportunities to practice, as well as time
for reflection, learning from one's mistakes, and new action. Workshops, college
classes, and team meetings are all opportunities to grow professionally as teachers
learn how to support each other's skill development in making good play happen.

Further Readings: Corsaro, W. A. (2005). *The sociology of childhood.* 2nd ed.Thousand
Oaks, CA: Pine Forge Press; Jones, Elizabeth (2003) Playing to get smart. *Young Chil-
dren* 58(3), 32–36; Jones, Elizabeth, and Cooper, Renatta (2006). Playing to get smart.
New York: Teachers College Press; Jones, Elizabeth, and Reynolds, Gretchen (1992).
The play's the thing: Teachers' roles in children's play. New York: Teachers College

Press; Monighan-Nourot, Patricia (1990). The legacy of play in American early child-hood education. In Edgar Klugman and Sarah Smilansky eds., *Children's play and learning: Perspectives and policy implications.* New York: Teachers College Press, pp. 59–85; Paley, Vivian (1986). *Mollie is three: Growing up in school.* Chicago: University of Chicago Press; Reynolds, Gretchen, and Jones, Elizabeth (1997). *Master players: Learning from children at play.* New York: Teachers College Press; Reifel, Stuart, and Brown, Mac H., eds. (2001). *Early education and care, and reconceptualizing play.* New York: JAI/ Elsevier Science Ltd; Van Hoorn, Judith, Nourot, Patricia M., Scales, Barbara, and Alward, Keith (1993). *Play at the center of the curriculum.* Columbus, OH: Merrill; Wing, L. (1995). Play is not the work of the child: Young childrens'perceptions of play and work. *Early Childhood Research Quarterly* 10(2), 223–247; Zigler, Edward F., Singer, Dorothy G., and Sandra J. Bishop-Josef, eds. (2004). *Children's play: The roots of reading.* Washington, DC: Zero to Three Press.

Gretchen Reynolds and Elizabeth Jones

Playgrounds

Playgrounds take many forms, including sports fields, festival grounds, carnivals, water parks, and indoor pay-for-play venues. The focus here is on playgrounds at schools, child care centers, public parks, and backyards that are intended for children's creative, spontaneous play.

No part of the world rivals Europe in early philosophical thought about the social, moral, physical, aesthetic, and pedagogical values of playgrounds as supports for children's play and early development. It was here that Plato, Martin Luther, John Amos **Comenius**, Jean-Jacques **Rousseau**, John Locke, Johann **Pestalozzi**, Friedrich **Froebel**, and other intellectual giants and reformers called the attention of the world to such values, and their ideas have influenced adult understandings of children's play and playgrounds to the present time. Guts Muth (1793) developed manuals and games for children's physical development in Germany during the early 1800s. These works were translated into many languages and were the basis for physical activities in schools worldwide. However, much of the early physical emphasis in Europe was on gymnastics for all ages and limited attention was given to children's free or spontaneous play. During the mid-1800s, the influence of physical development in Germany was transported to the United States through the "outdoor gymnasia," or indoor gymnastic equipment used outdoors. These first American organized outdoor playgrounds for children were complemented around the turn of the twentieth century by the introduction of "sandgartens," a concept borrowed from piles of sand in Berlin, intended initially for the play of very young children.

Child Development Center Playgrounds

During the early twentieth century, playground development in the United States followed two major paths. Playgrounds for child development centers for preschool and kindergarten children were patterned after the work of Pestalozzi, Froebel, and John **Dewey**, and were influenced by American child development research centers. These playgrounds featured materials and apparatus for several forms of play—dramatic play, construction play, exercise play, and organized games. Many also featured arts and crafts and nature areas. They were intended to enhance total development—social, cognitive, physical, and emotional—not just motor development. The general overall advantage of these playgrounds over those for public parks and schools is perhaps best explained by the training in child development and play value for adult caretakers of the children. As children entered elementary school, the emphasis by educators was increasingly placed on academics and much later on high stakes testing.

School and Park Playgrounds

A second distinct but parallel playground movement was taking place during the early twentieth century, resulting from the efforts of such educational reformers as Jane **Addams**, Henry Curtis, Luther Gulick, Jr., and Joseph Lee. These "play organizers" were intent on rescuing city children from social and economic hazards imposed on unsupervised children and youth roaming the city streets. These people included educators, psychologists, and social workers who organized the play of children on supervised, municipal playgrounds, initially in large northeastern cities and eventually throughout the United States. Working under the auspices of the Playground Association of America (PAA), organized in 1906, social reformers sought to influence and transform the behavior and moral attitudes of the young, especially the unsupervised and the immigrant, through programs of sports and rigorous physical conditioning.

As manufacturers saw the possibilities for sales of equipment used on "outdoor gymnasia," designers created steel jungle gyms, giant strides, see-saws, swings, and various other steel structures and outfitted public park and school playgrounds throughout much of the industrialized world. As sponsors intent on reducing maintenance installed asphalt and concrete under and around equipment, injuries multiplied and safety became a major issue. Typical early American municipal playgrounds featured about half a space for young children, with additional space for a wading pool in the center and sand bins around the sides. Separate areas were available for boys and girls, with most space reserved for boys. Additional space featured climbing, sliding, and swinging apparatus; a cinder track; handball and tennis courts; and a ball field that could be flooded in the winter for ice skating. Games fields and exercise apparatus, funded by local governments, and organized as municipal playgrounds spread rapidly. By 1905, thirty-five American cities had established supervised playgrounds supported by courses in play for training supervisors (Cavallo, 1981). By 1911, the PAA was deluged by letters requesting assistance in developing municipal playgrounds and the numbers had increased to 257 cities with 1,543 playgrounds. The official journal of the PAA, *The Playground*, is a rich source of early playground information.

Because of increasing interest in recreation, the name of the PAA was changed to Playground and Recreation Association of America (PRAA) and its journal was called *Recreation*. As interest in play declined, modifications and mergers of PRAA led to the formation of the National Recreation Association in 1930 and to the present National Recreation and Park Association (NRPA) in 1966. The energy of the early American playground movement declined as the focus on recreation held sway. The virtually indestructible, manufactured playground equipment remained in place during the world wars because steel was directed to the war efforts. This period was essentially devoid of any extensive energy for creating new playgrounds, perhaps in no small part due to the lengthy Great Depression, which was marked by hard work for children and limited economic resources to devote to children's play.

Following World War II, playground designers created a wide range of novel play equipment patterned after historical and fanciful devices such as animal figures, stagecoaches, and space rockets. Manufacturers reentered the field and began to produce and market these devices and the early see-saws, swings, merry-go-rounds, slides, etc.

Adventure Playgrounds

The concept of "adventure playgrounds" was created by a Danish landscape architect, C. Th. Sorensen, who was inspired by the energy and joy of children playing with scrap materials left on construction sites. His first "junk playground" or "adventure playground," was built by children assisted by adult playleaders in Emdrup, Denmark, in 1943. Adventure playgrounds spread throughout Scandinavian countries and eventually to other European cities, Japan, and the United States. These playgrounds feature trained playleaders, animal care, construction play using tools and scrap materials, contrived and organized games, gardening, and water play (Bengtsson, 1972).

Adventure playgrounds and "city farms" are popular in England, Denmark, Sweden, Norway, Germany, the Netherlands, and, to lesser degree, in Tokyo. Presently, about 1,000 exist in Europe, with about 400 in Germany. London has more than seventy scattered across seventeen boroughs. The short-lived American Adventure Playground Association (AAPA), formed in 1976 in southern California identified sixteen adventure playgrounds in the United States in 1977. Throughout the United States, designers and creative adults integrated some elements of adventure playgrounds into traditional playgrounds, but, by 2005, following the closing of the Houston Adventure Playground Association, only three in southern California and one in Berkeley continued to operate. The adventure playground concept failed to survive because of their "junky" appearance, growing concerns about safety, lawsuits resulting from the development and implementation of national playground safety standards, and the low value held for spontaneous play by the American public. The European playground safety standards exempt adventure playgrounds, and the prevalence of court judgments in playground injury lawsuits in Europe is significantly lower than in the United States.

The Playground Standards Movement

Playground injury data and pressure from private citizens led the Consumer Product Safety Commission (CPSC) to develop and publish national playground safety guidelines in 1981. The NRPA slowly turned attention back to playgrounds but focused primarily on safety. Currently, the major professional organizations concerned with children's playgrounds include the International Play Association, the Association for Childhood Education International, the National Association for the Education of Young Children, and the Association for the Study of Play.

The CPSC published *Handbooks for Public Playground Safety: Volumes I and II* in 1981. These volumes were revised in 1991, 1994, and 1997. In 1993, the American Society for Testing and Materials published *Standards for Public Playground Equipment* (revised in 1998 and 2001). Collectively, the CPSC and ASTM documents gradually became the "national standard of care" because of their influence in playground injury lawsuits and influenced the present "standardized" or "cookie-cutter" condition of most American playgrounds. Similarly, safety standards similar to the American standards were adopted by Australia and Canada, and the Europeans developed and adopted European playground safety standards. European adventure playgrounds were exempted from these standards.

Several American states enacted the CPSC guidelines into law and playground regulations for child care centers in all 50 states are inconsistent with national guidelines and standards. The number of playground injuries reported by the National Electronic Injury Surveillance System through CPSC has almost doubled since the CPSC guidelines were initiated, from about 117,000 during the mid-1970s to more than 200,000 during the early 2000s. The reasons for this increase are not clear but the decline of children's fitness levels may contribute to their inability to play safely on challenging playgrounds. Collectively, playground safety standards and regulations, coupled with increasing injury litigation, emphasis on academics and high stakes testing, and competition from technology (television, computers, and video games) for recess and free play time is contributing to a rapidly growing incidence of obesity, diabetes, early signs of heart disease, and poor fitness levels of children (Frost et al., 2005). Resistance to these counters to free, spontaneous play on playgrounds is resulting in a growing call for creativity in playground design, more time for free play and recess, and extensive modification of playground standards.

Playgrounds: Present and Future

Thought and action about children's playgrounds are in a state of flux perhaps unparalleled in history. Sponsors of playgrounds at child development centers for preschool children have managed to retain much of their broad developmental focus and provide both natural and manufactured materials intended to accommodate the broad play forms of young children.

The standardized, cookie-cutter playgrounds of most elementary schools contain a superstructure and swings designed primarily for exercise play with little or no provision for other forms of play. Community parks typically contain these same elements, complemented with games fields, swimming pools, and skate parks, focusing primarily on older children and adults.

Although restricted by safety standards, which are sometimes broadly misinterpreted to apply to natural materials, a growing number of independent playground developers are looking beyond manufactured or standardized equipment. Many of the professionals involved in developing safety standards are themselves having serious reservations about the unexpected consequences of perpetual standards revision and expansion, the power they hold in litigation, and the expansive interpretation of their meaning by designers, manufacturers, playground sponsors, inspectors, and expert witnesses (Frost, 2005).

The Community Built Association (CBA) is an organization of those interested in involving community groups in the design, organization, and creation of their own community built public spaces. Their spaces and works go well beyond traditional playgrounds to include parks, museums, public gardens, and historic restoration. Fortunately, many CBA members work to preserve adventure play elements, involve children in creating playgrounds, and feature natural elements such as plants, water, sand and soil, gardening, tools, and hand-made structures—elements featured on traditional adventure playgrounds. These "natural playgrounds" proponents frequently circumvent the "junk" appearance, opposed by many Americans, by employing professional landscaping and a focus on aesthetics. Meanwhile, children themselves increasingly turn to indoor sedentary technology games and only dream of the days of mud holes, tree houses, kick-the-can, tree swings, and hammers and nails.

Further Readings: Bengtsson, A. (1972). *Adventure playgrounds.* New York: Praeger Publishers; Cavallo, D. (1981). *Muscles and morals: Organized playgrounds and urban reform, 1880-1920.* Philadelphia: University of Pennsylvania Press; Frost, J. L. (2005). How play ground regulations are messing up children's play. *Today's Playground,* 5(7) 14-19. Frost, J. L., S. C. Wortham, and S. Reifel (2005). *Play and child development.* Columbus, OH: Merrill Prentice Hall; Muths, G. (1793). *Gymnastics for youth.* 1970 translation. Dubuque, IA: William C. Brown.

Joe L. Frost

Play Therapy

For decades, therapists have asserted that play therapy is the most effective medium for conducting therapy with children (Freiberg, 1965; Sandler, Kennedy, and Tyson, 1980). Play therapy is defined as "a play experience that is therapeutic because it provides a secure relationship between the child and the adult, so that the child has the freedom and room to state himself in his own terms, exactly as he is at that moment in his own way and in his own time" (Axline, 1950, p. 68). A more outcome-oriented interpretation of play therapy aims for symptom resolution and adaptive stability.

Play therapy originated in the psychoanalytic tradition as a method used to delve into the unconscious mind of children. Play was first used in therapy by Sigmund **Freud** in the early 1900s as a technique to understand children's unconscious fears. Free association, a technique used to explore the unconscious mind in psychoanalytic therapy with adults, was seen as an unsatisfactory tool for use with children. Psychoanalysts and child therapists began to use play in various ways in their therapeutic work with children (Dorfman, 1951). Dorfman describes Anna **Freud**'s use of play in therapy with children as a means to create an **attachment** between the analyst and the child, rather than as a central tool in therapy. Play allowed the child to develop a positive attachment to the therapist, thereby permitting actual therapy to occur. Some psychoanalysts saw children's play as analogous to free association. Similarly, child therapists who focused on a client-centered approach to therapy saw play as a central component of therapy. Play was considered a comfortable means of communication that allowed children to express themselves.

Amster (1943) identified six therapeutic uses of play: (1) play can be used for diagnostic understanding of children; (2) play can be used to establish a working relationship; (3) play can be used to restructure childrens negative functioning in daily life and defenses against anxiety; (4) play can be used to help children verbalize certain conscious material and the associated feelings; (5) play can be used to help children act out unconscious material and to relieve the accompanying tension; and (6) play can be used to develop children's play interests, which can carry over into daily life and which will enhance prognosis for future functioning.

As play became a more integral part of therapy with children, it became clear that play was the natural language of children. Because language development tends to be a slower process than cognitive development, as children engage in play during therapy, they are communicating information that they may not otherwise be able to express. Play in therapy is based on this developmental understanding that children do not understand or process information the same way as adults.

Numerous types of play therapy have emerged over the years. The major types of play therapy include Psychoanalytic, Directive, Nondirective, Release, Behavioral, Cognitive–Behavioral, Relational, Group, and Sand Tray.

Psychoanalytic Play Therapy was founded by Sigmund Freud, furthered by H. von Hug-Hellmuth, and formally structured by Melanie Klein. Play serves three primary functions in psychoanalytic play therapy sessions: (1) it allows a relationship to establish between therapist and child; (2) it allows the therapist insight into the child achieved through therapist interpretation of past experiences and memories and finally, (3) it serves as the medium for communication between child and therapist. Psychoanalytic play therapy occurs when the child is allowed to play with what he/she chooses, while the therapist interprets his or her preconscious and unconscious meanings out loud to the child—a technique labeled as "free association" (Klein, 1955).

Directive Play Therapy entails a series of therapist-structured situations specific to the child's current difficulties. In this type of therapy, the therapist is in charge of "setting up" the theme and content of play that will occur in the session. These structured situations are the vehicle to encourage the independent free play of the child, centered on the presenting difficulty (Hambridge, 1955).

Nondirective Play Therapy was pioneered by Virginia Axline, and allows the child to decide what to do in a session (within safe boundaries). Perhaps the most important aspect of nondirective play therapy is that the therapist must develop a warm and friendly relationship with the child. Child-centered, non-directive play therapy is based on Carl Rogers' philosophy of personality development and is based on the principle that "all individuals, including children, have the innate human capacity to strive toward growth and maturity if provided nurturing conditions" (Guerney, 2001).

Release Play Therapy is designed to allow children to act out their individual fears and concerns in a safe environment. Release therapy generates success by treating the child by utilizing his or her own methods of treating himself or herself (i.e., allowing the child to act out feelings of aggression through dolls, clay, etc.).

The role of therapist may be minimal, with little interpretation or guidance from the therapist.

Behavioral Play Therapy differs from other forms of play therapy in that the parents directly participate in the session—essentially assuming the role of "therapist." These therapy sessions occur in a typical play therapy room, with the parent engaging in activities chosen by their child. In these play sessions, operant conditioning is the primary technique used to effect behavioral change. Parent's administration of immediate and consistent reinforcement of appropriate behavior leads to an increasing frequency of this desired behavior. This also causes gradual extinction of the undesired behavior.

Cognitive-Behavioral Play Therapy is specifically created for preschool and school-aged children, and emphasizes the child's involvement in treatment by addressing issues of control, mastery, and responsibility for one's own change in behavior (Knell and Ruma, 1996). Techniques commonly employed in this type of play therapy are modeling, using puppets to demonstrate the behaviors the therapist wants the child to learn, and role playing, in which the puppets practice skills and receive feedback from the therapist.

Relationship Play Therapy was founded by Otto Rank and Carl Rogers and promotes full acceptance of the child as he or she is. The focus is on the importance and strength of the therapeutic relationship between child and therapist (Gil, 1991).

Group Play Therapy is defined by the modality of play; however, the focus of the therapy is on children interacting with each other. This therapy occurs with minimal interaction and guidance from the adult therapist and is based on the assertion children will change negative behavior to obtain acceptance from peers (Ginott, 1975).

Sand Tray Play Therapy was created by Dora Kalff. Sand tray play therapy is modeled after Jungian therapy, in that the sand tray represents the child's psyche. The child's placement of objects in the tray and use of symbols is interpreted as the child's passage through healing (Gil, 1991).

In summary, there are several reasons why play therapy has emerged as an important treatment approach for working with children. As stated previously, play is the natural language of children. Using play in therapy brings the therapist into the child's world and addresses issues in a language that is comfortable for the child. In a sense, children "play out" their issues or problems the same as adults "talk out" their problems. Developmentally, play is a means through which children are able to use concrete symbols (i.e., toys) to express their inner thoughts. Play therapy gives children the opportunity to exert some control in the therapeutic situation and a safe, supportive environment in which to express themselves.

Further Readings: Amster, F. (1943). Differential uses of play in treatment of young children. *American Journal of Orthopsychiatry* 13, 62–68; Axline, V. M. (1950). Entering the child's world via play experiences. *Progressive Education* 27, 68–75; Dorfman, E. (1951). Play therapy. In C. R. Rogers, ed., *Client-centered therapy: Its current practice, implications, and theory.* Cambridge, MA: The Riverside Press, pp. 235–278; Freiberg, S. (1965). A comparison of the analytic method in two stages of child analysis. *Journal of the American Academy of Child Psychiatry* 4, 387–400; Gil, E. (1991). *The healing power of play: Working with abused children*. New York: The Guilford Press; Ginott, H. G. (1975). Group therapy with children. In G. M. Gazda, ed., *Basic approaches to group psychotherapy and group counseling*. Springfield, IL: Charles C. Thomas, pp. 327–341; Guerney, L. (2001). Child-centered play therapy. *International Journal of Play Therapy* 10, 13–31; Hambridge, G. (1955). Structured play therapy. *American Journal of Orthopsychiatry* 25, 601–617; Klein, M. (1955). Psychoanalytic play technique. *American Journal of Orthopsychiatry* 25, 223–237; Landreth, G. (2002). *Play therapy: The art of the relationship*. 2nd ed. New York: Brunner-Routledge; Lebo, D. (1955). The development of play as a form of therapy: From Rousseau to Rogers. *Journal of Psychiatry* 112, 418–422; Sandler, J., H. Kennedy, and R. Tyson (1980). *The technique of child psychoanalyses*. Cambridge, MA: Harvard University Press.

Susan M. Swearer, Kelly Brey Love, and Kisha M. Haye

Portage Project

The Portage Project was developed in Portage, Wisconsin, in 1969 as a model early intervention program originally funded through the Handicap Children and Early Educational Program (HCEEP). Still a mainstay program in South Central Wisconsin, the Portage Project has grown and now offers training and replication services for other sites as well as a curriculum guide. The approach itself has also been widely disseminated as a model throughout the United States and many other countries. Since 1986 the International Portage Association has hosted conferences every two years.

Designed to deliver home-based services to children age birth to six years in rural areas with developmental delays and disabilities, the project promotes children's physical, self-help, social, academic, and language development. Based on the rationale that a parent is a child's first teacher, the Portage approach specifically teaches parents how to encourage their child's development through weekly home visits. These home visits, with their heavy parental involvement and the use of a behavioral method of instruction called precision teaching form the core of the Portage model of early intervention.

The home-based design is based on the beliefs that the home is the least restrictive environment for young children, a place that represents a wide range of natural behaviors, and the most practical arrangement for a rural model. In addition, the program's focus on training parents to support their child's development allows families to have a voice in what their children are learning with the understanding that helping parents to be advocates for their children will have long-term effects for their child's education.

Program services are delivered through weekly home visits, typically an hour and a half in length, by a teaching professional known as the home teacher. The home teacher has been trained to design individual curriculum for the child based on observations and parent input. Using the precision teaching model of behavioral analysis, the professional precisely defines targeted behaviors, breaks them down into smaller component tasks, and implements simple, highly repetitive teaching methods supported by continual assessment. To this end, each visit begins with the home teacher evaluating the child's progress on particular tasks from the week before, then developing new goals for the coming week, and teaching the parent how to engage in the prescribed activity with their child.

Three behaviors are targeted for development each week, with the goal of achieving a pattern of success that allows both child and parent to feel the benefits of continual progress. Assessment is an important part of the cycle and is based on formal, informal, curriculum-based, and ongoing observations.

In 1972, The Portage Project developed *The Portage Guide to Early Education* (revised 1976, 1996, 2003), a set of materials including a behavioral checklist and correlating activity suggestions meant to support home teachers in designing individualized curriculum. This guide is only a supplement to the program but is often confused as being the model in its entirety. During the 1970s, a wide body of research was completed documenting significant developmental gains for children who were provided Portage services. However, more recent reviews suggest that many of the studies were performed before today's more rigorous standards of evaluation were in place, and additional scientifically based research is needed to empirically demonstrate clear evidence of the program's effectiveness.

Further Readings: Brue, Alan W. (2001). The portage guide to early intervention: An evaluation of published evidence. *School Psychology International* 22(3), 243–252. Shearer, David E. and Darlene L. Shearer (2005). The portage model: An international home approach to early intervention of young children and their families. In Jaipaul Roopnarine and James E. Johnson, eds., *Approaches to early childhood education.* Englewood Cliffs, NJ: Prentice Hall, pp. 83–104. The Portage Project. Available online at http://www.portageproject.org/.

Lindsay Barton

Poverty, Family, and Child

The multiple stressors of poverty limit children's readiness for and ability to succeed in school. In the United States, the official poverty threshold was developed for the federal government in 1964. The poverty threshold is based on a formula that tripled the cost of a basic food plan because, at that time, the average household spent one third of its income on food. Every year, the poverty threshold is updated for inflation, and in 2006 it is equivalent to $20,000 for a family of four.

Using the official poverty definition, 18 percent of all children in the United States—13 million individuals—lived in poverty in 2003. These rates, however, have fluctuated over the past four decades, since the Census Bureau started tracking poverty rates. In 1959, 27 percent of children lived in poverty. The poverty rate declined through the 1960s to a low of 14 percent by the early 1970s. Poverty then began a steady increase, reaching a high of 22 percent by the early 1990s. From 1993 to 2001, poverty declined to 16 percent, but has since been rising.

Criticisms of the Poverty Definition

As early as 1965, experts began criticizing the poverty threshold. A 1995 report by the National Academy of Sciences recommended revising the poverty threshold because it did not include increases in child care costs, due to higher employment among mothers, medical costs, taxes, or noncash government benefits (e.g., food stamps) (Citro and Michael, 1995). Furthermore, the poverty threshold has not kept up with increases in living standards in the United States, which means that people in poverty are worse off relative to the rest of the population than they were forty years ago. A 2000 study of families' basic budgets for major expenses, including housing, child care, health care, food, transportation, and taxes, showed that families must earn twice the poverty line to provide a "safe and decent" standard of living for their children (Bernstein et al., 2000). For this reason, many analyses of child poverty in the United States, including those developed by the National Center for Children in Poverty, not only include those children who are in officially poor families, but those in families with incomes up to 200 percent of the poverty level.

Characteristics of Low-Income Children

In 2003, 37 percent of American children (26 million) lived in low-income families—defined as families with incomes less than twice the poverty threshold. That is more than one out of every three children in the United States. Minority children, children of immigrants, young children, and children living in southern states are much more likely to live in low-income families. Fifty-eight percent of black children and 62 percent of Latino children live in low-income families, compared to 25 percent of white children. Thirty-three percent of black children, 30 percent of Latino children and 9 percent of white children live in poor families. Two thirds of children of recent immigrants live in low-income families, compared to one third of children of native-born parents, despite high levels of work and marriage among immigrant parents. Thirty-three percent of children of recent immigrants and 15 percent of children of native-born parents live in poor families. Forty-one percent of children under six are in low-income families, compared to 36 percent of older children. Twenty percent of children under six and 15 percent of older children live in poor families. Rates of poverty and low-income status also vary among the states. More than half the children in some southern and southwestern states, such as Arkansas and New Mexico, live in low-income families.

Low parental education is a primary risk factor for low income. Eighty-two percent of children, whose parents lack a high school degree, are low-income, compared to 22 percent of children whose parents have at least some college education. Forty-eight percent of children whose parents lack a high school degree and 8 percent of children whose parents have at least some college education live in poor families. Employment does not prevent low incomes among parents with low education. Among children whose parents lack a high school degree, 72 percent remain low-income even though their parents work full-time and year-round. Parents' marital status is also an important risk factor for low income. Children of single parents are more than twice as likely to live in low-income families and three times as likely to be poor compared to children of married parents.

Hardship among Children in Low-Income Families

Children in low-income families experience many hardships that are a direct result of economic insecurity. They are more likely to suffer from poor health because they are less likely to have health insurance, less likely to go to the doctor or dentist, and less likely to have sufficient food to eat (Casey et al., 2001). Characteristics of neighborhoods contribute to children's poorer health. Children in low-income families are more likely to be exposed to environmental contaminants (Chuang et al., 1999) and to live in more violent neighborhoods (Evans), where they are disproportionately killed or injured as a result of that violence.

Decades of research suggest that poverty and low-income status is one of the greatest risk for children's poor performance in school. Children in low-income families score lower on standardized reading and math tests (Gershoff, 2003), in part, because they are less prepared to enter school. Low-income working mothers are more likely to rely on the less expensive child care provided by relatives, which is less likely to enhance school-readiness than the center-based care used by higher-income families (Cappizanno and Adams, 2004). Low-income mothers experience depression at twice the rate of mothers with higher incomes, which can lead to poor cognitive and behavioral outcomes for their children (Knitzer, 2002). Low-income children are more likely to engage in antisocial behavior, which compromises their ability to do well in school (Raver and Knitzer). Low-income families are more likely to move because of housing problems (Koball and Douglass-Hall, 2003), which can result in their children's falling behind in school because of frequent school changes (Pribesh and Downey, 1999).

Government Efforts to Address Poverty

Over the years, the federal government has tried many different approaches to combat poverty. Since the war on poverty, however, there has been no commitment to reducing poverty as a national goal, comparable, for example to the current policy in the United Kingdom. In the United States, the primary types of assistance for low-income children and families include cash benefits, such as **Temporary Assistance for Needy Families (TANF)**; in-kind assistance, which pay for specific supports, such as food stamps or housing subsidies; low-cost or free health insurance, such as Medicaid and the Children's Health Insurance program; and programs aimed at poverty prevention, such as Head Start, a preschool program to prepare low-income children for kindergarten and Pell Grants, which help low-income students pay for college. Other more recent poverty prevention programs focus on the dynamics of low-income families. These programs include marriage promotion, which aims to decrease divorce and increase marriage among low-income parents; fatherhood programs, which aim to increase father involvement and child support payments of low-income fathers; and teen pregnancy prevention programs.

As of fiscal year 2000, 6 percent of the United States budget was spent on means-tested programs, and an additional 7 percent of the budget was spent on Medicaid. Not all of this money was spent on low-income children and their families. For example, Medicaid also serves people with disabilities and senior citizens in nursing homes. One of the most important antipoverty programs is the federal Earned Income Tax Credit (EITC), which was created in the 1975, but greatly expanded in the early 1990s. It is the nation's largest cash program for low-income families—in 2002, it provided $37 billion to 21 million low- and middle-income families. It reduces the amount of tax that families with annual incomes of up to roughly $34,000 pay. The EITC is refundable, which means that families receive cash back if the credit is more than their taxes owed. Because families can only receive the tax credit if they earn income, the EITC is believed to encourage work among low-income and poor families. It is estimated that the EITC lifts over 2 million children out of poverty each year.

In recent years, there has also been new attention to policies directed at changing family formation and dissolution decisions. For example, marriage promotion efforts, ranging from public awareness campaigns about the benefits of marriage to individual marriage counseling, are being considered. Because research shows that the vast majority of low-income, unmarried, new parents want to marry, supporters believe that these programs will help parents reach this goal. Critics assert that since the effectiveness of marriage promotion programs is untested, such efforts should not be funded by a large sum of government money.

Poverty remains one of the greatest risk factors for children's poor health, poor school performance, and future poverty. Children are at risk of living in poor and low-income families simply because of their race, their parents' education levels, or even the state in which they live. Today, even full-time parental employment does not guarantee that a child will not face the risks of growing up in a poor or low-income family. Although government programs, such as **Head Start**, have been proven to lower the risks associated with low income, they remain in jeopardy of being cut or substantially changed. Other programs, such as the EITC, which have been shown to increase work and improve the financial well-being of low-income families, are also at risk. A national, comprehensive commitment to reducing childhood poverty is currently needed in the United States.

Further Readings: Bernstein, Jared, Chauna Brocht, and Maggie Spade-Aguilar (2000). *How much is enough? Basic family budget for working families.* Washington, DC: Economic Policy Institute; Cappizanno, Jeffrey, and Gina Adams (2004). *Children in low-income families are less likely to be in center-based care.* Washington, DC: The Urban Institute; Casey, P. H., K. Szeto, S. Lensing, M. L. Bogle, and J. Weber. (2001). Children in food-insufficient low-income families: prevalence, health and nutrition status. *Archives of Pediatrics and Adolescent Medicine*, 155: 508–514; Chuang, J. C., P. J. Callahan, C. W. Lyu, and N. K. Wilson (1999). Polycyclic aromatic hydrocarbon exposures of children in low-income families. *Journal of Exposure Analysis and Environmental Epidemiology* 9(2), 85–98; Citro, Constance, and Robert T. Michael (1995). *Measuring poverty: A new approach.* Washington, DC: National Academy Press; Evans, Gary (2004). The environment of childhood poverty. *American Psychologist* 59(2), 77–92; Gershoff, Elizabeth (2003). Low income and the development of America's kindergartners. New York: National Center for Children in Poverty; Knitzer, Jane (2002). *Building services and systems to support the healthy emotional development of young children—an action guide for policymakers.* New York: National Center for Children in Poverty; Koball, Heather, and Ayana Douglas-Hall (2003). *Where do low-income children live?* New York: National Center for Children in Poverty; Pribesh, S., and D. B. Downey (1999). Why are residential and school moves associated with poor school performance? *Demography* 36(4), 521–534; Raver, C. Cybele, and Jane Knitzer (2002). Ready to enter: What research tells policy makers about strategies to promote social and emotional school readiness among three and four year old children. New York: National Center for Children in Poverty.

Jane Knitzer and Heather Koball

Pratt, Caroline (1867–1954)

Caroline Pratt, with colleagues Lucy Sprague **Mitchell** and Harriet Johnson, founded the City and Country School in New York City in 1921. Pratt's distinctive educational philosophy, derived from direct observation of children, emphasized learning through play, field trips, open-ended materials, and children's self-directed planning and problem-solving. Pratt advocated the use of wooden blocks and carpentry in programs for young children and is credited with designing the first set of unit blocks in 1943.

Born in Fayetteville, New York, "Carrie," as she was known to her family, spent her early years participating in activities typical of village life after the end of the Civil War. Intellectually precocious, she attended local schools and taught for five years in the Fayetteville Union Free School after graduation. Pratt obtained a scholarship to begin kindergarten training at Columbia University in 1892. Soon disenchanted with Friedrich **Froebel**'s philosophy (which then dominated the field), Pratt decided to pursue manual training instead. During her formative years at Columbia, Pratt observed children using the Patty Smith **Hill** Blocks and, equally significant, learned to use tools and work with wood.

After traveling abroad to study Swedish *slöjd* (wood working or handwork), Pratt moved to Philadelphia, Pennsylvania, where she taught for several years (1894–1901). While in Philadelphia, Pratt encountered the problems of industrialization and became involved in social reform, most notably through her friend Helen Marot, a Quaker activist and social critic. Marot became Pratt's mentor and lifelong companion; their close association endured until Marot died of a heart attack in 1940. Their Massachusetts homes—first a farmhouse in the Berkshire Mountains and later a cottage on Memensha Pond on Martha's Vineyard—provided summer havens for like-minded friends and visitors. Pratt and Marot envisioned a world where educators and reformers would work in tandem to create thinking, responsible adults whose contributions, eventually, would improve society.

Social justice suffused Pratt's work, beginning at Hartley House, a settlement program where she taught carpentry after moving to New York in 1901. By 1914, Pratt had founded the Play School, a program where, she emphasized, experiments were done *by* children not *to* children (in contrast to Thorndike's "stimulus–response" experiments at nearby Columbia).

Pratt involved Greenwich Village artists (including Jackson and Charles Pollack) in teaching children. The Play School faculty also compiled collections of artwork to document children's growth. Pratt's resident artists and her documentation methods anticipated practices that are now associated with the **Reggio Emilia** preschools.

Caroline Pratt also emphasized field trips and dramatic play. The Play School curriculum often included "absorbing trips," experiences that lent themselves to reenactment and further play to deepen understanding. Her descriptions of excursions to the marketplace, construction sites, train stations, firehouses, and other places of interest firmly established the field trip as an important component of quality educational programming.

Pratt provided simple materials for children to use as they reenacted their adventures. Paper, clay, string, wood, and other malleable materials—transformed into dramatic play props—contrasted sharply with the highly structured pedagogical materials of the day, for example, the Froebellian gifts and Maria **Montessori**'s didactic materials. Pratt's materials demanded use of the imagination; yielded readily to children's play ideas; and provided an infinite number and variety of opportunities for expression.

Pratt's natural, hardwood blocks were intended for use by children of all ages. Noted for their mathematical properties and precision, the blocks designed by Pratt set a standard for manufacturing that survives today. Pratt also designed the first wooden block play accessories, including Do-Withs (jointed people and animal figures) and Wedgie People (community workers and family members). *The Art of Blockbuilding* (Johnson, 1933) and *The Block Book* (Hirsch, 1974; 1984) described the value of unit blocks for children.

Pratt's *New York Times* obituary (June 7, 1954) lauded her pioneering work in education. The inscription on her gravestone in Fayetteville, New York, reads "I learn from children," the title of her best-known book.

Further Readings: Caroline Pratt, educator, dead [obituary]. *The New York Times*, June 7, 1954. Hirsch, Elizabeth, ed. (1974; 1984). *The block book.* Washington, DC: NAEYC; Johnson, Harriet (1933). *The art of blockbuilding.* New York: The John Day Co.; Pratt, Caroline (1948). *I learn from children.* New York: Simon and Schuster; Pratt, Caroline, and Stanton, Jessie (1926). *Before books.* New York: Adelphi; Pratt, Caroline, and Lula E. Wright (1924). *Experimental practice in the city and country school.* New York: E. P. Dutton; Wolfe, Jennifer (2002). *Learning from the past: Historical voices in early childhood education.* Mayerthorpe, Alberta: Piney Branch Press.

Ann C. Benjamin

Prekindergarten. *See* State Prekindergarten Programs

Preschool Curriculum Evaluation Research Program (PCER)

In the United States today (NCES, 2001), more four-year-old children than ever before are attending some form of preschool program prior to entering **kindergarten**. There is a need to conduct rigorous research on the numerous curricula in use by preschool programs to provide scientific evidence on which policy makers and practitioners can base their decisions regarding curriculum selection. Given the emphasis in the **No Child Left Behind** (NCLB) legislation on "evidence-based" practices, **Head Start** and state-funded prekindergarten programs are increasingly scrutinizing research regarding the efficacy of their curricula in relation to their school readiness goals. To address this need, the Institute of Education Sciences (IES) in the U.S. Department of Education initiated the Preschool Curriculum Evaluation Research (PCER) Program, which was designed to conduct small-scale efficacy evaluations of available preschool curricula that had not been rigorously evaluated. The evaluations were conducted using a common assessment protocol and a randomized experimental design.

The PCER program began in 2002 when IES awarded grants to seven researchers to implement several widely used preschool curricula, with Research Triangle Institute (RTI) International serving as their national evaluation coordinator. In

2003, IES funded an additional five researchers, with Mathematica Policy Research (MPR) Inc. serving as their national evaluation coordinator. National evaluation data were collected in fall and spring of the preschool year. Children will be followed until the end of their kindergarten year. Data collection includes direct child assessments, parent interviews, teacher report on children's social skills, teacher interview, and direct classroom observations.

The final sample included Head Start, Title 1, State pre-K, and private preschool programs serving over 2,000 children in twenty geographic locations implementing thirteen different experimental preschool curricula. Participating classrooms or schools were randomly assigned to intervention or control conditions. Baseline assessments indicate that random assignment achieved equivalence at most sites, with some treatment-control variation by site. A report from the PCER Consortium outlining results from the preschool year and follow-up assessments at the end of kindergarten is anticipated to be released in 2006. *See also* Preschool/Prekindergarten Programs.

Further Readings: U.S. Department of Education (2001). National Center for Education Statistics, National Household Education Survey (NHES), 1991 and 1995.

Web Sites: PCER 2002 grantee information, http://pcer.rti.org/ PCER 2003 grantee information, http://www.pcer-mpr.info.

James A. Griffin and Caroline Ebanks

Preschool/Prekindergarten Programs

Preschool is a broad term that can be used to describe any school enrolling children prior to their entry into formal schooling. However, today in the United States, "preschool" most often refers to educational programs for three- and/or four-year-old children. Often distinguished from "**child care**," the term *preschool* denotes a program with an educational focus, although it is well established that a high-quality child care program provides the same educational and social–emotional curricula as a high-quality preschool program (Bowman, Donovan, and Burns, 2001). Unlike a preschool program, a child care program would likely be offered for more hours per day and more days per year in order to support parents' employment, as well as promote child development. The child care program would also be more likely to enroll infants and toddlers (i.e., children younger than three years of age). Despite these distinctions, preschool remains a general term applied to a range of early childhood education programs for children in the year or two prior to **kindergarten**.

Preschool programs may be located in public or private schools, child care centers, churches, synagogues, or other community-based organizations. They may be sponsored by for-profit or nonprofit organizations, and by school districts or other local, state, or federal governments. The services may be paid for through a combination of parent fees, foundation funding, private contributions, and employers, as well as through governmental funds. Some preschool programs enroll children for the full day, five days a week for the full year, while most operate for shorter periods of time (e.g., morning only, school-year only). Although the **curriculum** and structure of programs vary, they often emphasize social–emotional development (e.g., interpersonal skills, following directions) and early academic skills (e.g., concepts about print, counting).

In the United States, there has been a dramatic growth in preschool enrollment over the last half-century. Prior to the 1960s, enrollment in preschool never exceeded 10 percent of the total population of children aged three and four. By 1980, more than a third of children enrolled and attended preschool; and by 2000, more than half of three- and four-year old children attended preschool (U.S. Census Bureau, 2000). Increased enrollment has been fueled by greater interest among parents in enrolling their children in preschool, combined with efforts by the government to promote preschool enrollment through funding at the federal, state, and local levels. Since 1965, the federal **Head Start** program has provided comprehensive preschool programs for low-income children in an effort to increase their healthy development and school **readiness.** In 2004, this $6.7 billion program enrolled over 900,000 children (Head Start Bureau, 2005). In addition to Head Start, many states have also created state prekindergarten programs that use state funds to provide preschool in public schools and/or community-based organizations (e.g., child care centers, nonprofits). Additional governmental funding of preschool programs can also occur at the local level, where many school districts fund preschool programs in their schools using local funds—or opting to use federal (e.g., Title I) or state (e.g., funding formula) dollars to provide preschool programs. In fact, approximately 35 percent of all public elementary schools offer preschool classes—most often targeted to low-income children, children with special needs and/or four-year-old children (Wirt et al., 2004).

Data from the National Household Education Survey (NHES) highlight differences in preschool enrollment among diverse groups (as shown in the figures). Defining preschool attendance as any form of center- or school-based early care and education for three- and/or four-year-old children, NHES estimated that 56 percent of children were enrolled in 2001. However, four-year-old children were much more likely to participate (66%) than three-year-old children (43%), and children with working mothers were more likely to be in preschool (63%) than those with mothers not in the labor force (47%). Of particular concern from an educational equity perspective, children in families living in **poverty** were less likely to attend preschool (47%), as were Hispanic children (40%) and children with less-educated mothers (only 38% of children with mothers with less than high school degree were enrolled).

Since early childhood education programs such as preschool have been found to promote greater school achievement—particularly among at-risk children (Shonkoff and Phillips, 2000)—these discrepancies in preschool enrollment are troubling. Because poor and minority children are both less likely to attend preschool and less likely to come to school with basic readiness skills, increasing their preschool enrollment may be an important intervention to improve their school readiness and later school achievement. In fact, rigorous estimates of the effect of providing universal preschool enrollment for three- and four-year-old children in poverty suggest that this intervention could close up to 20 percent of the Black–White school readiness gap and up to 36 percent of the Hispanic-white

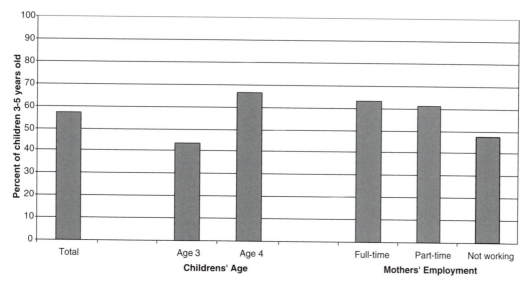

Enrollment in Preschool Programs in 2001 by Children's Age and Mothers' Employment Status.
Notes: Data from 2001 U.S. Department of Education, NCES, National Household Education Survey (NHES) Parent Interview; Preschool enrollment is assumed if the parent indicated that their three- or four-year-old child attended a "center-based program," which includes day care centers, Head Start, preschool, nursery school, prekindergarten, and other early childhood programs; Full-time work is defined as at least 35 hours a week.

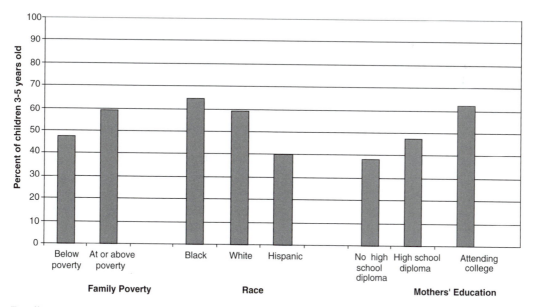

Enrollment in Preschool Programs among Population Sub-Groups.
Notes: Data from 2001 U.S. Department of Education, NCES, National Household Education Survey (NHES) Parent Interview; Preschool enrollment is assumed if the parent indicated that their three- or four-year-old child attended a "center-based program," which includes day care centers, Head Start, preschool, nursery school, prekindergarten, and other early childhood programs.

gap (Magnuson and Waldfogel, 2005). Yet these researchers also note the need to improve the educational quality of preschool programs to see these impressive impacts. Because preschool is such a broad term, applied to a wide range of programs, it should be noted that the quality of the early education services provided is much more important for children's development, learning, and health, than the program's label, whether preschool, nursery school, or child care. *See also* Academics; Curriculum, Emotional Development; Development, Emotional; Development, Social.

Further Readings: Bowman, B. T., M. S. Donovan, and M. S. Burns, eds. (2001). *Eager to learn: Educating our preschoolers.* Washington, DC: National Academy Press. Children's Defense Fund (2004). *Key facts in child care, early education, and school-age care.* Washington, DC: Author. Head Start Bureau (2005). Head Start program fact sheet. Available online at http://www.acf.hhs.gov/programs/hsb/research/2005.htm. Magnuson, K., and J. Waldfogel (2005). Early childhood care and education: Effects on ethnic and racial gaps in school readiness. *The Future of Children* 15(1), 169–196. Shonkoff, J., and D. Phillips (2000). *From neurons to neighborhoods: The science of early childhood development.* Washington, DC: National Academy Press. U.S. Census Bureau (2000). *2000 census—current population survey.* Washington, DC: Author. U.S. Department of Education, National Center for Education Statstics (2002). *Enrollment in early childhood education programs—the condition of education 2002,* NCES 2002-025. Washington, DC: U.S. Government Printing Office. Wirt, J., et al. (2004). *Prekindergarten in U.S. public schools, the condition of education 2004* (NCES 2004-077). U.S. Department of Education, National Center for Education Statistics. Washington, DC: U.S. Government Printing Office.

Elizabeth Rigby

Professional Development

Professional development encompasses both the formal education and specialized training of early childhood professionals. Studies have established formal education and specialized training as critical elements of high-quality early childhood education.

Formal education is defined as coursework that culminates in the receipt of a diploma or degree, including a high school diploma, an associate's degree, and a bachelor's or advanced degree from a postsecondary institution, irrespective of the field in which the degree is earned. Formal education can, but does not always, include specific courses in early childhood education. The term *formal education* implies the completion of a degree rather than short-term enrollment in degree-granting programs.

Specialized training in early childhood refers to education that is focused on the skills necessary to working in the field of early childhood. Such training can take the form of academic coursework in child development or a related field within the context of a degree-granting program (e.g., early childhood **teacher education**). It may also be offered outside an educational institution (e.g., by an association or resource and referral agency) and without formal education credits given for completion. Specialized training often takes the form of in-service workshops and mentoring opportunities.

Professional Development and Early Childhood Program Quality

Both formal education and specialized training are associated with the quality of early childhood education. A substantial body of research confirms the solid connection between formal education and effective job performance. Specifically, there is a strong relationship between the number of years of education and the qualities of teachers' behaviors in the classroom, suggesting that teachers who hold at least a bachelor's degree in any field are better equipped to provide high-quality early childhood education than those with fewer years of formal education.

In addition to research on teachers' general levels of education, there is evidence that specialized training in child development or early childhood education improves teacher performance. Some research has documented higher levels of teacher sensitivity and responsiveness, as well as greater overall quality, in classrooms in which teachers have at least a **Child Development Associate** (CDA) credential. A CDA is earned under the auspices of an organization or agency with expertise in early childhood teacher preparation (such as a postsecondary institution or resource and referral agency). It is awarded to individuals who have had training and experience in the field of early childhood education and have successfully completed the CDA assessment.

There is debate about whether specialized training on its own—without the benefit of a bachelor's or advanced degree—ensures high-quality early childhood education or better outcomes for children in early childhood settings. Some researchers argue that the nature of the specialized training is critical and that teacher effectiveness results only from involvement in formal programs of education in child development or a related field. For example, researchers who have observed teachers in child care centers with different levels and types of training and formal education (including, for example, a high school diploma with no specialized training, a CDA credential, and a bachelor's or higher degree in child development or a related field) have found that only teachers with a bachelor's degree or beyond are associated with classrooms regarded as high-quality. Although teachers with associate's degrees and CDA certificates prove to be more effective than those with only some specialized training in postsecondary institutions or a high school degree with some in-service training, they do not provide the "good-to-excellent" level of quality associated with children's future school success.

Family child care providers are less likely to have a bachelor's degree than center-based teachers. Nonetheless, the existing (but limited) studies of family child care homes reveal patterns of findings similar to those of centers. Family child care providers who are better educated and have received higher levels of specialized training create richer learning environments and provide warmer and more sensitive caregiving than providers with less education and training.

It should be noted that some very recent research on prekindergarten programs finds that teacher education and training are only modest predictors of observed classroom quality. This is in contrast with research on child care programs, for which such associations are greater in magnitude. These findings suggest that the importance of professional development to classroom quality might vary across types of early childhood settings.

Nonetheless, early childhood teachers and providers who possess *both* higher levels of formal education and specialized training in child development bring the most to early childhood education. They are generally more skilled at helping young children develop and achieve their potential. Their interactions with the children in their care are sensitive, warm, and intellectually stimulating—essential components of high-quality care. In particular, children whose teachers are well educated and specially trained have better prereading and premath skills, better social skills, and larger vocabularies. This link between teacher formal education and specialized training and children's school readiness is especially pertinent to children from low-income families, who are at high risk of academic failure if they enter elementary school without the social and cognitive skills necessary for adaptation to school.

The benefits to children of having well-qualified teachers in early childhood settings persist over time. For example, research suggests that the closeness of the early childhood teacher–child relationship is related to children's thinking skills, math skills, social skills, and language ability into the elementary school years. Children whose early childhood teachers have high levels of formal education and training are also more likely to cooperate with elementary-school teachers and, according to teachers and parents, have fewer behavior problems. Furthermore, the positive effects of high-quality early childhood teachers on low-income children can persist into young adulthood. In the care of well-trained early childhood teachers, children are more likely to grow up to be healthier and better adjusted, emotionally and socially. They are also less likely to need expensive remedial services, such as special education, and enter correction or welfare systems.

Professional Development Requirements in the United States

Many occupations, including architecture, electrical engineering, social work, and nursing, require individual credentials (e.g., a certificate or diploma) as a means of ensuring high-quality service. In most educational and human services, the conventional standard for professional preparation for practice is a bachelor's degree. Kindergarten and primary school teachers, for example, must have a bachelor's degree and earn **teacher certification** before they can teach. In its recent report on the care and education of preschoolers, the National Research Council recommended that each group of children in an early childhood program be assigned a teacher who has a college degree and specialized education related to early childhood (National Research Council, 2000).

While the early childhood field provides a mechanism for licensing facilities, it does not, as a profession, require credentials for the individuals who work with children. Instead, each state sets its own minimum qualifications, resulting in great variation in teacher preparation across states and program types (e.g., prekindergarten, child care). Twenty states and the District of Columbia require prekindergarten teachers to have a bachelor's degree. By comparison, only one state—Rhode Island—requires teachers in child care centers to have a bachelor's degree. In many states the maximum education requirement for teachers in child care centers is some early childhood coursework in a postsecondary institution. Thirty states require child care teachers to have no more than a high school diploma in order to teach. Family child care is another story. Only two states require family child care providers to have a high school diploma or its equivalent. Most states require providers to have some annual in-service training.

Professional Development Infrastructure

The professional development of early childhood teachers is dependent upon the accessibility and efficacy of the professional development system in place. An effective system of professional development requires an infrastructure. In the United States, the widespread and long-term professional development of early childhood teachers has led to the conceptualization of a *career lattice*, which depicts the knowledge, performances, and dispositions associated with the early childhood profession's various roles, levels, and settings. The career lattice fosters progression within the field by providing a logical sequence of roles and preparation that individuals can achieve. The lattice framework captures the diversity of roles and settings within the early childhood profession (represented by vertical strands) as well as steps toward greater preparation, tied to increased responsibility and compensation (represented by horizontal levels) within each role/setting. The lattice also allows for movement across roles (represented by diagonals). Each strand of the lattice is interconnected and all strands are part of the larger early childhood profession. By offering opportunities for advancement while early childhood professionals continue to work with children, career lattices serve as both support and advocacy for higher-quality services for children (**National Association for the Education of Young Children**, 1993).

Also critical to the professional development infrastructure are a *core body of knowledge* (specific knowledge) and a *set of core competencies* (observable skills) specific to the field of early childhood education and required to be an effective early childhood professional. Together, the body of knowledge and competencies distinguish early childhood professionals from other professionals. Finally, *articulation agreements* among institutions of higher education constitute another important component of the infrastructure. These allow early childhood professionals to transfer credit among schools, which makes it easier to earn a degree or pursue specialized education. Without articulation, teachers may have difficulty receiving credit for courses they have taken, which, in turn, makes it hard to earn a degree and advance in the field. *See also* Child Care, Families.

Further Readings: Burchinal, Margaret, Carollee Howes, and Susan Kontos (2002). Structural predictors of child care quality in child care homes. *Early Childhood Research Quarterly* 17(1), 87–105; Doherty, Kathryn M. (2002). Early learning: State policies. *Quality counts 2002: Building blocks for success. State efforts in early-childhood education* [Special Issue]. *Education Week* 21(17), 54–67; Howes, Carollee, and Jan Brown (2000). *Improving child care quality: A guide for proposition 10 commissions.* Los Angeles: UCLA Center for Healthier Children, Families and Communities; Howes, Carollee, Ellen Smith, and Ellen Galinsky (1995). *The Florida child care quality improvement study: Interim report.* New York: Families and Work Institute. Lowenstein, Amy E., Susan Ochshorn, Sharon Lynn Kagan, and Bruce Fuller (2004). *The effects of professional development efforts and compensation on quality of early care and education services.* Denver: National Conference of State Legislatures; National Association for the Education of Young Children (1993). *A conceptual framework for early childhood professional development* (Position Statement). Washington, DC: Author; National Research Council (2000). Eager to learn: Educating our preschoolers. Committee on Early Childhood Pedagogy: Barbara Bowman, M. Suzanne Donovan, and M. Susan Burns, eds., *Commission on Behavioral and Social Sciences and Education*. Washington, DC: National Academy Press; Pianta, Robert, Carollee Howes, Margaret Burchinal, Donna Bryant, Richard Clifford, Diane Early, and Oscar Barbarin (2005). Features of pre-kindergarten programs, classrooms, and teachers: Do they predict observed classroom quality and child-teacher interactions? *Applied Developmental Science* 9(3), 144–159; Vandell, Deborah Lowe, and Barbara Wolfe (2000). *Child care quality: Does it matter and does it need to be improved?* Washington, DC: U.S. Department of Health and Human Services; Whitebook, Marcy (2003). *Bachelor's degrees are best: Higher qualifications for pre-kindergarten teachers lead to better learning environments for children*. Washington, DC: The Trust for Early Education.

Amy E. Lowenstein

Professional Ethics

A commitment to ethical behavior is an essential component of every profession. Each profession (occupation with a commitment to a significant social value) has a unique conception of its ethical obligations based on the nature of its contribution to society, its history, and its values. Codes of ethics are part of the identity of the profession and provide guidelines for the ethical conduct of its practitioners. As an occupation that makes the significant contribution of educating and caring for the young in our society, the early care and education field is striving to become recognized as a profession. Part of this process is attention to professional ethics. Ethics is a particularly significant endeavor for the early care and education field because the children who are served are young and therefore vulnerable. The development of the **National Association for the Education of Young Children** (NAEYC) Code of Ethical Conduct was an important step in raising awareness of the moral and ethical dimensions of the early childhood educator's work and has provided a common framework for thinking about ethics and addressing ethical issues that arise in the work of early childhood educators.

Morality and Ethics

Morality refers to beliefs about right and wrong that guide an individual's behavior. Ethics addresses a range of values relating to morality and what is considered to be right and proper. Ethics can be defined as the explicit and critical reflection on moral beliefs. It is the study of right and wrong, duty and obligation. "Doing ethics" means making choices between values and examining the moral dimensions of relationships. Ethics builds on an individual's personal values and morality.

Professional ethics involves reflection on moral beliefs and practices, carried on collectively and systematically by the members of a profession. The goal of a profession is to meet the needs of clients and to use knowledge for the good of society. The responsibilities of a profession are set forth in a code of ethics—one of the hallmarks of a profession. A code assures the society that practitioners who perform a particular role will provide their services in accordance with high standards and acceptable moral conduct.

Codes of Ethics

A code of ethics reflects the shared understandings and combined wisdom of a group of professionals. A code acknowledges the obligations that individual practitioners share in meeting the profession's responsibility. A code, which lays out the profession's firmly held beliefs, can be a unifying force in a profession, providing a vision of what good professionals should be like and how they should behave. It also gives a framework for ethical decision making, offering guidance to practitioners in making choices that serve the best interests of their clients. It can also support a person who takes a risky but courageous stand and can provide the justification for a difficult decision.

A code of ethics helps people who work in a field to address issues that cannot be settled by research or by law and it supports them in doing what is right, not what is easiest, most comfortable, or will make them most popular. A code of ethics is not a legal or regulatory document. It differs from laws, policies, and regulations in that the code's focus is on individuals, not agencies, programs, or organizations. It guides but does not mandate professionals' efforts to address the most difficult situations of the workplace. Codes of professional ethics vary. Some are general and inspirational, while others are designed to provide specific guidance to practitioners in addressing ethical dilemmas that they encounter in their work.

The Naeyc Code of Ethical Conduct

The National Association for the Education of Young Children (NAEYC) has been involved in work on professional ethics since the 1970s. The first publication that focused on professional ethics, *Ethical Behavior in Early Childhood Education,* was authored by Lilian Katz and Evangeline Ward (1978/1991). In this work the authors describe several aspects of working with young children with significant ethical implications. The first and most compelling reason for early childhood educators to be concerned with ethics is the vulnerability of young children and the resulting power and status of the adults who work with them. Another reason is that early childhood educators serve many client groups (children, families, employing agencies, and the community) and therefore must be able to prioritize the interests, needs, and demands of one group over another. A third reason has to do with the ambiguity of the role of the early childhood educator who, in the course of the day, may assume many different roles, including caregiving functions that are much like those of a parent. It is to be expected that tensions sometimes develop between teachers/caregivers and children's parents when they have different views about how these children should be raised.

The Katz and Ward book, first released in 1978, served to document the field's need for a code of ethics to assist early childhood educators in fulfilling their many responsibilities and creating and maintaining multiple complex relationships while working effectively with young children and their families.

In 1984, NAEYC Governing Board created an Ethics Commission, chaired by Stephanie Feeney, which embarked on the task of exploring and clarifying the profession's understanding of its ethical responsibilities. The first edition of the code now in use was developed through a process led by Feeney and Kenneth Kipnis, a philosopher who served as a consultant during the development of the code. They began by publishing a survey in NAEYC's journal, *Young Children*. Results from that survey demonstrated that members agreed that the development of a code was an important priority. This began a two-year-long process during which workshops were held to reach consensus on the field's core values; vignettes were published in the journal, asking readers to send responses describing that they believed "the good early childhood educator" should do when faced with a variety of ethical dilemmas.

Working with the information gleaned from the membership through these efforts, Feeney and Kipnis presented the first draft of the code to the NAEYC Board in November 1988. After making the revisions recommended by the Board, the NAEYC Code of Ethical Conduct was approved in July 1989 and published in *Young Children* that November. The Code has been revised three times since its original adoption, in 1992, 1997, and 2005.

The NAEYC Code includes a Preamble; a list of core values; and sections exploring ethical responsibilities to children, families, community, and society. It also includes a statement of commitment—a personal expression of agreement with the values and responsibilities shared by all early childhood educators.

The core values articulated in the Code are firmly grounded in the history and literature of the field. They reflect members' central beliefs, their commitment to society, and a common purpose embraced by early childhood field. These core values are the foundation that makes it possible for early childhood educators to move from personal values and beliefs to a shared understanding of the professional values held by everyone in the field.

Each of the Code's four sections includes a brief introduction, a list of *Ideals* and a list of *Principles*. Ideals point the individual in the direction of desirable and exemplary professional behavior. The Principles identify practices that are required, those that are permitted, and those that are prohibited. Principles are the basis for distinguishing acceptable from unacceptable behavior. Typically the violation of such a rule involves betrayal of some core value of the profession.

In 2004, a Supplement for Early Childhood Adult Educators was released jointly by NAEYC, the **National Association of Early Childhood Teacher Educators** (NAECTE), and the **American Associate Degree Early Childhood Educators** (ACCESS). It addresses the unique needs of those who work with adult learners who are either working in, or preparing to work in, early childhood education.

The NAEYC Code Is a Living Document

Because NAEYC is a membership organization open to all who are interested in young children and early care and education, its code is not enforced as are those of professional groups like doctors and lawyers who have strong organizations charged with regulating the profession. But the NAEYC ethical guidelines have had a strong impact on practice in early childhood education. This influence can be attributed to NAEYC's commitment to making the Code widely available, building it into the association's activities and making it visible to members through regular publications and conference presentations.

The NAEYC Code of Ethics is available in the form of inexpensive brochures published by NAEYC in English and Spanish. And it is included in most basic texts in early childhood education. It can also be found on the NAEYC Web site (www.naeyc.org) by following links to Resources → Position Statements → Improving early childhood education and professionalism. NAEYC has invested in educating its members about the Code and in helping members learn how to apply it. They have published two books devoted to ethics: a basic text *Ethics and the Early Childhood Educator* (Feeney and Freeman, 1999) and *Teaching the NAEYC Code of Ethical Conduct: Activity Sourcebook* (Feeney, Freeman, and Moravcik, 2000), a book of activities and resources helpful to those teaching about the code and its application. These resources have been widely distributed and have played an influential role enhancing practitioners' professionalism.

The Code does not provide answers for all the thorny dilemmas of practice. The supporting and interpretive literature mentioned earlier does not play that role either—they offer neither cookbook formulas for finding one best solution, nor an exhaustive list of dilemmas and their "best" solutions. What these resources do offer, however, are tools to help early childhood educators approach difficult situations methodically and systematically, and to reach resolutions that are fair and defensible. It assures early childhood professionals that they are not alone when they take the moral high ground described by their Code of Ethics.

Further Readings: Feeney, Stephanie, and Nancy K. Freeman (1999). *Ethics and the early childhood educator.* Washington, DC: National Association for the Education for Young Children; Feeney, Stephanie, Nancy K. Freeman, and Eva Moravcik (2000). *Resources for teaching the NAEYC Code.* Washington, DC: National Association for the Education for Young Children; Katz, Lilian G., and Evangeline H. Ward (1978). *Ethical Behavior in Early Childhood Education.* Washington, DC: National Association for the Education for Young Children; Katz, Lilian G. (1995). Ethical issues in working with young children. In Lilian G. Katz, ed., *Talks with teachers of young children: A collection.* (pp. 237–252). Norwood, NJ: Ablex; Kidder, R. M. (1995). How good people make tough decisions: Resolving the dilemmas of ethical living. New York: Simon & Schuster; National Association for the Education of Young Children. (1989/1997). Code of Ethical Conduct. Available online at http://naeyc.org/resources/position_statements/pseth98.htm. National Association for the Education of Young Children, Code of Ethical Conduct: Supplement for Early Childhood Adult Educators 2004; Available online at http://naeyc.org/about/positions/ethics04.asp. Nash, Robert J. (1996). "Real world" ethics: Frameworks for educators and human service professionals. New York: Teachers College Press. Strike, Kenneth A., and J. J. Soltis, eds. (1992). *The ethics of teaching.* 2nd ed. New York: Teachers College Press.

Stephanie Feeney and Nancy K. Freeman

Program for Infant Toddler Caregivers (PITC)

The Program for Infant Toddler Caregivers (PITC) is the nation's major provider of infant/toddler caregiver training. WestEd, one of the nation's ten regional

Educational Research and Development Laboratories, launched PITC in 1986, working with the California Department of Education (CDE/CDD). PITC activities include creating and distributing video, print, and Web site materials, and providing institutes, graduate events, conferences, community outreach events, and locally based training of caregivers. PITC video and print materials are the most widely disseminated infant/toddler caregiver training materials in the United States. Between 1996 and 2003, PITC played a major role in providing training and technical assistance to the 700 **Early Head Start** and Migrant Head Start programs serving infants and toddlers. PITC has presented Trainer Institutes, along with graduate conferences and satellite trainings, in sixteen states. The Program for Infant/Toddler Caregivers training system has reached more than 100,000 caregivers nationwide.

The heart of the PITC philosophy is the development of warm, nurturing relationships between infants, their families, and their caregivers, and care that is individualized, culturally responsive, and respectful of the child's cues and natural desire to learn. PITC recommends six program policies that support relationships and early learning:

- The assignment of a *primary caregiver* to each child and family
- *Continuity* of caregiver assignments and groups over time
- The creation of *small groups* of children and caregivers
- Responsiveness to *individual needs,* abilities and schedules
- *Inclusion* of children with disabilities and other special needs,
- *Cultural responsiveness* through dialog and collaboration with families.

These policies are intended to promote the development of relationships and social skills as well as positive identity formation, along with cognitive, language, and physical skills. The physical child care environment is another critical element in the care of infants and toddlers. PITC recommends environments that are safe, healthy, comfortable, and convenient for both children and adults, encourage movement, allow for flexibility, are scaled to the children's size, and offer a variety of choices. An integral part of the Program's training philosophy is the concept of "Creating a Community of Learners," which focuses attention on the variety of learning styles, knowledge and experiences of adult learners, and emphasizes the value of supported, cooperative learning. An evaluation of PITC training has shown a positive impact on programs after completing the training. After attendance at PITC institutes, participants may become certified Program for Infant/Toddler Caregivers trainers in that module through the successful completion of a certification paper describing their training plans for each of the module's topics.

The PITC materials and trainings are organized into four modules.

- **Module I: Social–emotional Growth and Socialization** includes infant temperament, stages of emotional development, responsive caregiving, guidance, and discipline.
- **Module II: Group Care** includes caregiving routines, environments, group organization, and respectful care.
- **Module III: Learning and Development** includes brain development, cognitive learning, language and communication, special needs, and the role of culture in learning and development.

- **Module IV: Culture, Family, and Providers** includes culture and identity formation, parent–caregiver relations, and providing culturally sensitive care.
  See also Infant Care; Infant/Toddler Environment Rating Scale.
  Further Readings: Mangione, Peter L. (1990). A comprehensive approach to using video for training infant and toddler caregvers. *Infants and Young Children* 13(2), vi–xi.
  Web Site: PITC Web Site, www.pitc.org

J. Ronald Lally

Progressive Education

Progressive education is a term that refers to multiple and sometimes conflicting educational theories and practices. The term does not necessarily refer to one entity, and its origins are associated with many historical figures in the fields of education, child development, and philosophy. Although progressive education has manifested itself in a wide variety of teaching policies and practices, proponents of progressive education share a common desire to create schools that expand the concept of education beyond that of traditional schooling.

Progressive education was prominent in the early 1900s and began as an effort to use schools to improve each individual's life. This expanded the school's role to include addressing each child's health, improving the quality of family and community life, applying new pedagogical principles developed from the **child study movement**, and adapting instruction to accommodate the increasingly diverse populations of children attending public school. Progressive reformers believed that the schools should prepare citizens to be active participants in a democratic society.

John **Dewey** is often considered the founder of progressive education. Dewey himself, however, called Francis W. **Parker** the father of the movement. Progressive education also draws on ideas from Jean Jacques **Rousseau**, Johann **Pestalozzi**, and Fredrich **Froebel**, dating back to the late eighteenth century. Rousseau emphasized experiential learning, one of the hallmarks of progressive education. Pestalozzi was influenced by Rousseau's writings, and furthered the ideas of child-centered pedagogy and social justice through education. Froebel opened his own school that emphasized active cooperative learning after being inspired by Pestalozzi's ideas while working at a Pestalozzian school. Later, Parker and Dewey each integrated the concept that children learn best through actual performance and experimentation into their own work in the Quincy schools and the laboratory school at the University of Chicago, respectively.

Although the progressive education movement was not necessarily a cohesive effort toward a specific model of education, there are many philosophical foundations that pervade most progressive schools historically and in the present. Progressive educators attempt to educate the "whole child"—meaning children as intellectual, social, emotional, and physical beings—and view each child as an individual with a unique learning profile and unique needs. The progressive educator promotes adapting teaching methods to each individual child instead of forcing education on the child using the accepted methods of the time.

Progressive educators propose that education must differ for each student dependent on his individual needs, strengths, and weaknesses.

Progressive education claims to be child centered because it focuses on the needs of the individual child instead of the needs of the institution or the school. It rejects rote learning in favor of involving children in active learning by applying ideas to real-life situations. In this way, progressive education attempts to prepare children more fully to participate in society outside the school by placing academic skills in the context of the real world. In addition, progressive education promotes the value of **play**. In this sense, the early progressive education movement had a profound influence on today's preschools, where play is often the major vehicle used for teaching and learning. This aspect of progressive education draws heavily on Froebel's work, which led to the **kindergarten** movement in the United States. Play-based learning is closely connected to the idea of **emergent curriculum**, another aspect of progressive education, and involves the practice of creating curriculum based on children's interests. Close observation of children's play often reveals their interests and can allow the teacher to build curriculum that incorporates these topics that are important to her students. The progressive philosophy or principle is that children will be more invested in learning if they are interested in the topic and therefore motivated to participate in the learning experience. Progressive education also emphasizes self-discipline and does not use punishment as a way to encourage learning. The child is encouraged and allowed to progress at his own pace and teachers try to avoid competition.

Prior to World War I, the public was frustrated with classic curriculum, and was open to new ideas about schooling. Thus, Dewey and other progressive educators found an audience for their rejection of traditional rote learning in favor of a curriculum based on individual interests to prepare students for participation in a democratic society. Parker embraced an informal school environment as opposed to the traditional formal teaching techniques and Dewey later expanded upon Parker's ideas by writing about his belief that all areas of a child's life should be integrated into the school. Dewey was most influential after World War I when his philosophy that the school should be a microcosm of society coincided with public demand that education become more relevant to social needs.

Progressive education was most prominent from 1919 to 1955 when the Progressive Education Association was actively promoting its ideals. Stanwood Cobb founded the organization, and John Dewey served as honorary president from 1926 until his death in 1952. In 1924, the association began to publish *Progressive Education*, a quarterly publication that discussed the pedagogical practices of progressive schools. However, the association struggled to agree on a consistent philosophy of progressive education and was unable to create alternatives to the traditional curriculum that it criticized. Thus, in 1955, as progressive education became less popular, the association was dissolved.

Dewey in particular brought the ideas of progressive education to the world by writing many landmark books about it, including *The School and Society* (1899) and *Democracy and Education* (1916). However, some educators misinterpreted Dewey's writing and abandoned discipline completely in the name of progressive education. Some took Dewey's ideas about pupil freedom to such an extreme as to completely overlook the necessity of purpose, continuity, and structure in the learning process. Although Dewey himself criticized this practice, schools where pupils had complete control over their learning experience came to represent progressive education to numerous educators and laymen. This distorted public perception of progressive education led to rejection of progressive education by many who already opposed educational reform. However, the intent of Dewey's ideas about self-discipline were that children would learn more effectively through guided expression as opposed to authoritarian teaching.

Early progressive schools were characterized by unusually creative teachers and highly motivated students, which resulted in very effective and exemplary schools. However, owing to the lack of a standardized method, progressive education practices did not produce positive results when educators attempted to generalize progressive education into schools with typical teachers and students. In addition, the progressive education movement lost support in the 1950s owing to claims that it was tied to liberal and radical politics. In this era of cold war anxiety, anticommunism, and cultural conservatism, declarations that progressive education was un-American caused the public to reject it in favor of a return to traditional curriculum that focused on rigorous academic studies. In the mid-1950s the space race between the United States and the Soviet Union took over American political consciousness, causing many Americans to embrace stringent standards for education. Today, George W. Bush's **No Child Left Behind Act** continues to stress traditional methods of education as measured by standardized tests that will hold educators accountable for the education of American children.

Although progressive education is not as widely known today as it was in the early 1900s, many aspects of its philosophy have been integrated into a variety of educational settings, most notably contemporary preschools. Open classrooms, cooperative learning, multiage approaches, whole language, experiential education, and many forms of alternative schools all have philosophical roots in progressive education. In addition, many private and independent schools still exist that associate themselves with progressive education. The progressive education movement raised aesthetic standards for schools, increased the variety of pedagogical methods available to educators, and increased vocational and manual training opportunities. Although the demise of the Progressive Education Association in 1955 marked the end of the prominence of progressive education, its legacy lives on as educators continue to integrate aspects of this philosophy into modern schools.

Further Readings: Bortner, Doyle, M. (1950). Progressive education, what is it? *The Training School Bulletin* 47, 21–31; Cremin, Lawrence Arthur (1961). *The transformation of the school: Progressivism in American education, 1876–1957*. New York: Alfred A. Knopf; Dewey, John (1899). *The school and society*. Chicago: The University of Chicago Press. Dewey, John (1916). *Democracy and education*. New York: Macmillan; Dewey, John (1959) *Dewey on education. Selections with an introduction and notes by Martin S. Dworkin*. New York: Teachers College Press; Unger, Harlow G. (2001). *Encyclopedia of American education*. New York: Facts on File.

Joanna K. Nelson

The Project Approach

The Project Approach refers to that portion of the curriculum in which the children are encouraged to initiate, plan, and conduct in-depth investigations of objects and events from their own experience and environment. These investigations, usually referred to as projects, provide contexts for children to examine in depth and detail phenomena which are thought to be worthy of their fuller and deeper knowledge and understanding. In the United States, the project approach is most often found in preschool through the elementary grades.

The inclusion of projects in the curriculum for elementary school children was first reported in the United States early in the last century as applied at University of Chicago Laboratory School. Shortly thereafter this approach was promoted as a method of teaching in elementary schools by William Heard Kilpatrick (1922) under the title "The Project Method."

This method has a long history in the United Kingdom also, dating back to World War II until the 1980s, when it became a major component of preschool and primary education. Sometimes referred to as "the integrated day" (Katz and Chard, 1989), current interpretations of the project approach include many features associated with *progettazione*, one of many impressive components of the world-renowned preprimary schools of the small northern Italian city of **Reggio Emilia**. In addition to publications focused on this pedagogical approach, several Web sites with information, illustrations, and guidelines about implementation of the project approach are now available (cf. www.project-approach.com).

Current interpretations of the *Project Approach* suggest that projects are an important element of an early childhood curriculum that, when well implemented, are complementary to other elements of the larger curriculum. In project work, children frequently employ their growing academic skills purposefully in the service of their intellectual pursuits; it is assumed that the dispositions to master and use basic academic skills (e.g., reading, writing, graphing) are strengthened by their obvious usefulness in the eyes of the children themselves. Increasing awareness of the experience and practices of preprimary educators in Reggio Emilia has deepened their appreciation of how "graphic languages" such as observational drawing can enrich their project work. Reggio Emilia has also deepened an appreciation of the value of incorporating the careful **documentation** of the children's experiences to enhance all aspects of their learning, as well as to facilitate the involvement and appreciation of their parents.

Features of the Project Approach

Current interpretations of the project approach are more carefully structured than earlier implementations. Projects, defined as in-depth investigations of particular topics, are usually undertaken by a whole class, but in which small groups, or occasionally individuals, focus on subtopics related to the main one. The central feature of project work is that it involves children participating (with the adults) in the selection of the topic to be investigated, the formulation of the research questions, the gathering of the data they decide they will need in order to answer their questions, and in various ways summarizing and presenting their findings.

The Phases of Project Work

Katz and Chard (1995) and Helm and Katz (2001) recommend that projects be undertaken in roughly three sequential phases. This strategy helps young children gain a sense of the sequence and narrative of the experiences included in conducting investigations; it also enables the children to identify readily with the purposes of the work of each phase and to enjoy a sense of the progression as well as conclusion of their efforts.

Phase I—Getting Started: In phase I, a topic for the investigation is typically selected by the teacher in close consultation with the children. On the basis of discussions about possible phenomena to investigate, the teacher can assess the likelihood that the topic will be of interest to a sufficiently large proportion of the children in the class. During these early discussions, children are invited to share their own experiences, opinions, and current knowledge related to the topic.

Children are also encouraged to represent their own experiences related to the topic through drawings, paintings, dictating or writing stories, reporting their memories to each other. Throughout this period the teacher continues to assess which aspects of the topic are likely to be of greatest interest to most of the children, as well as which children might serve as leaders or resources because of their special experiences. The teacher also makes note of which aspects of the topic require further clarification and deeper knowledge and how the investigation can support this learning.

At the close of Phase I, the teacher helps the children formulate clearly their research questions and predict the answers; and share the basis for their predictions. The teacher also provokes the children to challenge each other's predictions and to think of ways to test them. Phase I concludes with a preliminary set of research questions, to be added to throughout the project. This phase may last several days, or a week or two, depending on how often the children are together, the scope of the topic, and their interests.

Phase II—Gathering the Data: During this period the main activity is conducting the investigation, doing the fieldwork involved in gathering data that will answer the previously generated questions. Depending on the ages of the children, and the nature of the topic, Phase II will include first-hand, direct exploration of the objects and environments related to the topic. During visits to relevant fields children might draw what they observe, asking questions of relevant on-site experts. Phase II also usually includes inviting experts into the classroom to answer prepared questions and to show and explain relevant items.

Many projects also include children's development of surveys and/or questionnaires related to the topic, and interviewing people who have something to say about the topic. Toward the end of this phase the children discuss with the teacher various ways of presenting the results of their research to peers, families, and others.

Many good projects have been conducted without field site visits and use data or pertinent objects collected and brought to classrooms from home. For example, several groups of preschoolers and kindergartners have participated in studies of balls that were part of home collections (sometimes as many as thirty different kinds). The topic "Water in Our Houses" has also involved kindergarten and primary grade children in different communities in bringing complex data from home to their classes to examine, analyze, and summarize together.

Phase III—Bringing the Investigation to a Conclusion: During the final period, the work of the investigation is brought to a close. The teacher involves the children in examining the findings as they correspond to their initial questions and predictions. During this phase a large part of the children's effort is devoted to deciding how to represent the story of their investigation during the project. Projects often conclude with an "open house" event to which parents and others in the community and in the school are invited to examine the children's work. These events often involve children in planning formal presentations, considering what their visitors will find most interesting about their work, and making decisions about what to include in the documentation of the project so as to show clearly what has been learned and accomplished. Many projects also produce class books, and photo albums that capture the children's experiences so that the children themselves can revisit them, and can share them with others who were not part of the actual experiences.

The Project Approach and Children's Development and Learning

Observing young children engaged in good project work makes it clear that development and learning can be supported by the activities and processes involved, as long as the topic under investigation is worthy of the children's energy and effort. As the teacher engages the children in discussions related to the topic, they have ample experience of expressing their views, listening to others' views, arguing, explaining, and engaging in the sort of **classroom discourse** that supports children's language development.

In conducting an investigation, children are active rather than passive learners, working in contexts in which they demonstrate their intellectual dispositions to theorize, analyze, hypothesize, make predictions, and to argue. This "active" versus "passive" role in the classroom is thought to be especially important in the development and learning of boys, who are more likely than girls to be expected to be assertive and active rather than passive in many cultures. In addition, children's emerging academic skills are purposefully employed during project work. The children readily take initiative and take responsibility for seeking answers to their questions by a variety of information-seeking strategies, for example, conducting interviews, surveys, making observational drawings and sketches that will serve as a basis for discussion, planning, and arguments. In other words, the purposes of these investigations and the usefulness of basic **literacy** and numeracy and other skills are clear to the children themselves.

Project Approach supports a number of dispositions identified as central to children's learning. Because investigations involve children in extended effort over time, rather than brief one-shot amusing activities, they are supportive of the disposition called *interest*, that is, the capacity to lose oneself in something outside of oneself. The Project Approach also emphasizes providing contexts that strengthen and support children's *intellectual* dispositions, in contrast to more formal instructional contexts that may damage important intellectual dispositions as a result of excessive academic pressure (see Golbeck, 2001 Marcon, 2003). *See also* Academics; Development, Language.

Further Readings: Golbeck, Susan L., ed. (2001). *Psychological perspectives on early childhood education: Reframing dilemmas in research and practice.* Mahwah, NJ: Lawrence Erlbaum Associates; Helm, Judith H., and Lilian G. Katz (2001). *Young investigators. The project approach with young children.* 2nd ed. New York: Teachers College Press; Katz, L. G., and S. C. Chard (1995). *Engaging children's minds. The project approach.* 2nd ed. Norwood, NJ: Ablex; Katz, Lilian G. (1997). The challenges of the Reggio Emilia approach. In Joanne Hendricks, ed., *First steps toward teaching the Reggio Way.* Upper Saddle River, NJ: Prentice; Kilpatrick, W. H. (1922). The project method. *Teachers college record,* 19(4), 319–335; Marcon, Rebecca (2002). Moving up the Grades: Relationship between preschool model and later school success. *Early childhood research and practice.* Available online at http://ecrp.uiuc.edu/v4/n1/marcon.html.

Lilian G. Katz

Project Zero (PZ)

Project Zero (PZ) is a research organization housed at the Harvard Graduate School of Education. PZ's mission is to understand and enhance learning, thinking, and creativity across the arts and other disciplines. At any given time, approximately ten to twenty separate investigations are underway in schools, museums, and other cultural and educational institutions in the United States and around the world. A primary focus of the research is creating communities of reflective learners and promoting critical and creative thinking for children, adults, and organizations.

PZ was founded in 1967 by the philosopher Nelson Goodman to study and improve education in the arts. Goodman believed that learning in the arts is a serious cognitive activity and should be studied as such, but that "zero" had been firmly established about the field (hence the organization's name). In 1972, Howard Gardner and David Perkins became codirectors, posts they held into the 1990s. In 2000, Steve Seidel assumed the directorship of the organization.

Three lines of PZ research are particularly noteworthy in the field of early childhood education. The Early Symbolization and Transition to Literacy Project (1976–1989) was a group of closely related studies that looked at young children's representational capacities. PZ researchers documented the maturation of young children's linguistic, artistic, and musical capacities in order to develop a model of early symbolic development in different areas. Researchers also investigated the onset and growth of symbol use in school-age children.

Based on Howard Gardner's theory of **multiple intelligences** and David Feldman's theory of development in nonuniversal domains, Project Spectrum (1984–1993) constructed an alternative approach to assessment and curriculum development for the preschool and early elementary years. Positing that each child has a unique profile (spectrum) of intelligences, and that these intelligences can be enhanced by educational opportunities, researchers used classroom observations to develop methods of assessing and promoting children's linguistic, mathematical, musical, artistic, social, scientific and kinesthetic knowledge.

The aim of the Making Learning Visible (MLV) Project (1997–present) is to understand, document, and promote learning groups in schools. MLV researchers investigate the power of the group as a learning environment and **documentation** as a way for students, teachers, and other interested adults to see how and what children are learning. Initially a collaboration with educators from the municipal preschools of **Reggio Emilia**, Italy, the project has also worked with teachers in the United States from preschool through graduate school to explore individual and group learning in a range of classroom settings.

Research directions at Project Zero are influenced by the interests of the principal investigators and priorities of funding organizations. The primary source of financial support comes from private foundations and individual philanthropists. Research findings are disseminated through publications, Web sites, and a variety of professional development formats such as an annual institute, seminars, and online courses.

Further Readings: Project Zero (2005). Available online at http://www.pz.harvard. edu/index.htm; Making Learning Visible (2005). Available online at http://www.pz. harvard.edu/mlv/index.cfm.

Ben Mardell and Mara Krechevsky

Psychosocial Theory

Noted child psychoanalyst Erik H. **Erikson** is often referred to as the father of psychosocial development. He was closely associated with psychoanalysts Sigmund **Freud** and his daughter, Anna **Freud**, during his stay in Vienna from 1927 to 1933, a period described as one of Freud's fame. Erikson, more than anyone else, made the most significant advances in the field of psychoanalytical theory. He viewed the psychoanalytic situation as a modern Western approach to humankind's attempts at introspection, beginning at first as a psychotherapeutic method and leading later to a broader psychological theory. Erikson's best-known work is *Childhood and Society* published in 1950.

Earlier, Freud had postulated that personality development was influenced by a sequence of stages in which the child's libido, or sexual energy, was centered on particular body zones, starting from the oral and moving through the anal, phallic, and genital regions of the body. Freud's approach to psychoanalysis was thus defined by a theory of psychosexual development. Erikson worked to broaden Freud's perspective after his study of the Sioux Indian children showed him the deep influence that social and historical change had on the human mind. Erikson himself had been greatly impressed by the work of anthropologists such as Ruth Benedict and Margaret Mead.

In his book, *Childhood and Society*, he made note of the fact that even anthropologists living for years among aboriginal tribes had been inattentive to the quality of child care within the tribes, and had failed to see that these tribes trained their children in some systematic way. In the same book, Erikson also presented an in-depth discussion on the Freudian concepts of the Id, the Ego, and the Superego. In doing so, Erikson made clear the continuity between the main ideas from his earlier training and his work later in life. These themes are integrated in the section in the book in which he formulated his discussion on the psychosocial nature of development, taking into account an understanding of general encounters between the child and the social world. Erikson, a Freudian ego-psychologist, basically widened the scope of psychoanalytic theory to give greater consideration to social, cultural, and environmental factors.

According to Erikson, human development takes place over eight psychosocial stages. At each stage, the individual faces a predominant "crisis," a turning point of enhanced potential. The more successfully the individual resolves the "crisis" at each stage, the higher will be the success rate at which the conflict at the next stage would be resolved and, subsequently, the healthier would be the development of the individual's overall personality. A successful resolution of a conflict results in the individual's developing a specific psychosocial virtue at the respective stage. The next section presents the eight stages in more detail.

Stages in Erikson's Psychosocial Theory of Development

Trust versus mistrust is the first conflict, or the first psychosocial stage, that an individual experiences in the first year of life. In this first year of life, infants depend on others for food, warmth, and affection and must trust their parents or caregivers for providing for their needs. If their needs are met in a responsive and consistent manner, infants will learn to trust their environment, and develop a secure attachment with their caregivers. If their needs are not responded to they will then develop mistrust toward people and things in their environment, and possibly even toward themselves. A positive resolution of the conflict of trust versus mistrust will result in the emergence of the psychosocial virtue of *hope*.

Autonomy versus shame and doubt is the second of Erikson's stages of psychosocial development and occurs between the ages of one and three years. During this period, toddlers begin to learn how to walk, talk, use the toilet, and do things for themselves. They begin to discover that their behavior is their own, and that they are able to control it. They begin to assert their sense of independence and autonomy. If parents encourage this assertion for independence and are reassuring when their child makes mistakes, the child will develop confidence in making future choices and decisions. If parents are overprotective, or disapproving of this assertion for independence, their child may become ashamed of being independent, or doubtful of his or her abilities. A positive resolution of this conflict enables a child to realize his or her *will*.

Initiative versus guilt is the third stage to occur between the preschool years of three and six. Children begin to develop and master motor skills and become more engaged in social interactions with people in their widening social world. This leads to an eagerness for more adventure in order to test the limits for their newfound skills. However, they also need to learn how to achieve a balance between their eagerness and their impulsiveness in making grandiose plans. If their parents and teachers are encouraging and can work with the children on realistic goals that can be achieved, children learn to feel confident in using their imagination. If, however, they are unsupervised by the adults and they continue to engage in impulsive fantasies that are doomed to fail, children begin to feel guilty and ashamed of taking risks and engaging in make-believe play. Positive experiences during this stage result in the development of the psychosocial virtue of courage and a sense of *purpose.*

Industry versus inferiority is the fourth stage that occurs between the ages of six and eleven years. Children of this age are in elementary school, and are beginning to make the transition into a world of academics and competing peers. Even as they are industriously learning new reading, writing, math, and social skills, they are evaluating their own abilities in the learning of these skills. If children find pleasure in intellectual stimulation and are able to master skills easily and earn praise for their efforts, they feel successful and productive. On the other hand, negative outcomes in the struggle to learn these skills can result in the child's feeling inferior to peers. A positive resolution of the conflict at this stage promotes the development of a sense of *competence,* yet another psychosocial virtue.

Identity versus role confusion occurs during adolescence and the individual now must integrate the healthy resolutions of all the previous stages in order to successfully answer the question "Who am I?" Individuals who have dealt with earlier conflicts successfully are ready for the "identity crisis" and emerge from this conflict with a strong sense of self, as well as the psychosocial virtue of *fidelity* and loyalty to one's self. If not, the individual will sink into confusion, unable to make decisions about one's own vocation, responsibilities, beliefs, and values.

Intimacy versus isolation is the sixth conflict and occurs during young adulthood. This stage is marked by intimate relationships. An individual who has not yet developed a sense of identity usually finds it difficult to enter into an intimate relationship or commitment and may retreat into isolation. Individuals who are able to form intimate and healthy relationships, and are able to share themselves with others, find the psychosocial virtue of *love.*

Generativity versus stagnation is the seventh stage and occurs during adulthood. By generativity, Erikson means the ability to look outside of one's self to care for and assist those from a different generation. During this stage, individuals not only feel the desire to create a living legacy and help the next generation, but also find themselves in the position of having to care for their ailing parents. Individuals can solve this crisis by having their own children or nurturing others in various ways. A successful resolution of this crisis results in the emergence of the psychosocial virtue of *care,* whereas a negative outcome in terms of the inability to assist others results in a sense of self-centeredness and stagnation.

Integrity versus despair is the last of the eight stages in the individual's development and occurs during old age. Old age is the time when individuals experience loss in various forms such as retirement, failing health, death of siblings and peers, and so forth. It is a time when the individual looks back and reflects upon his or her personal life and its role in the larger scheme of things. If the older person has experienced positive outcomes at the earlier stages of life, this retrospection will reveal a life well spent, and a feeling of satisfaction and a sense of integrity will prevail. If not, the individual will feel a sense of hopelessness and despair as the end of life approaches. This process of in-depth reflection and revelation leads to the development of the psychosocial virtue of *wisdom.*

Erikson did not believe that individuals must experience *only* the positive emotions. A positive outcome during each of the stages would result if the individual experienced more positive and fewer negative dimensions of the conflict. Some exposure to the negative emotions was also considered necessary. For instance, if a baby were to experience only trust and no mistrust, it would not prepare him or her to be able to discriminate whom to trust under different circumstances in order to survive in the world. Nevertheless, Erikson certainly believed that a positive resolution should dominate at each stage in order for the individual to develop a healthy personality.

Early childhood education in the United States became closely defined by Erikson's ideas. This theory of psychosocial development has had a profound impact on scholarly and lay interest in the social–emotional domain of children's development, and on a corresponding social–emotional curriculum for early childhood classrooms. Because the emerging psychosocial virtues for each stage would ultimately define the individual's identity, Erikson is often called the "architect of identity." He was concerned with the effect of rapid social changes in the United States, is credited for widening the scope of psychoanalytical theory to a greater consideration of social, cultural, and environmental factors.

It is interesting to note that Erikson's biographer, Robert Coles, noticed the effect of history, culture, and environment on Erikson's own work. Erikson's Danish parents were from Copenhagen, where the existentialist philosopher Kierkegaard had lived, and it is told that Erikson's mother had read books by Kierkegaard and Emerson during her pregnancy and Erikson's infancy. When Coles wrote that the roots of psychoanalysis were buried in nineteenth-century science and philosophy, he had traced a line of influence from Soren Kierkegaard, who examined the psychology of man from a theologian's perspective and believed that each man's mind had its own specific history and destiny; to the work of Viennese physician and psychoanalyst Sigmund Freud in his studies of the human mind; and, finally, to child psychoanalyst Erik Erikson, who years later would insist that it was necessary to pay attention to both the individual and society because "every life, every 'conflict,' every nation has a background and a future" (Coles, 1970, p. 42). *See also* Sex and Sexuality in Young Children.

Further Readings: Coles, Robert (1970). *Erik H. Erikson: The growth of his work.* Boston: Little, Brown and Company; Crain, William (2005). *Theories of development: Concepts and applications.* Upper Saddle River, NJ: Pearson Prentice-Hall; Erikson, Erik Homburger (1950). *Childhood and society.* New York: Norton; Friedman, Lawrence Jacob (1999). *Identity's architect: A biography of Erik H. Erikson.* New York: Scribner's Book.

Amita Gupta

Q

Qualitative Research

Qualitative research is empirically based inquiry through which researchers seek to understand the perspectives of human actors in social settings. Research is empirically based when data are collected and analyzed systematically. Data for qualitative studies usually include transcribed interviews, field notes from observations, and unobtrusively collected evidence such as documents and artifacts. Qualitative data analysis is inductive and interpretive in nature, and findings are grounded in the data that generated them. Understanding how individuals make sense of the natural contexts in which they operate every day is the aim of qualitative research, so studies are undertaken in natural settings, and capturing perspectives on the contexts in which participants act is essential to the research process.

Characteristics that distinguish qualitative from quantitative research include the following:

- **Natural Settings**—Qualitative researchers study social phenomena as they occur in everyday life because they believe human behavior cannot be understood outside the contexts of its natural occurrence.
- **Participants' Perspectives**—Describing the insider perspectives of actors in specific social settings is a primary concern of qualitative researchers.
- **Researcher as Instrument**—The principal data of qualitative studies are gathered directly by researchers themselves.
- **Extended Engagement**—Spending long periods of direct engagement in the contexts in which social phenomena are enacted is important to understanding participant perspectives.
- **Centrality of Meaning**—Understanding the meanings that individuals use to negotiate their social surroundings is an essential element of qualitative work.
- **Complexity**—Qualitative researchers assume that social settings are unique, dynamic, and complex, and they resist approaches that reduce complex settings to isolated variables.
- **Subjectivity**—Qualitative work is interested in inner states at the core of human activity, and bringing these inner states to light requires the application of researchers' subjective judgment.

- **Flexible Design**—Because the act of doing qualitative research often leads researchers in directions they did not anticipate, research questions, methods, and analysis procedures are sometimes altered as research designs are implemented.
- **Reflexivity**—Qualitative researchers acknowledge that they are part of the worlds they study, so systematically monitoring their influence and bracketing their biases is part of their research responsibility (Hatch and Barclay-McLaughlin, 2006).

While the use of qualitative methods is relatively new in applied fields such as education and early childhood education, the foundations of qualitative research were established in disciplines such as anthropology and sociology beginning in the early 1900s. Early anthropological work was characterized by ethnographic studies of "primitive" cultures in faraway places. Qualitative sociologists of the same period (many of whom were associated with "Chicago Sociology" at the University of Chicago) studied life experiences of working-class and poor immigrants in urban centers in the United States. Early qualitative studies in education settings were begun in the 1960s, mostly by sociologists and anthropologists interested in studying the social contexts of education.

Qualitative studies that focused on contexts involving young children began to be published in the 1980s. Early examples done in the United States include Corsaro's (1985) sociological analysis of peer culture in a preschool and Lubeck's (1985) comparison of how cultural values were transmitted in a Head Start serving African American children and a preschool program for white students. An important early childhood qualitative study in the United Kingdom was Pollard's (1985) examination of children's experience of primary schooling, and Davies' (1982) study of children's social interaction in classrooms and on playgrounds was an early qualitative study completed in Australia.

Given some shared foundations and overarching characteristics, many different approaches to doing qualitative research have evolved over the past four decades. Some of the approaches that have been used in qualitative early childhood studies are outlined below:

Ethnographies: Ethnography is a particular kind of qualitative research that seeks to describe culture or parts of culture from the point of view of cultural insiders. Ethnographers employ interviewing, observation, and artifact collection as their primary data collection techniques. Ethnography is the classic form of qualitative research that was developed by anthropologists who spend extended periods of time doing fieldwork within cultural groups. Contemporary ethnographers often study subcultures, communities, or classrooms, but their goals remain consistent with those of classic fieldworkers.

Participant Observation Studies: Participant observation studies use the same data collection tools as ethnographies, but they are not ethnographies because participant observation studies are much narrower in scope and usually involve less time in the field. Participant observation studies place researchers in social settings, but they do not have the broad purpose of capturing all of the cultural knowledge that insiders use to make sense of those settings. Researchers using this framework enter research settings with specific interests and specific questions in mind, and these interests and questions concentrate their studies in ways that ethnographers do not.

Interview Studies: While it is often a part of participant observation research, interviewing can be the primary data collection strategy in a qualitative project. Qualitative researchers utilize special interview strategies that are different in nature from interviews done in quantitative studies. Qualitative interviewers create a special kind of speech event during which they ask open-ended questions, encourage informants to explain their unique perspectives on the issues at hand, and listen intently for special language and other clues that reveal meaning structures informants use to understand their worlds.

Grounded Theory Studies: In *The Discovery of Grounded Theory*, Glaser and Strauss (1967) outlined a model that serves as a guide for collecting and analyzing qualitative data in rigorous, systematic, and disciplined ways. Grounded theory studies generate theories inductively derived from careful analysis of qualitative data. Vital to these procedures is the notion of constant comparison, through which researchers engage in detailed analytic processes that require repeated confirmations of potential explanatory patterns of meaning discovered in the data.

Narrative Studies: **Narrative** research is focused on gathering and interpreting the stories that people use to describe their lives. Different types of narrative studies include life histories, life story research, biography, personal experience methods, oral history, and narrative inquiry. All are based on the notion that humans make sense of their lives through story. Clandinin and Connelly (1994) identify the following methods for generating the data of narrative studies: oral history; annals and chronicles; family stories; photographs, memory boxes, and other personal/family artifacts; research interviews; journals; autobiographical writing; letters; conversations; and field notes and other stories from the field.

Case Studies: Researchers from many disciplines and many paradigms (qualitative and quantitative) call their work case studies. Qualitative case studies are a special kind of research that investigates a contextualized phenomenon within specified boundaries. Merriam (1988) offers examples of such bounded phenomena in education: "a program, an event, a person, a process, an institution, or a social group" (p. 13). Data collection and analysis procedures parallel those of other qualitative approaches. It is their focus on bounded systems that makes qualitative case studies different.

Those who hold traditional views of what constitutes research see limitations in the application of qualitative methods in early childhood education or other social science fields. These critics believe that any form of research should be measured against the tenets of quantitative approaches in terms of validity, reliability, and generalizability. They argue that the small samples in most qualitative studies, the subjective nature of data collection and analysis, and the lack of controlled variables make qualitative findings idiosyncratic, subject to researcher bias, and impossible to replicate. Qualitative researchers counter that the assumptions at the base of their research approaches are fundamentally different from those of quantitative methods, that different does not mean inferior, and that the worth of qualitative findings should be judged using criteria developed within qualitative research paradigms (Hatch, 2002).

Proponents argue that the strengths of early childhood qualitative research include its ability to reveal the experiences of those who live in the contexts in which early education and care happen. They claim that high quality qualitative studies provide vivid portraits of the how life unfolds in early childhood contexts. And, they say that qualitative approaches make possible an enriched understanding of the behaviors of actors as they negotiate the meaning structures of the settings that define early childhood. Qualitative researchers believe their contributions to early childhood theory, practice, and policy formation are at least as valuable as those of quantitative researchers.

Further Readings: Clandinin, D. J., and F. M. Connelly (1994). Personal experience methods. In N. K. Denzin and Y. S. Lincoln, eds., *Handbook of qualitative research.* Thousand Oaks, CA: Sage, pp. 413–427; Corsaro, W. A. (1985). *Friendship and peer culture in the early years.* Norwood, NJ: Ablex; Davies, B. (1982). *Life in the classroom and playground: The accounts of primary school children.* London: Routledge; Glaser, B. G., and A. L. Strauss (1967). *The discovery of grounded theory: Strategies for qualitative research.* Mill Valley, CA: Sociology Press; Hatch, J. A. (2002). *Doing qualitative research in education settings.* Albany, NY: State University of New York Press; Hatch, J. A., and G. Barclay-McLaughlin (2006). Qualitative research: Paradigms and possibilities. In B. Spodek and O. Saracho, eds., *Handbook of research on the education of young children.* 2nd ed. Mahwah, NJ: Lawrence Erlbaum, pp. 497–514; Lubeck, S. (1985). *Sandbox society: Early education in black and white America.* London: Falmer; Merriam, S. B. (1988). *Case study research in education: A qualitative approach.* San Francisco: Jossey-Bass; Pollard, A. (1985). *The social world of the primary school.* London: Cassell.

J. Amos Hatch

Quantitative Analyses/Experimental Designs

Quantitative (parametric) statistics are used to analyze data collected in group research designs, including nonexperimental designs as well as natural experiments, quasi-experiments, and randomized trial experimental designs (Shadish et al., 2002.) These are all multisubject designs in which characteristics of interest are measured systematically across a sample of participants. There are important differences between quantitative and **qualitative research** methodologies as they respond to education research questions.

In a recent monograph focused on scientific research in education, the National Research Council (2002) suggested that many education research questions can be characterized as addressing questions of "description—what is happening? cause—is there a systematic effect? and process or mechanisms—why or how is it happening?" (p. 99). Both quantitative and qualitative research methods are used in analyses of data collected to answer questions related to description. In general, experimental research methods and quantitative analyses are used to answer questions related to (a) relations among variables and (b) differences between groups.

Correlational studies are "quantitative, multi-subjects designs in which participants have not been randomly assigned to treatment conditions" (Thompson et al., 2005, p. 182). The analytic models applied with these designs are designed to evaluate the relations among two or more variables of interest. These analytic methods include multiple regression analysis, canonical correlation analysis, hierarchical linear modeling and structural equation modeling (Thompson et al.,

2005). Although they do not provide definitive causal evidence, results from correlational studies can offer directions for future experimental research designs. The use of sophisticated causal modeling or exclusion methods in correlational designs provides some basis through which "correlational evidence can at least tentatively inform evidence-based practice" (Thompson et al., 2005, p. 190).

In contrast to correlational designs, analyses of data collected using natural experiments, quasi-experimental or experimental designs typically focus on outcome differences between groups (e.g., analysis of variance, analysis of covariance, multivariate analysis of variance) or different rates of growth (e.g., growth curve analysis with multiple data points; multivariate repeated-measures analysis of variance). A brief description of each of these types of experimental designs appears below, followed by general comments on analytic strategies.

Natural experiments are group designs in which a "naturally occurring contrast between a treatment and a comparison condition" (Shadish et al., 2002, p. 17) is the focus of the research question. For example, the Swedish Adoption/Twin Study of Aging is a natural experiment in which data collected on pairs of twins separated at a young age and reared apart (46 identical, 100 fraternal pairs) are compared with data from matched pairs of twins reared together (67 pairs of identical and 89 pairs of fraternal twins). Data from this study have been used to understand genetic and environmental influences on cognitive and social behaviors (cf. Bergeman et al., 2001; Kato and Pedersen, 2005). Because it would be unethical to experimentally assign infants to be separated from their parents and siblings, twin studies such as this one rely on naturally occurring events in children's lives. Other examples of natural experiments include studies of children living in orphanages (e.g., Morison and Elwood, 2000) and of adults with mental retardation (Skeels and Dye, 2002). Natural experiments such as these often fit the definition of quasi-experimental research designs (described below) when there is a comparison group against which children in the intervention are compared. The Swedish Twin Study is an example of a natural quasi-experimental design.

Of particular interest in education and intervention research are answers to questions about the effects of interventions and the mechanisms through which those effects might occur. These are often referred to as "What works?" and "How does it happen?" questions (National Research Council, 2002). Quasi-experimental and experimental research designs are typically used to address these types of research questions. In quasi-experimental and experimental designs, researchers are interested in understanding different treatment or intervention effects across two or more groups. In a true experiment (described as a randomized controlled-trial design, below), participants are randomly assigned to an intervention or control (nontreatment, placebo) group. In contrast, assignment to group is by means of self-selection in a quasi-experimental design. In this case, unknown preexisting differences may be systematically associated with group selection. This makes it difficult to exclude all possible alternative explanations if different intervention outcomes are found across groups (Shadish et al., 2002). Many important and policy-relevant research questions, including questions about the effectiveness of intervention programs such as Head Start and the contributions of different types of early care to children's development, are addressed using quasi-experimental methods (cf. NICHD ECCRN, 2004; U.S. Department of Health and Human Services, 2005).

Randomized controlled trial designs are the best approach for understanding how specific intervention components are related to outcomes for children or families (Feuer et al., 2002). The unique strength of randomized experimental designs "is in describing the consequences attributable to deliberately varying a treatment" (Shadish et al., 2002, p. 9). In randomized designs, participants are assigned to experimental groups by chance. If done correctly, random assignment creates two or more groups that are probabilistically similar on average. When an intervention is applied to one group (the experimental group) but not to the other (control or placebo group), or when different types of interventions are applied across groups, and differences in outcomes are detected, such outcome differences can be attributed to the intervention (Gersten et al., 2005; Shadish et al., 2002).

Because there are at least two groups (treatment and comparison), analyses of data collected using natural experiments, quasi-experimental designs, or randomized controlled trials use general linear modeling techniques (including variations of analysis of variance, growth curve modeling, and hierarchical linear modeling) to compare group outcomes (Tabachnick and Fidell, 2001). Because there are often several potential units of analysis (e.g., data collected on children, teachers, and schools provide three different units of analysis), multilevel analyses (such as hierarchical linear modeling or growth curve modeling) are often most appropriate (Gersten et al., 2005). Current recommendations also require researchers to provide evidence that the research design has sufficient power to detect group differences and to provide evidence for the size of the intervention effect as well as evidence of significant differences between groups (Gersten et al., 2005; National Research Council, 2002).

In addition to the correlational and group designs described above, analyses designed to provide descriptive information, and analyses of the psychometric characteristics of assessment instruments, also fit within the broad category of quantitative analyses. Descriptive education research methods include those designed to allow statements about the characteristics of a population, descriptions of simple relationships between variables, or descriptions of special groups or populations (National Research Council, 2002). For example, information about the average level and variability of characteristics of interest is typically addressed by providing data on central tendencies such as the mean or median, and on variability such as standard deviation. Nonexperimental research designs also include procedures used in scale development. Analytic approaches may include factor analysis (including principal-components analysis and confirmatory factor analysis) and assessments of internal consistency reliability (calculation of Cronbach's alpha).

Further Readings: Bergeman, C. S., J. M. Neiderhiser, N. L. Pedersen, and R. Plomin (2001). Genetic and environmental influences on social support in later life: A longitudinal analysis. *International Journal of Aging and Human Development* 53, 107-135; Feuer, M. J., L. Towne, and R. J. Shavelson (2002). Scientific culture and educational research. *Educational Researcher* 31, 4-14; Gersten, R., L. S. Fuchs, D. Compton, M.

Coyne, C. Greenwood, and M. S. Innocenti (2005). Quality indicators for group experimental and quasi-experimental research in special education. *Exceptional Children* 71, 149-164; Kato, K., and N. L. Pedersen (2005). Personality and coping: A study of twins reared apart and twins reared together. *Behavior Genetics* 35, 147-158; National Research Council (2002). Committee on Scientific Principles for Education Research. In R. J. Shavelson and L. Towne, eds., *Scientific research in education. Center for education. Division of behavioral and social sciences and education.* Washington, DC: National Academy Press; NICHD Early Child Care Research Network (2004). Type of child care and children's development at 54 months. *Early Childhood Research Quarterly* 19, 203-230; Skeels, H. M., and H. B. Dye (2002). A study of the effects of differential stimulation on mentally retarded children. In J. Blacher and B.L. Baker, eds., *The best of AAMR: Families and mental retardation: A collection of notable AAMR journal articles across the 20th century.* Washington, DC: American Association on Mental Retardation, pp. 19-33; Tabachnick, B.G., and L. S. Fidell (2001). *Using multivariate statistic.* 4th ed. Boston: Allyn and Bacon. Thompson, B., K. E. Diamond, R. McWilliam, P. Synder, and S. Snyder (2005). Evaluating the quality of evidence from correlational research for evidence-based practice. *Exceptional Children* 71, 181-194; U.S. Department of Health and Human Services, Administration for Children and Families. (2005). *Head Start impact study: First year findings.* Washington, DC.

Karen Diamond

R

Race and Ethnicity in Early Childhood Education

Early childhood professionals working with young children in diverse settings have come to realize the salience of race and ethnicity in the lives of their students. It is important for teachers, caregivers, and parents to understand the impact of race and ethnicity in order to facilitate positive identity development, especially for children of color. This is particularly salient in the United States, unlike other homogeneous societies, because race matters as a sociopolitical construction and immigration policies are being constantly contested. Helping children of color and English language learners deal with prejudice and discrimination is a responsibility for all Americans.

Sometimes the terms race and ethnicity have been used interchangeably although they refer to different categories. Race is a complicated sociopolitical construct created by human beings and no longer defined by biology. In traditional sociology and anthropology race was associated with phenotype, or biological characteristics of hair texture and color, skin color, head shape, and other body features. Historically race had also been associated with intelligence and determined by blood quantum. These categorizations have led to stereotyping, racism, and discriminatory practices by individuals and institutions.

Ethnicity is expressed by cultural beliefs, values, language, and communication patterns brought by immigrants from throughout the world. Ethnicity has roots in countries of origin and reflects heritage, but it has evolved over generations in the United States. For example, a first-generation Asian American may speak the language of origin (Japanese, Chinese, Korean, Hmong) while a third- or fourth-generation child may not speak the language or know very much about the culture of his or her immigrant grandparents. Some African Americans prefer the term *black*, which has roots in American slavery, while others may call themselves African, having recently emigrated from an African country. American Indians and native Hawaiians fall into the category of indigenous peoples, and would not be considered ethnic groups.

In American society today, interracial, interethnic marriage has become common so there are a growing number of biracial, mixed-heritage children who may be struggling with their self-identity. It is important to let them self-identify and choose positive attributes from their family race and ethnicity rather than adopting a color-blind perspective. The salience of race, ethnicity, or native origin depends upon individual perceptions, group affiliation, and how one is constructed by others in their community. Children of color are more likely to be constructed as "other" in a race-conscious society. Children whose first language is not English are more likely to be considered "foreign" even if they were born in the United States.

Racial inequality continues to be a problem in American society. The State of America's Children 2005 produced by the Children's Defense Fund reports that black, American Indian, and Asian families have higher percentages of poverty compared to whites (whites 11.2%, blacks 33.1%, American Indian and Alaska Natives 31.6% and Asians 14.3%). Non-Latino black and Latino women are less likely to have prenatal care, while infant mortality before their first birthday for blacks is more than twice that of white babies (14.4 vs. 5.8 deaths per 1,000 live births). Inequality between white children and children of color exists in the number of children immunized, the number of children in foster care, and the number of children who are uninsured. In terms of education, there are more black and Latino children enrolled in Head Start (year 2003–2004) than white children (black 34.3%, Latino 37.2%, white 29.5%). And in terms of achievement in math and reading at the fourth-grade level, more black and Hispanic students scored below grade level compared to white students (Reading: white 61%, black 88%, Hispanic 85%. Math: white 53%, black 87%, Hispanic 81%). These statistics indicate that there is inequity in access to services and support for achievement by race.

In early childhood education, issues of racial identity development, antibias curriculum, and cross-cultural peer relationships are of concern. Consistent with Piagetian theory, the content of self-concept is linked to cognitive maturation and young children often identify themselves in terms of membership to certain groups defined by physical characteristics. Awareness of skin color and classification of others in the environment are common, but personality traits and psychological criteria associated with race develop later in middle childhood. In addition, children of color tend to have higher and earlier racial awareness than their white peers. Biracial children rely heavily on parental beliefs about the salience of race and modeling from family and communities of color.

A large body of research over several decades embodies the well-known findings that European American children prefer their own racial group and African American children also share that preference, sometimes misidentifying themselves as white. Research indicates that dark-skinned children are devalued as members of society and, contrary to common belief, there is little empirical evidence that cross-race friendships or voluntary associations are naturally made. Often these contacts are initiated by teachers or other significant adults. Children as young as three years old are *not* color blind and racism or negative meanings attached to racial difference is learned from environmental norms (school and home). A variety of research on black and white racial identity has presented stage theories of identity development that span a lifetime but little has been done on other racial groups such as Asian Americans or indigenous Americans (native Indians and Hawaiians).

In the future, early childhood professionals need to become cognizant of the research on white privilege since an overwhelming majority of teachers of young children in the United States are white and middle class. Resources for parents and caregivers on raising children in a multiracial, multicultural world, and on teaching tolerance have provided insight to real life incidents of racism and discrimination. Much more needs to be done by researchers and practitioners to assure that children of color develop positive racial identities and all children learn to value human differences and social justice for all.

Further Readings: Helms, J. E. (1990). Black and white racial identity: Theory, research, and practice. Westport, CT: Greenwood; Holmes, Robyn M. (1995). *How young children perceive race.* Thousand Oaks, CA: Sage Publications; Omi, Michael, and Howard Winant (1986). *Racial formation in the United States from the1960s to the 1980s.* New York: Routledge; Pang, Valerie Ooka (2005). *Multicultural education: A caring-centered, reflective approach.* 2nd ed. Boston: McGraw Hill; Ramsey, P. G. (1986). Racial and ethnic categories. In C. P. Edwards, ed., *Promoting social and moral development in young children: Creative approaches to the classroom.* New York, NY: Teachers College Press, pp. 78-101; Ramsey, P. G. (1987). Young children's thinking about ethnic differences. In J. S. Phinney and M. J. Rotheram, eds., *Children's ethnic socialization: Pluralism and development.* Newbury Park, CA: Sage Publications, Inc., pp. 56-72; Reddy, Maureen T. (1996). Everyday acts against racism: Raising children in a multiracial world. Seattle: Seal Press; Sheets, Rosa Hernandez, and Etta R. Hollins (1999). *Racial and ethnic identity in school practices: Aspects of human development.* Mahwah, NJ: Lawrence Erlbaum Associates; Tatum, Beverly Daniel (1997). *Why are all the black kids sitting together in the cafeteria?* New York: Basic Books; Van Ausdale, Debra, and Joe R. Feagin (2001). *The first R: How children learn race and racism.* New York: Roman & Littlefield Publishers, Inc.

Susan Matoba Adler

Read, Katherine (1904–1991)

Katherine Haskell Read influenced the field of early childhood education worldwide for over half a century. In 1950, she wrote the first textbook for college students preparing to teach young children, *The Nursery School: A Human Relationships Laboratory.* The ninth edition, coauthored with Pat Gardner and Barbara Child Mahler, was published in 1993 using an updated title, *Early Childhood Programs: Human Relationships and Learning.* Various editions of her text were translated into Danish, Hebrew, Italian, Japanese, Swedish, German, and Norwegian.

Katherine Haskell was born in Omaha, Nebraska, on April 10, 1904. After graduating from Mills College, Phi Beta Kappa, with a BA in political science in 1925, she worked as a psychologist at the Institute for Juvenile Research in Chicago from 1926 to 1928. She married George Read, who died several years after their daughter, Anne, was born in 1933. From 1929 to 1931 she taught nursery school at Purdue. After doing graduate work at the University of Chicago and Purdue, she received an MS from Purdue in 1938. She served as an instructor at Purdue from 1935 to 1940 and as supervisor of WPA nursery schools in Indiana in 1938. In 1941 she became an assistant professor of Household Administration at Oregon State University, attaining full professorship in 1948. During World War II she worked in the Kaiser Shipyards' famous Lanham Act child care facilities. She became professor of Child Development at Oregon State and headed the Department of Family Life and Home Administration from 1952 to 1965.

Throughout her life, Katherine embraced the perspectives of British psychoanalysts Anna **Freud** and David Winnicott, focusing—during the learning process—on the feelings and attitudes of children, of parents, and of adults who work with young children. She believed that self-understanding on the part of teachers was critical for helping young children to understand themselves. Her "Guides to Speech and Action" have endured and most are regarded as useful and appropriate today as they were fifty years ago (e.g., "State suggestions or directions in a positive rather than negative form," and "Give the child a choice only when you intend to leave the choice up to him"). Katherine was a major supporter of the **National Association for the Education of Young Children** (NAEYC), which published her articles and books. Katherine Read retired in 1965, married G. Maurice Baker, and moved to England. She died in 1991.

Further Readings: Baker, Katherine Read (1966). *Let's play outdoors.* Washington, DC: National Association for the Education of Young Children; Baker, Katherine Read (1972). *Ideas that work with young children.* Washington, DC: National Association for the Education of Young Children; National Association for the Education of Young Children (1992). In memoriam: Katherine Read Baker. *Young Children* 47(3), 33; Zavitkovsky, Docia, Katherine R. Baker, Jean R. Berlfein, and Millie Almy (1986). *Listen to the children.* Washington, DC: National Association for the Education of Young Children.

Carol S. Huntsinger

Read-Alouds and Vocabulary Development

Read-alouds, or reading aloud to children, is sometimes referred to as shared storybook reading. A common practice in many homes and early childhood settings, read-aloud time is a productive means for giving children opportunities to develop new meaning vocabulary. Because children's books present more advanced, less familiar vocabulary than everyday speech (Cunningham and Stanovich, 1998), listening to books being read aloud helps children go beyond their existing oral vocabularies; and it presents them with new concepts and vocabulary. Talking with children after shared storybook reading also gives children opportunities to use new vocabulary in the more decontextualized setting of a book discussion.

The variance in vocabulary knowledge of young children is well established. In 1995 Betty Hart and Todd Risley, two researchers at the University of Kansas who looked at parent–child interactions among different social groups, found some striking differences among preschoolers. On average, professional parents talked to their toddlers more than three times as much as parents of families on welfare did. Not surprisingly, that difference resulted in a big discrepancy in the children's vocabulary size. The average three-year-old from a welfare family demonstrated an active vocabulary of around 500 words, whereas a three-year-old from a professional family demonstrated a vocabulary of over 1,000 words.

Those differences become more pronounced as children get older—by the time the low-income children get to school and start to learn to read; they're already at an enormous disadvantage. It is estimated that children from economically privileged homes enter kindergarten having heard some 30 million more words than students from economically disadvantaged homes. Furthermore, the difference in time spent in "lap reading," sitting in the lap of an adult and listening to a book being read, may be of the magnitude of 4,000 to 6,000 hours.

Numerous studies have documented the fact that young children can learn word meanings incidentally from read-aloud experiences (Eller et al., 1988; Elley, 1988; Robbins and Ehri, 1994). In school settings, the effect is large for children age five and older and smaller for those under age four. Involving children in discussions during and after listening to a book has also produced significant word learning, especially when the teacher scaffolded this learning by asking questions, adding information, or prompting students to describe what they heard. Some (Whitehurst et al., 1994; Whitehurst et al., 1999) have called this process "dialogic reading."

Contrary to expectations, storybook reading with young children is not always a positive experience. Some read-aloud situations are less optimal than others and research also suggests that this scaffolding (providing explanations, asking questions, clarifying) may be more essential to those children who are less likely to learn new vocabulary easily. Children with less rich initial vocabularies are less likely to learn new vocabulary incidentally and need a thoughtful, well-designed, scaffolded approach to maximize learning from shared storybook reading (Robbins and Ehri, 1994; Senechal et al., 1995). Instructional strategies such as "text talk" (Beck et al., 2004) and "vocabulary visits" (Blachowicz and Obrochta, 2005) have been built on insights from this research.

De Temple and Snow (2003) draw the contrast between talk around shared storybook reading that is cognitively challenging and talk that is not. There has been substantial research on the nature and effects of storybook reading in both home and school settings which supports their view and suggests ways in which read-alouds can maximize student vocabulary learning (Neuman and Dickinson, 2001). This research suggests the following:

- Children can learn the meaning of unknown words through incidental exposure during storybook reading.
- With traditional storybook readings, unless there is attention to scaffolding for those with less rich initial vocabularies, the vocabulary differences between children continue to grow over time.
- Children learn more words when books are read multiple times.
- Children do not benefit from being talked at or read to, but from being talked with and read with in ways requiring their response and activity.
- Natural, scaffolded reading can result in more learning than highly dramatic "performance" reading by the adult
- Children learn more words when books are read in small groups.

In sum, most researchers agree on several principles related to developing vocabulary with read-aloud storybook reading in schools. First, there should be some direct teaching/explanation of vocabulary during storybook reading in school settings. Second, adult–child discussion should be interactive and discussion should focus on cognitively challenging ways to interact with the text rather than literal, one-word or yes/no questions. Children need to be able to contribute to the discussion in a substantial way, and smaller groups of five or six allow for this type of interaction. Third, the re-reading of texts in which vocabulary is repeated can maximize learning; informational texts and text sets can both capitalize on children's interest in "real" things (trucks, dinosaurs, pandas) as well as providing repletion on thematically related words. Lastly, the nature of the learning that occurs is different with familiar and unfamiliar books. In an initial reading the children may focus on the plot or storyline. In subsequent readings the reasons for characters' actions, especially unfamiliar vocabulary, may become the focus of their interest. Read-alouds can be a potent tool for exposing students to new vocabulary in a meaningful and pleasurable way.

Further Readings: Beck, I. L., M. G. McKeown, and L. Kucan (2002). *Bringing words to life: Robust vocabulary instruction.* New York: Guilford Press; Blachowicz, C. L. Z., and C. Obrochta (2005). Vocabulary visits: Developing primary content vocabulary. *Reading Teacher,* 59(3) November 262–269; Cunningham, A. E., and K. E. Stanovich (1997). Early reading acquisition and its relation to reading experience and ability 10 years later. *Developmental Psychology* 33, 934–945; DeTemple, J., and C. Snow (2003). Learning words from books. In A. V. Kleeck, S.A. Stahl, and E. B. Bauer, eds., *On reading storybooks to children: Parents and teachers.* Mahwah, NJ: Erlbaum, pp. 16–36; Eller, G., C. C. Pappas, and E. Brown (1988). The lexical development of kindergartners: Learning from written context. *Journal of Reading Behavior* 20, 5–24; Elley, W. B. (1988). Vocabulary acquisition from listening to stories. *Reading Research Quarterly* 24, 174–187; Hart, B., and T. R. Risley (1995). Meaningful differences in the everyday experience of young American children. Baltimore: P.H. Brookes; Neuman, S. B., and D. K. Dickinson (2001). *Handbook of early literacy research.* New York: Guilford Press. Robbins, C., and L. C. Ehri (1994). Reading storybooks to kindergarteners helps them learn new vocabulary words. *Journal of Educational Psychology* 86, 54–64; Senechal, M., E. Thomas, and J. Monker (1995). Individual differences in 5 year olds acquisition of vocabulary during storybook reading. *Journal of Educational Psychology* 87, 218–229; Whitehurst, G. J., J. N. Epstein, A. L. Angell, A. C. Payne, D. A. Crone, and J. E. Fischel (1994). Outcomes of an emergent literacy intervention in Head Start. *Journal of Educational Psychology* 86, 542–555; Whitehurst, G. J., A. A. Zevenberg, D. A. Crone, M. D. Schultz, O. N. Velting, and J. E. Fischel (1999). Outcomes of an emergent literacy intervention from Head Start through second grade. *Journal of Educational Psychology* 91, 261–272.

Camille L.Z. Blachowicz and Peter J. Fisher

Readiness

Readiness, as a general construct, signifies developmental status relative to some task or set of tasks. Children are ready for potty training, they are ready to spend the night at a friend's house, they are ready to crawl. In U.S. contexts, readiness has a specific meaning connected to the start of formal schooling. The definition provided here focuses on this type of readiness, examining the skills, dispositions, and abilities expected of children as they enter **kindergarten**.

The idea of readiness for school was created in the context of a developing system of formal education and more specifically the implementation of compulsory schooling (Snow, 2006). Entrance criteria for the early grades were developed to signal an idea of readiness—a model indexed to a particular age. Readiness gained both practical and scientific currency in the early twentieth century through the work of Arnold **Gesell**, who argued that readiness was essentially a biological construct, determined by the physical unfolding of the developing organism (Gesell, 1926). From this nativist and maturationist perspective teachers and families were cautioned to carefully assess children's readiness and to avoid "overplacement" in contexts that placed demands for which children were unready. Maturationist philosophy motivated a variety of practices designed to make sure that children were ready for the rigors of school. *Developmental screening* purportedly measured readiness for kindergarten, with the intention that unready children would wait a year. *Academic redshirting* called for delaying kindergarten entry for boys who were young relative to a kindergarten entrance cutoff, socially and emotionally immature, or physically small. *Kindergarten retention* places unready children in kindergarten for an additional year and *transitional programs* either before or after kindergarten were designed to create developmental curriculum for children who needed additional time to grow and develop. While these solutions to readiness problems had practical appeal, empirically, they have limited research support. Developmental screening poorly predicts kindergarten or later outcomes; children who are redshirted, retained, or attend transitional programs do not gain an advantage over their relatively younger peers and they have higher than expected incidence of social and emotional problems later in schooling (Graue and DiPerna, 2000; Meisels, 1999; Stipek, 2002). The lack of evidence to support maturationist practices parallels eroding support for maturationist theory as an explanatory tool for understanding child development. Rather than assuming linear maturation of individuals, theorists in areas as diverse as child development, psychology, literacy, and anthropology increasingly view development as multiply determined, occurring in specific contexts, and leveraged by specific expectations and resources. From this more socially oriented perspective, readiness is a contingent characteristic that certainly involves children but also requires attention to schools, communities, and families.

Current conceptions of readiness locate readiness dialectically, as a measure of the child relative to a particular historical and developmental context. For those who work from a developmental systems perspective, child readiness is considered in relation to the varied social systems in which a child lives and the degree to which these systems facilitate or constrain development (Mashburn and Pianta, 2006). Key to readiness are secure relationships among children, teachers, and families who support the growing child. Social constructivists assume that while readiness is expressed through child characteristics, it is a socially negotiated meaning held by stakeholders in local settings (Graue, 1993). When readiness is seen as socially constructed, it is entirely sensible that **assessment** of readiness will vary across raters, because the meanings they have for what constitutes a ready child vary as well. A related approach comes from evolutionary developmental psychology, which points to schools as culturally developed institutions into which human children are socialized (Bjorkland and Bering, cited in Snow, 2006).

Increasingly, policy concerns about readiness focus on its malleability, recognizing that readiness is developed in interaction with the environment across the preschool years. Initial definition by the **National Education Goals Panel** focused on a whole-child image of readiness, composed of (1) physical well-being and motor development, (2) social and emotional development, (3) approaches to learning, (4) language development, and (5) cognition and general knowledge (National Education Goals Panel, 1995), with attention to both ready children and ready schools. There is growing attention on programs that enhance readiness in the preschool years in indicator systems that track both institutional supports for children and families and child outcomes predictive of readiness, on developing definitions and measurements of readiness, and on the critical role that kindergarten plays in child readiness. These efforts work within a number of tensions: the incredible variability in the contexts experienced by young children prior to kindergarten, the diversity of kindergarten programs, and the developmental variation among children in the early years. This combination of variability makes defining a single set of readiness skills or characteristics a daunting task.

As the theoretical, conceptual, measurement, and instructional work continues, readiness practice focuses on providing adequate resources for children, families, and schools to support readiness across the developmental domains. Strategies that support readiness include responsive systems of early care and education that coordinate service delivery systems of health care, high quality child care, and publicly funded pre-K programs, and readiness indicator systems that track the availability of these resources. Receptive schools welcome all children when they are legally eligible to enter by being both developmental and inclusive in their approach.

Together, these viewpoints illustrate the importance of linking child and context in all considerations of readiness. Definitions of readiness need to consider ready children and ready schools, ready families and ready communities. Any conceptualization of readiness acknowledges its multidimensional nature, that it is a birth-to-five process that can be nurtured in diverse environments, and that it develops within an ecological system in which we all have responsibility (Snow, 2006). *See also* Constructivism; Grade Retention; Maturationism.

Further Readings: Gesell, A. (1926). *The mental growth of the pre-school child; a psychological outline of normal development from birth to the sixth year, including a system of development diagnosis*. New York: Macmillan Company; Graue, M. E. (1993). *Ready for what? Constructing meanings of readiness for kindergarten*. Albany: State University of New York Press; Graue, M. E., and J. C. DiPerna (2000). The gift of time: Who gets redshirted and retained and what are the outcomes? *American Educational Research Journal* 37(2), 509–534; Mashburn, A. J., and R. C. Pianta (2006). Social relationships and school readiness. *Early Education and Development* 17(1), 151–176; Meisels, S. J. (1999). Assessing readiness. In R. Pianta and M. J. Cox, eds., *The transition to kindergarten*. Baltimore: Paul Brooks Publishing, pp. 39–66; National Education Goals Panel (1995). *Reconsidering children's early development and learning: Toward common views and vocabulary*. Washington: National Education Goals Panel; Shepard, L. (1992). Retention and redshirting. In L. R. Williams and D. P. Fromberg, eds., *Encyclopedia of early childhood education*. New York: Garland, pp. 278–279; Snow, K. L. (2006). Measuring school readiness: Conceptual and practical considerations. *Early Education and Development* 17(1), 7–41; Stipek, D. (2002). At what age should children enter kindergarten? A question for policy-makers and parents. *Social Policy Reports* 16, 3–13.

Elizabeth Graue

Reconceptualists

The reconceptualist movement in early childhood education gained momentum in the 1980s, with conversations among scholars around the world who problematized the dominance of psychology and child development theory and drew from an array of other, more critical and postmodern perspectives in their work. These researchers, like those in a growing number of disciplines, are critical of the dominance of Enlightenment, modernist and western interpretations of the world that assume the existence of universal truths or natural laws as applicable and generalizable to all human beings. In the more specific case of early childhood education, contemporary reconceptualist scholars question the belief that scientific truths could or should be "discovered" about any individual or group of children and then applied to all younger human beings, no matter the culture, language, belief structure, or physical life circumstance. Many are feminists working with critical personal narrative and autobiography; some are engaged in contemporary, including postmodern, psychoanalytic scholarship; some work from a critical, poststructural lens; and still others are engaged in postcolonial critique as well as social justice work that focuses on decolonizing the field. Overall, reconceptualizing has come from within a context and value structure that strives to appreciate and support diversity in people, ideas, and ways of being, at the same time recognizing that privileging any particular set of beliefs and forms of knowledge can create power for certain groups of people and oppress and disqualify others.

The theoretical interpretations and forms of research employed in reconceptualizing the field of early childhood education have emerged from individuals and groups with personal and career histories focused on issues of social justice, equity, oppression and power, and diversity and opportunity. Reconceptualizing the field has included a focus on challenging grand narratives that serve to control and limit human beings, recognizing and embracing diversity in ways of living and being in the world, while acknowledging the sociopolitical, historical embeddedness in which human life resides. Reconceptualist work is concerned with revealing circumstances in which power and privilege are created for some groups of people while "others" are judged and disqualified as lacking or labeled as disadvantaged, yet continuously struggles to avoid the creation of new truths, or grand narratives, from reconceptualist perspectives. These concerns in the field of early childhood education have been addressed using various forms of critique, including qualitative naturalistic research that attends to the voices of peoples who are often underrepresented, historical genealogy, theory juxtaposition, and critical personal narrative.

An increasing number of early childhood educators are joining others in challenging European American discourses that have been generally accepted as universal truths. These "grand narratives"—which include everything from Western views of logic, to the Evangelical Christian discourse of salvation, to economic interpretations of human functioning whether Marxist or capitalist, to the imposition of Piagetian structuralism on all human cognition—have been questioned in a variety of fields and from diverse perspectives. The work of such scholars as Michel Foucault and Jacques Lyotard are good illustrations of the deconstruction of such dominant grand narratives.

Such challenges to universalist truths have been taken up by scholars in fields directly tied to early childhood education. Illustrations include the scholarship of Valerie Walkerdine and Erica Burman that directly challenges Piagetian developmental psychology and other developmental interpretations of the world. These examples illustrate the cultural embeddedness of the theories and the ways that human developmental perspectives have privileged Euro-American middle-class stereotypically masculine ways of interpreting and being in the world. In addition, various early childhood educators are influenced by the work of curriculum-studies scholars in education who, over the past 30 years, have reconceptualized the field from one of linear, determinist curriculum development to curriculum theory as understanding, human functioning, and learning—each as embedded within culture, history, politics, and social context.

Reconceptualist early childhood educators continue to address the grand narratives that dominate the field, illustrating the ways that beliefs in the "universal child" and universalist theories of thought and human change (e.g., developmental psychology, scientifically "discoverable" learning theories) actually place some groups of children into categories in which they are judged as normal, as on the "correct" human life path, and/or as even gifted—and "others" as delayed, slow, and possessing incorrect or less important knowledges and skills. As a critical example, much of the early reconceptualist scholarship (e.g., Kessler and Swadener, 1992) challenged the National Association for the Education of Young Children's *Guidelines for Developmentally Appropriate Practice*, charging that the perspective is monocultural and ethnocentric and ignores the range of life contexts and knowledges experienced by children from diverse cultural, ethnic, linguistic, and values contexts (e.g., individualistic orientations or connectedness of people as cultural ways of functioning). Applying a human or child development perspective on all people from all contexts, as if a natural universal human truth, has been revealed as privileging linear thought as well as privileging notions that define adults as superior to children, has been exposed as deterministic (and therefore limiting children), and ethnocentric (privileging Anglo, middle-class materialism and ways of life).

A large body of scholarly literature in education addresses cultural diversity in general, the recognition of diverse voices and knowledges, and the social and political embeddedness within which various groups function. Scholars whose work is often referenced by early childhood reconceptualists include Michael Apple, James Banks, Elizabeth Ellsworth, Michelle Fine, Paolo Freire, Geneva Gay, Madeline Grumet, Henry Giroux, Cameron McCarthy, Peter McLaren, Janet Miller, Christine Sleeter, and Joel Spring. Although surrounded by scholars in other areas of education whose work has been increasingly informed by cultural studies, feminist theory, critical perspectives, postmodernism, or poststructural theory, the field of early childhood education, in general, has continued to focus on individual, normative child development.

Reconceptualist early childhood educators and researchers have introduced these more diverse ways of understanding, questioning, and interpreting the world to the field. Much of the work envisions alternative perspectives in both theory and practice, demonstrates a willingness to ask difficult questions not previously addressed, integrates multiple voices (especially the voices that have so often been disregarded), and draws from a variety of human perspectives in order to better understand the complexities and socially/culturally constructed aspects of childhood (e.g., Cannella, 1997).

In recent years, early childhood educators have become increasingly involved in work that reveals power and privilege and that demonstrates children's awareness of gendered and colonialist impositions. Some of the earliest publications that could be identified as addressing power and privilege actually relate to poverty in the lives of young children (e.g., Polakow, 1993). In addition, an eclectic literature has emerged that uses postcolonial theory in early childhood education, and covers a wide range of power issues that include contradictions and challenges in indigenous education (e.g., Kaomea, 2003), the colonization of early childhood education through universal prescriptions for "quality" (e.g., Dahlberg et al., 1999) and decolonizing methodologies. Researchers have also demonstrated children's recognition of colonialist binaries (e.g., Tobin, 2000), feminist methodologies and gender issues (Hauser and Jipson, 1998; MacNaughton, 2000), and possibilities for transformational early childhood practices in a global context (e.g., Ryan and Grieshaber, 2005), to name just a few.

The three issues discussed thus far represent only major broad categories of concern for the field of early childhood education and should not be interpreted as placing limits on reconceptualist perspectives. Scholarly work and resultant practices labeled reconceptualist cannot easily be placed into any particular category. In addition, many researchers and educators who have been labeled "reconceptualists" might ultimately resist notions of labeling of any type. Rather, these scholars offer diverse questions, the recognition of autobiographical embeddedness within their own work, and attempt to increase possibilities for ways of viewing and understanding the world as well as approaches for living with and educating those who are younger.

Partly in response to frustrations in finding appropriate outlets for dissemination of reconceptualist work in dominant venues (e.g., conferences and journals), the first *Reconceptualizing Early Childhood Research, Theory and Practice Conference* was organized and held in Madison, Wisconsin, in 1991. Since that time, conferences have been held in locations across the United States and in Australia, Norway, and New Zealand. Recent meetings have drawn participants from over fifteen countries. In 1999, a Critical Perspectives on ECE special-interest group was founded within the American Educational Research Association. Several publishing companies now devote an entire series to reconceptualizing early childhood education scholarship, and reconceptualist scholars have published in a range of journals and implemented various forms of critical practice in education and public policy work. The range of scholarship, activism, and involvement in reconceptualization has provided new forms of praxis in the field of early childhood education.

Reconceptualist scholars see a compelling need for this work in the context of recent public policy practices in the United States as well as around the world. Neoliberal policies such as welfare "reform" in the United States and the United Kingdom have been critiqued by reconceptualists within a critical advocacy and postmodern discourse (e.g., Bloch et al., 2004). U.S. legislative mandates like **No Child Left Behind** in 2001, Smart Start, and the National Research Council Report on Scientific Research in Education demonstrate the ways that prevailing beliefs about "child," "family," and "education/care practices" are linked to sociopolitical agendas.

Reconceptualist perspectives and methodologies are oriented to and argue for "hope and possibility as we move toward a newly evolving, liberating 'third space,' an early childhood dreamscape of social justice and equity" (Soto, 2000, p. 198). Many reconceptualists believe that to ensure an equal and emancipatory early childhood education for both children and adults, all educators who are concerned about children and the future of human beings and the world, practitioners and theorists, teachers and parents, reconceptualists and developmentalists, must join together and take action in solidarity. *See also* Piaget, Jean.

Further Readings: Bloch, M., K. Holmlund, I. Moqvist, and T. Popkewitz, eds. (2004). *Restructuring the governing patterns of the child, education, and the welfare state.* New York: Palgrave Macmillan; Cannella, G. S. (1997). *Deconstructing early childhood education: Social justice and revolution.* New York: Peter Lang; Dahlberg, G., P. Moss, and A. Pence (1999). *Beyond quality in early childhood education and care: Postmodern perspectives.* London: Falmer Press; Hauser, M., and J. A. Jipson, eds. (1998). *Intersections: Feminisms/early childhoods.* New York: Peter Lang; Kaomea, J. (2003). Reading erasures and making the familiar strange: Defamiliarizing methods for research in formerly colonized and historically oppressed communities. *Educational Researcher* 32(2), 14–25; Kessler, S., and B. B. Swadener, eds. (1992). *Reconceptualizing the early childhood curriculum: Beginning the dialogue.* New York: Teachers College Press; Lubeck, S. (1985). *Sandbox society: Early schooling in black and white America.* London: Falmer Press; Mac Naughton, G. (2000). *Rethinking gender in early childhood.* Sydney: Allen and Unwin; Polakow, V. (1993). *Lives on the edge: Mothers and their children in the "other" America.* Chicago: University of Chicago Press; Ryan, S., and S. Grieshaber, eds. (2005). *Practical transformations and transformational practices: Globalization, postmodernism, and early childhood education.* Amsterdam: Elsevier; Soto, L. D., ed. (2000). *The politics of early childhood education.* New York: Peter Lang; Tobin, J. (2000). *Good guys don't wear hats: Children's talk about the media.* Chicago: University of Chicago Press; Viruru, R. (2001). *Early childhood education: Postcolonial perspectives from India.* New Delhi: Sage.

Gaile S. Cannella, Beth Blue Swadener, and Yi Che

Reggio Emilia Approach to Early Childhood Education

Reggio Emilia is a city in northern Italy where a volunteer group of educators, parents, and children came together after World War II with a shared vision for a new kind of school for young children. North Italy has a long history of civic engagement, trade guilds, and associations, and political activism and resistance to authoritarian government. At the war's conclusion, mindful of the devastation and suffering they had endured, they came together to try to improve the future for working families and their children. They did not want ordinary schools but ones where children could begin to acquire skills of critical thinking and cooperation essential to rebuilding and ensuring a democratic society. Under the leadership of its charismatic founding director, Loris **Malaguzzi** (1920–1994), the small network of parent-run schools in Reggio Emilia evolved first into a city-run system of preprimary schools (in the 1960s), and then added infant–toddler centers (in the 1970s). Even today the educators are evolving yet new forms of parent–professional and public–private partnerships to expand services to serve the whole city. Reggio Emilia educators have exercised a leadership role in educational innovation in Italy and Europe, and now increasingly the world. Their goal is for children to learn to engage in discussions and constructive play with others in a constructive and nonviolent way. Children (and families) are encouraged to express and discuss ideas in open meetings and to form close, long-term relationships with others in the school community. The Reggio Emilia preschools and infant–toddler centers are publicly supported and inclusive, giving first priority to children with disabilities and/or social service needs, such as low-income or immigrant status.

The Reggio Emilia approach is not an educational model in the formal sense, with defined methods, teacher certification standards, and accreditation processes. Instead, educators speak of their "experience" and how it can be a source of reflection or inspiration to others. Loris Malaguzzi was an integrative thinker, inspired by the great European progressive education tradition and by constructivist psychologists such as John **Dewey**, Jean **Piaget**, and Lev **Vygotsky**. He drew a powerful image of the child who comes into the world social from birth, intelligent, curious, and competent. Malaguzzi's vision of "education based on relationships" focuses on children in relation to people, things, and ideas. The goal is to activate and support children's rich network of associations and their participation in a world of family members, peers, community members, and the physical environment. Children, teachers, parents, and other citizens all have their respective rights to participate in such a system, to contribute to it, and to grow and learn within it. In fact, children are expected to be active and resourceful and to generate innovation and change in the systems in which they are involved. Teachers seek to hold before them this powerful image of the child as they support children in exploring and investigating. Children grow in competence to represent their ideas and feelings and to investigate concepts through many avenues/formats/media of expressive, communicative, and cognitive representation. Their "100 languages" may include speaking, writing, gesturing, drawing, painting, building, sculpting, collage, wire-work, shadow play, dramatic/role play, music, dance, puppetry, photography, and computers, to name a few **symbolic languages** that they may systemically explore and combine. Adults follow children's interests, and at teachable moments, they provide appropriate instruction in skills of reading and writing. They continually and indirectly foster language and **literacy**, counting, measuring, and problem-solving as children record and manipulate their concepts and communicate with others (including "writing" notes and letters). Teachers try to understand as fully as possible the children's viewpoints and abilities, seeing each child as full of strengths rather than full of needs.

Teaching and learning are negotiated, emergent processes between adults and children, involving generous time and in-depth revisiting and reviewing. These processes depend on the knowledge that teachers and children have of each other according to the school-level organization for continuity that keeps them together for two or three years. Parents and teachers also become closely acquainted, and this forms strong links between home and school. In such a context, long-term projects [*progettazione*] become important vehicles for open-ended investigations of subject matter, and these become longer and more elaborate as children grow older and more experienced in this way of learning. The classroom environment and arrangement of materials are carefully prepared to offer a sense of organization, comfort, and beauty and at the same time complexity and stimulation. The educators in Reggio Emilia believe the physical space should support children's communication and exchange of ideas; it has the features of a literacy-rich environment. It should also have emotional and aesthetic quality and use color, texture, and light to create values of transparency, reflectiveness, openness, harmony, balance, and softness. The environment makes a tangible statement to children, parents, and teachers that they are valued and respected. These are serious intentions, of course, yet the classroom atmosphere should be anything but sober and sedate. Rather, a classroom atmosphere of playfulness and joy should prevail in this kind of environment.

Time, too, is treated with special care. Children's own sense of time and their personal rhythm are considered in planning and carrying out activities and projects. When teachers lead activities, they provide enough time for spontaneous ideas to pop up and be discussed or explored. Children are given time to explore their ideas and hypotheses fully and in-depth. Projects and themes follow the children's ideas and development of concepts. Projects, activities and experiences such as field trips and celebrations build upon one another over time. Children review and revise their original work and ideas, refining them as they have further experiences, consider further questions, notice more details, make more connections, and acquire improved skills. Learning and development advance at their own pace, in widening and deepening cycles of understanding, not in prescribed, rigid sequences.

Teaching strategies are flexible and allow for input and decision making on the part of all participants. The Reggio Emilia approach is not a manual of strategies but instead a generalized way of working that must be adapted for each context and situation, because each one has its own unique history, constraints and problems, cast of characters, and assets and resources. For example, the format of parent–teacher partnership will vary from place to place, depending on the possibilities, negotiations, and preferences of the people involved. The most important principle is that teaching should be based on careful listening to and observation of children (and parents). Teachers begin by actively soliciting children's ideas and thoughts, considering what knowledge, questions, and preferences the children have before formulating plans and projects. Teachers usually work two to a classroom, and teamwork/mentoring is strongly promoted. A *pedagogista* (pedagogical specialist or education coordinator) works with several schools to guarantee high quality services. In addition, each school usually has a visual arts specialist (*atelierista*, or studio teacher) to work with teachers and children in classrooms as well as the *atelier* or studio to encourage expression through different media and symbol systems. Cooperation is encouraged among children through the use of small groups working together in common pursuit of an investigation or project. These can last for a couple of days, weeks, or months depending on the age and interest level of the children.

Teachers seek to be partners and guides to the children as they learn. They carefully prepare the environment to ensure that it provides strong messages about respect for the children and for their learning. In working with children, they play a delicate balancing act between engagement and attentive watching. They ask questions to draw out the children's ideas, hypotheses, and theories. Then teachers discuss together what they have recorded and make flexible plans and preparations for next steps in learning. They also act as recorders for the children, helping them to trace and revisit their words and actions. Teachers offer new ways of looking at things to children, and provide related experiences and materials. They provide direct instruction in tool and material use when needed, help children to locate materials and resources, and scaffold children's learning—sometimes coming in close and interacting actively with them, sometimes remaining attentively observing and listening nearby. They also nurture the children's emotional needs, and support and develop caring, individualized relationships with each family. They act as advocates for high-quality services to the public and the government. Malaguzzi summed up all of this complexity of the teacher's role in metaphoric language when he said that:

> We need a teacher who is sometimes the director, sometimes the set designer, sometimes the curtain and the backdrop, and sometimes the promoter. A teacher who is both sweet and stern, who is the electrician, who dispenses the paints and who is even the audience—the audience who watches, sometimes claps, sometimes remains silent, full of emotion, who sometimes judges with skepticism, and at other times applauds with enthusiasm. (Rinaldi, 2006, p. 73)

Children, clearly, are active participants in their learning. They make many choices throughout the day, including where to go in their classroom and building and on what to work. In addition to ongoing projects, children engage in many other forms of activity and play, including pretend play, singing, group games, storytelling, reading, cooking, outdoor play, rest, and relaxed and sociable meals together. They become part of a close-knit group, with their own unique routines and rituals and ways of expressing friendship and affection for one another.

Children's progress is observed and studied in nontraditional ways. **Documentation** is a cooperative practice that helps teachers listen to and see their children, thus guiding **curriculum** decisions and fostering **professional development** through collaborative study and reflection. Documentation helps teachers to follow, study, and make visible the ways that the group of children develops ideas, theories, and understandings. In Reggio Emilia classrooms, there are no checklists of skills, tests, or diagnostic evaluations, because the educators there believe that standardized assessments limit teaching too much by focusing on only a narrow range of what children do, not the whole picture of their strengths and potential. The American research community distinguishes between types of research based on the purposes for which it is conducted. The documentation favored by educators in Reggio Emilia promotes reflective practice and program improvement through formative methods that help educators better understand their problems, uncover the processes of teaching and learning, and analyze "what works and what does not" on an ongoing basis. It is intended to assist educators to refine and improve their work in process, not to allow outside audiences to understand outcomes and measure impacts over time. Formats and uses of documentation are continually changing as educators incorporate digital technologies that allow them to edit and combine images and share documentation in new ways.

In sum, the Reggio Emilia approach should be understood in the context of other Italian and European innovations in early care and education, as well as the historical context of progressive, child-centered educational models. Most of all, it offers a compelling example of what a city can accomplish when citizens, educators, and government come together to create what the Italians call a "culture of childhood," that is, a sustained community disposition to promote the educational rights and needs of children as an intrinsic good. *See also* Classroom Environments; Development, Language; Reggio Inspired Teacher Education; Standardized Tests and Early Childhood Education.

Further Readings: Cadwell, L. (2003). Bringing learning to life: The Reggio approach to early childhood education. New York: Teachers College Press; Ceppi, G., and M. Zini, eds. (1998). *Children, spaces, relations: Metaproject for an environment for young children.* Reggio Emilia, Italy: Reggio Children and Domus Academy Research Center; Dahlberg, G., P. Moss, and A. Pence (1999). *Beyond quality: Postmodern perspectives on early childhood education.* London: Falmer Press; Edwards, C., L. Gandini, and G. Forman, eds. (1998). *The hundred languages of children: The Reggio Emilia approach—Advanced reflections.* 2nd ed. Greenwich, CT: Ablex; Fu, V. R., A. J. Stremmel, and L. T. Hill (1992). *Teaching and learning: Collaborative exploration of the Reggio Emilia approach.* Columbus, OH: Merrill Prentice Hall; Gandini, L. (1993). Fundamentals of the Reggio Emilia approach to early childhood education. *Young Children* 49(1), 4–8; Gandini, L., and C. Edwards, eds. (2001). *Bambini: The Italian approach to infant/toddler care.* New York: Teachers College Press; Katz, L. G., and B. Cesarone, eds. (1994). *Reflections on the Reggio Emilia approach.* ERIC Clearinghouse on Elementary and Early Childhood Education; Milliken, J. (2003). *Reflections: Reggio Emilia principles within Australian contexts*; Castle Hill, New South Wales: Pademelon Press; New, R. (2000). Reggio Emilia: Catalyst for change and conversation. ERIC Digest EDO-PS-00-15. Available online at http://ericece.org; New, R. (2004). The Reggio Emilia approach: Provocations and partnerships with U.S. early childhood educators. In J. Roopnarine and J. Johnson, eds. *Approaches to early childhood education.* Ohio: Merrill/Prentice Hall; Project Zero, Harvard Graduate School of Education and Reggio Children S.r.l. (2001). *Making learning visible: Children as individual and group learners.* Reggio Emilia, Italy: Reggio Children S.r.l; Rinaldi, C. (2006). *In dialogue with Reggio Emilia: Listening, researching and learning.* London and New York: Routledge.

Carolyn Pope Edwards

Reggio-Inspired Teacher Education (RITE)

Reggio-inspired teacher education (RITE) is a term used to connote a group of early childhood educators who have been influenced by the work of Loris **Malaguzzi** and **Reggio Emilia**. It is also a term used to refer to specific principles and practices of early childhood teacher education in the United States that derive from this Italian city's municipal early childhood program. As described by its founders, RITE is really both more and less than a method.

Reggio-inspired teacher education, like the work taking place in Reggio Emilia, Italy, is actually best described as an *approach*. It is an approach to the way teachers construct curricula; it is an approach to the way teachers create and re-create the learning environment; it is an approach to the ways teachers collaborate with colleagues, parents, and children; it is an approach to how teachers can come to know the meanings children attribute to their educational experiences; and, it is an approach even to the very organization of the school itself. In other words, teacher educators adhering to RITE principles do not prescribe how these things are done but, rather, offer a perspective from which each of these topics can be considered.

This perspective is defined by six factors. First, the educational process, at any level, is embedded in a socially co-constructed context and as such must be responsive to the interests and needs of all the participants in the process, in particular, children, parents, and teachers (Smith, 2001). Second, children are recognized for their competence rather than for their limits, and as such curricula must be authentic, responsive, and build on this competence (Goldhaber and Goldhaber, 2000; Hull et al., 2002). One of the primary goals of a RITE program is to help new teachers understand the concept of curriculum as an emergent or negotiated experience involving others rather than a preplanned set of teacher-defined activities or lessons. A third critical component has to do with the assessment of children's progress, considered best done through the documentation and collaborative analysis of the products of children's educational investigations. Fourth, the physical and temporal arrangement of the classroom is an essential element in defining children's educational experiences. The environment must be accessible and responsive—the schedule allowing children ample time to become intellectually invested in their work. Fifth, teachers must come to see themselves as researchers and advocates as much, if not more, as they do directors of children's learning. They must be as intellectually engaged in learning as are their children. And sixth, RITE supports the principle that all these factors hold equally at all levels of the educational experience. The approach to preparing teachers and the approach to the organization of a school must be the same as the approach to the operation of a classroom. If the goal of a Reggio Emilia approach to children's education is to support the active intellectual engagement of children in worthwhile learning experiences, then the same set of considerations must equally be applied to the preparation of the teachers who will work with these children and to the organization of the schools in which this work will take place.

Further Readings: Burrington, B., and S. Sortino (2003). In our real world: An anatomy of documentation. In Joanne Hendrick, ed., *Next steps to teaching the Reggio Emilia way.* Columbus, OH: Prentice-Hall, pp. 224–238; Gandini, L., and J. Goldhaber (2001). Two reflections on documentation: Documentaation as a tool for promoting the construction of respectful learning. In Lella Gandini and Caroline Edwards, eds., *Bambini: The Italian approach to infant/toddler care.* New York: Teachers College Press; Goldhaber, D. E., and J. Goldhaber (2000). Education for all young children. In Colin Brock and Rosie Griffin, eds., *International perspectives on special educational needs.* London: John Catt

702   RESEARCH CONNECTIONS

Educational Ltd; Fu, V., and A. Stremmel (2001). *Teaching and learning: Collaborative exploration of the Reggio Emilia Approach.* Columbus, OH: Merrill-Prentice Hall, Inc.; Hull, K., J. Goldhaber, and A. Capone (2002). *Opening doors: An introduction to inclusive early childhood education.* New York: Houghton-Mifflin Co; Smith, D. (2001). Creating a community for infants: Hearing all the voices. *Innovations in early education: The international Reggio Exchange* 8 (2), 9–21; Smith, D., and J. Goldhaber (2004). *Poking, pinching, and pretending: Documenting toddler's experiences with clay.* St. Paul, MN: Red Leaf Press.

Dale Goldhaber and Jeanne Goldhaber

Research Connections. *See* Child Care and Early Education *Research Connections*

RITE. *See* Reggio-Inspired Teacher Education

Rogers, Carl (1902–1987)

Carl Ransom Rogers, an American founder of humanistic psychology, viewed human nature as essentially good. He developed a nondirective psychotherapy known variously as client-centered therapy, the person-centered approach, and person-centered psychotherapy. The phenomenological theory of personality that informed his clinical practice focused on subjective reality; central to subjective reality was the concept of *self*—Rogers' most important construct. He believed that a healthy self-concept would develop only if a person encountered unconditional positive regard, which is essential to achieving self-actualization.

Humanistic psychologists such as Carl Rogers and Abraham **Maslow** advanced the importance of enhancing children's self-esteem during the early years. "All About Me" curriculum units, for example, became very popular in early childhood education during the 1970s in part due to the impact of humanistic ideas. Early childhood practices that encouraged creativity and children's self-expression also flourished during this period because they related to actualizing one's human potential.

Carl Rogers was born on January 8, 1902, in Oak Parks, Illinois. His father, a civil engineer, provided well for the family, although fundamentalist Christian beliefs strictly controlled the Rogers household. When Carl was twelve, his family moved to the country, where he and his five siblings grew up isolated from harmful influences. Socially secluded and devoutly religious, Rogers pursued solitary activities, such as reading, that helped him graduate from high school with superior grades.

Rogers enrolled in 1919 at the University of Wisconsin, where he remained active in the church, hoping eventually to enter the ministry. He completed a BA in history in 1924 and, shortly thereafter, married Helen Elliot, a Wisconsin classmate and childhood friend. The couple subsequently had two children, David in 1926 and Natalie in 1928.

Although Rogers initially attended Union Theological Seminary in New York City, he became increasingly skeptical of religious doctrine. He transferred to Teachers College, Columbia University, to study clinical and educational psychology instead, completing his MA degree in 1928 and PhD in 1931.

Rogers' first professional position as staff psychologist at the Society for the Prevention of Cruelty to Children in Rochester, New York initiated his work with distressed children. The highly successful publication of *Clinical Treatment of the Problem Child* in 1939 led to a faculty appointment in psychology at Ohio State University, a move that launched Rogers' academic career. By 1945, he had become Professor of Psychology and Director of Counseling at the University of Chicago, where he completed his major work, *Client-Centered Therapy: Its Current Practice, Implications, and Theory* (Rogers, 1951).

Rogers returned to the University of Wisconsin in 1957, but, disillusioned with academia, he resigned his position in 1964 to become a resident fellow at the Western Behavioral Sciences Institute in La Jolla, California. In 1968, Rogers accepted a position at the Center for Studies of the Person, where he applied his theory to industry and education. He also became involved in the encounter group movement as a means of facilitating human growth and potential. Throughout his career, Rogers modeled compassion, empathy, and an unflagging commitment to helping others reach their full potential.

Further Readings: Kirschenbaum, Howard (1979). *On becoming Carl Rogers.* New York: Delacorte; Rogers, Carl (1969). *Freedom to learn: A view of what education might become.* Columbus, OH: Charles Merrill; Rogers, Carl (1961). *On becoming a person: A therapist's view of psychotherapy.* Boston: Houghton-Mifflin; Rogers, Carl (1951). *Client-centered therapy: its current practice, implications, and theory.* Boston: Houghton-Mifflin; Rogers, Carl (1939). *The clinical treatment of the problem child.* Boston: Houghton-Mifflin.

Web Site: Carl Roger Biography, http://www.nrogers.com/carlrogersbio.html

Ann C. Benjamin

Rousseau, Jean-Jacques (1712–1778)

Jean-Jacques Rousseau was born June 28, 1712, in Geneva, Switzerland, to a mother who died shortly after his birth. Some scholars (e.g., Dent, 2005) believe that this early loss of his mother had a significant effect on his personality and on his idealized form of human relationship, involving a "directness and immediacy he never experienced" (p. 8). At ten years of age, his father, a watchmaker, fled Geneva to avoid prison for a minor offense, leaving young Jean-Jacques to be raised by an uncle who eventually sent him to live with a Protestant pastor who became responsible for his education. Within a few years Rousseau was apprenticed to an engraver (Scholz, 2001). Rousseau left Geneva at sixteen, wandering from place to place, finally moving to Paris in 1742, where he converted to Catholicism. Rousseau earned his living working as a footman, music teacher, tutor, and personal secretary to the French ambassador to Venice.

For much of his adult life Rousseau was considered a brilliant, undisciplined, and unconventional thinker and a poor tutor. He spent much of his adulthood driven by sensuality and paranoia; he also suffered from an enlarged prostate. Rousseau spent his time between Paris and Geneva, writing both essays and music.

Many of the controversies associated with Rousseau's work were due to his unconventional beliefs about love, relationships, and his attempt to live by the principles he laid out in the *First Discourse*. He frequently initiated bitter quarrels with even supportive colleagues (www.philosophypages.com/ph/rous.htm). Somewhat complicated and ambiguous, Rousseau's general philosophy tried to grasp an emotional and passionate side of man, which he felt was left out of most previous philosophical thinking. In his early writing, Rousseau contended that man is essentially good, a *noble savage* when in the *state of nature* (the state of all the other animals, and the condition man was in before the creation of civilization and society), and that good people are made unhappy and corrupted by their experiences in society. He viewed society as *artificial* and *corrupt* and argued that the furthering of society results in the continuing unhappiness of man (www.lucidcafe.com/library/96jun/rousseau.htm). He minimized the importance of book learning, and recommended that a child's emotions be educated before his reason. He placed a special emphasis on learning by experience.

Rousseau eventually became famous as a French political philosopher and educator, even though he had no formal education. Many writers believe that the beginning of the field of child study as a discipline can be directly traced to the publication of Rousseau's beliefs in *Emile* in 1762. In *Emile*, Rousseau postulates that childhood is natural and a time important in itself, that a child will become increasingly fit to live in the world without adult supervision and direction, and that the child actively engages his environment, using it to suit his own interests. Although banned in France and burned in Geneva, this work was quickly translated into German and English and had a significant impact on practical reforms in educational practice. Some believe *Emile* was the most significant book on education after Plato's *Republic*.

It is somewhat ironic that Rousseau attempted to articulate the program of education that best fosters the true nature of man in his love of self (Scholz, 2001, p. 27), given that he refused to support the five illegitimate children he sired with Thérese Le Vasseur. All of his children were deposited at the local Foundling Hospital. It is also worth noting that the man who philosophized about social contracts had such a strong personal aversion to social interactions.

In his last years, Rousseau found solace in botany and solitude (Wokler, 1995). He died July 2, 1778, of apoplexy after his usual early morning walk, and an early breakfast, Thérese at his side. His remains were moved to the Panthéon in Paris in 1794 and placed close to those of Voltaire.

Further Readings: Cranston, M. (1991). *The noble savage: Jean-Jacques Rousseau, 1754-1762*. Chicago: University of Chicago Press; Dent, N. (2005). *Rousseau*. New York: Routledge; Riley, P. (2001). *The Cambridge companion to Rousseau*. Cambridge: Cambridge University Press; Rousseau, J. (1979). *Emile: or, on education*. Translated by Allan Bloom. New York: Basic Books. Originally published in London in 1762; Rousseau, J. (1987). *The social contract*. Translated by Maurice Cranston. London: Penguin. Originally published in 1762; Scholz, S. (2001). *On Rousseau*. Belmont, CA: Wadsworth; Stewart, P. (2000). Selected bibliography. Available online at www.c18.rutgers.edu/biblio/rousseau.html; Wokler, R. (1996). *Rousseau*. Oxford: Oxford University Press.

Michael Kalinowski

Ruggles Street Nursery School and Training Center
(Boston, Massachusetts)

Founded by Abigail **Eliot**, the Ruggles Street Nursery School and Training Center opened its doors at 147 Ruggles Street, Boston, Massachusetts, in January 1922. After studying at London's Rachel McMillan Nursery School and Training Centre, Eliot founded the school on the premise that young children were not receiving sufficient opportunities for cultural development, and physical and mental health, in the home environment. She also perceived a need for other nursery schools, but with qualified teachers rather than nurses who usually played this role. These initiatives led to a growing interest in training young women in the early childhood profession (Wertlieb, 2005). Started as a project of the Women's Education Association of Boston, 147 Ruggles Street became one of three nursery schools open in the United States; the others were in Detroit and in New York.

Ruggles Street was primarily focused on serving the low-income students; soon, the school became known as a safe educational home for children of all interests, economic backgrounds, and abilities. The school aimed at preparing the students individually and in group settings, working with children between the ages of two through five years. This devotion to educating all individuals became both the school's philosophy and the beginning of a shift in educational thinking in the United States toward a more holistic approach to teaching children.

By 1926, the Training School had grown to capacity, instructing fifty full-time education students. Mrs. Henry Greenleaf Pearson, Director of the Training School since its inception, realized that to continue as a training ground for exceptional early childhood educators, the school needed to expand beyond Ruggles Street. Moving to a double house at 355 Marlborough Street, Boston, the Ruggles Street School became the Nursery Training School of Boston. The school worked to educate students about the dynamics and principles of child development, emphasizing a **Montessori** style of teaching, learning through **play**, and strong parent–child as well as teacher–child relations.

Developing relationships with local universities was crucial to the continued success of the Training School program. In 1930, a reciprocal partnership was developed with the Boston University School of Education. In 1954, the Training School once again increased its connections with the Boston community, becoming affiliated with Tufts University. The Training School became a full department at Tufts University ten years later, renamed as the Eliot-Pearson Department of Child Study. Today it is known as the Eliot-Pearson Department of Child Development.

The Ruggles Street Nursery School no longer exists. In its place are the Eliot-Pearson Children's School and the Tufts Educational Day Care Center; each of these reflect new interpretations of the beliefs of Dr. Eliot and Mrs. Pearson. The Training School's idea of incorporating applied developmental research with field-based practicum experiences remains a cornerstone of all affiliates of the Eliot-Pearson Department of Child Development. This emphasis on "learning by doing" for students in the department's teacher education program remains a primary program characteristic—a principle and practice that can be traced back to the inception of the Ruggles Street Nursery School and Training Center in 1922.

Further Readings: Beatty, Barbara (2005). The rise of the American nursery school: Laboratory for a science of child development. In Pilleman, D. and S. White, eds., *Developmental psychology and social change: Research, history, and policy.* New York: Cambridge University Press, pp. 264–287; Eliot-Pearson Children's School (EPCS). (2005). *Eliot-Pearson children's school history.* Tufts University, Eliot-Pearson Children's School Web site. Available online at http://ase.tufts.edu/epcs/history.html; Eliot-Pearson Department of Child Development (EP). (2005). *Our department, Our history.* Tufts University, Eliot-Pearson Department of Child Development Web site. Available online at http://ase.tufts.edu/epcd/ourdepartment/aboutus/history.html; Manning, M., ed. (1982). *A heart of grateful trust: Memoirs of Abigail Adams Eliot.* Medford, MA: Tufts University; Nursery Training School of Boston 1939–1940 (NTSB 1939) (1939). *Nursery training school of Boston.* [Brochure]; Nursery Training School of Boston 1947–1948 (NTSB 1947). (1947). *Nursery training school of Boston, Ruggles street nursery school: 25th Anniversary.* [Brochure]; Wertlieb, D. (2005). Tufts University, Eliot-Pearson Department of Child Development. In C. Fisher and R. Lerner, eds., *Encyclopedia of Applied Developmental Science.* Vol. 2. Thousand Oaks, CA: Sage, pp. 1103–1105.

Sarah A. Leveque

S

School-Age Care

During the early school-age years, nonparental care during out-of-school time is a reality for millions of children in the United States. School-age programs provide academic and social activities for young school-age children while in a supervised environment during the hours they are not in school. With its dual role of enrichment and supervision, school-age care serves as a bridge between the nonparental child care arrangements of preschool-age children and the more structured school learning environment.

School-age care takes place during out-of-school hours before or after the regular school day, on school breaks, on weekends, and during the summer. The school-age care field often focuses on organized programs for school-age children in the hours before and after school, although care for school-age children is also provided in family child care settings (by both relatives and nonrelatives) and by in-home providers. Other common terms used to describe such care arrangements include out-of-school time, after-school care, school-age child care, extended day, extended services, expanded learning, and youth development activities.

Interest in and use of school-age care programs in the United States has grown in recent years because of factors such as increased female labor force participation, youth crime and risky behavior prevention efforts, concern that schools are not meeting the educational needs of children, and a decreased sense of supportiveness in the neighborhood environment. According to the National Household Education Surveys Program, 20 percent of Kindergarten through eighth-grade children have nonparental care arrangements before school. Nonparental school-age care is even more common in the hours after school, with estimates based on national samples ranging from 50 to 57 percent of school-age children in such arrangements (Kleiner, Nolin, and Chapman, 2004). A 2003 survey of U.S. households found that although 22 million families wanted after-school care for their children, only 6.5 million were participating, indicating that supply may not be meeting demand (Afterschool Alliance, 2004).

In the after-school hours, the most common type of nonparental arrangement is participation in a school- or community-based after-school program. While reported figures range from 11 to 26 percent, the exact percentage of school-age children using such arrangements varies slightly depending on the survey used and the specific ages and backgrounds of the children included in the sample. According to recent surveys, use is most prevalent among younger school-age children (age six to nine), African American children, children with employed parents, children from higher-income families, and children from single-parent homes. Considerable variation in program utilization also exists depending on state of residence. In a comparison of thirteen different states, participation of low-income children in before- or after-school programs ranged from 6 percent in Wisconsin to 17 percent in New Jersey (Sonenstein et al., 2002).

Other types of common nonparental care arrangements for school-age children include care by a relative or nonrelative adult in a family child care home, an in-home provider (e.g., nanny or babysitter), self care, and extracurricular activities used for supervision. Nearly one third (32%) of Kindergarten through eighth-grade children in nonparental arrangements before and/or after school have more than one arrangement, for example, grandmother care before school and school-age program after school (Kleiner et al., 2004).

After-school programs are typically housed in public schools where large cafeterias and gymnasium spaces, as well as ease in transporting children from school to after school, lend themselves to the operation of such programs. Programs are also found in a wide variety of other settings including child care centers, YMCAs, boys and girls clubs, religious institutions, parks and recreation departments, police athletic leagues, and private schools. There is great heterogeneity in after-school program goals, content, and services. However, most programs are open from 3 to 6 PM for 5 days a week with an average enrollment of 65 children. A typical schedule might include snack, homework time, academic activities (e.g., literacy skills training, mentoring, and tutoring), art activities (e.g., arts and crafts, music, dance, adventure education), recreation activities (e.g., outdoor playgrounds, organized sports), and service learning. Rates of participation are often sporadic, with individual children spending an average of 8 to 10 hours per week in a program (Afterschool Alliance, 2004; Kleiner et al., 2004).

Some evidence suggests that many after-school programs are of mediocre quality. For example, in the Making the Most of Out-of-School Time (MOST) evaluation, two thirds of observed programs were judged to be poor to fair in quality (Halpern, 1999). Quality is often hindered by high staff turnover rates, inadequate space, lack of interaction (or in some cases conflict) between the after-school program and the organization housing the program (e.g., public school). To help address the quality of after-school programs, the National AfterSchool Association (a professional organization with 7,000 members and thirty-six state affiliates) developed quality standards in 1998. These standards include thirty-six "keys of quality" in the areas of human relationships; indoor environment; outdoor environment; activities; safety, health, and nutrition; and administration (Roman, 1998). Using these standards, over 550 programs have been accredited in the United States by the National After-School Association as of April 2006.

Costs and Funding for After-School Programs

Costs for running a program vary tremendously, with estimates ranging from $700 to $6,600 annually per child depending on program features such as schedule, staff salaries, program size, and in-kind donations (Halpern et al., 2000). The greatest expense is staff compensation, with costs in this area typically accounting for 65–80 percent of total program operating expenses. Other costs for operating a program include facilities, supplies and equipment, food, capital costs, and infrastructure (including planning and evaluation, program development, licensing, transportation, and technical assistance).

After-school programs are funded through four main sources: parent fees, public money, private funds, and in-kind donations. A large part of funding for after-school programs typically comes from parent fees (15–25% of revenues), especially in more affluent communities. On average, parents pay $22 per week per child (Afterschool Alliance, 2004).

Federal funds also provide a significant source of revenue for school-age programs. For example, the 21st Century Community Learning Center program, the only federal program solely dedicated to funding after school, often provides funding for the start-up or expansion of after-school programs. Funds from this Department of Education program have increased from $750,000 in 1995 to just under $1 billion in FY 2004. The Child Care and Development Fund, administered through the Department of Health and Human Services, also provides funding to states for many after-school programs and represents a potentially sustainable source of funds for many child care programs. Approximately 35 percent of the $4.6 billion in FY 2003 federal money was spent on school-age children between the ages of 6 and 13. Other sources of federal funds for after-school programs include Temporary Assistance for Needy Families (through direct assistance and through transfer of up to 30 percent of funds to state block grants such as the Child Care and Development Fund or Title XX Social Services), and the Child and Adult Care Food Program that provides funding for meals, snacks, and nutrition education for programs serving low-income children.

After-school programs also tap other state, local, and private money to fund their operations. These resources are usually targeted toward direct services such as increasing quality, improving access, or expanding supply, with much smaller provisions made for financing infrastructure (e.g., facilities, professional development, technical assistance). Finally, in-kind contributions can be a significant part of after-school program operations. In-kind donations might include space, utilities, volunteer staff, materials, and tickets to events donated by community organizations (e.g., museums, sports teams).

Outcomes for Children

Research about the impacts of After-School programs on young school-age children has been mixed. A number of studies have demonstrated that participation in these types of programs, particularly those that provide a warm, positive and flexible environment, is associated with better academic grades, social relationships with peers, reading achievement, and emotional adjustment for first- to third-grade children (Mahoney et al., 2005; Pierce et al., 1999; Posner and Vandell, 1994). Similarly, Lauer and colleagues' meta-analysis examining out-of-school time activities indicates that such programs can have small, but positive, effects on reading and mathematic achievement of at-risk children and youth (Lauer et al., 2004). The largest gains in reading improvement were seen in the youngest children (grades K–2). A national evaluation of the 21st Century Community Learning Center after-school programs (including those for elementary and middle school students), however, found little relation between after-school participation and reading test scores, grades, problematic behaviors, goal setting, team work, or numbers of children in self-care (Dynarski et al., 2004). Findings from the NICHD Study of Early Child Care also suggest no relationship between before- and after-school program participation and cognitive and social development in first grade (NICHD Early Care Research Network, 2004).

Critics, including Kane, Mahoney, and Zigler, contend that evaluations of after-school programs to date suffer from methodological flaws that make it difficult to know exactly what impact after-school programs really have on child outcomes. Many evaluations rely on quasi-experimental designs in which no control group is included. The quality and appropriateness of comparison groups also varies from study to study. Results from the national evaluation of the 21st Century Community Learning Centers, despite the use of a strong experimental design using random assignment, have been criticized for other methodological problems including the premature nature of the evaluation (i.e., programs evaluated while still in the early stages of development), cross-over between program and comparison group participants (i.e., comparison group participation in the program), lack of representativeness in the elementary school sites included in the evaluation, lack of data gathered on possible key background and program variables, and reliance on unrealistic outcome measures. Additional research that addresses these methodological challenges is needed to further explore the true impact of school-age program participation on cognitive and social outcomes for children.

After-School Care Providers

After-school care providers include front-line teachers or assistants who work directly with children on a regular basis, as well as center coordinators and directors. Providers tend to work part-time for low wages and few, if any, benefits. These factors, combined with low professional status, a limited career ladder, and lack of a clear professional identity even within the school-age field itself, contribute to the 35–40 percent annual turnover rate.

Currently, no national professional development program exists for training school-age care professionals. Approximately one-half of states in the United States, however, have created or are exploring some form of credentialing for those individuals providing care for school-age children. For example, New York State offers an intensive, in-service credential specifically for school-age staff. Begun in 1998, the NYS School Age Care Credential (NYS SACC) is based on the U.S. Army School Age Care Credential, the first credential created for school-age care providers. The NYS SACC provides standards for training and recognition of staff members based on their ability to meet the unique needs of children aged five to thirteen. Similar to the Child Development Associate Credential for child care providers who work with children from birth through age five, the SACC process includes coursework, portfolio development, and parent feedback, as well as advisement and observation by knowledgeable school-age care professionals. SACC programs are offered throughout the state by local organizations such as Cornell University Cooperative Extension agencies, Child Care Resource and Referral agencies, and community colleges. In the first seven years of the NYS SACC, over 250 school-age care staff have been awarded their credentials.

Further Readings: Afterschool Alliance (2004). *America after 3 PM: A household survey on afterschool in America.* Available online at www.nmefdn.org/uimages/documents/CrtiHrsFS.pdf; Dynarski, Mark, Susanne James-Burdumy, Mary Moore, Linda Rosenberg, John Deke, Wendy Mansfield, and Elizabeth Warner (2004). *When schools stay open late: the national evaluation of the 21st century community learning centers program, new findings.* Washington, DC: U.S. Department of Education/Institute of Education Services, National Center for Education Statistics; Halpern, Robert, Sharon Deich, and Carol Cohen. (2000, May). *Financing after-school programs.* Available online at www.financeproject.org/financing_afterschool_programs.htm; Halpern, Robert (1999). After-school programs for low-income children: Promise and challenges. *The Future of Children* 9(2), 81–95; Kleiner, Brian, Mary Jo Nolin, and Chris Chapman (2004). *Before- and after-school care, programs and activities of children in kindergarten through eighth grade. 2001.* Washington, DC: U.S. Department of Education, National Center for Education Statistics; Lauer, Patricia A., Motoko Akiba, Stephanie B. Wilkerson, Helen S. Apthorp, David Snow, and Mya Martin-Glenn (2004). *The effectiveness of out-of-school time strategies in assisting low-achieving students in reading and mathematics.* Aurora, CO: Mid-continent Research for Education and Learning; Mahoney, Joseph L., Heather Lord, and Erica Carryl (2005). An ecological analysis of after-school program participation and the development of academic performance and motivational attributes for disadvantaged children. *Child Development* 76(4), 811–825; National Institute of Child Health and Human Development Early Child Care Research Network (2004). Are child developmental outcomes related to before- and after-school care arrangements? Results from the NICHD study of early child care. *Child Development* 75(1), 280–295; Pierce, Kim M., Jill V. Hamm, and Deborah L. Vandell (1999). Experiences in after-school programs and children's adjustment in first-grade classrooms. *Child Development* 70(3), 756–767; Posner, Jill D., and Deborah L. Vandell (1994). Low-income children's after-school care: Are there beneficial effects of after-school programs? *Child Development* 65, 440–456; Roman, Janette (1998). *The NSACA standards for quality school-age care.* Boston: National School-Age Care Alliance; Sonenstein, Freya L., Gary J. Gates, Stefanie Schmidt, and Natalya Bolshun (2002, May). *Primary child care arrangements of employed parents: Findings from the 1999 national survey of America's families.* Occasional Paper Number 59. Washington, DC: The Urban Institute.

Lisa McCabe

School Culture

"School culture" is a recognizable set of events (e.g., reading groups), routines (e.g., attendance count), artifacts (e.g., blackboard and chalk), norms and expectations (e.g., raise your hand for a turn to talk), concerns (e.g., standardized test scores), values (e.g., conformity), and roles (e.g., teacher and student) that are similar, pervasive, and socially constructed in schools throughout the country. Sociologists like Phillip Jackson (1968) recognized the special demands that a "life in school" places on students to use language in certain ways, behave in certain ways, and respond to the "hidden curriculum." While these sociologists did not use the term per se, their notion of schools' implicit demands to produce particular school behaviors to be successful as a student is the essential meaning of "school culture."

Judith Green was one of the first educators to look at the classroom with a cultural lens, more specifically with an interactive sociolinguistic and ethnographic perspective. In her prolific career with diverse collaborators, Green (1983) has examined various topics, including **curriculum** construction, language and **literacy** practices, and teacher and student roles, with the basic assumption that daily life in classrooms is socially constructed and negotiated over time in face-to-face interaction.

The notion of school culture was further developed by scholars whose primary interest was in understanding the difficulties experienced by marginalized groups of children in schools. Early on, Shirley Brice Heath (1983) studied the "ways of words" of several diverse communities in the Piedmont Carolinas, and emphasized the highly contextualized nature of communication across different cultural, socioeconomic, and linguistic communities. As she followed these groups of children into the school context, the mismatch between their community's cultural discourse patterns and those of the school became apparent. This mismatch established the idea that particular discourse patterns characterized school and might create an obstacle to participation, and thus achievement, for particular groups of children.

This insight was buttressed with a major finding from literacy researchers—that children socialized in diverse contexts come to school differentially prepared to respond to the demands of school culture (Jacobs and Jordan, 1993). Building upon Heath's seminal work, many scholars with multicultural and diversity interests have sharpened our understanding of the essentially middle-class nature of school discourse and literacy practices, and the challenge, therefore, to diverse learners, whose experiences at home do not provide an easy match with school (Delpit, 2002; Ladson-Billings, 1994; Moll, 1992; Finn, 1999). Furthermore, Scribner and Cole (1981) established the idea that there are multiple forms of literacy, including specialized forms of reading and writing, both in school and out. Researchers interested in the school context have focused on what has been called variously "school-based literacy" (Pellegrini, 2001), "schooled literacy" (Bloome, 1987), the "official" (versus the "unofficial") literacy practices found in school (Dyson, 1993), and "school culture literacy" (Kantor, Miller, and Fernie, 1992). Common across these terms are the notions that literacy practices are shaped by school culture in particular ways that reflect middle class-literacy, that school-based literacy is a specific variety of literacy that must be taught and learned by all students, and that it will be easier for those whose home experiences are seamless with the school context.

Understanding and accepting the power of the school culture context to shape and constrain school success reframes the discourse around many familiar topics, such as school **readiness**, **assessment**, culturally relevant pedagogy, and discipline and guidance. The idea that school culture is a relative term begs the question of the appropriate role for schools in supporting childhood socialization and the needs of diverse learners. Among the questions facing early childhood educators are how best to support various students as they come to school, and how—or if—teachers ought to change their **pedagogy** and curricula to help diverse students instead of requiring students to change in order to meet the requirements of the school-based context? Some propose that the primary challenge for schools is to expand the school culture so that it supports students and their families cross the bridge from home to school and become socially "bicultural" in the ways of their communities and their schools.

Further Readings: Bloome, D. (1987). *Literacy and schooling.* Norwood, NJ: Ablex. Corsaro, W. A. (1997). *The sociology of childhood.* Thousand Oaks, CA: Pine Forge Press; Delpit, L. (2002). *The skin that we speak.* New York: The New Press; Dyson, A. H. (1993). *Social worlds of children learning to write.* New York: Teachers College Press; Finn, P. (1999). *Literacy with an attitude: Educating working-class in their own self-interest.* New York: University of New York Press; Green, J. (1983). Exploring classroom discourse: Linguistic perspectives on teaching-learning processes. *Educational Psychologist* 18(3), 180–199; Heath, S. B. (1983). *Ways with words: Language, life, and working communities and classrooms.* New York: Cambridge University Press; Jackson, P. (1968). *Life in classrooms.* Holt, Rinehart & Winston. Jacobs, E., and C. Jordan, eds. (1993). *Minority education: Anthropological perspectives.* Norwood, NJ: Ablex; Kantor, R., S. Miller, and D. Fernie (1992). Diverse paths to literacy in a preschool classroom: A sociocultural perspective. *Reading Research Quarterly* 27, 185–201; Ladson-Billings, G. (1994). *The dreamkeepers: Successful teachers of African American children.* San Francisco: Jossey-Bass Publishers; Moll, L. (1992). Bilingual classroom studies and community analysis: Some recent trends. *Educational Researcher* 21(2) 20–24; Pellegrini, A. (2001). Some theoretical and methodological considerations in studying literacy in social context. In S. Neuman and D. Dickinson, eds. *Handbook on research in early literacy for the 21st century.* New York: Guilford; pp. 54–65; Scribner, S., and M. Cole (1981). *The psychology of literacy.* Cambridge, MA: Harvard University Press.

Rebecca Kantor, Melissa Schultz, and David Fernie

SECA. *See* Southern Early Childhood Association

Second-Language Acquisition in Early Childhood

All children are born ready to learn language to communicate with the significant people in their lives. Within the first few years of life, virtually all typically developing children master the basics of one language. Although this is a complex task that requires much effort, early language proficiency is expected and considered normal. Increasingly, in the United States, young children are in learning environments where more than one language is used. Internationally, it is estimated that there are as many children who grow up learning two languages as there are learning one. The number of children enrolled in preschool and Head Start programs whose home language is not English (English-language learners, ELL) has been steadily increasing over the past two decades. During the 2002–2003 program year, 27 percent of children enrolled in Head Start did not speak

English as their home language. Of these, the vast majority are from Spanish-speaking homes, with 139 other language groups also reported. There are now more Latinos (almost 40 million) than African Americans (almost 39 million) or any other ethnic group and they represent about 14 percent of the total population in the nation. Owing to immigration trends and child-bearing rates of Latina women, the number of Latino children as a proportion of all young children has also been steadily increasing. Currently, Hispanics make up about 26 percent of all children under the age of three.

Throughout the United States, the academic achievement levels, high school completion rates, and college attendance rates of English-language learners remain markedly below that of their white, English-speaking peers. These findings have led some to believe that second-language acquisition places children at risk for school success. Countering this concern is a growing and convincing body of research emphasizing that high-quality early childhood education can improve the educational achievement of children from diverse linguistic and cultural backgrounds and help to reduce this achievement gap before kindergarten. Therefore, it is important for the early childhood profession to have a clear understanding of how children acquire a second language in order to design high-quality learning environments for children who are in the process of acquiring English as their second language.

Will Two Languages Help or Hurt Young Children?

Research increasingly shows that most young children are not only capable of learning two languages, but that bilingualism confers cognitive, cultural, and economic advantages (Bialystok, 2001; Genesee, 2004; Hakuta and Pease-Alvarez, 1992). Bilingualism has been associated with a greater awareness of and sensitivity to linguistic structure, an awareness that is transferred and generalized to certain early literacy and nonverbal skills. There are several important implications of this research for early childhood professionals. Children who have the opportunity to speak two languages should be encouraged to maintain both, so they can enjoy the benefits that may accompany bilingual status. Children from homes where English is not the native language should be encouraged to cultivate their home language as well as English. Maintaining the home language is essential not just to the child's future academic and cognitive development, but also to the child's ability to establish a strong cultural identity, to develop and sustain strong ties with their immediate and extended families, and to thrive in a global, multilingual world.

How Do Children Learn a Second Language?

It is commonly assumed that preschool-aged children can just "pick up" a second language without much effort or systematic teaching. However, becoming proficient in a language is a complex and demanding process that takes many years. As with any type of learning, children will vary enormously in the rate at which they learn a first and a second language. The speed of language acquisition is due to factors both within the child and in the child's learning environment.

The child's personality, aptitude for languages, interest and motivation interact with the quantity and quality of language inputs and opportunities for use to influence the rate and eventual fluency levels.

Simultaneous vs. Sequential Second Language Acquisition

Barry McLaughlin (1984, 1995) has made a distinction between children who learn a second language *simultaneously* or *sequentially*. When a child learns two languages *simultaneously*, for example, before three years of age, the developmental pathway is similar to how monolingual children acquire language. However, there is some disagreement in the literature over whether bilingualism results in a slower rate of vocabulary development than when children are learning a single language. As children are in the process of acquiring two languages and becoming bilingual, one language may dominate. That is normal. It is rare for emerging bilinguals to be equally balanced in the development of both languages. Eventually, however, children who have the opportunity to acquire two languages simultaneously will become proficient in each language.

The language development of children who learn a second language after three years of age, or *sequentially*, follows a different progression and is highly sensitive to characteristics of the child as well as the language learning environment. At this point, the basics of the child's first language have been learned. They know the structure of one language, but now must learn the specific features, grammar, vocabulary, and syntax, of a new language. According to Tabors and Snow (1994), *sequential* second language acquisition follows a four-stage developmental sequence:

1. *Home Language Use.* When a child has become competent in one language and is introduced into a setting where everyone is speaking a different language, for example, an ELL entering an English-dominant preschool classroom, the child will frequently continue to speak his home language even when others do not understand. This period can be short or in some cases the child will persist in trying to get others to understand him for months.
2. *Nonverbal Period.* After young children realize that speaking their home language will not work, they enter a period where they rarely speak and use nonverbal means to communicate. This is a period of active language learning for the child; he is busy learning the features, sounds, and words of the new language (receptive language) but is not yet verbally using the new language to communicate. This is an extremely important stage of second language learning that may also last a long time or be brief. Any language assessments conducted during this stage of development may result in misleading information that underestimates the child's true language capacity.
3. *Telegraphic and Formulaic Speech.* The child is now ready to start using the new language and does so through telegraphic speech that involves the use of formulas. This is similar to a monolingual child who is learning simple words or phrases (content words) to express whole thoughts. For instance, a child might say "me down" indicating he wants to go downstairs. Formulaic speech refers to unanalyzed chunks of words or sometimes even syllables strung together that are

repetitions of what the child has heard. For example, Tabors (1997) reports that ELLs in the preschool she studied frequently used the phrase "Lookit" to engage others in their play. These are phrases the children had heard from others that helped to achieve their social goals, even though the children probably did not know the meaning of the two words.

4. *Productive Language.* Now the child is starting to go beyond telegraphic or formulaic utterances to create their own phrases and thoughts. Initially the child may use very simple grammatical patterns such as "I wanna play," but over time he will gain control over the structure and vocabulary of the new language. Errors in language usage are common during this period as children are experimenting with their new language and learning its rules and structure.

5. As with any developmental sequence, the stages are flexible and not mutually exclusive. McLaughlin and his colleagues (McLaughlin et al., 1995) preferred to describe the process as waves, "moving in and out, generally moving in one direction, but receding, then moving forward again" (pp. 3–4).

Sequential bilingual children may have somewhat different patterns of development than monolinguals in certain aspects of language development in the short term. This may include vocabulary, early literacy skills, and interpersonal communication. Young ELLs frequently know fewer vocabulary words in both English and their home language than monolingual children. This may be due to the limited memory capacity of young children or limited exposure to a rich and varied vocabulary. If they speak one language in the home and are learning English at preschool, the child may also know some words in one language and not the other. For instance, the child may have learned the English words *recess*, *chalk*, *line*, etc., at school, but never learned the corresponding words in Spanish because there was no need or opportunity to do so in the home. However, when the total number of words the child knows in both languages is considered together, it is comparable to the number and range of vocabulary words monolingual children know.

Code Switching/Language Mixing

It is important for early childhood educators to understand that *code switching* (switching languages for portions of a sentence) and *language mixing* (inserting single items from one language into another) are normal aspects of second language acquisition. This does not mean that the child is confused or cannot separate the languages. The main reason that children mix the two languages in one communication is because they lack sufficient vocabulary in one or both languages to fully express themselves. Research has shown that even proficient adult bilinguals mix their languages in order to convey special emphasis or establish cultural identity. In any case, code switching or language mixing is a normal and natural part of second language acquisition that parents and teachers should not be concerned about. The goal must always be on enhancing communication, rather than enforcing rigid rules about which language can be used at a given time or under certain circumstances.

Summary

Young children who have regular and rich exposure to two languages during the early childhood years can successfully become bilingual. Most research concludes that there are no negative effects of bilingualism on the linguistic, cognitive, or social development of children, and there may even be some general advantages in these areas of development. Simultaneous bilingualism follows a path similar to monolingual development; sequential second language acquisition occurs in a predictable series of stages or waves. Typically, at any given time, one language may dominate depending on the amount of time spent in each language. As early childhood programs become increasingly diverse, teachers will need to understand the process of second language acquisition and learn how to adapt their expectations and instruction accordingly. Increased understanding will lead to improved methods that will promote the learning and achievement of young children who are learning English as a second language.

A major implication of the increasing proportion of young children who are ELL is the composition and preparation of the early childhood workforce. All staff, teachers, support staff, and administrators will need to understand the developmental characteristics of dual language learners, effective instructional and assessment practices, and, most critically, the role of first and second language proficiency in long-term academic success. Ideally, the workforce will include professionals who are proficient in English as well as the children's home language and well trained in early childhood pedagogy. In order to realize the potential of early bilingualism, we will need highly skilled teachers who have achieved proficiency in bilingualism, multicultural perspectives, and effective teaching strategies. *See also* Bilingual Education; Development, Language; Language Diversity.

Further Readings: Bowman, B. T., M. S. Donovan, and M. S. Burns, eds. (2001). *Eager to learn: Education our preschoolers.* Washington, DC: National Research Council. Bialystok, E. (2001). *Bilingualism in development: Language, literacy and cognition.* Cambridge: Cambridge University Press. Espinosa, L., and S. Burns (2003). Early literacy for young children and English-language learners. In C. Howes, ed., *Teaching 4-8 year-olds literacy, math, multiculturalism, and classroom community.* Baltimore: Paul H. Brookes, pp. 47-69. Garcia, E. E. (2003). *Student cultural diversity: Understanding and meeting the challenge.* Boston: Houghton Miffin. Genesee, F. (2004). *Bilingual acquisition.* Available online at www://Earlychildhood.com. Genesee, F., J. Paradis, and M. Crago (2004). *Dual language development and disorders: A handbook on bilingualism and second language learning.* Baltimore: Paul H. Brookes. Hakuta, K., and L. Pease-Alvarez (1992). Enriching our views of bilingualism and bilingual education. *Educational Researcher* 21, 4-6. McLaughlin, B. (1984). *Second language acquisition in childhood: Preschool children.* Vol. 1. Hillsdale, NJ: Erlbaum Associates. McLaughlin, B., A. Blanchard, and Y. Osani (1995). Assessing language development in bilingual preschool children. Washington, DC: George Washington University. (The National Clearinghouse for Bilingual Education, #22, June). Tabors, P., and C. Snow (1994). English as a second language in preschools. In F. Genesee, ed., *Educating second language children: The whole child, the whole curriculum, the whole community.* New York: Cambridge University Press, pp. 103-125. Tabors, P. (1997). *One child, two languages: A guide for preschool educators of children learning English as a second language.* Baltimore: Paul H. Brookes Publishing Co.

Linda M. Espinosa

Self-Esteem and Self-Concept

Self-concept and self-esteem are considered important to children's development and education. These two terms are often mistakenly used interchangeably, yet they are in many ways inextricably intertwined. *Self-concept* is a broad category, of which *self-esteem* is a component. Self-concept refers to the perceptions, feelings, and attitudes that a person has about himself or herself. Self-concept includes how individuals see their personal characteristics such as empathy and caring, their moral virtues, their gender, ethnic, and religious identity, and their physical appearance and social power. Self-concept encompasses one's sense of competence in gradually differentiated domains such as cognitive, social, and physical realms. This sense of competence contributes to self-esteem. Self-esteem refers to the evaluations individuals make about themselves and encompasses their judgments about their self-worth. Self-esteem is thus an integral part of one's self-concept.

Although we often refer to a general level of self-esteem, on closer inspection, self-esteem may vary according to domain. For example, children may have high self-esteem based on their social skills and circle of friends, but they may have low self-esteem in academic or physical domains. Even more specifically, children may feel good about their reading ability, but have lower self-evaluations regarding their math ability. Low self-esteem in one domain, such as athletic ability, may have little effect on an individual if it is not considered important in a particular family, peer group, or culture. On the other hand, in families or cultures where athletic skills are important or where skills that underpin academic ability are highly valued, low self-esteem in these relevant areas may have increasingly devastating effects as children move through school.

Factors Affecting the Development of Self-Esteem and Self-Concept

The development of self-concept and self-esteem are influenced by a variety of factors. These include cultural values, the social context and significant others, the physical environment and opportunities to acquire skills and abilities as well as the individual's physical appearance. Parents' and teachers' expectations also contribute to the development of self-concept and self-esteem.

Views of self vary among cultures, subcultures, and families within cultures. Self-esteem and self-concept are affected by possessing culturally valued traits, such as striving or helpfulness. In Western cultures, one goal is to help children become more independent and to achieve—particularly in academic or athletic domains. In contrast to the importance of becoming independent and achieving for oneself, in some cultures and families, connectedness and relationships with family and community are more salient. For some, self-concept and self-esteem are based more on seeing oneself as a part of a web of relevant social relationships than on seeing oneself as unique. In some cultures, self-esteem may be based more on harmony, on fitting in with a relevant group, and on caring than on excelling and being competitive. These two contrasting views of cultural influences should not be taken as polar opposites, however. An alternative view of the self is possible wherein both autonomy and interdependence are important to varying degrees depending on the circumstances.

Self-concept and self-esteem develop largely within a social context. The interpersonal environment that caregivers provide influences the development of self-concept and self-esteem. The quality, consistency, and timing of adults' responses to infants may carry messages about trust, caring, and the value of the infant. Caregiver responsiveness may also convey information about young children's capacity to become competent and to control their environment. When caregivers respond positively and consistently to infants' cues, infants may come to learn that they are of value and that they can influence their social environment. This may contribute to beginning feelings of self-worth and competence.

Parental warmth, acceptance, and especially approval are associated with higher levels of self-esteem as children get older. The type and quality of parenting also affects self-esteem. Parents who make reasonable demands that are accepted by children, but who do not impose unreasonable restrictions and who allow their children some choice and control (often termed authoritative parenting), generally have children with higher self-esteem than parents who are authoritarian or permissive—at least in mainstream Western cultures. Consequently, training in effective parenting where parents learn to be more accepting of their children's feelings and behaviors may result in higher self-esteem for their children. On the other hand, what some view as authoritarian parenting may in other cultures be perceived as caring and loving and may, therefore, have beneficial effects on feelings of esteem in those cultures (Chao, 1994). Indeed, some researchers suggest that the construct of self-esteem is a particularly Western attribute.

Interestingly, regardless of gender, perceived physical attractiveness—even more than actual physical attractiveness—has been found to be the domain most highly correlated with self-esteem from early childhood onward. Furthermore, adults have been found to give more positive attention to physically attractive infants and toddlers than to those deemed to be less physically attractive.

The physical environment also contributes to self-concept and self-esteem. As children grow older, their self-esteem may increase if they are able to interact successfully with developmentally appropriate materials that provide a challenge within an encouraging environment. Their successful interaction with appropriately challenging materials as well as with supportive adults and peers allows for perceptions of competence and consequently enhanced self-esteem.

Parents' and teachers' expectations are likely to influence the development of children's self-esteem as well. The provision of materials and activities for children to learn and master new tasks not only provides opportunities for them to see themselves as competent but also conveys subtle clues about adults' expectations. Children who see that they are given less challenging materials than others may wonder whether adults do not expect them to succeed. They may suffer self-esteem decrements as a result. Although young children generally hold higher expectations for themselves than do their teachers, when teachers make their evaluations salient, such as pointing out children whose work is best, children's self-evaluations are more likely to reflect those of their teachers. In such an environment, children whose work is not praised or displayed may come to feel unworthy. Furthermore, teaching strategies, such as ability grouping and public comparison of children's work, also subtly reveal teacher expectations and often result in changes to children's perceptions of self-worth. Teachers' expectations and comments about children's qualities, such as kindness, helpfulness, and flexibility, as well as those about tangible successes, such as art projects or learning to read, also influence children's perceptions of their competence and self-worth.

In addition, learning academic and social skills so that children feel competent is likely to contribute to enhancing children's self-esteem. Evidence that teachers value all the cultures and families from which their children come also helps children feel worthy.

Effects of Self-Esteem and Self-Concept

Research suggests that both self-concept and self-esteem are related to how a child approaches a task. For example, children who see themselves as competent may approach tasks eagerly. In contrast, children whose self-esteem is less robust may shy away from approaching new tasks, events, or people. They become frustrated easily and see themselves as helpless. Consequently, self-esteem and self-concept have implications for motivation and learning—even for preschoolers as young as age two. Children will choose to engage in activities that make them feel worthy.

Self-Esteem Enhancement

Parents and teachers in a number of cultures often attempt to enhance children's self-esteem by praising them, though what is praised often varies. Several cautions are in order here. First, praising children's *ability* and telling them how smart they are may have devastating effects when they do not succeed. For children whose ability is praised, lack of success at a task is likely to make them question their ability and make them feel they are incompetent and unworthy. On the other hand, praising children's *effort* or the strategies they use rather than praising their ability has more positive long-term consequences for maintaining their persistence and consequently their self-esteem. In fact, Japanese children are more commonly praised for effort and are more likely to persevere. Children can modify their strategies and level of effort, whereas ability is something they cannot control. Second, what adults often overlook is that praise may make children dependent on adults for judgments about their self-worth. When this happens, children's self-esteem may suffer since they do not learn to judge their merits on their own. Third, sometimes when praise is used in a manipulative manner—as it is often done in American classrooms, to call attention to children who are doing what they are supposed to do, like waiting quietly—the praised child may feel embarrassed, negatively affecting self-esteem. Teachers who express sincere appreciation of children's positive qualities, such as helpfulness, persistence, interest or curiosity and who expand on these qualities are more likely to strengthen positive self-feelings.

In the United States, at least, many attempts have been made to develop educational programs to enhance self-esteem. Advocates for such programs have argued that by increasing self-esteem, children will be more likely to approach new tasks and learn better. Others have argued that acquiring the skills and abilities that are important within the culture enhances one's self-esteem and that therefore programs aimed specifically at improving self-esteem are unnecessary. They argue further that an overemphasis on self-esteem enhancement may divert time and attention from teaching important skills and abilities on which realistic self-esteem is based. Indeed, programs based on developing cognitive skills in domains of importance have been found to be more effective in increasing self-esteem than those that focus mainly on self-esteem enhancement.

Because the approval of significant others is highly correlated with high self-esteem, some have suggested that significant others be helped to find ways to demonstrate their approval or that other figures be found who can provide needed support. However, as noted above, effusive praise is likely to be counterproductive compared to recognition of genuine achievement or salient inner qualities.

In Western cultures, another way of enhancing self-esteem is to provide opportunities for self-direction as children mature. Children can be helped to expand their sense of participation and their sense of control and power over problems that they see in the larger environment. For example, children can be helped to take small steps toward overcoming prejudice, waste, poverty, and so on. The ensuing sense of accomplishment in areas of consequence are likely to influence children's sense of competence and their resultant self-esteem.

Further Readings: Chao, Ruth (1994). Beyond parental control and authoritarian parenting style: Understanding Chinese parenting through the cultural notion of training. *Child Development* 65(4), 1111-1119; Curry, Nancy E., and Carl N. Johnson (1990). *Beyond self-esteem: Developing a genuine sense of human value.* Washington, DC: National Association for the Education of Young Children; Harter, Susan (1998). The development of self representations. In Nancy Eisenberg, ed., *Handbook of child psychology: Vol. 3. Social, emotional, and personality development.* 5th ed. New York: Wiley, pp. 554-617; Marshall, Hermine H. (1995). Beyond "I like the way...." *Young Children* 50(2), 26-28; Marshall, Hermine H. (2001). Cultural influences on the development of self-concept: Updating our thinking. *Young Children* 56(6), 9-22.

Hermine Marshall

Sensory Integration. *See* Sensory Processing Disorder

Sensory Processing Disorder (SPD)

Sensory processing (also known as sensory integration) is the normal neurological process of organizing sensations for our use in everyday life. We use sensations to survive, to satisfy our desires, to learn, and to function smoothly. Sensory Processing Disorder (SPD), also called Sensory Integration Dysfunction, occurs when the brain inefficiently processes sensory messages coming from a person's own body and his or her environment. The person has difficulty responding in an adaptive way to everyday sensations that others hardly notice or simply take in their stride. These preschoolers described below all have SPD.

Darwin, 4, shrinks away from touch sensations, and his feet never leave the ground; he is a sensory avoider. Eddie, $3^1/_2$, needs sensory stimulation to get up and go but does not usually know how to go get it; he is a sensory disregarder. Ben, 3, constantly seeks all kinds of stimuli; he is a sensory craver. Andy, $4^1/_2$, has trouble differentiating between hot and cold, heavy and light, and other sensations; he is a sensory jumbler. Carrie, 5, with poor posture and no "oomph," is extraordinarily clumsy; she is a sensory fumbler.

Typically, the brain receives sensory information from the body and surroundings; interprets these messages; and organizes purposeful responses. As we climb the stairs, our brain senses that we're moving upward, forward, and from side to side. Usually without conscious effort, we make adaptive responses. We flex and extend our legs, alternate our feet, slide our hand along the banister, maintain our balance, keep upright, and watch where we are going. We are probably not even aware that our bodies are making these adjustments.

In addition to vision, hearing, smell, taste and touch, we have several other vital senses. According to the research of A. Jean Ayres, PhD, OTR, who formulated the theory of sensory processing, the fundamental sensory systems include the following:

1. The *tactile* sense, which provides information, primarily through the surface of our skin, from head to toe, about the texture, shape, and size of objects in the environment. It tells us whether we are actively touching something or are passively being touched. It helps us distinguish between threatening and nonthreatening touch sensations.
2. The *vestibular* sense, which provides information through the inner ear about gravity and space, about balance and movement, and about our head and body position in relation to the surface of the earth.
3. The *proprioceptive* sense, which provides information through our muscles and joints about where our body parts are, how they are stretching, and what they are doing.

These sensory systems develop prenatally. They interact with vision and hearing, smelling and tasting, which develop slightly later. As a result of typical sensory processing, self-control, self-esteem, motor skills, and higher-level cognitive functions can develop.

Sensory Processing Is Necessary for These Everyday Functions:

Academic skills	Hand preference
Attention	Healthy relationships with others
Auditory perception	Kinesthesia
Balance	Muscle tone
Bilateral coordination	Postural stability
Body awareness	Praxis,* including motor planning
Body position	Self-comforting
Emotional security	Self-esteem
Eye–foot coordination	Self-protection
Eye–hand coordination	Self-regulation
Fine-motor skills	Social skills
Flexibility	Speech and language skills
Force, or Grading of movement	Tactile discrimination
Gravitational security	Visualization
Gross-motor skills	Visual discrimination

*Praxis: the ability to conceptualize (or "ideate"), to plan and organize, and to carry out a sequence of unfamiliar actions; to do what one needs and wants to do in order to interact successfully with the physical environment.

Difficulty in these areas may be caused by sensory processing disorder. Generally, the red flags of SPD are unusual responses to tactile, vestibular, and proprioceptive sensations—the sensations of touching and being touched, of moving and being moved. The senses of seeing, hearing, smelling, and tasting may be involved, too.

Sensory processing disorder plays out differently from person to person. It can also vary in the same person from day to day, depending on factors such as fatigue, emotional distress, or hunger. It may coexist with attention deficit/hyperactivity disorder (ADHD), Asperger syndrome, autism, cerebral palsy, Down syndrome, fetal alcohol syndrome, fragile X, spina bifida, pervasive developmental delay (PDD), nonverbal learning disorder, bipolar disorder, and other problems. Sometimes SPD is severe, sometimes mild.

The child who avoids ordinary sensations or seeks excessive stimulation, whose body is uncooperative, whose behavior is difficult, and who doesn't "fit in" might be called an out-of-sync child. The out-of-sync child receives sensory information just like everybody else. He, too, receives tactile sensations about the clothes touching his skin. He, too, gets movement sensations on a playground swing. He, too, hears a dog bark, smells a banana, chews toast and sees people coming and going. But unlike most people, the child may misinterpret or be unable to use that information effectively. For instance, he may have a tantrum because the tag in his shirt scratches his skin—or, he may not notice that his pants are on backwards. He may feel seasick swinging for a few seconds—or persist in swinging for a "million minutes." He may panic when the dog barks a greeting—or ignore the dog's eagerness to knock him down. He may gag at food smells and textures— or cram all sorts of things, edible or not, into his mouth. He may shrink from visual stimulation such as flashing neon lights—or ignore the sight of rushing cars and run heedlessly into the street. Why is this child out of sync? The underlying problem may be one or more patterns of dysfunction.

1. If the child has *Sensory Modulation Dysfunction* (SMD), his reactions to stimuli may be out of sync because, deep inside, his central nervous system organizes and regulates them inaccurately. These physiological reactions are internal, unconscious—and out of the child's control. While what happens in his brain is invisible, his responses may be frequent, intense, long-lasting, and very noticeable, indeed.

One way this ineffective processing plays out is that the child like Darwin may be overresponsive, or "sensory defensive," to certain sensory stimuli. For example, a door clicking shut may sound too loud; a shimmering Christmas tree may look too bright; a rising elevator may move too fast; an elastic waistband may feel too tight. Usually, the overresponsive child is a sensory-avoider and tends to be either fearful and cautious, or negative and defiant.

Another way that out-of-sync processing plays out is that the child like Eddie may be underresponsive to certain sensory stimuli. He may be difficult to arouse or may withdraw from the scene because he does not know what to do. Sensations do not bother this sensory disregarder; they just do not seem to attract his attention.

A third outcome of SMD is that the child like Ben may be a sensory craver and constantly seek intense sensations, such as spinning, jumping, twirling, climbing, stuffing his mouth, turning up the volume, bumping and crashing into furniture and other people.

Another child with SMD may have a combination of over- and underresponsiveness to stimuli. This sensory fluctuator may avoid some stimuli, such as light, unexpected touch sensations, while craving other stimuli, such as intense proprioceptive and vestibular experiences.

2. If the child has *sensory discrimination dysfunction*, like Andy, he has difficulty differentiating among and between stimuli. His central nervous system inaccurately processes sensations, with the result that he cannot use the information to make purposeful, adaptive responses and get on with the day.

The child misgauges the significance and value of things. He may not "get" sensory messages that other children use to protect themselves, to learn about their world, and to relate successfully to other people. Is this an eraser—or a cookie? A snap—or a button? How hot is this birthday candle? How high is the curb? How loud is his voice? How full is his mouth? How full is his cup? How hard should he pedal? How soon should he brake? How low should he duck? How much force is he using to hold a pencil, draw with a crayon, change a doll's outfit, add blocks to a structure, kick a ball, stroke a kitten, or lean on a friend? For the child with poor sensory discrimination, interpreting such ordinary demands and responding appropriately may require enormous effort.

3. If the child like Carrie has *postural disorder* and/or *dyspraxia*—that is, dysfunction in praxis—she has difficulty conceiving of, planning, organizing, and carrying out a sequence of unfamiliar actions. Dyspraxia interferes with doing what one needs and wants to do to interact successfully with the physical environment. (The dyspraxic child often has poor sensory modulation and poor sensory discrimination, too.)

Performing unfamiliar actions is difficult for the dyspraxic child, and successfully going through all the steps of a familiar action may be difficult, as well. Getting dressed, pouring milk into the cereal bowl, climbing into the school bus, and opening her locker may be hard. Sharpening a pencil, putting papers in a three-ring binder, and organizing the steps to write a book report may be daunting. Tying shoes, kicking balls, and skipping ... making a sandwich and setting the table ... saying vocabulary words ... going after school to a new friend's house—all these undertakings may be troublesome, indeed. Struggling to keep up with other children can be discouraging and not much fun.

Sensory processing disorder is a complex problem. Unfortunately, children don't grow out of it; they grow into it, finding compensatory ways to cope with confusing, unpredictable, and threatening sensations. SPD may affect children's development, behavior, learning, communication skills, friendships, and play. It may affect one or all of their sensory systems and impede sensory-related skills needed for daily functioning. It may make children overly self-protective, or not self-protective enough. Their strongest sense may be a sense of uncertainty.

Sensory integration therapy. A child with SPD needs extra coping assistance. Sensory integration–based occupational therapy ("OT/SI") is highly recommended. Occupational therapy is the use of purposeful activity to maximize the independence and health of people with various physical, cognitive, psychosocial, or developmental needs. For a child, purposeful activities include swinging, climbing, jumping, buttoning, drawing, and writing—the child's "occupation." Other therapies are beneficial also, as increasing numbers of pediatric therapists receive added training in sensory integration theory and treatment. Therapy may take place at school, in a clinic, hospital, community health center, or home.

Under the guidance of a sensory integration–trained therapist, the child actively takes in movement and touch information in playful, meaningful, and natural ways. The child responds favorably to sensory integration treatment because it helps him learn to succeed—and he *loves* it!

Sensory-motor activities at home and school. Meanwhile, what can parents, teachers, and others do to help a child get in sync? At home and school, adults can incorporate sensory experiences into the day, as a "sensory diet." A balanced sensory diet, like a fitness plan, is a planned and scheduled activity program that a therapist develops to meet the needs of a specific child's nervous system. Its purpose is to help the child become better regulated and more focused, adaptable, and skillful.

A sensory diet includes a combination of activities. An alerting or calming activity may come first, depending on the child's needs.

Alerting activities help the child become effectively aroused:
- Crunching cereal, popcorn, nuts, pretzels, carrots, celery, apples, or ice cubes
- Bouncing on a therapy ball or beach ball
- Jumping on a mattress or trampoline

Organizing activities help regulate the child's responses:
- Chewing gum, granola bars, dried fruit, or bagels
- Hanging from a chinning bar
- Pushing, pulling, lifting or carrying heavy loads
- Getting into an upside-down position

Calming activities help decrease sensory overresponsivity or over-stimulation:
- Sucking a pacifier, hard candy, frozen fruit bar, or spoonful of peanut butter
- Pushing against walls with the hands, shoulders, back, buttocks, and head
- Rocking, swaying, or swinging slowly to and fro
- Cuddling or back rubbing
- Taking a bath or playing in water

At school, the child with SPD needs understanding and support to succeed. A teacher may want to help an out-of-sync student but lack training in the appropriate techniques. If so, the following suggestions may help:
- Reduce sensory overload
- Provide comfortable furniture
- Develop a consistent routine
- Plan transitions as carefully as lessons
- Inject movement breaks between and during activities
- Encourage students to be active rather than passive learners

- Give children plenty of time to answer or complete assignments
- Simplify instructions
- Give the child alternatives
- Emphasize the positive
- Provide physical feedback, with frequent "bear hugs" for soothing deep pressure

When the out-of-sync child begins to feel more in control, his schoolwork and social skills will improve. When he is less distracted, he distracts the other children less. Inclusive classrooms that have the support of **early childhood special education** professionals enhance the likelihood that all students are working to their best ability, amd that teachers can teach.

Indeed, at home and school, every child benefits from a safe, calm, and distraction-free environment. Every child requires frequent breaks from work to move and stretch. Every child needs to know that someone is paying attention to his strengths and weaknesses, likes and dislikes, ups and downs. Every child needs to be shown how to find solutions to problems. Every child needs assurance that his ideas have merit and that it's okay to have differing abilities. *See also* Inclusion.

Further Readings: Ayres, A. J. (2005). *Sensory integration and the child.* Rev. ed. Los Angeles: Western Psychological Services. Kranowitz, C. S. (2005). *The out-of-sync child: Recognizing and coping with sensory processing disorder.* Rev. ed. New York: Perigee; Kranowitz, C. S. (2005). Preschool sensory scan for educators (preschool SENSE), a collaborative tool for occupational therapists and early childhood teachers. Las Vegas: Sensory Resources; Kranowitz, C. S., Stacey Szklut, Jane Koomar, and Sharon Cermak (2004). *Making sense of sensory integration.* Las Vegas: Sensory Resources [compact disc]; Kranowitz, C. S., and Stacey Szklut, et al. (2001). *Answers to questions teachers ask about sensory integration.* Las Vegas: Sensory Resources; Miller, L. J. (2006). *Sensational kids: Hope and help for children with sensory processing disorder.* New York: Putnam.

Web Sites: www.SPDnetwork.org; www.SensoryResources.com; www.out-of-sync-child.com

Carol Kranowitz

SES. *See* Socioeconomic Status

Sex and Sexuality in Young Children

The story of sex and early childhood education is the story of its disappearance. These days, when sexuality is discussed in early childhood educational settings, it is most often in the context of danger and the need to protect children from sexual abuse and preschool teachers and directors from allegations of abuse. It has not always been this way. It need not be this way. And, many believe, it should not be this way.

Sex is an important topic for early childhood education because young children are sexual in the following four ways:

1. *Infantile sexual desires and interests.* One of Sigmund **Freud**'s most important contributions was to expand our understanding of sex from something that starts at puberty and involves only the genitals to a lifelong process of bodily

pleasures, attractions to others, and emotional attachments. Freud generally used the term *libido* rather than sex to refer to these feelings, desires, and attachments and he suggested that the libido is a force of energy that flows within us from the day we are born (indeed, if not earlier, for even in the womb a fetus can be observed sucking his or her thumb). For Freud, thumb sucking and more generally the pleasures associated with the mouth are the first stage of sexuality, a stage he called the oral stage. Freud suggested that as the child matures the oral stage is followed by the anal stage, which is a period from about the ages of two to four when children take a great interest in urination and defecation and bodily control. Next comes the oedipal or genital stage that begins around four years of age when children become interested in their own and each others' genitals, in the differences between the sexes, and with couples and romance, including the questions of what goes on between their parents, where babies come from, and who they will one day marry.

A century or so ago, when Freud was writing, these psychoanalytic ideas had a great influence on the field of early childhood education. In books for teachers and parents published in the first half of the twentieth century, Freud's work was often cited to encourage parents and teachers of young children to view children's sexual behaviors, interests, and questions as normal and healthy and to avoid repressive responses to young children's fledgling expressions of sexual curiosity. For example, in her 1920 book, *Nursery School Education*, Miss Grace **Owen** wrote as follows:

> What numbers of children have their development impeded and their tempers spoiled by their mothers' over-anxiety about furniture and clothes and respectability! We are just beginning to realize, largely through the work of Jung and Freud and other psychoanalysts, how great is the danger of the repression of the instincts and appetites— the dynamic forces of the mind. . . . What the nursery school teacher can do is to prevent unnatural repression of primitive impulses. . . . The morality of a civilized community must not be imposed on the child by the wholesale suppression of his natural instincts. (pp. 6, 53)

In the twenty-first-century early childhood setting, adults routinely monitor and restrict what Miss Owen considered children's "natural instincts." Today, four- and five-year-old children are vulnerable to accusations of sexually abusing their classmates. Kissing games and playing doctor, common activities of young children just a generation ago, are now activities that routinely lead to calls home, official reports, suspensions and, in rare cases, legal proceedings.

2. *Gender Formation.* By the 1950s, Freud's influence had receded in early childhood education as Freud's focus on the stages of young children's sexuality was replaced by Erik **Erickson**'s emphasis on the stages of the development of identity. For Erikson, a key dimension of what he called the quest for autonomy, initiative, and intimacy in young children is the formation of a gendered identity, an understanding of oneself as male or female. Erikson's influential book *Childhood and Society* (1950), which used to be a required reading for preservice early childhood educators, not only described what he called the "psychosexual

stages," but also presented case studies of young boys and girls who were struggling with problems of sexuality and gender. In the 1970s, the women's movement's focus on the formation of femininity under patriarchy led progressive early childhood educators to turn their attention to preschool classrooms as sites of gender formation. Teachers were warned of the dangers of sexism in the curriculum, and of the tendency to consciously or unconsciously pressure boys and girls to play out rigid, traditional notions of femininity and masculinity as, for example, in play in the housekeeping corner where only girls play at cooking and cleaning while only boys pretend to be firefighters, cowboys, and astronauts.

In recent writings, especially by reconceptualist scholars, concerns about sexism have expanded to include heteronormativity, a term used to describe the pressure put on us all, beginning with young children, to assume that the only normal family formation is one with a mother and father living in the same household and that the primary goal of life should be marriage with someone of the opposite sex (see Boldt, 1997).

3. *Embodiment.* Writing some fifty years ago, Jean **Piaget** taught us that preschool-aged children are in the sensory-motor stage, by which he meant that their primary way of thinking about and interacting with the world is through their bodies. Before we begin to think abstractly, only in our heads, we think concretely, by connecting what we are thinking about to what we are seeing and touching. Before we begin to think concretely, which happens around age six, we think through and with our bodies. Even though Piaget's project centered on **cognitive development**, his work taught early childhood educators to appreciate the importance of children's physicality. This emphasis reinforced the focus on movement, the senses, and the body that formed the beginnings of early childhood education in the work of Friedrich **Froebel**.

It is ironic that a field that has focused so closely on the importance of the body has recently shifted dramatically to an overemphasis on the mind, often to the detriment of the body. **No Child Left Behind** and **Brain Development** are used to justify more time spent on learning letters and less time on movement, more time in the classroom and less time on the **playground**, and more time sitting in front of computers and less time engaging in physical contact with others, of either the affectionate or rough-and-tumble variety. From a psychoanalytic point of view, this movement away from the body to the mind constitutes an unwise, unhealthy retreat from sexuality, broadly defined—a retreat contemporary feminist psychoanalytic writers call "disembodiment" (cf. Elizabeth Grosz, 1994).

4. *Sexual Danger.* There is now and presumably always has been **sexual abuse** of young children. This is a terrible thing, a far too common thing, but contrary to popular fears, not something that happens very often in early childhood education settings. Research suggests that the sexual abuse of children happens mostly at home, perpetrated mostly by family members, mothers' boyfriends, and, less often, neighbors. There are very few proven cases of the sexual abuse of children in early childhood education and care settings. And yet a few high-profile cases (e.g., the notorious McMartin case), based on allegations that turned out to have little or no basis in reality, have created the public misperception that young children are vulnerable to sexual abuse in preschools. While some families are likely reassured by the subsequent focus on finger-printing preschool teachers

and creating and enforcing rules about "safe touch" and "no touch" policies in early childhood education settings, others believe that such policies have had counterproductive effects on the lives of young children and the people who care for and educate them. Some blame this heightened focus on preventing sexual abuse in preschools on a society unwilling or unable to prevent the sexual abuse of young children in the home, where it actually occurs. Others point to a more pervasive problem in contemporary American society, not just of sexual abuse of young children but more generally of their hypersexualization, as can be seen, for example, in "Little Miss" beauty pageants, advertising, and internet pornography sites that turn children into objects of sexual desire.

Conclusion

Early childhood professionals have an ethical responsibility to advocate for policies that keep young children safe. In our zeal to protect young children, however, we must take care not to misplace our concerns and to thereby distort the world of the early childhood classroom. Fears connected with sexuality are negatively impacting early childhood education in several important ways. There were never many men in this historically female field, but now there are almost none. The **National Association for the Education of Young Children** (NAEYC) calculated that less than 4 percent of preschool teachers in the United States are men and they only represent about 1.3 percent of family home care providers. It is not uncommon for men teaching in preschool and lower elementary classrooms to be told by school directors that they need to be moved to a higher grade or to a job where they do not have direct contact with young children, thereby avoiding unwarranted accusations. While men in general are discouraged from working in the early childhood classroom, the situation is even more acute for gay men, who are constructed as sexual predators, unfit to work with young children (Silin, 1995; Tobin, 1997). In this climate of fear, female teachers are also suspect and limited in the ways they can interact with children. For example, many preschools have instituted rules that prevent preschool teachers from cleaning up students who soil themselves in bathroom accidents. Preschool teachers in many locales are required to attend "no touch" and "safe-touch" workshops where they are told to not hold children on their laps (Johnson, 2000), or if they do, to make sure the child sits "side-saddle" and not with legs apart and facing away rather than toward the teacher. These restrictions on adult behavior conjure images of children-at-risk. They also contribute to an image of children-as-*risky*. The early childhood education classroom has been turned into a "panopticon," a site where teachers feel they must continuously have all of the children in their class within their sight, to prevent sex play, sexual abuse, and other perceived dangers. In combination, these orientations to sex and sexuality represent a dramatic shift away from a view of sexuality as an essential component of the lives of young children and an important dimension of their healthy physical and mental development. *See also* Gender and Gender Stereotyping in Early Childhood Education; Parents and Parent Involvement; Reconceptualists.

Further Readings: Blaise, Mindy (2005). *Playing it straight: Uncovering gender discourses in the early childhood classroom.* New York: Routledge; Boldt, Gail (1997).

Sexist and heterosexist responses to gender bending. In J. Tobin, ed., *Making a place for pleasure in early childhood education*. New Haven, CT: Yale University Press; Grosz, Elizabeth (1994). *Volatile bodies*. Bloomington: Indiana University Press; Johnson, Richard (2000). *Hands off*. New York: Peter Lang; Jones, Alison (2001). *Touchy subjects: Teachers touching children*. Dunedin, NZ: University of Otago Press; Owen, Grace (1920). *Nursery school education*. New York: E.P. Dutton; Silin, Jonathan (1995). *Sex, death, and the education of children: Our passion for ignorance in the age of AIDS*. New York: Teachers College Press; Tobin, Joseph (1997). *Making a place for pleasure in early childhood education*. New Haven, CT: Yale University Press; Tobin, Joseph (2001). The missing discourse of sexuality in contemporary American early childhood education. In Jerome Winner and James Anderson, eds., *The annual of psychoanalysis*. Vol. 23: *Sigmund Freud and his impact on the modern world*. Hillsdale, NJ: The Analytic Press, pp. 179–200.

Joseph Tobin

Sexual Abuse

For thousands of years, sexual interactions by adults with children have been a regular occurrence. The social historian deMause (1974) noted that children of ancient Greece and Rome, especially boys, were frequently sexually exploited. Even today, there are those, such as members of the North American Man–Boy Love Association (NAMBLA), who believe adult–child sexual contact is appropriate and healthy. Entire industries have been created to support adult interest in child pornography, child prostitution, child sex tours, and other forms of sexual exploitation.

Child sexual abuse has only recently become recognized as an important social, political, and legal problem. The 1978 Protection of Children Against Sexual Exploitation Act and the 1986 Child Sexual Abuse and Pornography Act made it a federal crime to exploit a child sexually or to permit a child to engage in child pornography.

In the United States, the current definition of sexual abuse includes activities by a parent or other adult such as fondling a child's genitals, penetration, incest, rape, sodomy, indecent exposure, and exploitation through prostitution or the production of pornographic materials (Child Welfare Information Gateway, 2006). It is defined in CAPTA, the Federal Child Abuse Prevention and Treatment Act (U.S. House of Representatives, 2003, Title 42, Chapter 67, Subchapter I, §5106g) as follows:

a. the employment, use, persuasion, inducement, enticement, or coercion of any child to engage in, or assist any other person to engage in, any sexually explicit conduct or simulation of such conduct for the purpose of producing a visual depiction of such conduct; or
b. the rape, and in cases of caretaker or inter-familial relationships, statutory rape, molestation, prostitution, or other form of sexual exploitation of children, or incest with children.

Sexuality in young children is a natural occurrence leading unfortunately to millions of unnatural acts by pedophiles, particularly those aroused by prepubescent children. Of the estimated 906,000 children who were determined to be victims of child abuse or neglect in 2003, just 10 percent were sexually abused. Of all parents who were perpetrators of child abuse or neglect, fewer than 3 percent were associated with sexual abuse. More than three-quarters of perpetrators were friends or neighbors (National Clearinghouse, 2005). Many believe that most reports underestimate prevalence. While retrospective studies of adults suggest that ages seven to twelve is the period where children are most at risk of sexual abuse, more recent studies suggest that rates of sexual abuse have little variation for children three years of age or older.

Conceptual issues currently being discussed by professionals include (*a*) the cultural context, including normal patterns of touching and physical contact; (*b*) evaluating the intent of the perpetrator; (*c*) the exploitation of adult power and authority over the child; and (*d*) age or maturational differences between perpetrators and victims, especially given recent interest in adolescent and child victimizers (Miller-Perrin and Perrin, 1999).

Children have been sexually molested outside the home by Catholic priests, YMCA and Boy Scout staff members, and child care providers, as a weapon of war and may be associated with abduction and human trafficking. The first national study of sexual abuse in child care settings (Finkelhor et al., 1988) found children were at lower risk from sexual abuse in child care than in their own homes. In those cases where sexual abuse took place in a child care setting, the vast majority of cases (83%) involved single perpetrators, and child care staff and/or staff family members were most likely to be perpetrators. Few things predicted which children or families would be victimized. Abuse was most likely to occur in bathrooms or nap rooms. While the most common form of molestation was touching or fondling of children's genitals, penetration occurred in 93 percent of all cases in licensed child care settings. In considering prevention, several risk factors should be considered (Kalinowski et al., 1988). Urban settings, a heterogeneous staff, periodic but unpredictable supervised visits by parents, screening staff family members, and open parental access appeared to help reduce the incidence of sexual abuse. Facilities designed to minimize opportunities for inappropriate, hidden adult–child behavior may also reduce potential abuse.

Only 3 percent of confirmed child abuse cases in 1997 occurred in child care centers (Wang and Daro, 1998). Statistically, children have been safer in child care and other early childhood settings from the risk of sexual abuse than in their own homes. Molestation by family members, or boyfriends of the mother, is also likely to have greater posttraumatic stress disorder symptomatology. Many professionals believe false allegations of child sexual abuse against fathers stemming from divorce–custody situations are increasing.

It is also important to remember than many of the high-profile sexual molestation in child care cases in the 1980s were later found to have significant shortcomings, especially as a result of leading and suggestive interviews of children by case workers and law enforcement personnel.

Current research issues include the reliability of medical diagnoses and assessments; racial, ethnic, and gender differences in perpetrators and victims; attempts to better understand the roots of pedophilia; relationships between the age and severity of molestation and long-term health; where to locate convicted pedophiles after release from prison; and the advantages and difficulties of teaching children about their bodies, how to protect themselves, and how and when to inform adults about concerns.

Early childhood professionals, parents, and members of the community have a responsibility to protect children from sexual abuse, as well as a responsibility to guard against overreaction to a terrible but relatively rare occurrence, one consequence of which has been to effectively eliminate males from the out-of-home development of young children. *See also* Sex and Sexuality in Young Children.

Further Readings: Child Welfare Information Gateway (2006). *Child maltreatment 2004: Summary of key findings.* Washington, DC: National Clearinghouse on Child Abuse and Neglect Information. Retrieved June 19, 2006, from http://nccanch. acf.hhs.gov/pubs/factsheets/canstats.cfm. deMause, L. (1974). *A history of childhood.* New York: Psychotherapy Press; Finkelhor, D., L. Williams, and N. Burns (1988). *Nursery crimes.* Newbury Park, CA: Sage Publications; Kalinowski, M., L. Williams, and K. Gartner (1988). In D. Finkelhor, L. Williams, and N. Burns, eds., *Nursery crimes.* Newbury Park, CA: Sage Publications; Miller-Perrin, C. L., and R. Perrin (1999). *Child maltreatment: An introduction.* Thousand Oaks, CA: Sage Publications; National Clearinghouse on Child Abuse and Neglect Information (2004). *What is child abuse and neglect?* Washington, DC: Author. Available online at http://nccanch.acf.hhs.gov/pubs/factsheets/whatiscan.cfm; National Clearinghouse on Child Abuse and Neglect State Statutes Series (2005). *Definitions of child abuse and neglect.* Washington, DC: Author. Available online at nccanch.acf.hhs.gov/general/legal/statutes/define.cfm; U.S. House of Representatives (2003). *Child abuse prevention and treatment act.* Ithaca, NY: Cornell University Legal Information Institute. Available online at http://www.law. cornell.edu/uscode/html/uscode42/usc_sup_01_42_10_67_20_I.html; Wang, C. T. and D. Daro (1998). *Current trends in child abuse reporting and fatalities; The results of the 1997 annual fifty state survey.* Chicago: National Center on Child Abuse Prevention Research.

Michael Kalinowski

Skinner, Burrhus Frederic (1904–1990)

B. F. Skinner founded a movement in the field of psychology called *radical behaviorism.* He won numerous awards in his lifetime, including the National Medal of Science, which was presented to him in 1968 by President Lyndon B. Johnson, and the first Citation for Outstanding Lifetime Contribution to Psychology, which he received from the American Psychological Association (APA) shortly before his death. B. F. Skinner is now universally regarded as the most influential behavioral psychologist of the twentieth century. More than any other behaviorist, his view of human development stimulated research that had very important implications for teaching practices in the fields of early childhood regular education and early childhood special education.

Skinner was born in Susqehanna, Pennsylvania. As a young man he had aspirations of becoming a writer and enrolled in Hamilton College in New York, where he received a BA in English literature in 1926. He spent nearly a year in Greenwich Village working as a bookstore clerk and writing fiction in his spare time, but soon became disillusioned with his literary skills. At the age of twenty-four, he decided to pursue graduate work in the Department of Psychology at Harvard University. He received his PhD in 1931 and remained at Harvard until 1936. It was during this postdoctoral period that he conducted a series of animal experiments using a method he called the *experimental analysis of behavior*. Based on this work, he formulated several *principles of operant reinforcement theory*, described various *schedules of reinforcement*, and demonstrated how new behaviors could be learned through processes such as *shaping*, *fading*, and *chaining*.

In 1936, Skinner married Yvone Blue. The couple moved to Minneapolis, where he taught and continued to conduct research at the University of Minnesota. In 1938, they had their first child, Julie. Skinner also published his first book, *The Behavior of Organisms: An Experimental Analysis*, which contained findings from animal experiments that he used to support his theoretical arguments. In 1943, toward the end of his tenure at the University of Minnesota, Skinner's wife gave birth to a second daughter, Deborah. Two years later he accepted the position of chair of the Department of Psychology at Indiana University. In 1946, he and a small group of behavior analysts arranged the first meeting of the Society of the Experimental Analysis of Behavior, which eventually led (twelve years later) to the establishment of the *Journal of the Experimental Analysis of Behavior*. In 1948, he returned as a tenured professor to Harvard, where he remained for the rest of his career.

During his lifetime, Skinner published dozens of theoretical and empirical journal articles as well as several important books. In 1948, he published *Walden Two*, which described a visit to an imaginary utopian community where U.S. citizens lived far better than people in the outside world. Skinner wrote the book because he wanted to demonstrate the advantages of a society based on scientific social planning and reinforcement principles of human development. In 1957, he presented an operant analysis of language development in a book titled *Verbal Behavior*, which was not particularly well received in the scientific community and strongly criticized by the noted linguist, Noam Chomsky. In 1971, he published *Beyond Freedom and Dignity*, which proved to be very controversial and prompted a series of university lectures and television appearances. Skinner continued to feel that his ideas were often misrepresented, which prompted him to write *About Behaviorism* in 1974. Toward the end of his life, he remained very active and wrote a three-volume autobiography, *Particulars of My Life: The Shaping of a Behaviorist*, and *A Matter of Consequences*. Skinner was diagnosed with leukemia in 1989 but continued to work productively. He presented his last talk to a standing-room-only crowd at the August 1990 meeting of the American Psychological Association. Ten days later he finished the manuscript from which he had taken many of the ideas for his presentation, then quietly died a few hours later.

Further Readings: Skinner, B. F. (1974). *About behaviorism.* New York: Alfred A. Knopf. Skinner, B. F. (1987). Whatever happened to psychology as a science of behavior. *American Psychologist* 42, 1–70.

Web Sites: B. F. Skinner Foundation, http//:www.bfskinner.org; Buzan, Deborah Skinner, Guardian Unlimited, http://books.guardian.co.uk/departments/healthmindbody/story/0,6000,1168052,00.html; Rachlin, Howard. National Academy of Sciences, Biographical Memories, http:www.nap.edu/reacingroom/books/biomems/bskinner.html

Vey M. Nordquist and William Bryan Higgins

Social Cognitive Theory

Social cognitive theory is "a framework for analyzing human motivation, thought, and action" (Bandura 1986, p. xi). First proposed in 1963 by Albert **Bandura** and Richard Walters, this theory outlines a process by which people learn through direct experience and observing others. Since introducing this theory, Bandura has changed its name several times to emphasize its evolution. Because Bandura and his colleagues broadened its perspective to include concepts beyond observational learning, it was renamed social learning theory in the 1970s. In 1986, Bandura again revised and renamed it **social cognitive theory**. However, many people and textbooks continue to use the older names.

Concepts central to contemporary understandings of this theory include reciprocal determinism, modeling, self-efficacy, and self-regulation. As is the case with the theory itself, reciprocal determinism is referred to by different names, including triadic reciprocality, reciprocal causation, and reciprocal determinism. According to social cognitive theorists, human functioning can be explained by the interactions of three factors: behavior, person, and environment. The behavioral factors are the observable behaviors of the individual. Personal factors include an individual's thoughts, beliefs, personality traits, emotions, and biology (e.g., sex, race/ethnicity, disability). Environmental factors include both the social (e.g., peers, parents, teachers) and physical (e.g., schoolroom, house/apartment, playground) environments. The following example of a three-year-old girl illustrates how these three factors combine and interact to influence the development of children. A three-year-old girl who attends a preschool (physical environment) will play (behavior) with many peers (social environment). This interaction may increase her skills (person) in dealing with social conflict, which are manifested in the behavior of talking to, rather than hitting, another child who takes the toy she was playing with. This change in behavior, in turn, can influence her peers' attitudes and behaviors (her social environment) toward her and her attitude (person) toward her peers. As this scenario shows, all these elements directly and indirectly cause changes in the other elements and illustrate the principle of triadic reciprocal determinism.

Modeling is also a major concept of social cognitive theory. "If human behavior depended solely on personally experienced consequences, most people would not survive the hazards of early development" (Bandura 1986, p. 283). People learn the vast majority of their behaviors through a combination of experience and modeling. Modeling occurs when a person observes someone else's actions and the consequences of those actions, which in turn influence his or her behaviors, cognitions, or emotions. Bandura identified three important functions of modeling: response facilitation, inhibition/disinhibition, and observational learning. Response facilitation occurs when an observer exhibits a previously learned behavior in response to a modeled action. Observing a model can also inhibit or disinhibit someone from behaving in a similar way. People might become inhibited after observing the negative consequences of a modeled event in that they do not perform the modeled activity themselves. People might become disinhibited after observing a modeled prohibited activity that is not punished if they in turn perform the modeled activity themselves. Response facilitation and inhibition/disinhibition are similar in that they relate to previously learned behaviors. The difference is that response facilitation involves socially acceptable behaviors while inhibition and disinhibition involve what usually are considered negative actions.

The final function is observational learning, which is how people learn new behaviors. In Bandura's famous experiment, children watched a film of a woman playing with a bobo doll (a blow-up clown that pops back up when hit). Typically, children punched the bobo doll; however, this woman hit it with a toy hammer, kicked and threw it. After observing this filmed behavior, when the children were given the opportunity to play with the bobo doll, they displayed similar behaviors, thus supporting the hypothesis that observational learning had occurred. However, children who also saw the filmed woman scolded for the inappropriate play with the bobo doll did not spontaneously display these same behaviors when given the opportunity. But, when asked to show what the woman on the film did, they could perform these behaviors. Therefore, although they still had learned through observation, these behaviors were inhibited through punishment of the model.

Whether newly learned behaviors are exhibited or previously learned behaviors are facilitated, inhibited, or disinhibited depends on the consequences of those behaviors. Consequences can be enactive or vicarious and can be either reinforcing or punishing. Enactive consequences are those that occur after a person's own behaviors while vicarious consequences are those that happen after a model's actions. Reinforcement is anything that increases the chances of the behavior occurring again and punishment decreases the chances of the behavior occurring again (this is a similarity to **behaviorism**). In Bandura's bobo experiment, the children who watched the filmed woman get scolded experienced vicarious punishment. A common occurrence in preschool settings is that after a preschool teacher praises a child for putting away some blocks, he and his two friends hurry to pick up the trucks. The first child was enactively reinforced while his friends were vicariously reinforced. Reinforcement and punishment indirectly influence behavior through expectations of future consequences (part of the person in reciprocal determinism). If people's behaviors are reinforced (punished), they expect the same consequence for the same, or similar, behaviors in the future. Therefore, these behaviors should reoccur (or not occur) in similar circumstances.

People do not model everyone that they observe. There are four conditions that observers must meet, plus three characteristics that potential models must have for modeling to occur successfully. Firstly, observers must pay attention to the modeling event, especially the relevant details of the behavior. Secondly, observers must retain this information correctly within their long-term memory. Thirdly, observers must have the motoric ability to produce the behavior. Finally, observers must be motivated to perform the behavior. As mentioned previously, consequences of the modeled behaviors can increase or decrease observers' motivation to exhibit the behavior.

There are three elements—perceived similarity, competence, and status—that characterize individuals who are effective models. Typically, perceived similarity relates to age, gender, personal background, ethnicity/race, and interests. People tend to emulate models they think are competent and they ignore incompetent potential models. Even though adults might not consider a kindergartner competent, a four-year-old might. Observers also tend to emulate someone who has a higher status than they do. Many children hold teenagers in awe and believe that they have very high status. Adults may emulate people with money, prestige, or fame due to the high status that our society accords them. Regardless of the actual degree of similarity, competence, or status, if observers believe a potential model has all these elements in some combination they are more liable to pay attention to, retain in memory, and be motivated to emulate the model's behaviors or thinking patterns.

Many aspects associated with human functioning, such as thinking patterns, attitudes, or beliefs, cannot be directly observed. However, they can be learned through cognitive modeling or rule learning. With cognitive modeling, people verbalize their thinking patterns, thereby making these unobservable thoughts, attitudes, or beliefs observable to someone else. For instance, many teachers and parents point to items and count aloud because they want young children to learn this thinking strategy. With rule learning, people observe the behavioral manifestations of covert elements (e.g., beliefs, attitudes) and infer the rule behind these occurrences. For instance, a child whose parent is easily angered and stomps around, swears, or throws things may learn to be easily angered also.

In addition to reciprocal determinism and modeling, beliefs of self-efficacy influence the nature and extent of learning through experience and observation. Self-efficacy (part of the person in reciprocal determinism) was defined by Bandura as a person's belief about his or her capability to perform a specific action to attain a goal. Self-efficacy affects human functioning in all areas of life through four psychological processes: cognitive, motivational, affective, and selective.

When faced with obstacles, more self-efficacious people think analytically and adapt their strategies, while less self-efficacious people begin to think erratically and choose less effective strategies. More self-efficacious people think about success and the steps they will take to reach that positive outcome while less self-efficacious people think about failure and how they and others will react to that negative outcome. These differing cognitions enhance more self-efficacious people's chances of overcoming difficulties but exacerbate the negative situation for less self-efficacious people.

People motivate themselves through forethought and their beliefs about their chances of success and failure. People with high self-efficacy tend to maintain or even increase their motivation and efforts after difficulties, viewing them as temporary setbacks rather than failures. They attribute these setbacks to insufficient effort or uncontrollable factors and their successes to sufficient effort, good strategy use, or high ability. On the other hand, people with low self-efficacy quickly give up when faced with difficulties. They attribute their failures to low intelligence or ability and their successes to uncontrollable factors, such as luck or other people.

Children develop self-efficacy beliefs through the natural consequences of and other people's reactions to their own behaviors. Positive outcomes can enhance positive self-efficacy while negative outcomes can decrease self-efficacy. Parents, teachers, and other adults can increase young children's positive self-efficacy beliefs through enhancing opportunities for positive outcomes, being responsive to and encouraging children's positive behaviors, and attributing setbacks to lack of effort or wrong strategy use rather than to lack of intelligence or ability. Peers and siblings can also affect a child's self-efficacy beliefs through modeling and social comparisons.

The fourth major concept of social cognitive theory is self-regulation, which is the process through which people control their thoughts, feelings, and actions that help them progress toward their goals. The four phases of self-regulation are goal setting, self-observation (or self-monitoring), self-judgment (or self-assessment), and self-reaction.

Some goals are more effective in enhancing self-regulation than others. Although long-term goals are very important, they are more effective when divided into shorter-term or sub-goals. Specific goals are better than vague or general goals. An effective goal also needs to be attainable but challenging to be motivating.

During the self-observation phase, people monitor their behaviors related to their specific goal. They can do this through a physical record of progress, or lack of progress, toward the goal. People who physically record or chart their progress might spontaneously change their behavior due to this record keeping.

During the self-judgment phase, people compare their self-observations to their goals and determine whether they are progressing or not in several ways. Firstly, people can compare their current behaviors directly to their goal. For example, if a second-grader's goal is to read a chapter book this week, she can gauge how much progress she has made on Friday. Secondly, people can compare their current behaviors to their own previous behaviors. A six-year-old knows he can tie his shoes now, although last month he could not. Thirdly, people can compare themselves to other people. An eight-year-old can ride a two-wheeler while her friend still has training wheels. Finally, people can compare themselves to an absolute standard. A junior in high school compares his cumulative grade in his biology class to that which is required for an A.

After people self-observe and self-judge, they must decide what to do next. If the goal has been reached or adequate progress is being made, people might self-reinforce. This self-reinforcement can be praise, a feeling of satisfaction, or a tangible reward. One potential hazard with tangible self-reinforcements is choosing a self-defeating reinforcer. For instance, if dieters chose to reinforce themselves with a banana split, this could cause them to go off their diet and gain some weight back. If people are not progressing toward their goal, there are several possible reactions. Based on the judgment that the goal was not appropriate to begin with, they may change the goal by making it more specific or less challenging. If the goal is appropriate but they still are not progressing adequately, people could decide to put forth more effort or change the strategies involved in reaching the goal. These four phases of self-regulation are cyclical in that people continuously move back and forward from one phase to another.

In summary, social cognitive theory explains human functioning through analyzing how people's behaviors, personal characteristics, and environment interact. Some of the major elements of these reciprocal determinants are the behaviors and thinking patterns of effective models (social environment), and a person's self-efficacy and self-regulation (person). Through using social cognitive theory, teachers and parents can become effective models for young children and can aid them in developing positive self-efficacy and self-regulation.

Further Readings: Bandura, Albert, and Richard Walters (1963). *Social learning and personality development.* New York: Holt, Rinehart, & Winston; Bandura, Albert (1986). Social foundations of thought and action: A social cognitive theory. Englewood Cliffs, NJ: Prentice Hall; Bandura, Albert (1994). Self-efficacy. In V. S. Ramachandran, ed., *Encyclopedia of human behavior.* Vol. 4. New York: Academic Press, pp. 71–81; Pajares, Frank M. Available online at http://www.emory.edu/EDUCATION/Bandura.html; Schunk, Dale H. (2000). *Learning theories: An educational perspective.* Upper Saddle River, NJ: Merrill; Zimmerman, Barry, J., Sebastian Bonner, and Robert Kovach (1996). *Developing self-regulated learners: Beyond achievement to self-efficacy.* Washington, DC: American Psychological Association.

Sherri L. Horner and Srilata Bhattacharyya

Social Competence

Early social competence has been linked to later successes, not just in social and psychological domains but also in academic, behavioral, and other aspects of well-being and adjustment. Although a long history of research has focused on the socioemotional, physiological, and cognitive correlates of early social competence, a unitary working definition of 'social competence' remains elusive. Because of the complexity of the construct, researchers have used a wide range of criteria, referring to specific social skills (e.g., social information processing), the impact of behaviors on others (e.g., sociometric ratings, popularity), and children's success in achieving goals in social settings (e.g., resource control).

Despite the lack of a common definition, most agree that socially competent children show positive behaviors toward others, are able to develop healthy social relationships, are seen favorably by others, and have "accurate social information processing" skills (Creasey et al., 1998). Researchers also suggest that "competence" is a subjective evaluation of the child's overall effectiveness in navigating social worlds, and includes adaptive behaviors (i.e., skills, physical development, language skills, academic skills), social skills (i.e., interpersonal behavior, self-related behaviors, task-related behaviors), and the results of actions, particularly peer acceptance (Gresham and Reschly, 1987).

The complexity of the construct and the lack of an accepted definition of social competence are paralleled by a divergence of instrumentation and methodology used to study it (McConnell and Odom, 1999). Methods to study social competence have included direct observation, peer nominations, self-report, and surveys. Measures also vary in focus—with some targeting performance and skills (e.g., ability to cooperate) and others examining outcomes, for example, how much children are liked (Hubbard and Coie, 1994).

While varying significantly in focus and scope, measures overlap significantly. Children who achieve high scores on certain measures (e.g., emotional regulation) tend to receive high scores on others (e.g., academic success, sociometric ratings). And while researchers and practitioners understandably rely on particular measures of competence depending on their specific interest, attempts to comprehensively measure social competence should include a combination of instruments.

The Development of Social Competence—Infancy to Childhood

Social competence is tied to cognitive and socioemotional skills, and social competence is related to the child's developmental stage. In infancy, social competence includes awareness of the environment and the ability to engage in meaningful interactions with others, particularly caregivers. Infants can be quite active and responsive to the environment. They smile to caregivers, open and close their mouths, blink their eyes, wave their hands, and even imitate adults' behaviors. Such interactions help infants communicate needs to caregivers and can influence caregiver responses. Such meaningful interactions ideally help to establish a secure attachment to a caregiver, considered by many to be one of the most significant experiences in a person's lifetime—possibly forecasting the quality of later relationships (Oden, 1999).

With age, sociocognitive and emotional skills become more sophisticated, and social worlds become more complex. Children begin to interact with different companions and gain access to more contexts (e.g., school, playground, and neighborhood). They become increasingly able to choose what contexts to participate in and with whom to interact. In other words, children begin to take a more active role in determining and navigating their own social worlds.

Peer relationships come to the forefront as the child encounters peers at school and tin he neighborhood. Peer interactions are integral to the development of social competence—influencing school performance and adjustment, and providing emotional support and a sense of belonging (Ladd, 1999). In the context of peer relationships, a child learns to negotiate and manage conflicts, to argue and experience success and frustration, to understand others' opinions, and to take others' perspectives. In other words, during childhood, even while the family continues to be a significant arena in which aspects of social competence are developed, peer interactions increasingly become an important venue through which skills and social competencies emerge.

Influences on Social Competence

Multiple factors contribute to young children's social competence. Parents in particular contribute to children's social competence both through their genetic legacy and the nature of their social interactions. Effective parental interactions, including involvement in play, and direct teaching and encouragement, promote children's social competence with peers. For instance, preschoolers who are rated as popular by teachers often have parents who are more involved in their social play. Likely, through observing and imitating the roles of important adult figures, children learn accepted social norms associated with socially competent behavior (Creasey et al., 1998). Parents can also arrange, provide opportunities for, and facilitate children's play with peers. For instance, mothers can enhance the quality of toddlers' play with unfamiliar peers by giving positive feedback. It is not hard to imagine how parents are able to help children seek out experiences and enhance their interactions with others. Conversely, stressful home environments can have adverse effects on social competence. High levels of marital conflict have been linked to higher rates of children's problematic behaviors. This might be partly due to a disruption of parental practices, as well as the weakening of the child–caregiver **attachment** bonds.

Although parents are the primary source of social and emotional support for young children, peers also play an ever-increasing role in promoting children's competence. The implications of peer interactions for social competence have already been discussed. But in addition, peers can also serve as a protective factor against many stressors that might impede the development of social competence, including parental discord (Oden, 1999).

Negative peer experiences can have adverse effects on social competence. Rejection or victimization can become a source of significant stress, contributing to feelings of loneliness and low self esteem. In addition, peer rejection can escalate in a negative developmental spiral. When less socially competent children are rejected by peers, they have limited positive social interactions, which adversely impacts social competence. As a result, they are less willing to interact with peers (Ladd, 1999).

Another important component related to social competence is the quality of the early childhood environment (that the child care setting can serve as a protective factor for children who might have insecure attachments with caregivers). Experiencing high-quality child care has also been shown to facilitate secure attachments between children and their teachers—in turn promoting social competence and other positive outcomes (Howes and James, 2002).

Children are also active agents in their own socialization. They are not passive recipients of socialization influences, but instead show ever-increasing agency in architecting their own experiences. Thus, the child is a significant influence on the development of his own social competence.

Finally, one cannot try to understand social competence without taking into consideration the cultural background of the child. Cultural groups vary in innumerable ways, particularly in the experiences of children as well as what is considered as "competent" in specific settings (Tietjen, 1994). For instance, Schneider (1993) found important differences in the levels of aggression and play behaviors of African American and Hopi Indian children—with the latter being more interested in group success than the former. In recent years, research on parental ethnotheories has also revealed interesting cross-cultural variation in expectations and ideals for their children. Unfortunately, the consideration of **culture** in studies of competence has been infrequent.

In summary, early social competence is a significant facet of children's development that has important implications for both current functioning in the social setting, as well as in forecasting later successes. There is no commonly agreed-upon definition of social competence, and this is reflected in the diversity of measures and instruments used to assess social competencee. Moreover, because social competence is intertwined with cognitive, socioemotional, and physical skills, what is considered as "social competence" also changes with age—from simple interactions with caregivers, to more complex relationships and experiences with a broader range of people. And while there are some limitations in the current literature on social competence, scholars recognize the importance of the topic and are working in many ways to better understand this aspect of children's development. *See also* Classroom Environments; Parents and Parent Involvement; Peers and Friends.

Further Readings: Creasey, G. L., P. A. Jarvis, and L. E. Berk (1998). Play and social competence. In O.N. Saracho and B. Spodek, eds., *Multiple perspectives on play in early childhood education*. Albany, NY: SUNY, pp. 116-143; Edwards, C. P., M. R. T. de Guzman, J. Brown, and A. Kumru (2006). Children's social behaviors and peer interactions in diverse cultures. In X. Chen, D. French, and B. Schneider, eds., *Peer relations in cultural context*. New York: Cambridge University Press, pp. 23-51; Gresham, F. M., and D. J. Reschly (1987). Dimensions of social competence: Method factors in the assessment of adaptive behavior, social skills, and peer acceptance. *Journal of School Psychology* 25, 367-381; Howes, C., and J. James (2002). Children's social development within the socialization context of child care and early childhood education. In P.K. Smith and C.H. Hart, eds., *Blackwell handbook of childhood social development*. Malden, MA: Blackwell, pp. 137-155; Hubbard, J. A., and J. D. Coie (1994). Emotional determinants of social competence in children's peer relationships. *Merrill-Palmer Quarterly* 40, 1-20; Katz, L.G., and D. E. McClellan (1997). *Fostering children's social competence: The teacher's role*. Washington, DC: National Association for the Education of Young Children; Ladd, G. W. (1999). Peer relationships and social competence during early and middle childhood. *Annual Review of Psychology* 50, 333-359; McConnell, S. R., and S. L. Odom (1999). A multimeasure performance-based assessment of social competence in young children with disabilities. *Topics in Early Childhood Special Education* 19, 67-74; Oden, S. (1999). The development of social competence in children. Urbana, IL: ERIC Clearinghouse on Elementary and Early Childhood Education. (ERIC Document Reproduction Service No. ED. 281610); Ogilvy, C. M. (1994). Social skill straining with children and adolescents: A review of the evidence of effectiveness. *Educational Psychology* 14, 73-83; Schneider, B. H. (1993). *Children's social competence in context: The contributions of family, school and culture*. Oxford: Pergamon; Tietjen A. M. (1994). Supportive interactions in cultural context. In F. Nestmann and K. Hurrelmann, eds., *Social networks and social support in childhood and adolescence*. Berlin: Walter de Gruyter & Co., pp. 395-408.

Maria Rosario T. de Guzman, Cixin Wang, and Toni L. Hill-Menson

Social Constructionism

Social constructionist theory suggests that psychological phenomena (e.g. emotions, self, and the mind) are not individual but social in nature; they are transmitted, created, maintained, and constructed through language and discourse. Social constructionism as a theory has been influenced by a number of multidisciplinary and transdisciplinary traditions, including sociology (Berger and Luckmann, 1966), critical theory (Foucault, 1976), and literary theory (Derrida, 1976). Contemporary interpreters of social constructionism in the psychological realm, including Kenneth Gergen and Rom Harré, emphasize the role of language and discourse in the construction of psychological processes such as the self, emotions, memory, and attitudes. Social constructionism came about as a challenge to empiricism and positivism and the notion of objectivity. A major assumption is that traditional notions about truth, knowledge, and the nature of reality should be examined critically, as all knowledge is historically and culturally specific.

Social construct*ionism* as a theory of knowledge construction is distinct from, although conceptually related to, the theory of social construct*ivism*. They differ with respect to a fundamental tenet having to do with the role and place of the individual mind. Social constructivism (see Lev **Vygotsky** entry) focuses on how the individual mind is first social and then individual and highlights the importance of language in the process. In social constructivism, the individual mind internalizes ways of being through the social and cultural tools of the society. Social constructionism, in contrast, places a primary emphasis on discourse as a vehicle for constructing self and ways of knowing the world. Social constructionists eschew the notion of the mind as an individual container and instead focus on what happens outside of the mind between people. From this perspective, people are not born as individuals with inner states, but rather the individual and inner states are socially constructed through moment-to-moment interactions. A major aim of social constructionist research is to uncover the ways that constructs such as knowledge, emotions, cognition, self, gender, and sexuality are socially constructed through social, cultural, and ideological discourses.

Social constructionist theory views language as a critical feature of the construction process, such that the underlying assumption is that all meaning is brought into being through language. Kenneth Gergen (1999) posits, "If language is a central means by which we carry on our lives together—carrying the past into the present to create the future—then our ways of talking and writing become key targets for concern. It is not only our grand languages of self, truth, and morality at stake; our futures are also fashioned from mundane exchanges in families, friendships, and organizations, in the informal comments, funny stories, and the remainder of the daily hubbub" (p. 62). This statement suggests that ways of talking and using language in everyday interactions shape ways of knowing, being, and doing. However, language is not simply a way to express what we see in the world, it is "the doing of life itself" (Gergen, 1999, p. 35).

Larger discourses also play a key role (e.g., discourses about gender or sexuality) and contain "frames" within which words shape meaning. For example, the larger discourse frames tell us what it means to be male, female, heterosexual, homosexual, student, teacher, black, white, poor, rich, Republican, or Democrat. These larger discourse frames provide "ways of being" that are grounded in what these terms mean in our society. As such, discourse provides a way for us to interpret the world. Through various discourses we form notions of self and identity, which are bound by power, history, culture, and ideology.

Social constructionists also suggest that research paradigms are socially constructed and built from discourses about knowledge, truth, and reality. For example, social constructionists consider how scientific knowledge is socially constructed though discourses about science, rationality, and logic. Other social constructionist critiques focus on how knowledge is located in particular historic and cultural contexts. Other areas of social constructionist inquiry include questions of how inner states such as emotions are known and regarded as true and how they are related to the power structures and ideology of a culture. How is truth related to our subjective experience? Is all truth subjective in nature? Is there a bounded individual self? If so, how is it contextual, political, and historical? What is the role of discourse and language in the construction of reality, truth, and knowledge? These are some of the questions asked by those who study social constructionism.

Early childhood scholars with interests in classroom processes have studied what gets accomplished by children in their daily lives as students and peers through a social constructionist lens. Traditional topics in the psychological literature such as gender and identity, social competence, friendship processes, and social isolation have been reexamined not as stable internal traits but as constructs that are constantly being created and recreated as children engage with each other and with adults. Bronwyn Davies and Rom Harré (1990), for example, see gender as constructed by multiple subject positioning that are taken up by children as they negotiate who they are in social interactions. Subject positioning are fluid and open to change in moment-to-moment discursive practices. Similarly, applying the notion of subject positioning to children's social status within peer groups, Scott (2003) also interpreted children's rejection and isolation not as an outcome of enduring poor social skills, but as a positioning constructed through discourse and social interaction.

A central criticism of social constructionism is the notion of agency. Is agency a top-down or bottom-up process? Do everyday ways of talking, being, and doing determine the larger discourse frame or does the larger discourse frame determine everyday ways of talking, being, and doing? How much of a role do humans have in shaping their ways of talking, knowing, being, and doing if everything is socially constructed? It is still unclear how much influence the larger discourse frames have on everyday interactions, as well as how much everyday moment-to-moment interactions have on the construction of the larger discourses of our society. This is an issue that is debated within social constructionist theory and is problematic. In the top–down view, humans are locked into the roles set by the larger discourse frames of the society, which leaves little room for change at the micro level and little human agency. While the bottom–up view positions humans as actively constructing and reconstructing discourse, according to Burr (2003), "The individual is a 'given' from which society arises, and therefore cannot be said to be constructed by that society" (p. 183). Thus, the notion of agency and the process of construction (e.g., Is it a top–down or bottom–up process?) is one aspect of social constructionism that is still under debate. *See also* Constructionism.

Further Readings: Berger, P., and T. Luckmann (1966). The social construction of reality: A treatise in the sociology of knowledge. New York: Doubleday; Burr, V. (2003). *Social constructionism.* New York: Routledge; Davies, B., and R. Harré (1990). Positioning: The discursive production of selves. *Journal for the Theory of Social Behavior* 20(1), 43–63; Derrida, J. (1976). *Of grammatology.* Baltimore: Johns Hopkins University Press; Foucalt, M. (1976). *The history of sexuality: An introduction.* Harmondsworth: Penguin; Gergen, K. J. (1999). *An invitation to social constructionism.* Thousand Oaks, CA: Sage Publications; Gergen, K. J. (1994). *Realities and relationships: Soundings in social construction.* Cambridge, MA: Harvard University Press; Harré R., and P. F. Secord (1972). *The explanation of social behaviour.* Oxford: Blackwell; Scott, J. A. (2003). The social construction of "outsiders" in the preschool. In R. Kantor and D. Fernie, eds., *Early childhood classroom processes.* Cresskill, NJ: Hampton Press, pp. 63–98.

Samara Madrid and Rebecca Kantor

Social Constructivism

Social constructivism is an educational theory with roots in both cognitive **constructivism** (Piaget, 1950; Piaget and Inhelder, 1969) and **socio-cultural theory** (Vygotsky, 1978); and conceptual links to the theory of discourse known as **social constructionism** (Gergen, 1999). The discourse which shaped social constructivism dates back to the 1970s when a community of educators raised their concerns with transmission models of teaching and learning that emphasize rote memorization and decontextualized tasks. At its core, social constructivism rests on the theoretical assumption that reality and knowledge are emergent and situated in social context and constructed as people engage with others in joint activity (Cobb, 2002; Cole and Wertsch, 1996; Wells, 2000).

Social Constructivism as Distinct from Constructivism

While social constructivism shares some epistemological notions with cognitive constructivism, within the field of early childhood education it was also a response to this theory. Specifically, social constructivism in educational settings arose out of a concern about the teacher's role in the classroom. For example, in the application of constructivist theory in classrooms, interaction and **direct instruction** between children and teachers is played down in favor of an emphasis on the child's exploration of the physical environment. *Social* constructivism, in contrast, emphasizes the importance of collaboration between the teacher and student, and students with each other, as social interaction is viewed as the primary means for children to construct new meanings. As such, social constructivism and constructi*vism* differ in a fundamental tenet; constructivism views learning as *following* development and the disequilibrium that occurs as children act upon the physical environment, whereas social constructivism views learning as *leading* development and as something that occurs as children engage in social activities with others.

According to social constructivist theory, cognition and learning exists in a dialectical relationship with the social world. Dialectical process is a term used both by social constructivists and constructivists to describe how children resolve cognitive conflicts to produce higher levels of mental functioning. Constructivists suggest that cognitive conflicts are resolved through the child acting on the physical environment, and the child gradually comes to understand how things work—practically and in the abstract, types of knowledge that Piaget referred to as "physical knowledge" and "logico-mathematical knowledge." Social constructivists interpret conflicts and knowledge differently, suggesting that conflicts are resolved through social processes; knowledge is something that is distributed across, between and within individuals and the collective. However, knowledge is not simply transmitted to the child from the social world, but rather it is appropriated and transformed as children engage with others, making children active agents in the learning process. The underlying assumption is that knowledge is always emerging as the child acts upon the social context and the social context acts upon the child, which allows for new meanings to be constructed as they influence one another. According to the social constructivist, then, knowledge is "(re)created in a specific activity setting, involving particular individuals who have a common goal, or at least a set of overlapping goals, to which they are all orienting" (Wells, 2000, p. 71).

Social Constructivism as Distinct from Sociocultural Theory

Social constructivism is also conceptually related, but distinct from, sociocultural theory (Vygotsky, 1978) and activity theory (Leont'ev, 1981). One notable distinction is how each theory views the contextual nature of learning and the construction of knowledge. For example, sociocultural theory places an emphasis on the mediating role of historically situated cultural tools and artifacts. In other words, it is not the social context alone that produces new understandings, but also the cultural tools and artifacts within it that produce and shape new knowledge: "artifacts clearly do not serve simply to facilitate mental processes that would otherwise exist. Instead, they fundamentally shape and transform them" (Cole and Wertsch, 1996, p. 252). Similarly, social constructivism and activity theory differ in that activity theory examines not only the immediate social and cultural context and the historical context but also how the production of knowledge is both constrained and shaped by history, which informs present "activity systems" (Cole, 1995). The central focus of activity theory is on systems of activities, which are bound by history and culture and have primacy over the individual cognitive functioning as the unit of analysis. The important point is that the collective systems located in social, cultural, and historical contexts override the notion of the isolated individual mind.

Social Constructivism as Distinct from Social Constructionism

A final distinction that is important to note are the differences between social constructivism and social constructionism (Gergen, 1999). Social constructi*vism* and social constructio*nism* differ in that social constructivism focuses on the Vygotskian notion that the individual mind is first social and then individual and the importance social context has in learning. In contrast, social constructionism places a primary emphasis on discourse as a vehicle for constructing knowledge (Gergen, 1999). The important distinction rests on the role and place of the individual mind. In social constructi*vism*, the individual mind internalizes ways of being through collaboration with others in social context, while social constructio*nism* eschews the notion of the mind as an individual container and instead focuses on what happens between the minds of people.

Social Constructivism and Educational Practice

Paul Cobb's work (2002) on mathematical learning is an example of the evolution from constructivism to social constructivism as the theory has been applied to education. Cobb's framework is derived from both constructivism and social interaction, and "together, the two perspectives treat mathematical learning as both a process of active individual construction and a process of enculturation into the mathematical practices of wider society" (McClain and Cobb, 2001, p. 105). The focus is not on the development of mathematical knowledge in isolation, but rather on understanding how mathematical learning and cognitive growth are grounded in classroom communities. Within classroom communities, sociomathematical norms and practices are constructed, accepted, and/or rejected by teachers and students, processes that affect cognitive growth and mathematical understandings. Within this perspective the learner and the teacher, as well as the individual and the collective, are seen to exist in a reflexive relationship in which "one does not exist without the other" (McClain and Cobb, 2001, p. 105).

Given that the role of the social context and interactions with others is central in social constructivism, practical applications have also focused on joint activity between learners and teachers. According to Wells (2000), "Vygotskian theory, or social constructivism, as we might call its educational application, thus calls for an approach to learning and teaching that is both exploratory and collaborative" (p. 61). Learning and teaching from this perspective views both the teacher and the students as active agents in the construction of knowledge. Content should not be taught in a rote linear fashion but should be explored and examined in a holistic, emergent manner so that the focus is on the process of joint activity rather than on specific predetermined outcomes. An **emergent curriculum** allows for dialogue and diversity in ways of solving problems that supports and builds on the prior knowledge that teachers and students bring with them in order to create shared understandings. In this view, each learning event is seen as unique, and the teacher and the students both take the position of the learner. This differs from other views that position the teacher as someone who imparts knowledge to the less advanced students.

In a social constructivist classroom, knowledge is always in the process of being constructed; both the teacher and the students are always constructing new ways of thinking about and solving problems. Thus, practical applications of social constructivist teaching are grounded in the notion that learning is a reciprocal and collaborative process among all members. *See also* Vygotsky, Lev Semenovich.

Further Readings: Cobb, P. (2002). Reasoning with tools and inscriptions. *The Journal of the Learning Sciences* 11(2&3), 187–215; Cole, M. (1995). Cultural-historical psychology: A meso-genetic approach. In L. Martin K. Nelson and E. Tobach, eds., *Sociocultural psychology: Theory and practice of doing and knowing.* Cambridge: Cambridge University Press, pp. 168–204; Cole, M., and J. Wertsch (1996). Beyond the individual-social antinomy in discussions of Piaget and Vygotsky. *Human Development* 39, 250–256; Gergen, K. (1999). *An invitation to social constructionism.* Thousand Oaks, CA: Sage Publications; Leont'ev, A. N. (1981). *Problems in the development of mind.* Moscow: Progress Publishers; McClain, K. and P. Cobb (2001). Supporting students' ability to reason about data. *Educational Studies in Mathematics* 45, 103–129; Piaget, J. (1950). *The psychology of intelligence.* New York: Hartcourt, Brace; Piaget, J., and B. Inhelder (1969). *The psychology of the child.* New York: Basic Books; Vygotsky, L. S. (1978). *Mind in society: The development of higher mental functions.* Cambridge, MA: Harvard University Press; Wells, G. (2000). Dialogic inquiry in education: Building on the legacy of Vygotsky. In C. Lee and P. Smagorinsky, eds., *Vygotskian perspectives on literacy research: Constructing meaning through collaborative inquiry.* Cambridge: Cambridge University Press, pp. 51–85.

Samara Madrid and Rebecca Kantor

Social Studies Curriculum. *See* Curriculum, Social Studies

Socioeconomic Status (SES)

Socioeconomic status (SES) is commonly used in the early childhood field to describe the social class level of an individual or family, typically taking into account income, accumulated wealth and assets, and educational background. This article summarizes the definitions and measurement of SES, as well as the implications of SES for early childhood development and policy implications for early care and education (ECE).

Definition and Measurement

There is no standard definition or formula for defining SES. Income, wealth, and educational background are typically used to calculate SES level, and can be defined as annual income, monetary value of assets, and formal educational degrees. In much of the research that utilizes this variable, statistical procedures control for effects of SES in order to measure the effects of another variable, such as a treatment in an experimental design. Because SES has many implications for child outcomes, it is also important to consider as a source of influence. Historical and cultural contexts help determine the appropriateness of the various scales used to measure SES. For example, in the nineteenth century few Americans had college degrees, making the use of formal degrees as an educational scale inappropriate for this time period. Similarly, using an American asset or income scale would be an inappropriate measure of SES in another country.

Because income and educational attainment are positively correlated, this measure works in most circumstances. However, certain circumstances or occupations can create problems for measuring SES, such as the temporary status of graduate student or clergymen who are well-educated but generally low-income. Researchers and demographers must be careful to state their definition of SES in their studies, and readers must be cautious when making comparisons and generalizing across contexts.

The concepts of **poverty** and SES often overlap but are defined differently. Poverty is calculated using absolute income whereas SES is measured relative to others. Educational level can be measured using formal degrees (e.g., a bachelor's or master's) or by other variables, such as the number of books in the home. The federal poverty line in the United States is a specific dollar threshold, defined as the amount of money required to adequately feed a family for a year (as determined by the United States Department of Agriculture) multiplied by three. In 2005, the U.S. poverty level for a family of four was $19,350. If a family's income falls below this threshold, the family is considered poor. If a family's income falls below 200 percent of the poverty line ($38,700 for a family of four in 2005), the family is considered low-income. Compared with income, SES is generally a more stable measure across time. While income may change drastically each year, SES takes into account more constant variables such as educational attainment and accumulated wealth.

Demographics

Educational attainment. Eighty percent of the U.S. population over age 25 have graduated from high school, and about one-quarter hold a bachelor's degree or higher. Less than 10 percent of the population holds a postgraduate degree (master's, professional, or doctorate degrees).

Income. In 2004, the median annual household income in the United States was $44,473. For the most part, the income distribution is concentrated in the middle. In 2000, 12 percent of the U.S. population had annual household incomes of $100,000 or more while 16 percent had incomes less than $15,000.

Characteristics of Low-SES children. Demographers and researchers, including the U.S. Census Bureau and the National Center for Children in Poverty (NCCP) have found that a large and increasing number of children in the United States live in low-SES homes. The likelihood of living in lower-SES families varies according to children's age, ethnicity, family structure, and geography. Young children are even more at risk of living in poverty. In 2005 nearly 20 percent of children under age six lived below the poverty line. In 2000 the NCCP reported that the poverty rate for children under three was found to be 80 percent higher than the rate for adults. Black and Hispanic children are more likely to live in lower-income households than Asian or white children. In addition, single-parent households and families with young parents are significantly more likely to be low-income. Southern and western states in the United States have higher rates of childhood poverty than northern or eastern states.

The Implications of Low Socioeconomic Status

Low-SES home environments tend to be less stimulating for young children than mid- and upper-SES homes, often due to a lack of resources or education. Several studies have investigated the impacts of socioeconomic status on children's development (for reviews, see Brooks-Gunn and Duncan, 1997, and McLloyd, 1998). Children in low-SES homes are at greater risk for inadequate nutrition and obesity, cognitive developmental delays and inadequate health care, increased exposure to environmental toxins such as lead (Evans, 2004), and a higher incidence of and exposure to abuse or neglect. Parents with income below the poverty line tend to be less responsive to their young children and use more punitive parenting techniques than those with income above. In addition, lower family income may lead to living in neighborhoods with higher crime rates, inadequately funded schools, and fewer resources for child development. Research has linked neighborhood influences with parenting practices and child outcomes. Several studies suggest that, in the long term, family income may have negative implications for adolescent well-being, particularly cognitive outcomes and school achievement.

Early care and education options are limited for low-income families, largely due to their high cost, and the few options available to low-SES families tend to be low-quality. In child care centers that serve low-income families, caregivers tend to display less warmth and responsiveness to children, and speak to children in more authoritarian ways than caregivers in centers serving middle- and upper-income families. Low-SES families are more likely to use informal child care (i.e., family, friend, and neighbor care or kith and kin care), which is unregulated and often low-quality.

Socioeconomic Status and Early Care and Education

Because of the few options available to low-SES families, public early care and education programs have been developed to serve low-income children. **Head Start** is a federal program established in the 1960s to provide preschool services to low-income families, and **Early Head Start** was developed more recently to serve low-income infants and toddlers. The recent wave of state universal prekindergarten programs has expanded services to more children. Child care subsidies help low-income families afford early care and education programs, and have been significantly increased to better serve more families since welfare reform in 1996.

Research has shown that high quality early care and education experiences can mitigate the negative effects of low SES (for reviews, see Barnett, 1998; Devaney et al., 1997). In the short term, participation in Head Start can enhance children's cognitive, social, and physical development. Long-term effects of intensive, high quality early childhood programs, such as the **High/Scope Perry Preschool** and the Abecedarian Project, include higher rates of high school graduation and reductions in the use of special education services in addition to enduring social benefits such as increased labor market productivity and higher taxable earnings. Children from low-SES families show greater gains than children from middle- and upper-SES homes when provided with high-quality early care and education.

While public early childhood programs are important to and beneficial for low-income children, children from the working poor class are often caught in the middle—unable to afford high-quality care but ineligible for public options. In addition, targeted programs further segregate low-SES children. As a result, six states have recently established universal prekindergarten programs or are moving toward universal access for all children, regardless of SES.

In addition to providing or subsidizing direct ECE services, the SES of children and their ECE providers has policy implications. Policy makers must consider provider's SES when creating trainings. Low-SES providers may not have the funds to attend trainings, or may lack Internet access for on-line courses. In addition, the match in SES between provider and child has implications for home–school relations; families and their early childhood teachers must be able to relate and successfully communicate with each other.

Although there is no standard definition of socioeconomic status, recent research emphasizes the importance of SES for children's development. Living in low-SES homes is a risk factor for young children, affecting physical, cognitive, and social–emotional development. However, these effects can be partially mitigated by early interventions that include high quality early care and education. Considering the large numbers of American children living in low-income homes, the expansion of high-quality early care and education programs is necessary to ensure that all young children have a healthy start in life. *See also* Preschool/Prekindergarten Programs.

Further Readings: Barnett, W. S. (1998). Long-term effects on cognitive development and school success. In W. S. Barnett and S. S. Boocock, eds., *Early care and education for children in poverty*. Albany: State University of New York Press, pp. 11–44; Brooks-Gunn, J., and G. Duncan (1997). The effects of poverty on children. *The Future of Children* 7(2), 55–71; DeNavas-Walt, C., B. D. Proctor, and R. J. Mills (August 2004). *Income, poverty, and health insurance coverage in the United States: 2003*. United States Census Bureau, U.S. Department of Commerce. Available online at http://www.census.gov/prod/2004pubs/p60-226.pdf; Devaney, B. L., M. R. Ellwood, J. M. Love (1997). Programs that mitigate the effects on poverty for children. *The Future of Children* 7(2), 88–112; Evans, G. W. (2004). The environment of childhood poverty. *American Psychologist* 59(2), 77–92; Helburn, S. W., and B. R. Bergmann (2002). *America's child care problem*. New York: Palgrave; Hsien-Hen, L., and H. Koball (August 2003). *Living on the edge: The changing demographics of low-income families and their children*. National Center for Children in Poverty, Mailman School of Public Health, Columbia University. Available online at http://nccp.org/media/lat03d-text.pdf; McLloyd, V. C. (1998). Socioeconomic disadvantage and child development. *American Psychologist* 53, 185–204; National Center for Children in Poverty. (2002). *Early childhood poverty: A statistical profile*. Mailman School of Public Health, Columbia University. Available online at http://nccp.org/media/ecp02-text.pdf.

Taryn W. Morrissey

Southern Early Childhood Association (SECA)

The Southern Early Childhood Association (SECA) is a national organization that strives to improve the lives of the children and families of the South and to support the over 19,000 professionals who are members of the Southern Early Childhood Association. SECA encompasses 14 states in the Southern region: Alabama, Arkansas, Florida, Georgia, Kentucky, Louisiana, Mississippi, North Carolina, Oklahoma, South Carolina, Tennessee, Texas, West Virginia, and Virginia. SECA brings together preschool, **kindergarten**, and primary teachers, administrators, caregivers, program directors, and individuals working with and for families to promote quality care and education for young children.

SECA is committed to providing leadership and support to individuals and groups by doing the following:
- enhancing the quality of young children's lives through early childhood care and education;
- supporting families in their roles of caring for their children;
- fostering the professional growth and status of individuals working with young children and their families;
- increasing public understanding and support for policies and programs that ensure developmentally based services to young children and their families;
- focusing on Southern issues concerning children and families.

The Southern Early Childhood Association provides the following services to members of the Association and to state affiliates:
- Three issues of *Dimensions of Early Childhood*, a refereed professional journal which helps translate research into practice
- Three issues of the *SECA Reporter*, the professional's guide to what's happening in the South in early childhood education
- Support for state efforts to develop positive policy agendas for children
- Member benefit programs, including discounts on training and conferences
- Specialized publications that assist professionals and practitioners in working with young children.

For more information on SECA, visit the organization's Web site at www.SouthernEarlyChildhood.org, or write to or call the following address or phone number: Southern Early Childhood Association, P.O. Box 55930, Little Rock, AR 72215-5930, 1-800-305-SECA

Glenda Bean

SPD. *See* Sensory Processing Disorder

Special Education. *See* Early Childhood Special Education

Spiritual Development

Children's spiritual development has rarely been a topic of study or investigation in the fields of child development and early childhood education in the United States. Given the increasing numbers of children from homes with diverse religious beliefs amid the strong resistance to public discussion of religious be-liefs and values, many adults believe that questions of spirituality are better left to children's families, religious leaders, and institutions (Banks and Banks, 2001). However, this omission from knowledge about child development limits practi-tioners' ability to develop fully integrated interventions with children and fami-lies. Furthermore, the lack of study of children's early experiences in religious and spiritual development may impact children's comprehensive development.

Although there is a lack of consensus on issues pertaining to spiritual devel-opment, key distinctions can help frame the issues and help develop practical approaches to working with children and families.

Significance

People of various religious faiths share the belief that spiritual development is central for the positive development of the individual and of society. Spiritual de-velopment may contribute to a moral system that promotes charity, compassion, and justice. Spiritual development may also help individuals and groups of individ-uals adjust positively to life circumstances, as indicated by studies of adolescents that report positive correlations between spirituality and adolescent thriving in-dices such as school engagement and the possessing of what researchers refer to as a moral compass (Dowling et al., 2004).

Spiritual development may prove important for addressing global issues having to do with religious differences. Sociopolitical events around the globe are often fueled by religious differences. Meanwhile, increased immigration and changes in religious experiences in families over time have made nations, and sometimes inhabitants in the same home, increasingly diverse in terms of religious traditions and spiritual values. Statistics about the number of adherents to particular faith traditions are controversial due to the interests and capacity of any authorizing group to measure religious behavior, particularly given the multiple criteria for determining religious group membership. Eileen Linder, the editor of the 2000 Yearbook of American and Canadian Churches, suggests that comparing statistics is not the best way to understand our increased religious pluralism: "We now have a critical mass of people from different religious traditions. Whether we have the numbers or not . . . we need to learn ways to engage with them" (Pluralism Project, 2006).

Early childhood educators are challenged to become familiar with a wide va-riety of religious and spiritual traditions. Competence around diverse religions and diverse approaches to spirituality can equip educators to serve children and families in more comprehensive and adequate ways, and such competence may generate support for scholarship.

The Distinction between Faith and Belief

There are general and historical distinctions between faith and belief. Wilfred Cantwell Smith describes faith as neither rare nor automatic, but rather as a ubiquitously prodigious hallmark of being human; faith is "the human potentiality for being human" (Smith, 1998, p. 142). As such, faith is sufficiently broad to encompass any symbol system, be it religious or secular. Faith refers to the actual involvement and interaction with dogma, beliefs, and symbols, whereas belief refers only to tenets and dogmas. In this way the concept of belief is too narrow to encompass all that is spiritual.

When faith and belief are conflated, both are relegated to a lower level of existence characterized by a type of mysticism that is the product of some irrational feeling or exercise of the mind. Attention to human potential and social action shifts instead to private contemplations in the mind. The likelihood that a person's faith manifests itself in action that transforms the world is, then, lessened considerably.

The distinction between faith and belief has important implications for whether and how they are topics of discussion in public spheres. When thinking about faith as belief, educators may be hesitant to inquire about a family's faith, for fear of generating disagreement. However, the distinction between faith and belief facilitates public conversation, because faith is a dialectical relationship between self and widely held norms of compassion, generosity, and justice. No matter what the specific beliefs may be, then, there is apt to be considerable common ground between educator and family.

Organizing Frameworks for Understanding Development

The dominant framework for understanding religious and spiritual development has been the stage theory of development, which, with respect to spirituality, argues that humans follow a fixed trajectory of stages that develop toward an ideal type or universal endpoint. The stage theories of Jean **Piaget** and Lawrence **Kohlberg** are prime examples. Stage theories, then, share the idea that development is linear and normative.

Alternatives to stage theories view development as multidirectional movement toward many possible endpoints. The possibility of there being a range of endpoints shifts attention from the individual to the individual's interacting with his or her faith tradition or culture. The individual, positioned within complex social and cultural systems, develops both spiritually and otherwise as a composite of transactions and experiences. Using this frame, the individual develops spiritually to the extent that there is a good match between individual, faith tradition, and culture. This developmental–cultural approach allows for development to take on different meanings depending on faith tradition and culture.

Alternatives to stage theories also emphasize quantitative rather than qualitative changes in a person's faith. For instance, Kwilecki (1999) focuses on the role the supernatural has for the individual and how, with development, the supernatural becomes functional in multiple ways. What matter are how important the supernatural becomes in a person's life and the strength of a person's convictions, not qualitative changes in how a person thinks. Although spiritual development can be charted as qualitative change over time (from immature to mature), spiritual development also means a deepening and strengthening of faith and an approximating to ideals that are both culturally situated and universal.

An increasing amount of scholarship is expanding to include the religious and spiritual life of young children. An exploration of children's God concepts based on the social learning and projection theories finds that children's beliefs are highly influenced by the beliefs of the mother (De Roos et al., 2004). A longitudinal study of mother–child dyads, with children entering at 14 months, finds positive links between committed compliance and internalization (Kochanska, 2002). Further collaboration between practitioners and researchers may help provide a deeper understanding of religion in the lives of young children, particularly because young children may not conform to the boundaries that adults erect between sacred and secular settings (Myers, 1997).

Further Readings: Banks, J., and C. McGee Banks (2001). *Multicultural education: Issues and perspectives.* New York: John Wiley & Sons, Inc.; De Roos, S., Iedema, J. and S., Miedema (2004). Influence of maternal denomination, God concepts, and child-rearing practices on young children's god concepts. *Journal for the Scientific Study of Religion* 43(4), 519–535; Dowling, E., S. Gestsdottir, P. Anderson, A. von eye, J. Almerigi, and R. Lerner (2004). Structural relations among spirituality, religiosity, and thriving in adolescence. *Applied Developmental Science* 9(1), 7–16; Kwilecki, S. (1999). *Becoming religious.* Cranbury, NJ: Associated University Press; Myers, B. K. (1997). *Young children and spirituality.* New York: Routledge. Pluralism Project, Harvard University, www.pluralism.org (2006) Scarlett, W. G. (2006); Toward a developmental analysis of religious and spiritual development. In E. C. Roehlkepartain, P. E. King, L. M. Wagener, and P. L. Benson, eds., *The handbook of spiritual development in childhood and adolescence.* Thousand Oaks, CA: Sage Publications, pp. 21–34; Smith, William C. (1998). *Faith and belief: The difference between them.* Oxford, UK: Oneword Publications.

Mona M. Abo-Zena and W. George Scarlett

Standardized Tests and Early Childhood Education

A test, as defined by the *Standards for Educational and Psychological Testing* (1999), is "an evaluative device or procedure in which a sample of an examinee's behavior in a specified domain is obtained and subsequently evaluated and scored using a standardized process." In test administration, standardization refers to "maintaining a constant testing environment and conducting the test according to detailed rules and specifications, so that testing conditions are the same for all test takers" (AERA, APA, and NCME, 1999).

The use of standardized tests with very young children has caused considerable controversy in the field of early childhood education and psychology (Dyer 1973; Shepard 1994). Educators of young children have raised concerns about the appropriateness of engaging young children in formal testing situations, the limitations of standardized test scores in describing young children's growth and development, and the use of test scores to evaluate the effectiveness of a range of programs that serve young children and their families.

In 1991, the Association for Childhood Education International (ACEI) issued a position statement that called for an immediate halt to "*all* testing of young children in preschool and in grades K-2 and the practice of testing every child in the later elementary years" (ACEI and Perrone, 1991). This position reflected the following several concerns:

- The inability of very young children to fully participate in most standardized assessment conditions, which require focused attention, a specific set of responses, and, in some instances, timed responses to a set format of questions and tasks. The major concern was whether young children were developmentally able to understand the task and to participate in standardized testing procedures.
- The failure of standardized test scores to provide classroom teachers with instructionally useful information about individual children, although the test scores were often used to make important inferences about the status of young children's growth and development.
- The use of potentially problematic inferences in making high-stakes decisions about children's entry into **kindergarten,** promotion and retention in the early grades, placement in special classes, etc., and
- The increasing pressure on early childhood educators to depart from what they considered sound curriculum practices to prepare children to take the tests.

A report to the National Education Goals Panel (Shepard et al., 1998) outlined the following set of general principles in early childhood assessment:

- Assessment should bring benefits for children.
- Assessments should be tailored to a specific purpose and should be reliable, valid, and fair for that purpose.
- Assessment policies should be designed recognizing that reliability and validity of assessments increase with children's age.
- Assessments should be age-appropriate in both content and the method of data collection.
- Assessments should be linguistically appropriate, recognizing that to some extent all assessments are measures of language.
- Parents should be a valued source of assessment information, as well as an audience for assessment results. (pp. 5–6)

In addition, the report presented four major assessment purposes: (1) to support learning, (2) identification of special needs, (3) for program evaluation and monitoring trends, and (4) for high-stakes accountability. However, the report cautioned that, "Before age 8, standardized achievement measures are not sufficiently accurate to be used for high-stakes decisions about individual children and schools. Therefore, high-stakes assessments intended for accountability purposes should be delayed until the end of third grade (or preferably fourth grade)" (Shepard et al., 1998, p. 21).

Ironically, as the movement to expand access to quality state-funded preschool education to all children grew in the 1990s, so did the calls for increased accountability and testing of young children. Under the **No Child Left Behind** Act of 2001, testing in reading and **mathematics** was required of all students in grades 3–8 by the 2005–2006 academic year. With sanctions in place for schools in which children's test scores did not indicate progress, programs for young children were under increasing pressure to "get children ready" for the third-grade assessments.

In addition, in September of 2003 the **Head Start** Bureau implemented its own pre-k standardized test. The Head Start National Reporting System (NRS) was the first nationwide skills test to be administered to over 400,000 four- and five-year-old children enrolled in Head Start–funded programs (Government Accountability Office, 2005).

The **National Association for the Education of Young Children** (NAEYC) and the National Association of Early Childhood Specialists in State Departments of Education (NAECSSDE) issued a revised position statement in which they called for appropriate use of standardized measures in the assessment of young children (NAEYC/NAECSSDE 2003). The 2003 position statement did not call for a halt to standardized testing of young children. Rather, the document outlined the following set of guidelines intended to promote appropriate use of standardized tests:

Considerations in using individual norm-referenced tests. In general, assessment specialists have urged great caution in the use and interpretation of standardized tests of young children's learning, especially in the absence of complementary evidence and when the stakes are potentially high (Jones, 2003; National Research Council, 1999; Scott-Little et al., 2003). All assessment activities should be guided by ethical standards of quality (AERA, APA, and NCME 1999). The issues are most pressing when individual norm-referenced tests are being considered as part of an assessment system. In those cases, the standards set forth in the joint statement of the American Educational Research Association, the American Psychological Association, and the National Center for Measurement in Education (AERA, APA, NCME, 1999) provide essential technical guidelines (NAEYC and NAECSSDE, 2003, p. 10).

Although controversy continues to surround the use of standardized tests with young children, it is important to remember that assessment can provide valuable information for teachers and parents. Attention is now being focused on the development of a new breed of instruments that are sensitive to young children's developmental levels as well as to variations in cultural and linguistic background and to the use of comprehensive assessment systems that include evidence of young children's development from standardized tests as well as well-designed classroom-based assessments. It is important, as well, for teacher preparation programs to include "assessment literacy" as a competence in early childhood programs.

Further Readings: ACEI and Perrone, V. (1991). *ACEI position paper on standardized testing.* Olney, Maryland: Association for Childhood Education International; AERA, APA, and NCME. (1999). *Standards for educational and psychological testing.* Washington, DC: American Educational Research Association; Dyer, H. S. (1973). Testing little children: some old problems in new settings. *Childhood Education* 49, 362–367; Government Accountability Office (2005). *Head Start: Further development could allow results of new test to be used for decision making.* Washington, DC: Government Accountability Office; NAEYC and NAECSSDE. (2003). *Early childhood curriculum, assessment, and program evaluation: Building an effective, accountable system in programs for children birth through age 8.* Washington, DC: National Association for the Education of Young Children; NAEYC and NAECSSDE. (2003b). *Early Childhood Curriculum, Assessment, and Program Evaluation: building an effective, accountable system in programs for children birth through 8 (with expanded resources).* Washington, DC: National Association for the Education of Young Children; Shepard, L. A. (1994). The challenges of assessing young children appropriately. *Phi Delta Kappan,* 75(6), 206–212; Shepard, L. A.,

S. L. Kagan, and Wurtz, E. (1998). *Principles and recommendations for early childhood assessments*. Washington, DC: National Education Goals Panel.

Jacqueline Jones

Standards

Early childhood stakeholders use the term *standards* to define a range of issues within the field, such as licensing standards, accreditation standards, standards of best practices, standards of quality, curriculum standards, performance standards, and proficiency standards. Moreover, the nation in which one is examining the issue of "standards" alters their definition, their history of development, their use by practitioners, and their effects on the lives of young children.

The term *standards* has particular significance within the context and the history of early childhood education (ECED) in the United States. Unlike many nations throughout the world, the United States does not have a national curriculum at any level of education. Local governments typically decide upon the educational policies, practices, and curricula of their communities. However, recent reform initiatives, such as the federal government's reauthorization of the Elementary and Secondary Education Act (ESEA) in 2002, commonly referred to as the **No Child Left Behind Act** (NCLB), have shifted the power over decisions about **curriculum**, **assessment**, and student proficiency from the local community to the federal and state governments. Yet, many early childhood education services in the United States exist outside of the confines of public education policy, particularly programs serving children ages birth to five. This intertwining structure of early education services and education reform complicates a definition of standards and the standards-based accountability (SBA) systems in early childhood education.

Defining Standards

Three types or forms of standards are typically utilized in U.S. early childhood education. *Content standards* refer to the knowledge and skills that students are to attain at particular points within their early childhood career. *Performance standards* define what assessment measures are to be used to determine whether the child is acquiring the content standards. *Proficiency standards* indicate how well the student must perform on that assessment measure to be deemed proficient in acquiring the content standard.

Dissecting the range of content, performance, and proficiency standards that exists in the field of ECED depends upon where the program is physically located, its funding agency, and the range of children it serves. For example, President George W. Bush's *Good Start, Grow Smart* initiative requires state agencies that receive federal dollars through programs such as the **Child Care and Development Fund** (CCDF) to develop a set of voluntary early learning guidelines or content standards for literacy, language, and math activities for children ages three to five. These early learning guidelines are to align with their state's K-12 content, performance, and proficiency standards (Office of the White House, 2002). State agencies currently decide how to implement these early learning standards and, in most instances, they affect only those programs that receive federal and/or state monies.

History

Understanding where these standards come from is as important as defining what they mean. Standards in early childhood education emerged from and in response to the trajectory of K-12 education reform.

While the idea of pursuing national curricula has existed in the United States since the Eisenhower Administration, the National Commission on Excellence in Education (NCEE) publication of *A Nation at Risk* (1984) spurred the first of three waves of reform that led to the current state of standards-based accountability reform in the United States. The importance of the NCEE's document is that it claimed that the United State's system of education was a systemic failure. To solve this problem, the commission recommended the implementation of rigorous academic standards and increased student performance requirements for such things as high school graduation and college admission.

While the Reagan Administration (1981–1989) reduced federal funding, support, and involvement in national education policy issues, the nation's governors, primarily in the South, through organizations such as the National Governor's Association (NGA) and the Southern Regional Educational Board (SREB) took up education reform and pursued initiatives that went beyond the recommendations of the NCEE. They promoted a second wave of reform that substituted less academic governance over local school districts, with increased accountability for student performance.

This rise in academic requirements and accountability measures that resulted from these two waves of reform intensified the educational demands of young children. In the latter half of the 1980s, school districts increased their use of readiness tests to determine whether students were prepared to enter kindergarten or first grade and districts escalated their curricular expectations for the early grades (e.g., Meisels, 1989). This emphasis on accountability and formal academic instruction in the early years led NAEYC to develop and eventually publish its guidelines for what it labels developmentally appropriate practices for young children (Bredekamp, 1987).

Even though publications from NAEYC and other research-based organizational responses (e.g., American Educational Research Association, the American Psychological Association, and the National Council on Measurement in Education, 1999) helped delineate the appropriate curricular and assessment expectations for young children, policy makers continued to position ECED as an educational tool to "ready" students for academic learning in K-12 schooling. For instance, President H. W. Bush (1989–1993) with the support of the NGA promoted national education goals, which included the call for voluntary national standards and assessments. While President Bush's **National Education Goals Panel**'s (NEGP's) *America 2000* legislation failed, President Clinton incorporated these goals into his administration's *Goals 2000* legislation. For both of these policies, the first goal was for all students by the year 2000 to start school ready to learn.

The *Goals 2000* legislation and the reauthorization of the federal government's Elementary and Secondary Education Act in 1994 titled the *Improving American School Act* (IASA), reframed readiness through the context of standard-based accountability reform, the third wave of reform. Polices at the federal and state levels that followed this legislation led to the development of content, performance, and proficiency standards in various subject areas. Originally, this wave of reform promoted the implementation of "world-class" content standards and the use of performance-based assessments, which asks students to perform an activity or a task to demonstrate their understanding of the question. Controversy over cost and the reliability of the administration of performance-based assessments led to their demise. Multiple choice, fill-in-the-blank, and short-answer standardized tests replaced them. Similarly, the federal government began to examine the idea of including "opportunity to learn" standards with the *Goals 2000* legislation, which would set basic requirements for providing resources, funding, and training to insure that all students receive equal access to the conditions and resources for learning (Lewis, 1995). However, controversy over funding and the reach of the federal government into local issues defeated such proposals.

Current "Standards" Requirements in the Various States

In spite of continuing controversies, standards-based reforms at the state and local level now shape curricular and performance expectations of young children as early as age three. Moreover, the NCLB Act of 2002 escalated this demand for SBA reform in America's K–12 school systems. For instance, NCLB requires that by 2006 each state have content, performance, and proficiency standards for each grade level for grades 3–8 in reading and math. Moreover, states must have academic standards in science that cover grade spans 3–5, 6–9, and 10–12, and by 2007–2008, the state must administer annual assessments in science at least once in grades 3–5, 6–9, and 10–12 to assess student proficiency levels. Failure to achieve NCLB's demands for improved annual yearly performance in reading, math, and science for all students in grades 3–8 will result in a series of sanctions for the school, the district, and the state while invoking a series of choice options for the students.

In addition to NCLB, some state departments of education (e.g., Texas and Florida) or local school districts (e.g., Chicago) use these standardized **assessments** to determine whether students meet that agency's proficiency standards. Third-grade students who fail to meet these states' or districts' proficiency standards can be retained. Such a result is referred to as a high-stakes consequence.

Thus, as this demand for annual yearly progress advances for students in K–12 education, schools, districts, and state departments of education will pay further attention to what types of learning experiences students are having before they enter the third grade.

For children ages 3–5, the type of standards that exists is dependent upon the specific program and its funding agency. For instance, beginning with their

2004–2005 biennium budget requests for federal funds through the CCDF block grant, state agencies had to include a plan for establishing voluntary early learning guidelines or content standards in literacy, language, pre-reading and numeracy skills for children ages 3 to 5 that align with the state's K-12 standards. Currently, forty-three states have these early learning guidelines for preschool and prekindergarten programs in place. Additionally, in 2003, the *Good Start Grow Smart* initiative required agencies that operate **Head Start** programs to implement the Head Start Outcomes Framework, which includes 100 indicators of what children in Head Start should know and be able to do when they leave the program to enter kindergarten. Head Start also developed its controversial National Reporting System, which uses an assessment tool to measure students' literacy and math skills.

Future of Standards in ECED

As standards-based reforms become a permanent fixture of early childhood education, organizations (e.g., the **National Association for the Education of Young Children** [NAEYC] and the National Association of Early Childhood Specialist in State Departments of Education, 2002; National Institute for Early Education Research) and early childhood researchers (e.g., Kagan and Scott-Little, 2004) have outlined guidelines for and raised issues about developing early learning standards for young children.

These organizations and researchers hope that by developing early learning standards stakeholders will make a sincere effort to develop a continuous system of ECED for the child from birth through elementary school. Unfortunately, implementing SBA reform in the current structure of ECED in the United States has the potential to split early childhood programs into two distinct systems: publicly funded systems that must adhere to state and federal SBA reforms and a private system that must only meet licensure regulations.

A primary concern of these organizations and researchers is that current policies, such as the Bush administration's *Good Start, Grow Smart* initiative, fail to address all areas of a child's development—cognitive, language, physical, social, and emotional. Fostering a child's emotional, regulatory, and social development skills is important in assisting that child to develop into a curious, confident, and persistent student in the classroom (Bowman et al., 2000).

Furthermore, standards fail to address such issues as the funding disparity that exists between early childhood programs and the fostering of professional development so that all children have high-quality early learning experiences. Research makes clear that such experiences provide an immediate and lasting effect on a child's academic and life experiences.

Finally, the history of SBA reform raises the question over the use of assessment measures to evaluate students and programs. Currently K–12 SBA reforms use student performance data to evaluate the effectiveness of their programs, teacher qualifications, and student learning. If ECED follows this trend, many fear SBA reform will resurrect the concerns that arose in the 1980s over appropriate curriculum, **readiness** tests, and approaches to **curriculum**, and stakeholders will fail to use these assessments to foster child and program development (Kagan and Scott-Little, 2004).

The challenge for the field of early childhood education is to find a means to work with diverse stakeholders to ensure that these policies create a system that actually promotes continuous improvement for children birth through grade 3. Such a system that enables all students to reach the defined proficiency standards, assesses progress toward those benchmarks, and uses results to improve the performance of all members of the system, can only be developed if policy makers proceed with caution (Baker, 2002). *See also* Curriculum, Emotional Development; Standardized Tests and Early Childhood Education.

Further Readings: American Educational Research Association, American Psychological Association, and National Council on Measurement in Education. (1999). *Standards for educational and psychological testing.* Washington, DC: American Educational Research Association; Baker, E. L. (2002). The struggle to reform education: Exploring the limits of policy metaphors. CSE Technical Report 576. Los Angeles: University of California, National Center for Research on Evaluation, Standards, and Student Testing; Bowman, B. T., M. S. Donovan, and M. S. Burns (2000). *Eager to learn: Educating our preschoolers.* Washington, DC: National Academy Press; Bredekamp, S., ed. (1987). *Developmentally appropriate practice in early childhood programs serving children birth through age 8.* Washington, DC: National Association for the Education of Young Children; Kagan, S. L., C. Scott-Little (2004). Early learning standards: Changing the parlance and practice of early childhood education. *Phi Delta Kappan* 85, 388–396; Lewis, A. C. (1995). An overview of the standards movement. *Phi Delta Kappan* 76, 744–751; Meisels, S. J. (1989). High stakes testing in kindergarten. *Educational Leadership* 46, 16–22; National Association for the Education of Young Children, and National Association of Early Childhood Specialist in State Departments of Education (2002). *Early learning standards: Creating conditions for success.* Available online at http://naecs.crc.uiuc.edu/position/creating_conditions.pdf; Accessed March 20, 2004; National Commission on Excellence in Education (1984). *A Nation at Risk: The Full Account.* Cambridge, MA: USA Research; Office of the Whitehouse (2002). *Good start, grow smart: The Bush Administration's early childhood initiative.* Available online at http://www.whitehouse.gov/infocus/earlychildhood/sect1.html.

Christopher Brown

State Licensing Standards

The licensing of early care and education programs in the United States is authorized by law in each of the fifty states and the District of Columbia. Licensing rules set each state's floor, or foundation, of acceptable quality. Programs below that floor will not be permitted to exist. Other types of standards defining other levels of quality also apply.

Each of the licensing rules is a right that children and parents have to a defined level of quality, backed up by the state in its policies for responding to complaints. The rules must be met by all private centers and home-based early childhood programs as defined by the state, regardless of subsidy. They are used to implement a basic consumer protection principle, "First, do no harm." Licensing policy is intended to reduce the risk of harm from fire, unsafe buildings or equipment, spread of epidemic disease, any form of disaster, and developmental impairment.

The licensing laws often abolish early care and education programs altogether, then restore the right to operate such a program only to those who have state permission. Requiring a license is a powerful intervention by government on behalf of children and their families. Balancing this power, operators of programs have many rights to be treated fairly.

The word "standards" in this article is used generically to include all the varying terms that are used in connection with state law, federal law, and professional guidance. Mandatory standards for licensing are usually called "requirements" or "rules and regulations." There is no common use of many other regulatory terms, such as guideline, registration, and certification, since some states and the federal government use them differently.

The Licensing Rules

The licensing law in each state specifies what rules may be written by the agency. The rules cover all aspects of a program—building and grounds, equipment, qualifications of teachers, directors, and family child care providers; health and safety procedures, the program of activities, schedule, developmental curriculum, discipline, and the role of parents.

Prior to granting a license, the states usually require a building safety inspection and approval, a public health inspection and approval, and initial criminal records checks of licensees and their employees. These baseline approvals linked to the license are part of the necessary floor. The licensing rules themselves are usually established as "minimums," which means "at least." They are not program specifications because programs are encouraged and expected to go beyond what is required. They are not ideals because there are serious penalties for failing to meet them. Licensing requirements differ from other types of standards because they have the force of law. As with any law, enforcement requires strong public support.

Most States rewrite their rules fairly frequently. Since they do not all make their changes in the same month or year, any comparison of the states' rules must be made as of the same date to be accurate. Comparative data that are in print are probably incorrect. Updated comparisons are posted on the Web site of the National Child Care Information Center (NCCIC) (http://nccic.org,)

Task forces or advisory groups within the state reach consensus on proposed rules, usually based on new research findings, changes in the field of practice, and comparative data on what other states are doing. Their consensus-building process is essential to enforcement of the rules. Rule-writing groups compare their state's rules with current rules in other states to identify where their own rules need strengthening, and to see how their own state ranks with other states. The rules themselves are posted on the Web site of the National Resource Center for the Health and Safety of Children in Child Care (NRC) (http://nrc). Over time, the level of quality in the field tends to improve as a result of funding, accreditation, training, college scholarships, and consumer demand.

When new rules are being considered, many existing programs may already meet a higher standard. When a proposed new rule is controversial, the states may grandfather the rule (permit existing programs to waive it), or they may grandmother the rule (set a later date by which all programs must meet it.) The rules most likely to create controversy are those that affect cost, particularly staffing ratios, group size, and the qualifications of staff.

Licensing as policy is typically American, with its emphasis on regulating private services. Rather than operating services by government, and rather than relying entirely on forces in the private market to create an acceptable supply of services, these state laws have created a third possibility, a *regulated market*. Early care and education in the United States is not affordable for all children. However, children at all income levels are protected through licensing.

Levels of quality in early care and education programs

Types of Regulation	Standards Used	Levels of Quality
Continuous improvement	Expert Guidance Standards Curriculum Guidelines, Departments of Education	Excellent level to guide continuous improvement
Credential	Standards for credential for roles in the field	Good to excellent
Accreditation by professional organization	Standards for accreditation	Good to excellent
Tiered funding	Funding source establishes two or more levels of quality	Good
Rate setting	Enable programs to meet funding standards	Good
Quality rating	Research rating scale	Rating scores from good enough to excellent
Licensing and other required approvals	Minimum ("at least") level of quality acceptable to the state	Good enough to reduce risk of harm.

Different types of standards

Type of Standard	Applied To?	By What Agency	Using What Power?
Licensing Requirements	All children in all programs defined in the licensing law	State licensing agency, sometimes delegated to county	Power of the people delegated from the Legislature
Funding Specifications	All programs receiving a particular funding stream	Administering agency of the funding stream	Contract agreement
Program accreditation	Programs meeting a higher professional standard	National professional organization, or state	Contract agreement that allows the program to display the accreditation

Type of Standard	Applied To?	By What Agency	Using What Power?
Tiered levels of quality	Programs recognized at a higher level than licensing	Licensing agency, funding agency, or a collaboration	Contract agreement with source of subsidy or quality initiative
Teacher license	All teachers in public schools	State Department of Education	DOE ability to enforce without waivers varies
Specialized early childhood credential	Staff who earn the credential	National Department of Labor; Child Development Associate (CDA); or state credential for a role	Power or the reputation of the credential. May be a licensing requirement
Higher education degrees	Directors or teachers in early childhood programs in states that require degrees	Degree granted by accredited colleges, checked by licensing agency	Delegated power under the licensing law

Coverage

In 1994, states licensed 117,284 centers, and 300,032 homes. If a program is not required to be licensed, but receives state or federal dollars, the state may require it either to apply for a voluntary license, or meet the licensing rules, or meet higher standards to receive funding.

All states cover full-day centers, but a few do not cover part-day programs. School system, public, private, or even faith-based schools are usually not covered by the licensing agency. The states' Departments of Education have been considered responsible for their quality.

Fourteen states exempt faith-based early childhood centers that apply for and are granted an exemption. Most exempt faith-based programs do have to meet some state standards for health and safety. Only one state exempts programs that are accredited by or are members of an organization that has its own accreditation standards.

Large family child care homes, usually seven or more unrelated children with more than one caregiver, are covered in most states. Licensing is seldom applied to small family child care homes when only one or two children are included. The caregiver's own children are usually counted in the number. Care by a child's parent or relatives is not required to be licensed, although funding standards may apply to it.

Ratios and Group Sizes

Since 1986, states have moved toward greater uniformity in their staffing requirements for the youngest age groups. For children at age nine months, the child/staff ratio in 2004 is 4:1 in thirty-five states, with a group size limited to eight in twenty states. No state has a ratio greater than 6:1. In 1986, ratios varied up to 12:1; and thirty-five states either permitted groups larger than eight or did not regulate group size at all. Ratios varied up to 12:1. The shift to smaller ratios for infants has been gradual, and the shift to setting limits on group size has been even slower. There are still eleven states that do not limit the size of groups of nine-month-old infants.

Toddler staffing patterns have also been improved across the states, although not as rapidly as those for infants. However, as children become two, there is cause for concern that staffing may not adequately protect children in all states. When children are twenty-seven months old, there is wide variability of rules. There is no ratio for children at this age that is the same in more than nine states. Other states divide in more or less equal numbers, ratios of 8:1; 7:1, 6:1; 5:1 and 10:1.

There is a little greater consistency in staffing requirements for four-year-olds. The largest number of states, seventeen, require a group size of twenty with two caregivers. Twenty-three states permit groups of thirty or more. In most states, the staffing requirements result in at least two teachers/caregivers in each group. However, in fourteen of the states, one qualified person without an assistant can be solely in charge of fifteen or more four-year-olds.

Alternative Qualifications

Staff qualifications in state licensing rules for early childhood programs usually require one or both of two different types of professional preparation: (1) preservice qualifications for specific roles: degrees, courses, credit hours, or credentials prior to employment in the role; (2) specified number of hours of training for all staff in all roles every year.

The content of both pre-service and annual continuing education is primarily child development or early childhood education. Two-year degrees with that specialization are offered at many public community colleges or technical colleges, but four-year degree programs with early childhood specialization are more rare. At the four-year level, the early childhood degrees are likely to be in private colleges, making articulation with the two-year programs difficult.

A single requirement of a four-year degree in child development would have to be widely waived. There are not enough college degree programs to meet this specification. States sometimes accept degrees in "related fields." Other states may require graduates in related fields to have course credits in early care and education and/or direct experience with young children as well as the degree.

States usually identify a number of alternative ways of meeting their required qualifications for roles. Some of the alternatives permit some direct service experience to substitute for some of the academic qualifications. States use these alternatives both to avoid granting waivers and also to ensure that individuals have knowledge of children younger than kindergarten age.

Annual ongoing training may be counted by teachers as pre-service training for the director role, or by assistants as pre-service training for teaching or other roles; but it is not, by definition, pre-service preparation for the role a person already fills. Only thirteen states require twenty or more hours of training every year. A handful of states require a larger number of hours every other year, so that one credit-bearing course could be used to meet the rule. Community-based training is beginning to be offered for credit.

The qualifications for directors are strongly focused on child growth and development and early childhood education. Only twenty-six states, roughly half, even mention additional administrative content among their qualifications for training for directors. Seven of them have developed a director credential.

The minimum alternative qualification is the least required amount of academic coursework, or specialized education in early care and education. Direct experience with young children under qualified supervision is not counted as an educational pre-service qualification, because it is not an educational qualification.

For directors, the range of alternative ways of qualifying, across the states, is from two ways to eighteen ways. One state has only one alternative. Qualifications in early care and education are higher for directors than for teachers. Only three states set no educational requirements for directors. Some states set more stringent pre-service qualifications for directors of larger centers. The range of the minimum alternatives for directors is as follows:

Minimum alternative director qualifications, 2004

Minimum Pre-service Educational Alternative	Number of States	% of States
Pre-service only	6	12%
Pre-service and annual ongoing training	32	62%
Only annual ongoing training	10	19%

Pre-service minimums may be college degree or certificate programs, courses or credits, or clock hours of training. The highest academic alternatives for directors are as follows:

Highest alternative director qualifications, 2004

Maximum Pre-service Educational Alternative	Number of States	% of States
MA/MS/PhD	6	12%
BA/BS	29	57%
AA/AS	4	8%
CDA credential	0	0%
Specified number of college credits short of degree	7	13%
State director credential	4	8%
Ongoing annual hours of training only	1	2%
	51	100%

For teachers, too, there were a number of alternatives, ranging to eight options. Twenty-nine states had either no academic qualifications, or required only a high school degree with direct experience or basic orientation for teachers. Some states link an alternative to a size of center, that is, requiring that larger centers must employ some percentage or some required number.

Minimum alternative qualifications, all teachers 2004

Minimum Alternative	Number Of States	Percent Of States
Bachelor's degree	1	02 %
Associate's degree	0	0
Child Development Associate	11	21%
College credit hours	6	12%
Clock hours prior to employment	2	04%
Two-year vocational early childhood program	3	05%
No training qualifications other than basic orientation	29	57%
	51 states	100%

Maximum alternative pre-service qualifications, teachers and master teachers 2004

Maximum Academic Alternative	Number Of States	% Of States
MA/MS	3	5%
BA/BS or "higher" degree	16	31%
AS	5	9%
CDA credential	4	8%
Specified number of college credits short of degree	8	15%
State DOE certification as public school teacher or other	5	9%
State Credential or Approved Training Programs	12	23%
Ongoing only	51	100%

Fourteen states identify two levels of teachers. They may call the more qualified teachers group supervisor, lead teachers, or other name, and require one of them for a specified number of children, such as every forty-five children. These "master teachers" are not included in the table of minimum alternatives because they are not the lowest alternative for a teacher.

A small number of states now issue an official certificate of some kind to teachers and directors in licensed programs so that their qualifications are portable to other licensed programs. At least twenty-two states have established registries that track a person's changing qualifications. Five states mention some state-level credential or approved training program among the maximum alternatives for teachers. Teacher licenses are seldom mentioned.

Tiered Strategies

A recent approach both to personnel qualifications and to program standards is to define different levels of quality, and to offer supports and incentives to help programs and their employees move to higher levels of quality. Thirty-five states have adopted tiered quality improvement strategies for centers, and thirty-two have adopted them for family child care homes. Some examples of innovation, implemented differently in different states, are

state financial support for accreditation;
bonus incentives for teachers to add to their qualifications;
scholarship help to individuals employed in early care and education programs;
funding incentives for programs to reach defined higher levels of quality;
new credentials, for infants/toddlers, directors, and teachers;
registries of personnel and their updated qualifications;
rated licenses; and
tiered funding levels in subsidy policy.

These new policies represent an enormous stride forward for states in implementing both their licensing rules and their funding standards through interagency collaboration. The first few states to develop differentiated rates identified two levels of program quality: the required licensing level and accreditation. Finding that the gap between the two was difficult for programs to bridge, some of the states invented middle levels of quality that take into account the record of compliance and set progressively lower ratios and higher staff qualifications.

The higher levels of quality are not enforced through the use of licensing power, but rely on contract agreements. A program that cannot maintain its level will keep its license, but may not keep its quality rating or its funding level. To implement this kind of policy, someone must go to the program, determine their level, and connect them to sources of help. The early childhood licensing staff may be the visitors to recommend approval as meeting a higher level, in addition to their licensing responsibilities, or states may design other models for implementing these policies.

Case Loads for Licensors

Compliance with licensing rules is significantly higher if someone from the licensing office routinely inspects the licensed center or home. In some states the case loads are so high that it is unlikely that the licensee will be visited during the period covered by the license. In other states, an adequate number of staff are able to visit regularly, issue correction orders, follow up to see that corrections were made, and investigate complaints.

Most licensees want to meet the licensing rules. When visits are rare, they may slip out of compliance when distracted by other urgent issues. There is a very small number of programs that have no intention of complying with the rules. They may enroll more children than their license permits, and conceal broken equipment and fire hazards. They will be out of compliance, come into compliance temporarily after a licensing visit, and then fail to comply again and again. Unless there is adequate staff and legal power to follow up, this small group of noncomplying programs will be permitted to continue to create risks for children.

Examples of states with large case loads of centers are Massachusetts, Maine, and Minnesota. States with much smaller case loads are Florida, South Carolina, and Oklahoma. These states have employed enough staff to carry out their licensing responsibilities, and also to inspect for tiered levels of quality. By creating a single system for visiting programs, the state can have adequate staff to enforce the licensing rules and also to implement funding levels and quality incentives.

History

The first of the states to write a licensing law for children's services was Pennsylvania in 1883. Prior to that time, many states had voluntary standards that were advisory, not mandatory. Pennsylvania pioneered the first real licensing law for children. Other states began to adopt this enforceable type of law. Early care and education programs were not subsidized other than by private charity.

In most states infants and toddlers were prohibited altogether from programs until the mid-1960s. As these states began to permit programs to include these vulnerable age groups, they set ratios and group size low to avoid plentiful but harmful services.

However, other states already had a large number of existing programs with high numbers of infants per staff, and large groups. As these states tried to write more stringent rules, existing programs feared that rules would add higher costs to parents and reduce the supply of services. It took many years for states to resolve issues between costs, supply, and potential harm.

In 1962, most of the states without such laws enacted one in anticipation that the federal government would require it as a condition for funding. There has been a clear emphasis on child development in the licensing rules for all children, stressing the inseparability of strands of cognitive, emotional, social, and physical development since the 1930s.

Research on the effectiveness of programs for poor children received widespread public attention in the 1960s. Head Start was created in 1965 as a federally managed comprehensive program for poor children and their families, with its own performance standards. In 1967, open-ended federal funding under the Social Security Act became available for child care. Standards for funding became an issue.

In the 1967 Social Security Act, the Congress mandated "a common set of program standards" for all programs receiving federal dollars. Federal Interagency Day Care Requirements (FIDCR) were written. FIDCR history was characterized by controversy, revised versions, increasing distrust among advocates, and decreasing numbers of participating federal agencies.

Part of the controversy stemmed from confusion over the difference between state licensing and federal funding standards. Some of the licensed programs feared that FIDCR would apply to all programs for all children, without funding. To add to their confusion, child advocates wanted the federal government to set standards for all children, rather than funding standards for some children. However, federal interagency standards were very clearly standards for funding.

Debates became polarized, pitting "quality" federal standards versus "minimum state standards." Federal standards were finally abolished by the Congress. Later, in 1991, Congress mandated that federal Child Care and Development funds must be spent in programs that meet "health and safety" standards. More important, they also mandated that a percentage of the funds be set aside for "quality improvement."

Trends

The federal funds for quality improvements under CCDBG led to a decade of innovative new policies and interagency collaborative efforts. Thirty-five states have implemented innovative policies that recognize a progression of levels of quality. In at least some of the states, debate has moved from polarized arguments over "quality" versus "minimum" to defining levels of quality, and collaborating across agencies to help programs move to higher levels. Licensing offices have moved from exclusive focus on baseline permits to a broader state vision for levels of quality implemented collaboratively.

In some states, the laws for licensing now express the states' broader vision. Moving from licensing to state goals for quality goes beyond the power delegated for licensing, but not beyond the power of the state. Agencies that administer child care funds can offer incentives in contract agreements.

Issues for the Future

The peculiarities of U.S. policy, with licensing for all children but subsidy only for poor families, will continue to affect their implementation. It is clear that a collaboration between licensing and funding policy can result in better licensing and also higher levels of quality. It is an open question, and probably a question to the Congress, whether quality initiatives in the future will be for all children, or whether a narrower focus on poor children will dominate.

Federal funding for future quality initiatives is uncertain after 2004. If funds continue, most states will create or continue their innovations, and new models will emerge for implementing them. Without continued available funding, these initiatives could lose momentum at least temporarily. States that are paying more for higher quality will badly need to create or improve accountable ways of determining the quality level of programs.

Professional development planning groups in the states have made substantial progress in creating career pathways and a lattice across all the different roles that are filled by early childhood professionals. There is work to be done in some states to integrate these policies with the teacher license granted by the Department of Education for one of the roles.

Progress has been made in articulating levels of education from entry level up to the two-year degree. Articulation between that degree and a four-year degree in the same field is much more difficult. Higher education will need to offer more degree programs, better articulation and much better advisement for those who work with children at these younger ages.

Further Readings: American Academy of Pediatrics, American Public Health Association, and the National Resource Center for the Health and Safety of Children in Child Care. (2002) *Caring for our children: National Health and Safety Performance Standards: Guidelines for Out-of-Home Child Care Programs,* 2nd ed. Elk Grove Village, IL: AAP; Collins, Judy, Sarah LeMoine, and Gwen Morgan. (2004). *Child Care Licensing Trends.* Vienna, VA: NCCIC. Class, Norris. Levels of Standards. Presentation at NAEYC Conference. Seattle, Washington, November 1973; Class, Norris E., and Richard Orton (1980). Day care regulation: The limits of licensing. *Young Children* (September), 12–16; Gormley, W. T. (1991). Day care in a federal system. *Social Service Review* (December), 582–596; Lazar, Irving R., H. M. Darlington, J. Royce Murray, and A. Snipper (1982). "Lasting effects of early education: A report from the Consortium for Longitudinal Studies." *Monographs of the Society for Research in Child Development,* 47I: Serial No. 201; Morgan, G. (1996). Licensing and accreditation: How much quality is quality? In Susan Bredekamp and Barbara A. Willer, eds., *NAEYC accreditation: A decade of learning and the years ahead.* pp. 129–138; USHEW, Office of the Assistant Secretary for Planning and Evaluation (1977). Policy Issues in Day care: *Summaries of 21 papers.*

Gwen Morgan

State Prekindergarten Programs

State prekindergarten programs are state-funded initiatives in the United States that provide classroom-based early education services to young children prior to kindergarten entry. The structure and focus of these programs vary among the states. In most cases they are voluntary preschool programs provided free of charge to eligible children three to four years of age. Although usually administered by the state Department of Education, in many states prekindergarten programs may be located in public or private schools, community-based organizations, within Head Start programs or in other settings. Some states have chosen to create their own prekindergarten program (e.g., North Carolina's "More at Four") while others have contributed state funds to supplement federal Head Start funding. Both approaches are considered state prekindergarten programs since they are state-funded educational programs for three- to four-year-olds. In each case, state-funded programs increase the supply of early education programs in the state.

During the last twenty years, many states in the United States have adopted or expanded their prekindergarten program to promote children's school readiness and eventual academic success (as depicted in the figure). Prior to 1980, only seven states funded programs. By the early 1990s, this number had grown to twenty-seven states serving 290,000 children. By 1998, forty states had prekindergarten programs, serving more than 700,000 children. Less growth has been seen in recent years, which may be due to the budget crises states are facing.

A primary rationale for both the development and expansion of state prekindergarten programs has been the promotion of children's school readiness and later school success. Research on school readiness and early intervention programs has

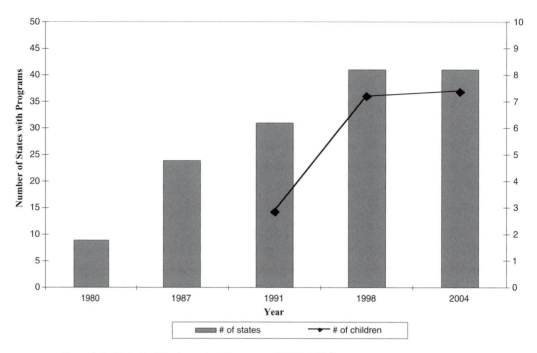

Growth in State PreKindergarten Programs (1980–2004)
Sources: Adams and Sandfort (1994); Barnett et al. (2003); NIEER (2004). Data on the exact number of children enrolled in state prekindergarten programs was not available for 1980 or 1987.

fueled this national attention. In particular, studies of children entering kindergarten have found that family risk factors (e.g., low maternal education, welfare dependency, low income) are associated with lower proficiency in early reading, math, and general knowledge. This is consistent with earlier findings that low-income children are less likely to arrive at school ready and are more likely to be educationally disadvantaged or have difficulty in school. For many policy makers, this learning gap upon school entry indicates a need to intervene earlier in children's lives. Evidence from early intervention, such as the Perry Preschool Program, Abecedarian Project, and Chicago Child–Parent Centers, demonstrates that one way to better prepare children for kindergarten is to offer school readiness skills in high-quality preschool settings. This approach has been demonstrated to be cost-effective, producing far greater gains for society than the cost of the investment, and thereby providing an economic incentive to invest early in children's lives (see Shonkoff and Phillips, 2000).

This push for school readiness was manifest in national policy in 1989 when President Bush and the nation's governors announced six national education goals, the first being, "By the year 2000, all children in America will start school ready to learn." This goal included three objectives—one of which was as follows: "All children will have access to high-quality and developmentally appropriate preschool programs that help prepare children for school." And the states have responded. Today, the vast majority of states fund a prekindergarten program.

Yet most state programs serve only a small percentage of children or only fund a part-day program that fails to meet the needs of parents who work full-time. A recent survey of state prekindergarten programs by the National Institute for Early Education Research (NIEER) (Barnett et al., 2004) concluded that only 10 percent of the nation's three- to four-year-olds were enrolled in state prekindergarten programs and that the vast majority of these children are four-year-olds in the year prior to kindergarten.

Most states do not offer access to all preschool-aged children, choosing to target their prekindergarten programs to children in low-income families or those who have other factors that place them at greatest risk of educational difficulties and school failure. A few states, however, have established or are taking steps toward establishing universal prekindergarten. For example, Georgia currently provides funding for all four-year olds, while Oklahoma reimburses school districts (that choose to provide prekindergarten) for all four-year-olds. New York has also established a universal prekindergarten program. However, the program has not received funding increases as originally scheduled, so it generally remains available only to children in low-income families and children who have other risk factors.

NIEER concluded that all states need to improve their quality standards for prekindergarten programs. For example, only 18 states required prekindergarten teachers to have the four-year college degree that every state requires of kindergarten teachers and that has been recommended by the National Research Council for every preschool education classroom. NIEER also found that although total state spending for state-funded prekindergarten exceeded $2.5 billion in 2002–2003, three-fifths of this spending was from five states—California, Georgia, New Jersey, New York, and Texas. Also, in most states, spending per child was too low to ensure quality.

The NIEER report identified three states with exemplary prekindergarten programs: Georgia, Oklahoma, and New Jersey. Interestingly, each state uses a different approach to finance and structure its program. Georgia offers preschool in a range of early childhood settings to all four-year-old children, funded by lottery funds, but does not require that teachers have a bachelor's degree. Oklahoma has a universal program for four-year-olds that is based on district-level provision of prekindergarten. As a result, the program is not available everywhere in the state. All preschool teachers are certified and receive the same salaries and benefits as other public school teachers. State funding is provided through the regular education funding formula, which lends financial stability to the program. New Jersey's "Abbott District" preschool program provides prekindergarten services to both three- and four-year-olds in the state's largest and most disadvantaged school districts. The program is the combined result of a court order and legislation. The "Abbott District" preschool program requires the highest standards in the nation (e.g., a certified teacher who is paid a public school salary, and an assistant teacher in each class of fifteen children). New Jersey also provides funds for half-day preschool to 102 other school districts, with somewhat lower quality standards.

Other states continue to expand their state prekindergarten programs. In 2006, the majority of state legislatures increased funding for their state's prekindergarten program—resulting in a cumulative $14.1 billion across the fifty states and the District of Columbia (PreKnow, 2006). It is the hope of many child advocates that these state prekindergarten programs will continue to be critical building blocks of the early care and education system in the United States. *See also* Preschool/Prekindergarten Programs.

Further Readings: Adams, G. (1994). *First steps, promising futures: State prekindergarten initiatives in the early 1990s.* Washington, DC: Children's Defense Fund, Barnett, W. S., K. B., Robin, J. T. Hustedt, and K. L. Schulman (2004). *The state of preschool: 2004 state preschool yearbook.* Rutgers, NJ: The National Institute for Early Education Research; Children's Defense Fund (2003). Key facts in child care, early education, and school-age care. Washington, DC: Author; Lee, V. E., and D. T. Burkam (2002). Inequality at the starting gate: Social background differences in achievement as children begin school. Washington, DC: Economic Policy Institute; Mitchell, A., et al. (1998). Early childhood programs and the public schools: Between promise and practice. Dover, MA: Auburn House Publishing Company; National Child Care Information Center (June 2004). *Information products: State funded prekindergarten initiatives.* Available online at www.nccic.org; PreKnow (2006). *Votes count: Legislative action on Pre-K, Fiscal Year 2006.* Washington, DC: Author; Shonkoff, J., and D. Phillips (2000). *From neurons to neighborhoods: The science of early childhood development.* Washington, DC: National Academy Press.

Elizabeth Rigby

Steiner, Rudolf (1861–1925)

Rudolf Steiner is best known as the founder of the Waldorf School movement (see **Waldorf Education**). Arising from the social chaos of post–World War I Germany, Waldorf Education sought to establish a school, open to all children, that would set a foundation for social and cultural renewal. Steiner also made fundamental contributions to the fields of medicine, social theory, art, movement, pharmacology, agriculture, architecture, and theology.

Steiner was born in 1861 in Kraljevek, now known as Croatia, to Austrian parents. In 1889 he moved to Weimar, Germany, where he edited the scientific works of Johann Wolfgang von Goethe. In Weimar he was able to meet many of the prominent artists, thinkers, and cultural figures of his time. After receiving a Doctorate in Philosophy at the University of Rostock in Germany in 1891, Dr. Steiner lectured extensively on a new science of the spirit, which he called Anthroposophy (wisdom or knowledge of man). Anthroposophy attempts to generate a "science of the spirit," broadening materialistic views of nature and humankind to learn to perceive the forces that work within and behind them. In 1894, Steiner wrote one of his seminal works, *A Philosophy of Freedom* (published in German as *Die Philosophie der Freiheit*). In this book, he sets out to describe how the human ability to think creatively and intuitively can be a liberatory act, allowing us to move beyond mere materialism.

Following the chaos and destruction of World War I, Steiner began lecturing and writing about social renewal. From 1919 until his death in 1925 he lectured to a wide variety of groups across Europe. He guided the renewal of many areas of human, social, cultural, and scientific activities, including art, education, sciences, social life, medicine, pharmacology, therapies, agriculture, architecture, and theology. Steiner's guidance resulted in many practical endeavors such as sculpting and painting influenced by Goethe's theories of color and form, Waldorf Education, the Camphill movement, biodynamic agriculture, and Anthroposophic medicine and remedies. Rudolf Steiner helped to develop new techniques for painting, modeling, sculpting, and a new form of movement known as eurythmy—a way to make speech and music visible. His lectures about social life led to the formation of the worldwide Camphill movement. First established in Scotland in 1940 and based on Steiner's ideas, there are now more than ninety Camphill communities in twenty-two countries around the world. Camphill communities house and work therapeutically with children, youth, and adults who have developmental disabilities. Volunteer coworkers live, learn, and work together with disabled people in a self-sustaining community. Residents live in extended family settings where relationships are cultivated. Volunteers and residents perform meaningful work together such as candle making, stained glass, bookbinding, weaving, woodworking, and biodynamic farming. Biodynamic agriculture is based on a series of lectures by Rudolf Steiner encouraging farmers to work actively with the forces of nature, free of chemicals. Lectures by Dr. Steiner inspired the development of a new practice of medicine. This holistic approach attempts to work out of an integrated image of the whole human being in illness and health.

In 1919, Rudolf Steiner was asked to give a series of lectures to help guide the opening of a new school for children of the workers of the Waldorf-Astoria cigarette factory in Stuttgart, Germany. Steiner subsequently became the director of this first "Waldorf" school, a position he held until his death in 1925. There are now more than 600 Waldorf schools all over the world. Waldorf education attempts to educate the whole child: head, heart, and hands. Through imbuing lessons with each of these elements children are helped in developing their own innate capacities. On the basis of Steiner's notions of child development, Waldorf kindergartens are distinctive in their belief that early childhood is a time for the development of the physical organism rather than the cognitive abilities of the young child. Waldorf kindergartens and nursery classes are founded upon Steiner's recognition that the child absorbs a host of sense impressions and naturally imitates them. The attitudes of caregivers as well as the physical environment have profound influences upon the child. Thus, a great deal of care is given to create a warm, nurturing environment filled with objects from the natural world. The curriculum reflects the rhythms of the natural world rather than the intellectual work of learning to read and write. Teachers of Waldorf kindergartens and nursery classes are specifically trained in the development of the young child, with a strong emphasis on the importance of story, song, and movement for the nurturance of the young child.

Rudolf Steiner left a huge body of work. During his lifetime he wrote twenty books, gave over six thousand lectures (most of which were transcribed and published), and wrote many essays. Initiatives stimulated by his insights can be found in many diverse disciplines in countries all over the world. Steiner died in 1925.

Further Readings: AWSNA. (2004). *Association of Waldorf Schools in North America*. Available online at http://www.awsna.org; Setzer, V. W. (2003). *Rudolf Steiner chronological biography*. Available online at http://www.sab.org.br/steiner/biogr-eng.htm; Steiner, Rudolf (1894). *A philosophy of freedom* (M. Lipson, Trans. 1995 ed.). Herndon, VA: SteinerBooks; Steiner, Rudolf (1928). *The story of my life.* Translated by H. Collison. London: Anthroposophical Publishing Co; Stewart, James (2004). *Rudolf Steiner Archive*. Available online at http://www.elib.com/Steiner/.

Eric Gidseg

Subsidies. *See* Child Care Subsidies and Tax Provisions

Symbolic Languages

One of the central tenets of sociocultural theory is the vital importance of symbols as they mediate relationships between the mind and the environment (Bruner, 1990; Kozulin, 1990). When educators speak of the symbolic languages of children they are referring to the ways in which children make visible, or represent, their ideas. A language may be defined by its uses: to express, to communicate, and to work things through. Talk, for example, may be used to make one's thoughts and feelings known to the self and others (express and communicate). Talk is but one of many languages available to us. We can also express and explore ideas through graphic languages such as drawing, painting, sculpting with clay or wire, weaving, construction, and shadow, and through more temporal languages such as movement and music. Early Childhood educators are learning from **Reggio Emilia** that children are able to articulate and explore their most profound ideas best when they are able to represent those ideas in those many languages, the "one hundred languages of children" (Malaguzzi, 1998).

Though some call "paint" or "clay" or "drawing" a language, that is an incomplete, and therefore inaccurate, characterization. Paint as an entity is not a language, nor is drawing, wire, or clay. They are media only … until the child *uses* them as symbolic languages … to express, communicate, or figure things out. Examples of children using drawing as a language might be the five-year-old who draws her memory of the merry-go-round she rode at the amusement park the day before; the boy who is fascinated with airplanes draws what he knows about the different types of airplanes; the six-year-old who has been thinking about shadows draws a series of theories about how shadows work, beginning with her idea that all shadows occur in daylight and on the ground.

A child must know a medium well before it becomes a language for her. Children come to know a medium through many experiences with it. Often in early encounters with a medium a child explores, testing what the medium will do, how it feels, how it looks, and how it responds to her actions (learning the "affordances" of the medium; Forman, 1994). Such exploration might look like scribble. Or it might be more of a "formula" representation. For example, a child who knows how to draw houses well, who is comfortable drawing houses, and who feels no need at present to challenge herself when drawing houses might draw house after identical house after identical house as she learns a new type of pen, or she might translate this familiar subject into paint to explore the paint, and so forth. As the child learns what a particular medium will do, how it will respond to her actions upon it, and what it will allow her to do, she acquires proficiency, confidence, and understanding about the medium. Eventually we see her begin to use that medium to represent that which she does not yet know how to represent, or to explain her thinking about a particular idea through the medium. It is then that we might say the child is using that medium as a symbolic language. Such familiarity with media requires both frequent access to the media and time. This is why it often does not satisfy either child or teacher when a teacher asks a child to represent a new idea with an unfamiliar medium. Over time, as children come to know the media and to use them as languages they also learn to value the media as tools for making their ideas visible, discovering, for example, that some are better suited to representing certain ideas than others.

Children are full of ideas, theories about how the world works, and full of imagination. It is not only satisfying to represent those ideas, theories, and imaginings, but also vital to the learning process. When children represent an idea, either through reading, writing, or talking, through graphic media, or through more temporal media such as music and movement, their understanding of the idea grows. High school and college students take notes during lectures, partly so that they will have them as referents when studying. But the act of taking the notes itself ... representing what the professor is saying ... also supports the student's making sense of what he is hearing. In the same way, every time young children draw, paint, sculpt, construct, and act out their ideas, they develop a deeper understanding of those ideas (as well, of course, as honing their proficiency with and control of the media). Understanding grows even further when children represent an idea in multiple languages. For example, to draw a chair one must consider angles, number of legs, and the size of the parts of a chair in relation to each other (the legs all reach the baseline, for example). But when trying to construct or sculpt a chair in three dimensions, one must also consider how the chair manages to stand. When a child represents a thing, he "defamiliarizes" it—makes it new for himself, in a way. According to Giovanni Piazza, studio teacher (atelierista) in Reggio Emilia, this gives the child more images of the subject of her representation, and, he says, we want children to "have more images of one thing, a wealth of images" (Rabitti 1994). Symbolic representation also has a fundamental role in small-group project work. Often the foundation upon which such collaborative work rests is spoken language. Children pose their ideas, challenge each others' ideas, negotiate point and counterpoint, make plans, and so forth—in words. However, sometimes words seem to be inadequate to the idea at hand. As Loris **Malaguzzi** points out, "graphic representation is a tool of communication much simpler and clearer than words" (1998, p. 92). Children might draw or otherwise represent graphically an idea that they have struggled to express verbally. They might draw to understand more completely the idea of another. While the *act* of representing an idea can help clarify it for the individual, the *product* of the representation can help others understand her idea, and it can support the development of a shared, larger idea.

Teachers can support children's use of symbolic languages by doing the following:

- Providing good quality materials for representation. For example, paintbrushes in a variety of sizes and with a variety of brush tips can give children the control they need to make their ideas visible. Paper that both stands up to the rigors of different media and that makes the representation look its best is more likely to call to children than, for example, newsprint. Real potters' clay (e.g., white or red low fire clay) supports more detailed representation than does, for example, play-dough.

- Making sure the *media are accessible* to the children as they need it. Teachers will want to keep in mind that children may need many, many experiences with a medium before they use it as a language. Many teachers store media in well-organized low shelves so that children can both find and reach what they need when they need it.

- Providing *time* for children to invest energy and emotion in their representation, and to navigate the problems they encounter as they work to make their ideas visible.

- *Supporting* children's learning about representation directly. A child may have a desire to represent before he has the necessary techniques or control or perhaps even knowledge of the media to accomplish his goals. Without support the child may come to expect less of himself and resort to coping strategies that don't necessarily help him learn to represent his ideas, for example choosing to draw only what he knows how to draw or throwing attempt after attempt away in frustration. A sensitive teacher can recognize the dichotomy for the child, work to help the child make his idea visible, and even help him develop strategies for the next time around.

- *Displaying* children's representation prominently and with care, sending the message, "Your work is important to us all." Teachers can also make children's representation public by taking it to a class meeting, inviting others to seek out the artist for advice if they would like to try something similar, thereby affirming the artist and inspiring his classmates.

- Supporting each child's establishment of a "satisfaction bar," and the disposition to persevere until she is satisfied that she (or the group with which she is working) has made her/their mental image visible. The teacher's response to the child's work can send a strong message. Because one goal is to encourage children to revisit their work, teachers might respond with "What's happening here?" rather than evaluative comments about the child's work and "Are you satisfied?" rather than, for example, "Are you finished?" Noticing when the child needs adult support for technique, tools, or moral support also helps the child sustain effort toward making her idea visible.

- Encouraging the *flow of ideas* in the classroom. As children represent their ideas teachers can encourage others inspired by those ideas, note the evolution of the idea as its representation flows from one child to another, and pay attention to the way such ideas become part of the shared language of the classroom. For example, Mary draws a king and queen. Nearby Charles and Jamal, inspired by Mary's drawing, begin to make paper crowns. Others join them. The teacher notes this flow of ideas and makes the children's work public in a class meeting. Later that day the teacher notices that a small group is making a castle for kings and queens on the block platform. King-and-queen play draws in more children over many days, and soon it becomes part of the group's shared language and a way of sustaining relationship for the children. All this happens in a classroom where children are encouraged to represent their ideas, have learned how to do so, and where the flow of ideas from one child to another is treasured.

Further Readings: Bruner, Jerome (1990). *Acts of meaning.* Cambridge, MA: Harvard University Press; Kozulin, Alex (1990). *Vygotsky's psychology: A biography of ideas.* Cambridge, MA: Harvard University Press; Malaguzzi, Loris (1998). History, ideas, and basic philosophy, An interview with Lella Gandini. In Edwards Carolyn, Gandini Lella, and Forman George, eds., *The hundred languages of children. The Reggio Emilia approach—advanced reflections.* 2nd ed. Greenwich, CT: Ablex Publishing Corp., pp. 49—97; Forman, George (1994). Different media, different languages. In Lilian Katz and Bernard Cesarone, eds., *Reflections on the Reggio Emilia approach.* Urbana, IL: ERIC, pp. 37-46; Rabitti, Giordana (1994). An integrated art approach in a preschool. In Lilian Katz and Bernard Cesarone, eds., *Reflections on the Reggio Emilia approach.* Urbana, IL: ERIC, pp. 51-68; Cadwell, Louise (2003). Bringing learning to life: The Reggio approach to early childhood education. New York: Teachers College Press; Edwards, Carolyn, Gandini, Lella, and Forman, George, eds. (1998). *The hundred languages of children. The Reggio Emilia approach—advanced reflections.* 2nd ed. Greenwich, CT: Ablex Publishing Corp; Gandini, Lella, Hill, Lynn, Cadwell, Louise, and Schwall, Charles (2005). *In The Spirit Of The Studio: Learning from the Atelier of Reggio Emilia.* New York: Teachers College Press; Hendrick, Joanne, ed. (2003). *Next steps toward teaching the Reggio way: Accepting the challenge to change.* Upper Saddle River, NJ: Pearson Merrill Prentice Hall. The Hundred Languages of Children: Catalogue of the Exhibit (2nd ed.). 1997. Reggio Children; Topal, Cathy (1992). *Children and painting.* Worcester, MA: Davis Publications, Inc. Vecchi, Vea, and Guidici, Claudia, eds. (2004). *Children, art, artists: The expressive languages of children, the artistic language of Alberto Burri.* Reggio Emilia: Reggio Children.

Pam Oken-Wright

T

TANF. *See* Temporary Assistance to Needy Families

Tax Provisions. *See* Child Care Subsidies and Tax Provisions

Teacher Certification/Licensure

Teacher certification or licensure is the process by which individuals become fully qualified to teach. In the field of teacher education, the terms certification and licensure are typically used synonymously. For the purposes of this entry, teacher certification will be used. Teacher certification is the responsibility of each state, province, and territory, resulting in different certification requirements across states, provinces, and territories. Certification requirements are delineated in legislation, with oversight and implementation by a designated governmental entity. Although variation exists, certification requirements typically specify the age range or grade level for which the individual is being certified, the standards that the individual must demonstrate to be qualified to teach, and the measures used to document that the standards have been mastered. Some states require individuals to complete an induction year before becoming fully certified.

Certification may be at the initial or advanced level. Initial certification refers to the initial license to practice as a professional in the field, whether that license is obtained at the undergraduate or graduate level. Advanced certification is obtained at the graduate or inservice level and is based on more in-depth study in the chosen field. The focus of this entry is initial certification.

For over a decade, the **National Association for the Education of Young Children** (NAEYC), the Association of Teacher Educators (ATE), and the **Division for Early Childhood** of the **Council for Exceptional Children** (DEC/CEC) have jointly advocated that states develop free-standing certificates for educators working with all children birth through age eight, with the age range and standards for certificates being congruent across states in order to promote reciprocity (Hyson, 2003; Sandall, Hemmeter, Smith and McLean, 2000). Other professional organizations, such as the **Association for Childhood Education International** (ACEI), Association for Supervision and Curriculum Development (ASCD), the National Association of State Boards of Education (NASBE), and the American Federation of Teachers (AFT) have also developed recommendations urging creation of uniform and distinctive early childhood certification.

Early childhood education (ECE) and **early childhood special education** (ECSE) are distinct fields and thus, certification separate from elementary, middle grades, and secondary certification is essential for several reasons. First, theory and research support the early childhood years as a unique developmental phase that has implications for developing and implementing effective learning environments, curriculum, and assessment. A distinct body of research also provides guidance as to how children with disabilities birth through age eight develop and learn and thus, what adaptations may be necessary in early childhood settings. Families play a significant role in early childhood programs, with the family and home being the primary context for learning and development. Understanding cultural and linguistic diversity, as well as the importance of collaboration with families and other professionals are central to effective early childhood services. In addition, the preference for early childhood services in inclusive settings and natural environments requires that all early childhood educators possess knowledge and skills in working with young children with disabilities and their families.

Second, early childhood educators work in a variety of settings (e.g., **child care,** public and private preschools and **kindergartens, Head Start, Early Head Start, early intervention**). They may also be employed in a variety of roles in which they provide direct or indirect services to children and families (e.g., lead teacher, consultant, home visitor, program administrator, staff development specialist). Although the majority of entry-level professionals are in lead teacher roles, certification standards must take into account these possible roles and employment settings.

Third, several researchers have concluded that the quality of early childhood staff is, if not the most important, one of the most important factors in determining program quality and outcomes for children (e.g., Buysse et al., 1999; Cost, Quality, and Child Outcomes Study Team, 1995). In addition, a statistically significant correlation between specialized education and the quality of learning environments has been reported. On the basis of a review of research investigating the relationship between formal education and professional experience to quality, Kontos and Wilcox-Herzog (2001) concluded that (a) formal education positively correlates with classroom quality, (b) specialized education is positively correlated with teacher behavior, and (c) experience is not consistently correlated to program quality or effective teacher behavior.

Finally, federal legislation, if not mandating certification, suggests that early childhood educators obtain specialized education in the field and move toward full certification. Head Start required that at least 50 percent of its teachers have an associate's degree by Fall 2003. Part C of the **Individuals with Disabilities Education Act** (IDEA) requires that early interventionists possess the highest entry-level degree for state certification as a minimum standard for providing services to infants and toddlers with disabilities and their families. The **No Child Left Behind Act** (U.S. Department of Education, 2002) requires every state to ensure that all teachers are highly qualified, with *highly qualified* defined as having obtained full certification in the field in which the individual is teaching or having passed a state teacher licensing examination.

It has been consistently recommended that ECE and ECSE certification focus on ages birth through eight and that within that age range individuals specialize in two of the three age spans—infant/toddler, preschool, or primary. This would result in a broad knowledge base regarding development and learning and the implications for assessment and curriculum across the age range from birth through eight. Specialization in two of the three subperiods would allow for in-depth knowledge and skills based on career choices and workplace needs.

Consistent recommendations have also been made regarding the content of ECE and ECSE certification. Most states base certification on the standards of the professional associations representing the various disciplines within teacher education (CEC, 2003). Through the National Council for the Accreditation of Teacher Education's (NCATE) State Partnership Program, forty-eight states have developed partnerships with NCATE through which joint accreditation reviews of teacher education programs within institutions of higher education (IHEs) are conducted according to state and national standards. Within those states, teacher education programs are reviewed using both state and national standards even though an individual IHE may not seek NCATE accreditation. Thus, an ECE program would be based on state and NAEYC standards, whereas an ECSE program would address state and DEC/CEC and CEC Common Core standards. Blended ECE and ECSE programs would include state standards and all three sets of professional association standards.

Standards identify the knowledge, skills, and dispositions (i.e., values, attitudes, beliefs) that early childhood and early childhood special educators must possess in order to work effectively with young children and their families. Thus, standards define what early childhood professionals must know and be able to do. The standards across the professional associations identified above emphasize that all early childhood educators must demonstrate a common core of knowledge and skills for working with all young children and their families. These standards are typically organized by the following categories: child development and learning; family and community relationships; observation and assessment; curriculum, teaching, and learning; and professionalism. Field experiences are emphasized and integrated throughout the standards. The CEC Common Core standards are organized similarly, but in more discrete categories: foundations, characteristics of learners, individual differences, instructional strategies, learning environments and social interactions, language, instructional planning, assessment, ethics and professional practice, and collaboration.

Age and content congruency is advocated to promote reciprocal agreements across states, provinces, and territories. Certification configurations tend to be separate ECE and ECSE, in which individuals specialize in one of the two disciplines, dual ECE and ECSE in which individuals complete separate preparation programs but qualify for both certifications, or blended ECE/ECSE in which individuals complete a common program of study resulting in depth and focus in both ECE and ECSE. Blended certification should include state standards, as well as all NAEYC, DEC/CEC, and CEC Common Core standards. Because of the trend toward inclusive settings for young children, states, provinces, and territories that choose to maintain separate ECE and ECSE certificates are encouraged to develop linkages between those certifications to support the option for IHEs to develop blended preparation programs.

Professional literature identifies several trends and issues related to ECE and ECSE certification. Because certification is the responsibility of states, provinces, and territories, there is great variation across those jurisdictions resulting in issues regarding reciprocity. In a review of early childhood certification in the United States, Ratcliff et al. (1999) reported that few states adhere to recommendations for a birth through age eight certification. They found that states' definitions of the early childhood age span and its subdivisions vary greatly, with at least twelve different licensure configurations identified. For thirty of thirty-eight states reporting, Dannaher and Kraus (2002), identified six different age configurations between birth and age eight (e.g., birth through eight years, birth through five years, three through eight years) for ECSE certification and seven for blended ECE/ECSE certification.

Although research links the quality of programs and outcomes for children with increased qualifications for early childhood educators, many early childhood programs do not require staff to have college degrees, certification, or demonstrate competence in the recommended standards. Yet, in the United States, all fifty states and territories provide services to children ages birth through five with disabilities under the requirements of the IDEA. Most have used existing certifications to meet the "minimum highest entry" requirement for personnel under IDEA, with many of those certifications not including the infant/toddler age range. In their annual review of preschool programs for children with disabilities, Dannaher and Kraus (2002) reported that only thirty of the thirty-eight states providing data have an ECSE certification or a blended ECE/ECSE certification. This report does not indicate if certification is required in those states to work with preschool children with disabilities.

A variety of programs exist for children who are developing typically (e.g., child care, private and public preschool programs, Head Start, Early Head Start), with many of these programs being inclusive. In the United States, forty-six states and the District of Columbia fund some type of preschool program for children younger than age five (AFT, 2002). Some fund only one type of program, while others fund multiple types of programs (e.g., public preschool for all three- and four-year-olds, preschool for children identified at-risk). The AFT's review of policies regarding state-funded early childhood programs indicated that only thirty-two states and DC require a bachelor's degree for lead early childhood teachers, while all states require a bachelor's degree for kindergarten teachers. That same report indicated that fifteen states and D.C. require a bachelor's degree and certification for all state-funded early childhood settings, with another ten states requiring a bachelor's degree and certification only in selected settings. When considering early childhood programs in addition to state-funded programs, forty states require no college education for licensed child care staff and less than one-half of teachers working with three- and four-year-olds have a college degree (NIEER, 2003).

To address the above inconsistencies in certification, as well as the requirement for certification, numerous groups have recommended that early childhood educators in lead teacher roles have a minimum of a bachelor's degree and certification (e.g., ACEI, AFT, ASCD, ATE, DEC/CEC, NAEYC, NASBE). The following recommendations may assist states, provinces, and territories in developing certification requirements, ensuring that all lead teachers are fully qualified, and supporting higher education in developing and offering early childhood teacher education programs:

1. Include the birth through eight age range and standards developed by professional associations in certification requirements.
2. Develop career ladder or lattice systems that allow for upward mobility and increased compensation as early childhood educators increase their preparation, and support movement across programs/systems for horizontal movement of personnel.
3. Enhance collaboration between IHEs and governmental agencies involved with certification.
4. Support IHEs in developing or expanding programs to meet certification requirements. This should include incentives to develop new courses and programs; employ adequate numbers of qualified faculty, including those from culturally and linguistically diverse backgrounds; and develop articulation agreements between two- and four-year institutions.
5. Provide resources to improve working conditions, salaries, and benefits of early childhood educators as a means to attract qualified personnel.
6. Provide incentives for newly employed personnel and currently employed personnel to obtain certification. This may include provisional certifications; financial assistance for tuition, books, child care, etc.; and "grandfathering" clauses.

Further Readings: American Federation of Teachers (2002). *At the starting line: Early childhood education programs in the 50 states.* Washington, DC: American Federation of Teachers; Buysse, Virginia, Patricia W. Wesley, D. M. Bryant, and D. Gardner (1999). Quality of early childhood programs in inclusive and noninclusive settings. *Exceptional Children* 65, 301–314; Cost, Quality, and Child Outcomes Study Team (1995). *Cost, quality, and child outcomes in child care centers public report.* Denver: Economics Department, University of Colorado at Denver. Available online at http://www2.acf.dhhs.gov/programs/hsb/regs/hsactogc.htm; Council for Exceptional Children (2003). *What every special educator must know: Ethics, standards, and guidelines for special educators.* 5th ed. Arlington, VA: Council for Exceptional Children; Dannaher, J., and R. Kraus, eds. (2002). *Section 619 profile.* 11th ed. Chapel Hill: University of North Carolina, FPG Child Development Institute, National Early Childhood Technical Assistance Center; Hyson, M., ed. (2003). *Preparing early childhood professionals: NAEYC's standards for programs.* Washington, DC: National Association for the Education of Young Children; Kontos, Susan, and A. Wilcox-Herzog (2001). How do education and experience affect teachers of young children?" *Young Children* 14, 54–64; National Institute for Early Education Research (NIEER) (2003). America shortchanges its preschoolers: Few states require teacher training; *Preschool Matters* 1(1), 3, 8. Ratcliff, N., J. Cruz, and J. McCarthy (1999). *Early childhood teacher certification licensure patterns and curriculum guidelines: A state-by-state analysis.* Washington, DC: Council for Professional Recognition; Sandall, S., M. L. Hemmeter, B. J. Smith, and M. E. McLean (2005). DEC recommended practices: A comprehensive guide for practical application in early intervention/early childhood special education. Longmont, CO: Sopris West. U.S. Department of Education. *No child left behind.* August 2002. Available online at http://www.NoChildLeftBehind.gov.

Vickie D. Stayton

Teacher Education and Compensation Helps (TEACH)

The TEACH (Teacher Education And Compensation Helps) Early Childhood® Project is a professional development support system for teachers and directors working in early care and education programs or family child care homes with children ages birth through five years. The project is based on a scholarship program that links increased education of teachers and directors with increased compensation, a commitment to their employer, and reduced turnover.

The TEACH Early Childhood Project began in 1990 as a pilot developed by and operated through Child Care Services Association (CCSA), Chapel Hill, North Carolina. The TEACH Project was developed as a reaction to a North Carolina child care workforce study that reported, on average, child care teachers made little more than minimum wage, few had earned degrees beyond high school diplomas, and child care programs did not offer teachers any support for continuing education. The report also noted that the statewide annual turnover rate for teachers working in early care and education was 40 percent. The initial pilot was successful in providing twenty-one scholarships to teachers working in child care centers. Initial funds were provided through a variety of community and family foundations (Child Care Services Association, 2000). In 2004, the TEACH Project was institutionalized in the State of North Carolina and is now available in every county. The North Carolina Project operates on an annual budget of $3.4 million that is funded through federal, state, and private funds.

Since its inception in North Carolina, the project has been adopted by twenty-two other states. It is supported by a variety of state government and community agencies in those states. Currently, twenty-two states have a licensed TEACH scholarship program and they are supported through the TEACH Early Childhood Project Technical Assistance and Quality Assurance Center located in Chapel Hill, North Carolina (TEACH Early Childhood Project Technical Assistance and Quality Assurance Center, 2003).

The Project is evidence of public and private partnerships that are initiated by local early care and education advocates. The Project is flexible enough to be adopted by the individual states yet fixed in key areas to maintain the integrity of the program. The adaptation of the Project in other states came after local advocates developed an awareness of the growing problems of poor quality child care in that area. Opportunities to expand this professional development support system have come as a result of the availability of federal funds in the area of **Child Care and Development Funds** and increases in the **Temporary Assistance for Needy Families**' funding (Kerlin, 2003).

All TEACH Early Childhood Projects include four components; however, the details of each component may vary among different licensed programs. First, the scholarship is usually a partial one for tuition, books, and a travel stipend for a teacher to attend a credentialing program in early childhood education (state credential, child development associate credential, associate's degree, or bachelor's degree). Many scholarships also include funds for paid release time so the teacher can attend classes during the day, study, or take care of personal business. The cost for tuition and books that is not covered by the scholarship is usually provided by the scholar and their employer. The second component is the requirement of a specified amount of educational coursework that is outlined in the TEACH contract and must be completed in a specified timeframe. Following completion of the required education, the teacher is granted a compensation incentive in the form of a raise or bonus. Some compensation incentives are paid wholly by the TEACH Project, others are paid wholly by the employers, and others represent a mixture of funding between the employer and the TEACH Project. Finally, the teacher makes a commitment to remain in the early care and education field, and most commonly, with their sponsoring child care program, for a specified period of time.

The impact that the TEACH Early Childhood Project has had on the early care and education field varies based on the length of time that a Project has been operating and the amount of funds available to teachers through the Project. In North Carolina, approximately 5,000 teachers participate in the TEACH Project each year, their earnings increase by an average of 10 percent, and the turnover rate for teachers averages less than 10 percent annually. Statewide turnover rates for all early childhood care and education teachers have dropped to 24 percent a year. Similar results have been reported by every state operating a TEACH Project. In addition to the impact on individual teachers, the Project has been a catalyst for system changes that require public policy and law makers to consider professional development of teachers to include not only scholarship money to take college courses, but a complete system that recognizes the difficulty that teachers have in going to school, working full-time, and supporting their own family. Another system that has been impacted is the higher education system as more teachers take college-level courses and demand alternative delivery models, flexible days and times that courses are offered, more variety of courses, and course content that addresses the needs of experienced adult learners. For more information, contact Child Care Services Association at www.childcareservices.org.

Further Readings: Child Care Services Association (2000). *T.E.A.C.H. Early Childhood®: Celebrating ten years July 1, 1990-June 30, 2000.* Chapel Hill, NC: Child Care Services Association; Kerlin, Janelle (2003). The transfer of child care worker education and compensation policy across states: The TEACH. Early Childhood® Model. The Urban Institute. October 2003. Available online at www.urban.org/UploadedPDF/410890_TEACH_Report.pdf. TEACH Early Childhood® Project Technical Assistance and Quality Assurance Center (2003). *What we've learned. Providing strategies and solutions for the early childhood workforce.* Annual Report, 2002-2003.

Susan Catapano

Teacher Education, Early Childhood

Among the pressing educational issues facing our nation is an alarming shortage of qualified classroom teachers. Since the publication of the Report of the

National Commission on Teaching and America's Future (1996), debates on educational reform have focused on the preparation and continuing education of
teachers and the impact of well-qualified teachers on students' learning. Teacher
quality is a major priority of the reform agenda because what teachers know and
learn how to do as a result of their own professional preparation significantly
influences children's success in school. Teacher education has thus assumed an
unprecedented importance at the level of national policy and within the field of
educational research and practice.

Teacher education in the United States refers to postsecondary coursework and
classroom experiences that help develop and deepen both the content and the
pedagogical skills necessary to ensure that all children learn. Within the field of
early childhood as well as other divisions in the broad field of education, teacher
education occurs at both the *initial* and *advanced* levels. *Initial* early childhood
teacher education consists of general education as well as domain-specific content preparation and specific methodological preparation. Guidelines for such
programs of study, often described as preservice teacher education, are generally
linked to state licensing requirements and result in an initial teaching license,
thereby making one eligible to teach. *Advanced* early childhood teacher education consists of professional development that increases the skill and knowledge
of licensed practicing teachers. Although requirements vary from state to state,
advanced teacher education programs often lead to a permanent or professional
state license. Whether the program of study is for initial or advanced licensure, the
primary aim of teacher education programs is the improvement of student learning and achievement through the improvement of teachers' skill and knowledge.
Effective teacher education programs entail rigorous and relevant preparation for
the contemporary realities of teaching. These realities include teaching children
from diverse backgrounds, addressing children's individual abilities, working in
partnership with children's families, having a deep knowledge of the content they
teach, and being able to articulate what and why they teach as they do. These
new demands have exacerbated decades-old controversies about the nature of
and need for early childhood teacher education.

The criticism of teacher education was originally focused on the education of
elementary and secondary teachers. Since the 1990s, however, early childhood
teacher education has become an essential part of the school reform agenda as
the public addresses the educational needs of the very young. The next section
highlights the unique traditions in early childhood teacher education that are
related to preparation of early childhood teachers.

Historical and Philosophical Traditions of Early Childhood Teacher Education

While issues of teacher quality and higher standards are dominating the educational debates, controversies regarding the content and means of early childhood
teacher education are not new. Rather, they began in the nineteenth century
and continue today as the cornerstone of our field just as they did when the
Committee of Nineteen of the International Kindergarten Union was forced to
issue three reports because it could not come to consensus on the **kindergarten**

curriculum in the early 1900s. For most of the twentieth century, early childhood teacher education programs prepared young females in programs that emphasized knowledge in child development as its core knowledge base. Child development knowledge and the knowledge of developmental norms became the cornerstone of most early childhood teacher education programs. Yet, within the field of early childhood teacher education itself, there has been a continuing distinction in teacher education programs for child care staff, preschool and kindergarten teachers, and primary teachers, all of whom are being educated as early childhood professionals. The history of early childhood teacher education is long and rich and provides a historical and philosophical perspective from which to consider contemporary issues in the preparation of qualified teachers for young children.

High-Quality Teacher Education for Initial Preparation

The publication *What Matters Most: Teaching and America's Future* (National Commission of Teaching and America Future, 1996) marked a decade of national reports that addressed issues of quality in American education. Its leading recommendation called for higher standards for teachers linked to standards for students, and for teacher education at all levels to be standards-based to obtain a cadre of highly qualified teachers.

Consistent with this recommendation and beginning in the early 1990s, the National Council for the Accreditation of Teacher Education (NCATE) began raising standards for entry into the profession through rigorous new standards for accreditation, licensing, and advanced certification. Teacher education as a field raised the standards for accrediting its programs. The NCATE devised a new performance-based accreditation system that many regard as helping to raise the level of teacher preparation. Institutions of higher education that choose to seek NCATE approval must now provide evidence that their candidates can perform well in the classroom and on licensing examinations. In states with NCATE-approved programs, there is an increasing alignment between teacher education accreditation standards, beginning teacher licensing standards, and advanced certification standards, thus providing a more coherent system of teacher preparation and development. NCATE-approved programs also are seen as providing the public with evidence that the institution is capable of delivering well-qualified teachers for all children.

Other sources of influence on teacher education come from the field of early childhood education. In response to the call for standards-based education reform, the **National Association for the Education of Young Children** (NAEYC) has revised its standards for the colleges and universities that prepare early childhood teachers. These *Standards for Early Childhood Professional Preparation* provide research-based program guidelines to institutions of higher education that prepare initial teacher candidates and advanced practicing professionals. The revised standards focus more deeply on academic content, cultural and linguistic diversity, children with special needs, practical experiences and preparation, and outcomes of teacher education (i.e., their impact on young children's learning). Many U.S. early childhood professionals consider the use of NAEYC standards as a crucial step in raising the quality of programs for all young children by improving the preparation of early childhood teachers.

Guidelines from these (NAEYC, NCATE) and other (e.g., the **Association for Childhood Education International** [ACEI]) professional organizations that develop standards for the preparation of early childhood teachers converge with a growing body of research on teacher characteristics and preschool quality. Combined, these sources suggest that good early childhood teachers should have a minimum knowledge of (1) child development, (2) an understanding of developmentally appropriate practice and assessment, (3) knowledge and understanding of the foundations of literacy and numeracy, (4) knowledge and skill in appropriate methodology that fosters skill and concept acquisition, and (5) understanding of the children and families with whom they work. This core knowledge should inform all early childhood teacher education programs regardless of the credential being sought (i.e., Child Development Credential [CDA], associate, bachelor's, or advanced degree) or the focus of the teacher education program (i.e., programs for children from birth through age five, programs for children ages five through eight).

Despite the existence of these forms of professional recognition, not all early childhood teachers are prepared in programs that are explicitly influenced by such standards. Some programs may be situated in institutions that do not belong to NCATE or have not adopted the Interstate New Teacher Assessment and Support Consortium (INTASC) principles. Others may be in specialized institutions or may primarily aim to prepare teachers for careers other than that of public school teacher. Thus, the diversity of teacher professional preparation and professional roles is a major factor on the career continuum.

If these recommended guidelines are not sufficient to inspire reform in university teacher education programs, there is an additional incentive. The federal government's first dramatic entry into teacher quality, Title II of the Higher Education Act, increased accountability requirements for colleges of education. Colleges must now report institutional pass rates on the teacher preparation examination used in their state. This data is publicly available and is used as a requirement in professional accreditation decisions.

Literature on Teacher Education and Teacher Learning

Research has long supported the view that the teacher is the single most important variable in student learning (Cochran-Smith and Zeichner, 2005; Darling-Hammond, 2001; Darling-Hammond and Bransford, 2005). The literature also clearly points out that many teachers are being asked to work in ways for which they have not been prepared—"to engage in the systematic, continuous improvement in the quality of the educational experience of students and to subject themselves to the discipline of measuring their success by the metric of students' academic performance" (Elmore, 2002, p. 3). Some research concludes that high quality teacher preparation has a positive influence on student achievement at both the individual and classroom levels. Conversely, teachers who do not hold a teaching certificate or who are teaching in a field for which they were not prepared, have students who do less well than students taught by teachers prepared in high-quality teacher preparation programs (Goldhaber and Brewer, 2000; Educational Testing Service, 2000).

Other research (Darling-Hammond and Bransford, 2005; Cochran-Smith and Zeichner, 2005) synthesizes teacher education research concerning the effectiveness of formal teacher preparation. Findings show that well-prepared teachers demonstrate a common set of agreed upon essential knowledge and skills, are more likely to stay in the profession, and produce more student learning. The studies also report that program components related to a clear, articulated vision of teaching and learning are related to the quality of teachers as well as student achievement.

Still other literature (Cochran-Smith and Zeichner, 2005; Wilson et al., 2001, 2003) synthesizes research on key issues in teacher education. The results for issues related to pedagogical preparation, and clinical experiences show a positive relationship between teacher preparation and student achievement whereas results on arts and science preparation of teachers indicate that knowledge may affect teachers' performance through stronger verbal, writing, and critical thinking skills.

Finally, there is a body of teacher education research that addresses the preparation of teachers with a critical, multicultural perspective to meet the changing cultural and linguistic demographics of today's school population (Banks, 2005; Cochran-Smith and Zeichner, 2005; Sleeter, 2001; Seidl and Friend, 2002; Zeichner, 1996). Much of this work shows short term impact and lacks longitudinal, empirical evidence that tracks changes in teacher candidates' attitudes, beliefs, and dispositions as they work in classrooms with underserved populations of children. The existing studies find that those preparing to teach often have a monolithic perspective and believe that children from other culture are the problem (Florio-Ruane, 2001, Zeichner, 1993). Sleeter's research (2001) notes the widening cultural gap between today's diverse population of children and those that teach them, because most teacher candidates are white, female, and middle-class and bring a superficial understanding of cultural issues into their teaching.

To reduce this gap and address the changing cultural makeup of today's schools teacher preparation programs began making programmatic changes. Many introduced multicultural education courses or targeted at least one clinical placement in a school with diverse population. Florio-Ruane (2001) suggests the need to go beyond courses and placement and to address students beliefs about diversity early in their teacher preparation programs by embedding multiple voices and personal stories that help teacher candidates view culture as something all people hold. By developing critical reflective educators who value multiple perspectives, teacher candidates can begin their journey to becoming multiculturally competent teachers.

In sum, the research literature on teacher education shows that the most powerful learning opportunities for teachers are anchored in student learning, include high standards, are content-focused, develop ongoing collaboration and networks across teachers, share common norms of beliefs, and provide in-depth, focused learning experiences that relate closely to the classroom (Elmore, 2002). While the research base provides ways to design and deliver high-quality teacher preparation, it is limited in identifying a large body of empirical evidence on its effects on teachers' practice or its impact on student learning.

Career Continuum

The National Commission on Teaching and America's Future (1996) recommended that "school districts, states, unions, and professional associations cooperate to make teaching a true profession, with a career continuum that places teaching at the top and rewards teachers for their knowledge and skill" (p. 94). In support of these aims, voluntary standards have been set by a number of professional groups (e.g., National Association for the Accreditation of Teacher Education (NCATE), National Association for the Education of Young Children (NAEYC), Interstate New Teacher Assessment and Support Consortium (INTASC) and the National Board for Professional Teaching Standards to ensure teacher quality across levels and settings. Conceptually, these standards are closely aligned, providing a consistent framework for the continuum of teachers' professional development. This continuum of standards is focused on a set of shared knowledge, skills, and commitments to ensure that accreditation, licensing, and advanced certification standards are compatible and together form a coherent system of quality assurance for the profession.

Contemporary Influences on ECE Teacher Education

Three major events in the last decade highlight the growing importance attributed to well-qualified early childhood teachers and are associated with specific and sometimes controversial changes in teacher education programs. These include a federal literacy initiative, the release of a national report on prevention of reading difficulties, and increased attention to early brain development. In particular, a new emphasis on student performance is profoundly influencing the ways teachers are selected, prepared, licensed, and evaluated. Teacher effectiveness is increasingly measured by what students learn, and teacher quality is measured by both content and pedagogical knowledge. Such conditions necessitate that teacher education programs examine their models of teacher education to ensure that they are meeting the changed emphases on accountability, assessment, and standards and teaching appropriate content to young children.

National initiatives are not only increasing quality demands on teacher education programs; they are also increasing demands for the quantity of such programs. For example, the federal **No Child Left Behind Act** (2001) requires that states have a highly qualified teacher in every public school classroom by 2006. The government definition of "a highly qualified teacher" is one that is licensed or certified by the state, holds at least a bachelor's degree, and has passed a rigorous State test on subject knowledge and teaching skills. Achieving this goal will require a greater conformity to previously described reform initiatives in early childhood teacher education; it will also require greater attention to the recruitment of college students into the field of teacher education; and increased collaboration between universities and public school professional development programs.

Summary and Conclusions

The increased demand for more well-qualified teachers who are knowledgeable about what they teach, skilled in how to teach children of different backgrounds and abilities, and deeply committed to whom they are teaching translates into a need for more high-quality programs of teacher preparation and development. The challenge for teacher education programs in the twenty-first century will be to maintain a dual focus on the heightened expectations on teachers and schools in light of changing understandings about adult and child learning and effective teaching. This dual focus naturally evokes tensions that have ramifications for early childhood teacher education programs and for teacher educators. Some of these tensions are conceptual in nature (e.g., inquiry-oriented practice versus technical practice, philosophy and reality conflicts, content versus pedagogy) and are voiced differently from policy makers, parents, and administrators. Others are based in the teacher education research and practice literature (e.g., traditional versus alternative certification and the increased coursework in leadership and advocacy and personal belief systems that drive program development and change) and others are political (responding to federal, state, and local mandates), Teacher education, in general, and early childhood teacher education, in particular, continues to be plagued by competing loyalties in an effort to prepare the best teachers for all of the children in the United States. *See also* Child Development Associate (CDA) National Credentialing Programs.

Further Readings: Banks, J. A. and C. A. Banks, eds. (2005). *Multicultural education: Issues and perspectives.* 5th ed. Hoboken, NJ: John Wiley & Sons. Cochran-Smith, M., and K. M. Zeichner (2005). Studying teacher education: The report of the AERA panel on research and teacher education. *American Educational Research Association*; Mahwah, NJ: Lawrence Erlbaum Associates, Inc. Darling-Hammond, L., and J. Bransford, eds. (2005). Preparing teachers for a changing world: What teachers should learn and be able to do. *National Academy of Education, Committee on Teacher Education*; San Francisco: Jossey Bass, Inc. Florio-Ruane, S. (2001). *Teacher education and the cultural imagination: Autobiography, conversation, and narrative.* Mahwah, NJ: Erlbaum. Elmore, R. F. (2002). Bridging the gap between standards and achievement: The imperative for professional development in education. Washington, DC: The Albert Shanker Institute; Isenberg, J. P., and Jalongo, M. R., eds. (2003). *Major trends and issues in early childhood education.* New York: Teachers College Press. National Association for the Education of Young Children (2001). *NAEYC standards for early childhood professional preparation: Initial licensure levels.* Washington, DC: Author. National Association for the Education of Young Children. (2002). *NAEYC standards for early childhood professional preparation: Advanced programs.* Washington, DC: Author. National Board for Professional Teaching Standards (1998). *What every teacher should know and be able to do.* Southfield, MI: Author. National Commission on Teaching and America's Future (1996). *What matters most: Teaching for America's future.* New York: Author. National Staff Development Council (2001). *Standards for staff development.* Oxford, OH: Author; Wilson, Suzanne M., Floden, Robert E., and Ferrini-Mundy, Joan (2001). *Teacher preparation research: Current knowledge, gaps, and recommendations.* Michigan State University, under the auspices of the Center for the Study of Teaching and Policy, University of Washington. Suzanne M. Wilson, and Robert E. Floden (2003). *Creating effective teachers: Concise answers for hard questions*. ERIC Clearinghouse. Washington, DC: American Association of Colleges for Teacher Education.

Joan Isenberg

Teacher Research

Teacher research is generally defined as the "systematic and intentional inquiry carried out by teachers" (Cochran-Smith and Lytle, 1993, p. 7) and is described by a wide range of labels, including practitioner research, teachers-as-researchers, **action research**, partnership research, and teacher inquiry. Teacher researchers study and analyze a wide range of questions and aspects related to their classroom practice, typically resulting in new plans of action and new knowledge about the teaching learning process. Current school reform efforts and recommendations to raise professional standards for teacher certification in the United States include the provision of teaching experiences that move teachers beyond a dependence on organized knowledge (generated from outside schools and classrooms) and the transmission of this knowledge, toward new understandings developed through critical thinking and teacher research. While this "call to action" might seem relatively recent, teacher research in the United States is not.

Historically, evidence of teacher research has spanned more than a century of work among teachers and teacher educators who have inquired alone and in collaboration, utilized diverse, yet related, methodologies, and engaged in a range of traditions in which teacher research and practice are mutually informing, nested endeavors. The many forms of teacher research have included and continue to include both empirical and conceptual studies and utilize an array of data sources such as reflective journals, oral inquiry, case studies, classroom-based research, and autobiographical accounts of teaching, learning, and schooling. Regardless of the label used or form taken, teacher research positions teachers as producers as well as consumers of knowledge—knowledge that is situated and constructed in classrooms and schools, focused on pedagogical, social, and political issues, and informed by the learning lives of children and teachers. Noted educator Eleanor Duckworth (1987) wrote the following about her vision of researchers who also teach:

> This kind of researcher [cares] about some part of the world and how it works enough to want to make it accessible to others; he or she would be fascinated by the questions of how to engage people in it and how people make sense of it; would have time and resources to pursue these questions to the depth of his or her interests, to write what he or she learned, and to contribute to the theoretical and pedagogical discussions on the nature and development of human learning. (p. 140)

Within the wide array of qualitative or interpretive studies, teacher researchers' aims include understanding the complexity of the teaching and learning process, addressing the need to study contexts of learning that are particular and situated, and including diverse sources of data for creating thick descriptions of learning. In these studies, methodologies typically include in-depth interviews, observational field notes, and a diversity of classroom documentation (work samples, photographs, video tapes, transcriptions). At times, similar to the above-mentioned product–process studies, teacher researchers have participated in interpretive studies alongside university researchers. Yet, even when teachers are members of such research initiatives, the struggle continues today to situate teacher researchers in positions of equal or shared authority for contributing to the knowledge base that informs practices, policies, and programs in schools.

During the past century in the United States, there appears to be at least three periods when teacher research has gained a prominent foothold in the professional literature, taking center stage in the dominant discourse, and legitimatizing the researching lives of early childhood teachers. These include the Progressive Era early in the twentieth century, the action research and collaborative action research movement spearheaded by Kurt Lewin midcentury, and practitioner research during the 1970s and 1980s to the present.

The roots of teacher research in the United States go back to the Progressive Education Era, led by John **Dewey,** when he called for teachers to engage in "reflective action" that would lead toward inquiry-oriented practice (1933). Progressive educators' research and practice focused more on the child rather than curriculum content as the source of direction for the creation of relevant teaching and learning experiences. Teacher reports were the cornerstone of the model of inquiry in Dewey's laboratory school, informed by documentation including teachers' field notes, classroom experiments, and teachers' collective debriefings of the daily learning experiences of children and teachers. Attention was on the study of how to provide for, promote, and investigate the active engagement of children in authentic classroom experiences and to share knowledge learned from these classroom studies with others in the field of early childhood education.

The early efforts by teacher researchers of the Progressive Era to critically study children's learning lives in naturalistic, school settings were expanded upon and to some degree elevated by the work of Kurt Lewin in the 1940s and 1950s, who coined the phrase "action research." Action research is one form of teacher research in which teachers study classroom problems or questions and act to change practice in response to the analyses of their data. Subsequently, action researchers have investigated a wide range of topics, including pedagogical (e.g., impact of teaching strategies on children's learning, content-specific studies such as teaching writing), organizational (e.g., the role of open classrooms on children's learning), and community-focused (e.g., home–school relations, parent participation) aspects of teaching and learning. The practice of action researchers is characterized by movements through iterative cycles of critical observation and documentation, reflection, planning, acting, revising, and acting. Engagement in such cycles of inquiry typically results in a heightened awareness of decision making, problem posing, and problem solving. Teacher researchers are sometimes referred to as reflective practitioners because they reflect *on* action and *in* action to frame, critique, and respond to problems or questions (Schon, 1987).

Consequently, teaching is praxis because teachers examine theory in light of practice, through recursive cycles of reflection and action.

While teachers can engage in action research alone, often teachers conduct research with others through research collaboratives, study groups, or critical friend partnerships. It was Lewin who first sought to bring researchers and teachers together to engage in collaborative action research, where the mechanism and potentials of the social construction of knowledge are made visible and diverse and complementary perspectives contribute to new, shared understandings. From these earliest years to today, university researchers and teachers form action research groups in which teachers learn to conduct research, contribute new insights and knowledge to the field, and view teaching and researching as mutually informing inquiry. In addition to collaborative action research other research partnerships have developed over the years including those created by Professional Development Schools (PDS) and developed by the Holmes Partnership, Research is a fundamental cornerstone of these university-public school partnerships in which classroom teachers, preservice teachers, and university faculty research together, shaping the policies and programs of local schools while educating young novice teachers toward inquiry-oriented practice.

Teacher researchers have not always partnered with university researchers, but have also formed research collaborations within and across classrooms and schools, utilizing a form of systematic and intentional inquiry not necessarily representative of action research. For example, during the 1980s and 1990s a number of research collaboratives developed, including the research communities such as Patricia Carini and colleagues at the Prospect School in Bennington, Vermont, and Steve Seidel and others at Harvard Project Zero in Cambridge, Massachusetts. In these collaborations, teachers generated and used protocols to guide their analyses and interpretations of a wide range of classroom records, including photographs, transcriptions of children's conversations, videotapes, work samples, and teachers' field notes. For example, at the Prospect School, teachers created the *Descriptive Review of the Child* process to frame and systematize their careful investigations of children's early learning experiences, inviting teachers from throughout the school to participate in the collective analyses and interpretations of rich and diverse classroom records. Educators at Project Zero created an inquiry process called the *Collaborative Assessment Conference*. Teachers come together to talk about children's learning and use this tool or framework to systematically guide their conversations related to how children work on problems or explore interests and the role of teachers in their efforts to improve contexts for learning.

Research collaborations similar to these developed concurrently, focused on particular curriculum content areas, with early literacy and children's oral and written language taking the early lead in the 1970s and 1980s, including play, storying, and drama, followed by, most notably, mathematics and science instruction. Such research groups have grown during the past two decades due, in part, to the support and encouragement by professional organizations such as the National Council of Teachers of English (NCTE), the National Writing Project, the Critical Friends' Groups (CFGs) of the National School Reform Faculty's (NSRF) group, the International Reading Association, to name a few, and the Teachers Network Leadership Institute (TNLI). These national and international initiatives aimed at facilitating teachers' research together, have been joined by a plethora of local and statewide groups aimed at creating contexts for studying teacher practice, children's learning, and the impact of policies and practices on schooling in specific locales.

Beginning in the mid to late 1980s, similar work by educators in the more than thirty municipal infant–toddler and preprimary schools of **Reggio Emilia**, Italy began to influence the work of U.S. teacher-researchers' generation and use of classroom **documentation**. Documentation is not only a compilation of classroom records but also a spiraling process in which teachers collaboratively use documents to inform and guide teacher practice; reveal children's construction of knowledge; demonstrate a respect for children's work; validate the competencies of children, and communicate teachers' ideas for and understanding of children's learning lives to each other, to parents, and to the larger community. Through this approach to early education, Reggio-inspired teachers and teacher educators in the U.S. have developed research collaboratives (e.g., **Reggio-Inspired Teacher Education** (RITE) and the Informed Practice Collaboratives) and meet regularly to share and engage in collective reflections from which collaborative decisions are made for how to challenge, deepen, and extend children's learning. Among the functions of documentation for teacher inquiry are (*a*) representational (creating meaning), (*b*) mediational (linking thought to action), and (*c*) epistemological (providing a source of new knowledge). Across these examples of research collaboratives, early childhood teachers engage in research with others to chronicle, "make visible," and disseminate new understandings about children's learning even as they create contexts and constructs for research that are inclusive, deliberate, and embedded within the practice of daily teaching.

Concurrent with the emergence of research collaboratives in the United States, a rich reservoir of teacher research (both conceptually and empirically based) by individual teachers has developed. Nevertheless, evidence of empirical studies by individual teachers is more difficult to find in the literature than conceptually based research. Yet, the creation of new professional journals aimed at publishing the writings and the research of teachers (e.g., *Voices of Practitioners: Teacher Research in Early Childhood Education*, now a special section of the **National Association for the Education of Young Children**'s (NAEYC) journal *Young Children*, the online journal of *Early Childhood Research and Practice*, and the journal *Theory into Practice*) during recent decades have become more plentiful. Teachers' conceptual studies have been most evident through the narratives and autobiographical accounts that describe the complex and multifaceted nature of teaching and learning.

These chronicles of teachers' and children's educative experiences may be considered by some researchers and educators as more teacher stories rather than serious research. However, if one applies Cochran-Smith and Lytle's (1993) definition of teacher research (noted at the beginning of this entry) then the writings of well-known teacher researchers such as Vivian Paley, Sylvia Ashton-Warner, and Francis Hawkins clearly represent deliberate and systematic inquiry, often conducted over long periods of time, and informed by the analyses of a diversity of documentation. These accounts of teacher inquiry are squarely aimed at answering important questions focused on understanding the emergence of early literacy, investigating children's friendships, rights, and moral dimensions in the classroom, and facing the challenge of how to reach troubled and impoverished children, for example. Such questions and teachers' written accounts of their studies are focused on real problems that subsequently frame teacher research, inform teacher practice, and contribute new knowledge to the field of early childhood education.

As evidenced in the teacher research described here, teachers over the past millennium in the United States have continued to take steps away from a position of "the researched" toward one of "researcher," who contribute new knowledge to the field of early education. The work of teacher researchers includes both how teachers construct new knowledge and which knowledge they choose to pursue. Here, teacher knowledge refers to a range of foci from personal, practical knowledge to pedagogical content or subject matter knowledge to propositional knowledge. Thus, knowledge includes two distinct and related moments in learning, researching, and teaching. These include both the process of constructing new knowledge and the realization that certain knowledge already exists (Shor and Freire, 1987). The disposition to continually inquire, to seek, and to connect ways of knowing is one that views the teacher as a lifelong learner or student of teaching, committed to generating practical theories and "local knowledge" (Cochran-Smith and Lytle 1993, p. 45) with others and sharing that knowledge with the broader field of education.

Regardless of the focus or form of research or type of knowledge produced and used, teacher researchers are influencing reform in the field of early childhood **teacher education** as well as within classrooms and across schools. This is occurring even as the debate continues on whether knowledge generated by authorities outside teachers' classrooms holds more weight (as scientific knowledge) than knowledge generated by classroom researchers. Nevertheless, the evidence of teachers' movement away from roles characterized by passivity from which they receive knowledge from "outsiders" without question, deliberation, or challenge has shifted toward one characterized by systematic and intentional research, resulting in inquiry from which new knowledge and ways of knowing emerge. Thus, teacher researchers today are actualizing what John Dewey (1929) noted early in the twentieth century of the teacher research movement—that the most important act of a teacher is to investigate pedagogical problems through inquiry.

Further Readings: Cochran-Smith, Marilyn, and Susan Lytle (1993). *Inside/outside: Teacher research and knowledge.* New York: Teachers College Press. Dewey, John (1929). *Experience and nature*; La Salle: Open Court. Dewey, John (1933). *How we think: A restatement of the relation of reflective thinking to the educative process.* Lexington, MA: D.C. Heath. Duckworth, Eleanor (1987). *"The having of wonderful ideas" and other essays on teaching and learning.* New York: Teachers College Press. Himley, Margaret, and Patricia F. Carini, eds. (2000). *From another angle: Children's strengths and school standards.* New York: Teachers College Press; Schon, Donald (1987). *Educating the reflective practitioner: Toward a new design for teaching and learning in the professions*; San Francisco: Jossey-Bass. Shor, Ira, and Paulo Friere (1987). *A pedagogy for liberation: Dialogues on informing education.* South Hadley: Bergin and Garvey.

Mary Jane Moran

Teaching Exceptional Children (TEC)

Teaching Exceptional Children (TEC) is a journal published by the Council for Exceptional Children (CEC) for teachers and administrators of children with disabilities and children who are gifted. A peer-reviewed journal, it primarily publishes articles about practical methods and materials that can be used in classrooms, as well as articles on current issues in special education learning and teaching. The journal also provides information on the latest technologies, techniques, and procedures developed for teaching exceptional students. *TEC* has a practical focus aimed at helping teachers of exception children to put new practices and technologies into immediate application. Articles applicable to infants, young children, and families frequently appear in this journal, although *TEC* is not specifically an early childhood journal. The journal has been in continuous publication since November 1968 and now publishes six issues a year. All members of the CEC receive the journal as part of their membership, but nonmembers can also subscribe. The full-text of the journal is also available online. For more information, see the CEC Web site at www.cec.sped.org.

Samuel Odom

TEC. *See Teaching Exceptional Children*

Technology and Early Childhood Education

Broadly defined, technology in early childhood education includes a variety of media: computer-mediated software programs, video/audio learning instruments, robotic building kits, and electronic toys. Technology can be used as stand-alone classroom-based learning material in the form of a **technology curriculum** or can be integrated into other classroom curricula. Technology can also be used at home to supplement and augment children's experiences in the classroom.

Advances in technology provide new potentials in classroom learning, and make possible new ways for peer social interaction to take place inside and outside the classroom. As such, the body of research in technology and early childhood education has multiple foci, including the impact of technology on early **cognitive development**, personal–social development, language and **literacy**, numbers and **mathematics**.

Educational technologies that are used in early childhood classrooms to enhance classroom learning can be categorized into the following four groups, depending on the pedagogical goal of the tool and the design features of the software:
- computer-assisted instruction (CAI),
- intelligent tutoring systems (ITS),

- constructionist learning materials,
- and computer supported collaborative learning (CSCL).

While technologies developed within these four paradigms all have the goal of enhancing children's cognitive development, they differ in their theoretical stance of how that goal is reached. Computer-assisted instructional instruments (such as computer software that teaches numbers and vocabularies) take a drill and practice approach, whereas intelligent tutoring systems, which could be either computer software or electronic hardware in form, iteratively adapt their inherent, computerized educational curriculum to match the ability of the student users. Both computer-assisted instructional instruments and intelligent tutoring systems are usually stand-alone learning materials that may or may not require close supervision from teachers or adults.

Constructionist learning materials are technological tools that allow children to become designers and creators of their own personally meaningful computer-based projects. These tools are often open-ended and serve children to start developing technological fluency as well as to reflect about their own thinking and learning. Finally, computer-supported collaborative learning instruments provide means for communication and collaboration among students and between students, parents, and teachers. Technological tools developed within both the constructionist and the computer supported collaborative learning paradigms are usually open-ended educational tools meant to be integrated into the classroom curriculum, and therefore the content areas to explore with those tools is flexible and can be determined by the teacher. In contrast, software developed within the CAI and ITS paradigms involves content already produced by the designer of the computational tool.

A large body of interdisciplinary research on technology and early childhood education has been conducted in the past three decades. Early research efforts focused on the impact of technology on children's cognitive and **academic** development. In early childhood, for example, research has shown the benefits of CAI type drill and practice software in assisting children to complete counting and sorting tasks. Beyond simple drill and practice, technologies, especially computer simulations, have also shown potentials for supporting children's *mental actions*, or mental object-manipulation tasks, such as rotating objects or identifying patterns. Through simulations, both on the computer and through electronic hardware and toys, technology affords the ability to concretize abstract cognitive tasks that were previously thought to be unreachable for young children.

Constructionist types of technological environments, such as Logo, or the language of the turtle, were developed by Seymour Papert and his colleagues in the 1960s. These materials are now widely used in early childhood classrooms. Research has shown the benefits of these experiences, for example, when young children learn how to program a computer while exploring powerful ideas about mathematics. New types of robotic technologies allow children to manipulate technology in the same way they play and learn with pattern blocks or other manipulative toys frequently used in the early childhood setting.

Using technology in early childhood classrooms can also help foster peer collaboration among students and promote positive social development. Research has shown that working with technology, especially computer-related educational tools, instigates new forms of collaboration among students, such as helping and instructing behaviors, discussion, and cooperation. Technology can also be a medium through which interaction between children with special needs and their peers can be facilitated. Several types of technology are specifically designed to promote social interaction among student users. Computer supported collaborative learning tools are purposefully set up to promote communication and peer learning among young children by encouraging group work and sharing. With proper instructions from teachers, children can use CSCL tools to learn to collaborate, to problem-solve, and to work on tasks that may be otherwise too difficult to do alone.

However, different types of technology foster different levels of social and personal development. The literature has raised concerns for technologies that do not promote positive interactions between children and computers and among children using technology in the classroom. Some uses of technology, while effective in promoting cognitive development, may not be ideal for social and prosocial development. For example, although technologies that promote drill and practice may foster self-efficacy and promote turn-taking and sharing, they may also engender competitiveness in children. Moreover, using technology as a standalone tutor without proper and planned integration with classroom curriculum may result in isolation among students and hinder peer collaboration and learning. The integration between technology and classroom curriculum and management is vital to the successful use of technology in early childhood education classrooms

Technologies that effectively facilitate social interaction also promote language and literacy development. Activities around technologies that support interactions among student peers by encouraging peer learning, peer teaching, and cooperation inevitably become venues for language-rich exchanges. At the computer, for example, research has shown that children speak twice as many words per minute than at other non–technology-related play activities such as playdough and building blocks. The abstract and open-ended nature of many educational technologies, such as computer simulation software or electronic and robotic construction kits, has been shown to effectively engender imagination, creativity, and language exchanges that are rich with emotion and interpersonal understanding. However, as with any other benefits of using technology in early childhood education, effective use of educational technologies as a tool to promote literacy and language development depends greatly on the curriculum used along with the technology. While even stand-alone drill and practice computer software can help children read and strengthen their vocabulary recall, the impact of technology is greatest with regard to language development when it is also used to facilitate peer interaction rather than as a replacement for teachers or tutors.

Therefore, educational technology should not be seen as a stand-alone tool to be set aside in the classroom. Effective use of educational technology requires a well-planned and supported technology–classroom integration. Although educational technology has been traditionally seen as a tool to provide cognitive and academic exercises, educational technology also requires adult attention to ensure that it is used in a way that does not interfere with children's peer and teacher-child interactions. However, when properly introduced to the classroom, technology can be a great asset to early childhood education in facilitating children's cognitive, personal–social, and language development. *See also* Constructionism.

Further Readings: Bers, M., I. Ponte, K. Juelich, K. Viera, and J. Schenker (2002). Teachers as designers: integrating robotics in early childhood education. *Information Technology in Childhood Education, AACE* 123–145; Bers, M., R. New, and L. Boudreau (2004). Teaching and learning when no one is expert: Children and parents explore technology. *ECRP* 6(2); Clements, D. H., and B. K. Nastasi (1992). Computers and early childhood education. In M. Gettiger, S. N. Elliott, and T. R. Kratochwill, eds., *Advances in school psychology: Preschool and early childhood treatment directions.* Hillsdale, NJ: Lawrence Erlbaum, pp. 187–246; Papert, S. (1991). What's the big idea: Towards a pedagogy of idea power. *IBM Systems Journal* 39(3–4); Genishi, C., P. McCollum, and E. B. Strand (1985). Research currents: The interactional richness of children's computer use. *Language Arts* 62(5), 526–532; Koshmann, T. (1996). *CSCL: Theory of practice of an emerging paradigm.* Hillsdale, NJ: Lawrence Erlbaum Associates.

Marina Umaschi Bers and Clement Chau

TECSE. *See* Topics in Early Childhood Special Education

Television

Television viewing is a part of the regular daily routine of most American children. Despite the recommendations of the American Academy of Pediatrics that young children below the age of two years should not watch television, a report funded by the Henry J. Kaiser Family Foundation indicated that 74 percent of children below age two have watched television, and, on a typical day, 59 percent watch an average of two hours and five minutes. In a national survey including 145 families with two- and three-year-olds, parents reported that their child watches an average of about two hours (159 minutes) each day. School-age children spend almost three hours per day watching television. Thirty percent of children up to age three and 43 percent of children four to six years old have televisions in their bedrooms. A more recent survey of parents found that the mean age infants and toddlers began watching videos and television was about six months and nine and three-quarter months respectively. The mean number of hours that infants and toddlers under two years watched television per day was about one hour and twelve minutes, slightly less time than two- and three-year-olds watch television (Singer and Singer, 2005).

Formal Features and Special Characteristics of Television

Properties, conventions, and formal features that distinguish television from other media, and that affect children's comprehension are (1) *attention demand*—the continuous movements on the screen that evoke an orienting response; (2) *brevity of sequence*—the brief interactions among people, brief portrayal of events, the brief commercials (10–30 seconds long; (3) *interference effects*—the rapid succession of material that interferes with rehearsal and assimilation of material; (4) *complexity of presentation*—the cross-modality presentation of material (sound, sight, and printed word, especially in commercials); (5) *visual orientation*—television is concrete, oriented toward spatial imagery; and 6) *emotional range*—the vividness of action (special effects, music, lighting).

It may be difficult for a young child to comprehend slow motion or speeded motion, the juxtaposition of scenes or split-screen technique, the use of subliminal techniques (two scenes to be viewed simultaneously, used often in dream sequences), special effects such as zooming in, making things appear small, or growing gradually in front of your eyes. Other television features include "magical" effects involving distortions, fades, or dissolves, changes in figure and ground, and the rapid disappearances of persons or objects.

Research Methods

There are numerous techniques used to study the effects of television on young children: *survey* research, *laboratory studies* dealing with experimental and various control conditions, *cross-sectional field studies*, and *longitudinal* approaches in which data obtained are examined for their possible effects on overt behaviors over an extended period of time. *Meta-analysis* is a technique for examining an accumulation of separately conducted studies that have comparisons between experimental and control conditions, or of contrasting groups with respect to relevant cognitive and behavior variables.

Results of Television Exposure

In the 1980s, a series of experimental studies examined the effects of television on preschool children with a particular emphasis on imagination and aggression. Highly imaginative children tended to watch programs chiefly on the Public Broadcasting System (PBS) and had parents who also valued imagination. Children who were watching at least three hours or more a day were *less* imaginative than those children who only watched one hour a day. The less imaginative children had a history of watching action/adventure TV programs and cartoons, all associated with high levels of rapid activity and **violence**. Their parents also proved to be less likely to control their children's TV viewing (Singer and Singer, 1981). Children who watched action detective programs or particular cartoons or programs with superheroes were more likely to be aggressive both verbally and physically in the day care centers and at home than children who were lighter television viewers and whose parents controlled the kinds of programs and number of hours that children viewed television. Researchers followed children over a year to four or five years later, and found that early heavy TV viewing of more violent programming was associated with subsequent overt aggressive behavior at home and in school (Singer and Singer, 2005).

Another example of a longitudinal approach involved a long-term follow-up from preschool-age to middle and high school and included children who predominantly watched programs on Public Television such as *Sesame Street*. These children performed better in school academically and behaviorally than children who chiefly watched commercial programs. Large-scale longitudinal studies have presented evidence linking frequent exposure to violent media in childhood with aggression later in life (Anderson et al., 2003).

Educational programs that include fantasy elements and offer solutions to problems have been shown to foster imagination and creativity and prosocial behaviors such as sharing, taking turns, and cooperation. Research, however, employing a content analysis of the five most popular prime-time family sitcoms among children ages two to eleven years found that, while sitcoms featured child characters in the major story line, the emphasis was primarily on negative emotions such as fear and anger. In experiments with infants aged ten to twelve months, the older children showed increases in negative emotions after viewing an actress who vividly expressed these negative emotions. It appears from this study that by one year, a child is able to process the social information and the emotional state of people depicted on television (Singer and Singer, 2005). Research concerning television's effects on children's fears has been summarized by Cantor (2006). As children grow older, they become more responsive to realistic dangers than to those depicted in fantasy programs.

In terms of health, studies have found that viewing frightening material raised children's heart rates and that the more children watched television the less likely they were to engage in physical activity (Durant et al., 1994). **Obesity** and its relationship to television is being investigated by researchers, but most of the data reported are correlational rather than causal. Young children are influenced by advertising of toys and food products, and children as young as two years already have established beliefs about particular brands (Hite and Hite, 1995).

In a meta-analysis of twenty-three studies, television was found to be negatively correlated with reading ability; the magnitude of the correlation rises sharply after 20 hours of television viewing (Walberg and Haertel, 1992). Viewing more than three hours per day seems to be the critical peak in the decline of reading ability. It may be that television viewing displaces the time needed for practicing reading. Researchers have found a significant association between the amount of television watched between ages one and three, and subsequent attention problems at age seven (Christakis et al., 2004). Children who watch heavy amounts of television tend to have shorter attention spans.

In a longitudinal study by Lemish and Rice (1985), observations of children's behaviors were recorded while they watched television in their own homes. The children were newborn to three years of age, actively involved in the process of language acquisition. The main categories of children's verbalizations were as follows: labeling objects on the screen, asking questions about the program, repeating television dialogue or parent comments about the content, and describing the content. Parents acted as mediators, with their verbalizations paralleling the child's. Linebarger and Walker (2005) concluded from experimental studies with babies observed every three months from age six months to the age of two that programs featuring tight narrative structures that used language-promoting strategies predicted greater vocabulary and more expressive language development than did programs like Teletubbies that emphasized baby talk and looser story content.

Controlling Television

Since broadcast television encompasses stations that transmit their signals through a technology that uses publicly owned airwaves, the Federal Communications Commission (FCC) has the power to grant broadcast licenses and to create regulations that are related to public interest. The Children's Television Act of 1990 enacted by Congress and implemented by the FCC led to the requirement that broadcasters include three hours per week of educational programming for children aired between six in the morning and eleven in the evening. Cable and other nonbroadcast technologies are not bound by any obligation to serve the public interest since they do not use the broadcast airwaves for distribution of their programming.

The V-chip, a filtering device that parents can use to block material that has the potential of harming children, became part of the Telecommunications Act of 1996 stipulating that all new television sets must be so equipped. Commercially produced devices include lock boxes that parents can purchase to block out programming that they consider inappropriate for their children. Program ratings by age, violence, sex, adult dialogue, and fantasy violence are supposed to appear in the corner of a TV screen at the start of each show; they are inconsistently applied and there are no content descriptors. There are discrepancies often between ratings offered in newsprint, guides, and those appearing on the television screen (Singer and Singer, 2001).

Specific curricula using specially prepared manuals (and sometimes video accompaniments that explain the electronic workings of television's special effects), that discuss commercials, violence, and fantasy/reality distinctions, and the different genres (news, drama, documentary, cartoon, quiz show) are available to schools and to parents for controlling and mediating children's television viewing. Research indicates that children who are exposed to such curricula have a clearer understanding of how television transmits information and entertainment than children who have not been exposed to such curricula (Singer and Singer, 2001).

In addition to the industry monitoring the quality of television, a parent or other caregiver has a significant role to play concerning the content and age appropriateness of the material that a child watches. Adult caregivers can mediate by explaining TV content, asking questions to determine how accurately a child has processed the material, controlling the number of hours a child views each day, and selecting programs that are age- and content-appropriate. When the parent is an active participant with the child, television has the potential to be a good teacher. *See also* Attention Deficit Disorder/Attention Deficit Hyperactivity Disorder; Development, Language; Parents and Parent Involvement.

Further Readings: Anderson, C. A., L. Berkowitz, E. Donnerstein, L. R., Huesmann, J. D. Johnson, D. Linz, N. M. Malamuth, and E. Wartella (2003). The influence of media violence on youth. *Psychological Science in the Public Interest*. December; Cantor, J. (2006). Protecting children's welfare in an anxiety-provoking media environment. In Nancy E. Dowd, Dorothy G. Singer, and Robin F. Wilson, eds., *Children, culture and violence*. Thousand Oaks, CA: Sage Publications, pp. 163–178; Christakis, D. A., F. J. Zimmerman, D. L. DiGiuseppe, and C. A. McCarty (2004). Early television exposure and subsequent attentional problems in children. *Pediatrics* 113(4), 708-713; DuRant, R. H., T. Baranowsk, M. Johnson, and W. O. Thompson (1994). The relationship among television watching, physical activity, and body composition of young children. *Pediatrics* 94(4 Pt 1), 449-455; Hite, C. F., and R. E. Hite (1995). Reliance on brand by young children. *Journal of the Market Research Society* 37 (2), 185; Lemish, D., and M. L. Rice (1985). Television as a talking picture book: A prop for language acquisition. *Child Language* 13, 251-274; Linebarger, D. L., and D. Walker (2005). Infants' and toddlers' television viewing and language outcomes. In E. A. Wartella, E. A. Vandewater, and J. Rideout, eds., "Electronic Media Use in the Lives of Infants, Toddlers, and Preschoolers." *American Behavioral Scientist* 48(5), 624-645; Singer, Dorothy G., and Jerome L. Singer (1981). *Television, imagination and aggression: A study of preschoolers.* Hillsdale, NJ: Erlbaum. Singer, Dorothy G., and Jerome L. Singer, eds. (2001). *Handbook of children and the media.* Thousand Oaks, CA: Sage Publications. Singer, Dorothy G., and Jerome L. Singer (2005). *Imagination and play in the electronic age.* Cambridge, MA: Harvard University Press. Walberg, H., and G. Haertel (1992). Educational psychology's first century. *Journal of Educational Psychology* 84, 6-21.

Dorothy G. Singer and Jerome L. Singer

Temperament

Temperament is a set of personal characteristics and patterns that emerge early in life and persist over time. Most researchers and clinicians interpret temperament as the result of innate biological and heritable predispositions. Lists of temperamental traits vary, including characteristics as disparate as activity level and introversion or shyness. Combinations of temperamental characteristics are often grouped together to describe a child's personality profile, an "easy child" or "the difficult child." Although seen as long-standing, such traits are not immutable. At any given time, a child's temperament represents both constitutional predispositions and the history of how the child's environment has responded to those traits.

The uniqueness of individual temperament has been recognized throughout history and across cultures. Stories about people almost always involve description of temperament; Shakespeare's Hamlet, for example, was impulsive and indecisive at the same time. A person's temperament can be what attracts others or pushes them away. An understanding of temperament can help early childhood educators identify children's learning styles, communicate more effectively with parents, and reflect on their own expectations of children.

Among the most thorough longitudinal investigations of temperament is that of Thomas and Chess. These researchers followed children from early infancy into adulthood periodically rating their subjects on nine characteristics, activity level, rhythmicity, adaptability, approach-withdrawal, mood, intensity of reaction, attention span–persistence, distractibility, and threshold of response. Over the years they have found that these traits tend to persist over time; they are not entirely immutable, and certain clusters of traits may make success in school more difficult to achieve. For example, a highly active child who is both distractible and not persistent at tasks may have difficulty in a structured school setting. Some children diagnosed with **Attention Deficit Disorder/Attention Deficit Hyperactivity Disorder** (ADD-ADHD) may be at the extreme end of what Thomas and Chess have described as a pattern of behavioral characteristics.

One characteristic that has received a great deal of attention by both developmental psychologists and early educators is shyness or introversion. Every group that an early childhood educator encounters will include some children who are outgoing and gregarious and others who are passive and avoid social contact. The research of Jerome Kagan demonstrates that babies who respond to novel experiences with fussiness at 4 months tend to be shy children in their preschool and early school years. According to Kagan, these children have a physiological response to what they experience as stressful. The resultant behavior pattern may vary from immediate withdrawal to cautious approach depending on how the child has been supported throughout childhood in new situations, but the underlying physiological response reflects an innate predisposition.

Temperamental characteristics carry different meanings in different cultural settings. For example, among the Inuit studied by Jean Briggs (1998) the degree of desired fearfulness of adults contrasts with the gregariousness encouraged in many European American families. In another example, Chinese child-rearing practices seem to support reticence as a strength, whereas shyness is seen as undesirable in Canadian families (Chen et al., 1998).

Parents may respond differently to children with different temperaments. Babies born with a tendency to be irritable may have parents who respond to these traits with their own discomfort and even anger or they may provide a soothing environment. Over time these children may look very different from each other despite their innate temperamental tendencies. One expresses irritability in responding to new situations, the other mediates her emotional response with the self-regulating strategies she learned from responsive caregiving. The behavioral match or mismatch between parents and children is partly attributable to temperament. Such match or mismatch may also operate in teacher–child interactions.

In many early childhood classrooms it is the active, gregarious children that draw attention from the teacher and the quiet, passive children who seem to carry on without much teacher involvement. An understanding of the temperamental profile of each child can help avoid such inequity in classrooms. As it relates to learning, for example in how a child approaches new curriculum materials, an understanding of temperament allows the teacher to support each child's learning process. One child may be very persistent to the point of not wanting to clean up when the time for project work is over; another child may require a good deal of support to stay with an activity. Such understanding may also help in managing peer interactions; an impulsive child who approaches other children with passion and energy may require help in softening his approach so that other children can tolerate his play. Conversely, the more socially passive child may need support in entering a mutual play situation.

Temperament is also a useful topic for communication with parents. Parents want teachers to know their children as people. A simple description of the child's developmental progress according to standard sets of milestones rarely convinces parents that the teacher truly knows the child. Temperament provides a vehicle for a more complete communication about the child and what the child is capable of. T. Berry Brazelton's Touchpoints approach utilizes temperament as a particularly effective way of establishing common understanding of the child in developing a relationship with a parent.

Temperament tells a teacher how a child operates in the world of materials and people. As such it provides an essential means for understanding children as unique individuals rather than as a collection of skills or developmental competencies. *See also* Parent and Parent Involvement.

Further Readings: Bates, J., and M. Rothbart, eds. (1989). *Temperament in childhood.* Chichester, England: Wiley. Briggs, J. (1998). Inuit morality play: The emotional education of a three-year-old. New Haven, CT: Yale University Press; Chen, X., K. Rubin, G. Cen, P. Hastings, H. Chen, and S. Stewart (1998). Child-rearing attitudes and behavioral inhibition in Chinese and Canadian toddlers: A cross-cultural study. *Developmental Psychology* 34(4), 677–686; Kagan, J., and N. Snidman (1991). Temperamental factors in human development. *The American Psychologist* 46(8), 856; Kristal, J. (2005). The temperament perspective: Working with children's behavioral styles. New York: Paul H. Brookes Pub. Co. Miller, Peggy J., R. Potts, Heidi Fung, Lisa Hoogstra, and Julie Mintz (1990). Narrative practices and the social construction of self in childhood. *American Ethnologist* 17, 292–311; Thomas, A., and S. Chess (1977). *Temperament and development.* New York: Brunner/Mazel.

John Hornstein

Temple, Alice (1871–1946)

Early in the twentieth century, the Alice Temple program was a vital element in the integration of **kindergarten** and elementary schools and in the training programs for their teachers. She became a model for those working at both levels of the educational system.

From birth until her retirement in 1932, Alice Temple lived and worked in Chicago. Her kindergarten teacher training began in the Chicago Free Kindergarten Association program at age eighteen. In 1904, she enrolled as a full-time student at the University of Chicago, where John **Dewey** and Anna Bryan had established a curriculum reflecting children's interests. She continued there as a teacher, developing a model kindergarten-primary program and becoming chairman of their new Kindergarten-Primary Department in 1929.

Kindergarten, originally for children aged three to six or seven, had functioned outside the public school system after its introduction in the 1870s. In the early 1900s, it was accepted as the "first step on the ladder" for the public elementary schools of Illinois, but was limited to one or two years before first grade. Temple based the integration of kindergarten and primary grades upon Dewey's idea of continuity between these two levels, a proposal that fit into the public and professional discourse about social efficiency and scientific measurement. Her system, coauthored with Samuel Parker, was published in 1928 as *Unified Kindergarten and First Grade Teaching*.

Temple joined the **International Kindergarten Union** (IKU) in 1900. She was identified as a "Liberal" when divisions developed between those who maintained a structured use of curriculum materials and those who credited Friedrich **Froebel** for originating the kindergarten in the 1830s but were heeding his directives to modify it through continued study. She advocated free play with building blocks, a "housekeeping area" with miniature utensils and dolls, and varied art activities to be used creatively. She emphasized, however, that some subject matter should be determined by the teachers and that appropriate assistance and guidance be given to the young students.

Temple was involved with many IKU committees and activities, with elective offices including vice-president (1923–1925) and president (1925–1927). She was instrumental in establishing their journal, *Childhood Education*, in 1924. After the IKU merged with the National Council of Primary Education to become the Association for Childhood Education in 1930, she served on its Advisory Board until her death in 1946. "She was always ready to throw in her efforts with those of others wherever she could serve. *Cooperation* was the keynote of her working methods as were *unity* and *continuity* the theme of her motivation." (Snyder 1972, p. 212)

Temple had a major influence upon students who became leaders in the IKU and the emerging nursery school movement, not only from the course content but by patterning their own professional lives upon hers. Perhaps her lifetime is best summarized in Snyder's list of *Dauntless Women in Early Childhood Education:* "Alice Temple, a great teacher. Her students spoke of her reverently, as they acclaimed the lasting influence she had exerted on them and then found it difficult to recall specific things she had said" (1972, p. 360).

Further Readings: Mayhew, Katherine Camp, and Anna Camp Edwards (1936). *The Dewey school: The laboratory school of the University of Chicago: 1896-1903*. New York: Teachers College Press; Parker, Samuel C., and Temple, Alice (1925). *Unified kindergarten and first grade teaching*. Boston: Ginn and Co. Snyder, Agnes (1972). *Dauntless women in early childhood education—1856-1931*; Washington, DC: Association for Childhood Education International. Weber, Evelyn (1984). *Ideas influencing early childhood education*. New York: Teachers College Press.

Dorothy W. Hewes and Shunah Chung

Temporary Assistance to Needy Families (TANF)

The Temporary Assistance to Needy Families (TANF) program is a federal block grant that provides financial assistance and work opportunities to families in need by allowing states the freedom and flexibility to determine how best to meet citizens' needs. Enacted in 1996 as part of welfare reform, TANF funding may be used to provide cash benefits to low-income families, funding for child care activities, and support for other work-related activities. With over 3.6 million children receiving some type of TANF support each month during FY 2004, it is clear that this program has a significant impact on a large number of children in the United States (Administration for Children and Families, 2005).

TANF was established through the Personal Responsibility and Work Opportunity Reconciliation Act (PRWORA) of 1996. In 1992, presidential candidate Bill Clinton gave a campaign speech proclaiming the need for drastic changes in welfare policy, asserting that "no one who works full-time and has children at home should be poor anymore. No one who can work should be able to stay on welfare forever" (Danziger, 1999, p. 1). After President Clinton took office, he appointed an interagency task force to study possible solutions to this problem, and develop legislation to reform welfare policy. Although there was much controversy surrounding the bill, in August of 1996, Congress passed PRWORA and President Clinton signed the act into law (Danziger, 1999).

Welfare reform under PRWORA represents a dramatic change in the way cash assistance and support services are delivered to children and families. The TANF block grant, administered by the Office of Family Assistance, replaces the previous Aid to Families with Dependent Children (AFDC), Job Opportunities and Basic Skills (JOBS), and Emergency Assistance (EA) programs (Administration for Children and Families, n.d.a). The general mission of TANF is to move welfare recipients to work and self-sufficiency, and to ensure that welfare receipt is short-term and not "a way of life." The four stated purposes of TANF are as follows:

- to assist needy families so that children can be cared for in their homes;
- to reduce dependency [upon government] of needy families by promoting job preparation, work, and marriage;
- to prevent out-of-wedlock pregnancies;
- to encourage the formation and maintenance of two-parent families.

The legislation encourages states to be flexible, innovative, and creative in the ways in which they provide supports to working families. However, the legislation also establishes some basic requirements for the program. For instance, TANF recipients must begin working as soon as they are job-ready, or no more than two years after they began receiving cash assistance. Work activities under TANF are broadly defined, and include education or training programs, subsidized or unsubsidized employment, community services, and job search. Finally, adults who are eligible for cash benefits may only receive them for up to 60 months (and often less, at each state's discretion).

States received $17 billion in fiscal year 2004 for activities related to the four purposes of the block grant. States can use TANF to support low-income families by providing monthly cash benefits, child care subsidies, transportation assistance, tax credits, and assistance related to work activities. These activities directly affect children whose families are eligible for TANF support. Primarily, children benefit from the monthly cash benefits their families receive, and also from the child care subsidies that allow children to attend child care activities while their parents work or attend education or training programs. TANF dollars can be used directly for child care, or can be transferred to states' Child Care and Development Funds (CCDF) for child care subsidies (Administration for Children and Families, n.d.b). TANF funding can also be transferred to the Social Services Block Grant (SSBG) and used for activities related to social services for adults and children, including services related to preventing or remedying abuse or neglect of children. Much of the funding allocated under SSBG is spent on protective services for children, foster care services, and services for disabled children. SSBG funding is also used for child care subsidies and other child care activities (Administration for Children and Families, n.d.c).

As TANF represents a complete overhaul of the welfare system of the past few decades, numerous studies have been conducted measuring the various effects of the program. In general, results from these studies of TANF are mixed. While welfare reform has resulted in decreased caseloads and increased employment of single mothers (largely due to the 60-month time limit for benefits), not all families who get off of TANF experience an improved financial situation once they begin working (Fremstad, 2004; Haskins et al., 2001). Currently, the federal government is in the process of working on TANF reauthorization, and many research and advocacy organizations have suggested modifications to the current policy to make TANF more effective for the children and families it affects. These modifications include changes to specific aspects of the law, such as the number of weekly work hours required for parents with children, programs and policies related to adolescents and especially to teen parents, and policies related to child care and the choices parents face when returning to work (Levin-Epstein, 2002).

Further Readings: Administration for Children and Families (2005). *Caseload data: TANF: Total number of child recipients FY 2004.* Available online at http://www. acf.dhhs.gov/programs/ofa/caseload/2004/children04tanf.htm. Administration for Children and Families (n.d.a.) *Fact sheets: Office of family assistance.* Available online at http://www.acf.hhs.gov/opa/fact_sheets/tanf_factsheet.html. Administration for Children and Families (n.d.b); *Fact sheets: Welfare.* Available online at http://www.acf.hhs.gov/news/facts/tanf.html; Administration for Children and Families (n.d.c). *SSBG 2003.* Available online at http://www.acf.hhs.gov/programs/ ocs/ssbg/annrpt/2003/chapter2.html; Danziger, S. H. (1999). Introduction: What are the early lessons? In Danziger, S. H., ed., *Economic conditions and welfare reform*; Kalamazoo, MI: W.E. Upjohn Institute for Employment Research, pp. 1-14; Haskins, R., I. V. Sawhill, and R. K. Weaver (2001). Welfare reform: An overview of effects to date. Available online at http://www.brook.edu/es/research/projects/ wrb/publications/pb/pb01.htm; Levin-Epstein, J. (2002). Testimony of Jodie Levin-Epstein, Senior Policy Analyst, Center for Law and Social Policy. Available online at http://www.clasp.org/publications/Levin-Epstein_4-11-02_testimony.pdf.

Abby Copeman

Thorndike, Edward L. (1847–1949)

Edward Lee Thorndike was a leader in educational psychology at the turn of the twentieth century. Thorndike grew up in New England, where his father was a Methodist minister. He attended Wesleyan University in 1891 and showed intellectual independence from his father when writing for the Eclectic Society and by later referring to himself as an agnostic. While at Wesleyan, Thorndike studied the work of William James and later credited James for his own devotion to psychology. Thorndike later attended Harvard for two years, then Columbia University. At Columbia, Thorndike found a second mentor in James Cattell. Thorndike's thesis was entitled "Animal Intelligence, An Experimental Study of the Associative Processes in Animals," wherein he explained learning as the forming of associations between situations and impulses to action within that situation. Thorndike's thesis is noted as a starting point for experiments in animal psychology.

Thorndike accepted a teaching position at Western Reserve's College for Women, where he taught two courses on education and teaching theories. In 1899, Thorndike returned to Columbia University and was selected for Teachers College as Associate Professor of Genetic Psychology. Thorndike also taught child psychology but held that courses were generally a waste of time because education came best through personal reading and study. He married in 1900 and subsequently wrote *Human Nature Club*, *The Elements of Psychology*, and *Principles of Teaching*.

Thorndike spent a decade researching animal and human psychology. He believed that progress in science led to social advance. He studied monkeys, wrote the article "The Evolution of Human Intellect," and conducted experiments with A.R. Woodworth. In 1903, Thorndike published *Educational Psychology* and, later, *An Introduction to the Theory of Mental and Social Measurements* as the first complete theoretical and statistical handbook in social science. Thorndike believed that individuality was the key concept of school theory and practice and stated that the school must respect the needs and capacities of individual students. "Individuality" was his first extended statement about differential psychology, and his three-volume series on *Education Psychology* was published at the peak of his influence. This volume focused upon learning as the central issue of psychology and asserted that man is by nature a connection-forming creature with many possibilities. Thorndike later discovered high correlations between reading and intelligence tests. His *Thorndike Arithmetics* became adapted as a statewide text and was widely used.

Thorndike was elected to the National Academy of Sciences in 1917. He became more involved in research when Teachers College established its Institute of Education Research. Receiving honors at the international level in 1937 and 1938, he became President of the American Academy of Arts and Sciences. Thorndike was known for the extension of measurement to all education and for his learning theory. He believed education to be a theory, an art, and a science.

Further Readings: Joncich, Geraldine (1968). *The sane positivist: A biography of Edward L. Thorndike.* Middletown, CT: Wesleyan University Press; Weber, Evelyn (1984). *Ideas influencing early childhood education.* New York: Teachers College Press.

Charlotte Anderson

Topics in Early Childhood Special Education (TECSE)

Topics in Early Childhood Special Education (*TECSE*) is one of the leading scholarly, peer-reviewed journals in the area of early intervention and early childhood special education. Its mission is to communicate information about early intervention, which is defined as services to infants, toddlers, and preschoolers at risk for, or who display, developmental disabilities and their families (Carta,

2005). The journal publishes empirical research, policy analyses, literature reviews, and position papers. Beginning in April 1981, it originally published four topical issues each year, and has evolved into publishing annually three topical issues and one open or nontopical issue. Articles from *TECSE* have influenced policy and practices for infants and young children with disabilities and are often cited by authors of papers in other journals. *See also* Special Education, Early Childhood.

Further Readings: Carta, J. J. (2005). Editorial policy. *Topics in early childhood special education* 25, 123–125.

Samuel Odom

Touchpoints

Touchpoints is a strength-based practical approach of working with families of young children and is based on Dr. T. Berry Brazelton's forty years of clinical and research experience as a pediatrician. The central notion around which this approach is organized is that of "Touchpoints," or the predictable bursts, regressions, and pauses that occur over the course of a child's development. Touchpoints typically precede a spurt in a particular line of development, and are often accompanied by parental frustration and self-doubt. For practitioners concerned with the health and well-being of the child and family, these Touchpoints can be seen as points of change for the child and the parent, as well as for the family as a whole. While the Touchpoints approach was initially implemented in health care settings, it was also originally intended, and has since been adapted, for use in a variety of settings including early intervention, social services, public health, and early child care and education organizations.

The Touchpoints program is designed to help family-serving professionals in such multidisciplinary settings build their knowledge about child development and develop collaborative strategies for working with families. A particular goal of the program is to help professionals use these strategies to foster a sense of competence in parents and empower them in their parenting abilities. Thus, the Touchpoints program operates from the framework that each and every parent is the expert on his or her child. Through this process, the approach seeks to optimize child development, support healthy families, and enhance professional development.

The Touchpoints framework has both developmental and clinical components. The program recognizes that early childhood is a time of great change for both children and families. The approach views development as a discontinuous process rather than a linear progression of attaining developmental milestones. However, while development is not viewed as a linear or continuous process, there are many periods of change that can be predicted. These predictable periods of change are often accompanied by disorganization as children may learn new skills in one area, but simultaneously regress in other areas of development. For example, when a child is learning to walk, he/she may not be able to remain on a regular sleep schedule. These times of change may affect not only the child's behavior, but also the entire family system.

Because "Touchpoints" are predictable, the approach views such times of disorganization as valuable opportunities to help parents anticipate and plan for the challenges they face in raising young children). By providing such "anticipatory guidance" (Stadtler et al., 1995), family-serving professionals, including early childhood educators, can help parents recognize the strengths they already have and gain confidence in their own parenting abilities and instincts. The Touchpoints approach, then, operates from a clinical framework that assumes that, if parents can anticipate and better understand the periods of disorganization in their children's development, then they will feel more empowered in their abilities to effectively respond to such challenging times.

The Brazelton Touchpoints Center offers a training specifically designed for early child care and education providers to help enhance their knowledge of child development and develop collaborative strategies for working with the families in their programs. The trainings are organized around a set of guiding principles, and assumptions about families and professionals, which serve as a framework for reflective practice for early child care and education providers. The training encourages providers to avoid advice-giving and prescriptive approaches to communication, and instead employ collaborative approaches to help parents gain confidence in their own decisions and parenting strategies. Ultimately, parents' recognition of their own strengths should, ideally, have a positive effect on their children's well-being and development.

The Touchpoints early child care and education training also focuses on the entire family system. Touchpoints in Early Child Care and Education represents a shift away from the idea of a *child* attending child care, and toward the goal of child care providers joining and supporting every *family* as a system of care around their child. Thus, the trainings provide strategies designed to not only improve parent-provider communication and relationships, but also to promote positive parent–child relationships. The Touchpoints approach recognizes that parents may often feel ambivalent about placing their children in out-of-home care, and that some may feel threatened by the relationships that their children are forming with their child care providers. Thus, while the Touchpoints approach values the parent–provider relationship, the ultimate goal of the program is to focus on and enhance relationships within the family.

By training teams of professionals from around the country, the Touchpoints approach has built a national network of training sites. Some of these sites focus primarily on training for early care and education professionals. Others are multidisciplinary and encourage the use of the Touchpoints approach in helping professionals who work with families communicate with each other, as they join families in systems of care. The approach has also been specifically adapted for use with families of children with special needs. Finally, an American Indian initiative (Mayo-Willis and Hornstein, 2003) has prompted further review and adaptation of the approach based upon cultural variation in child-rearing beliefs and practices.

The Touchpoints approach draws from Urie **Bronfenbrenner's** (2001) ecological systems theory which views development as the product of interactions that take place between children and the multiple environments in which they live. According to this theory, stronger linkages between the various environments in which a child lives, such as between home and child care, and more specifically between parents and child care providers, should have a positive influence on children's development and well-being. With the increasing numbers of families in the United States that are coming to rely on early child care and education services, Touchpoints provides a way to enhance provider–parent relationships, and ultimately promote the healthy development of young children and their families.

Further Readings: Brazelton, T. Berry (1994). *Touchpoints: Your child's emotional and behavior development.* Cambridge, MA: Da Capo Press. Brazelton Touchpoints Center (2005). *Touchpoints in early care and education reference guide and participant training materials.* Version 1.0. Boston, MA: Brazelton Touchpoints Center; Bronfenbrenner, Urie (2001). Ecological models of human development. In Mary Gauvain and Michael Cole, eds., *Readings on the development of children.* 3rd ed. New York: Worth Publishers, pp. 3–8; Mayo-Willis, L., and J. Hornstein (2003). Joining native American systems of care: The complexities of culturally appropriate practice. *Zero-to-Three* 23(5), 36–39; Stadtler, A., M. O'Brien, and J. Hornstein (1995). The touchpoints model: building supportive alliances between parents and professionals. *Zero-to-Three* (15)1, 24–28.

Mallory I. Swartz and John Hornstein

Transitions/Continuity

Transitions are a part of everyone's life. Generally, a transition refers to the process in which an individual participates when moving from one setting to another. Changing schools or communities, entering the job market, marriage, and retirement are examples of normative, positive life transitions. At times, transitions may negatively impact an individual and/or family, such as divorce, death of a family member, or loss of a job. In the field of early childhood and early childhood special education, families and children experiencing transitions when leaving one program and entering another may encounter a smooth transition or one laden with difficulties. When transitions are supportive, the gaps that may have existed between the two programs are bridged, resulting in continuity (SERVE, 2002). Continuity refers to an uninterrupted connection or flow of services, such as a child leaving a Head Start setting and enrolling in a new preschool, or a child with special needs moving into another setting and receiving his therapy sessions without disruption. Continuity is critical to the success of transitions.

Transition considerations for typically developing children and their families must not be overlooked, as this time is critical in setting the stage for successful school experiences. Each child and family's transition experience is unique and, thereby, cannot be characterized by specific standards or procedures. However, Pianta and Kraft-Sayre (2003) developed five guiding principles that may be applied to transition planning for all young children. These include fostering relationships as resources, promoting continuity from preschool to kindergarten, focusing on family strengths, tailoring practices to individual needs, and forming collaborative relationships. The literature regarding transitions mirrors the principles described above. In addition, parents must be recognized as experts and empowered as advocates for their children. Although these principles may be attainable, they require much preparation from all parties involved in transition planning.

Often parents of children with special needs experience a myriad of transitions long before their youngster reaches school age. Premature infants and those with birth complications may require the hospital's neonatal intensive care unit (NICU) and subsequent referral for early intervention services. Children diagnosed with developmental delays and their families must transition from early intervention provided in the home to an early childhood special education program in the local elementary school. The transition journey will continue as the child moves throughout school and into adulthood, each transition bringing its own challenges and successes.

Whether a child is transitioning from early intervention to preschool or preschool to kindergarten, transitions for some families may be matter of fact, while others are quite complex. Often concerns and stress are heightened during the process, and must be addressed accordingly. Issues such as differences in program philosophy and expectations, services provided, the level of parent involvement, and concerns related specifically to the child are only beginning points for transition planning. Specifically, a child's preschool program may permit parents to volunteer in the classroom, but in his new kindergarten classroom, the policy might not include parent volunteers except for field trips. The preschool curriculum may differ significantly from that of the kindergarten, and the focus may be more academic than developmental. Class size differs, parents may receive progress reports quarterly rather than weekly, and the child's classroom expectations will change. In the case of a child moving from early intervention to an early childhood special education classroom, children and families must adapt to an entirely different environment. Instead of a case manager or physical therapist coming to a family's home each week, a school bus transports the young child to an elementary school for his education. Rather than addressing a concern during a therapy session, a parent must contact her child's teacher to set up a conference among the child's service providers at school. These examples are part of the transition process and program continuity and will require some adjustment on the part of all parties involved with the child.

An effective transition serves as a bridge between two programs, going from the familiar and comfortable to the unknown and uncharted course. Some educators perceive transition as an ongoing effort to link a child's natural environment (home and family) with a support environment (the child's program) (Kagan and Neuman, 1998). In some instances, transitions consist of a series of activities that take place prior to a child's leaving one setting and entering another, characterized by a visit to the new placement, a meeting with parents, and an exchange of the child's records. Other transitions may include an interagency agreement between the sending agency and receiving program. The goal is to provide as smooth as possible transition with no disruption in services (continuity) for the child and family.

Part C, Public Law 105-17 (IDEA, 1997) provides early intervention services for children with disabilities birth through age two, and Part B regulates the delivery of services for children ages three through five. Within the child's Infant Family Service Plan (IFSP) and/or **Individualized Education Plan** (IEP), a transition plan must be addressed in order to meet federal laws. A timeline serves as a roadmap for implementing the transition plan and should be established as early as the child's enrollment in the early intervention program. Although transition procedures are not mandated until 90 days prior to the actual transition, agencies, schools, parents, and children need much more than three months to put all the pieces in place for an effective transition. When considering a preschool-to-kindergarten transition, educators should contact parents at the beginning of the preschool year to initiate a connection between families, schools, and agencies in order to plan transition activities for families and children during the course of that year (Pianta and Kraft-Sayre, 2003).

Many states and individual school divisions or agencies have developed their own particular procedures for the implementation of transition plans. These plans often include specific timeframes for each aspect of the transition, such as dates set aside for parents and children to visit programs, deadlines for sending children's records, and/or guidelines for a transition coordinator to follow. Professionals involved in planning should guard against the transition becoming a series of events rather than a process that takes time and is intended as an individual plan for each child and family.

Because transitions are different for each child and family exiting one program and entering another, it is imperative that those identified as stakeholders periodically evaluate the effectiveness of the system. The input of parents, teachers, administrators, therapists and community agencies must be considered in the process to accommodate the needs of children and families. The ultimate result will be improved transitions for all persons involved.

The literature offers numerous suggestions of activities and procedures designed to prepare families, children, and receiving agencies or schools for the successful, smooth transition from the current program to the new program. The following suggestions serve as a starting point for planning transitions, and are applicable to most early childhood transitions. It is important to note that extenuating circumstances may arise in which much different activities would be more appropriate.

Transition planning for children with developmental delays must begin early in the child and family's interaction with the initial agency or program. It is as if parents should be told at the onset of services that the transition process will be initiated immediately to prepare them for future changes. For example, parents of infants and toddlers with disabilities need to be aware of services available to them when their child reaches age two or three. Although their child may or may not require further services beyond the early intervention program, parents should be prepared to consider alternatives available to them. A case manager, generally the early interventionist, should either serve as the transition coordinator or maintain close contact with that individual during the child's early intervention services. It is advisable to develop a transition timeline, even though some changes will most likely take place. Stakeholders will demonstrate a stronger ownership if a plan is visible and each person is included in the process.

The participation of parents is key to successful transitions. Parents need to be recognized for their expertise and concerns and priorities must be addressed at the onset. Agency and school personnel should protect parent and child confidentiality, ensure compliance with federal and state mandates, and encourage and respect parental input. Parents should consider themselves partners in the process.

In transitions for typically developing children, such as home or preschool to kindergarten, or those for children with special needs, receiving programs should be aware of prospective students in order to be prepared to meet their needs should they be placed in their care. Staff members of sending and receiving programs should be introduced to each other to begin collaborative relationships. Where feasible, these individuals should be participants in assessments and meetings, striving to increase their visibility, knowledge, and involvement with children and families. When families visit programs they most likely will feel comfortable, welcomed, and willing to participate in the program activities with their children. Introducing parents to the principal, school nurse, office staff, therapists, and paraprofessionals, along with a tour of the facility, should help in alleviating fears of a large building for their little child. Inviting parents for a return visit or telephone call signifies openness on the part of staff.

An evening should be designated for meeting other perspective and current parents and staff members on an informal basis. Children and siblings should be invited to attend, and babysitting and refreshments provided. Parents should have an opportunity to learn about program curriculum and materials, participate in activities with their children, and to ask questions. A highlight for the evening could be the arrival of a school bus and driver inviting parents and children to board. At the end of the school year parents may be guests at graduation or a picnic, and during the summer months sending and receiving teachers might conduct home visits to new families. Finally, parents can be invited to attend an open house prior to the opening of school. Kindergartens may choose a staggered enrollment for the first few weeks of school in order to introduce the children to school on a gradual basis, or permit parents to spend the first several mornings in the classroom with their children.

Transition services are not achieved without careful planning, involvement of all stakeholders, an evaluation component, and the establishment of a timeline. Recognizing transition as a process instead of a series of activities, as individualized for each child, and as subject to change, will result in a smooth transition and continuity of services for everyone.

Further Readings: Kagan, S. L., and M. J. Neuman (1998). Lessons from three decades of transition research. *The Elementary School Journal* 98(4), 365–379; Pianta, R., and M. Kraft-Sayre (2003). *Successful kindergarten transition*; Baltimore: Paul H. Brookes. Rosenkoetter, S. E., A. H. Hains, and S. A. Fowler (1994). *Bridging early services for children with special needs and their families*; Baltimore: Paul H. Brookes. SERVE (2002). *Terrific transitions*. The School of Education, University of North Carolina at Greensboro.

Lucy Kachmarik

U

United Nations Children's Fund (UNICEF)

Whenever one hears the two words *children* and *international*, UNICEF immediately comes to mind. First established in 1946, the acronym stood for the United Nations International Children's Emergency Fund. In 1953, the words *International* and *Emergency* were officially dropped but the full acronym has remained the term used to refer to the United Nation's Children's Fund. In many parts of the world, UNICEF is much more than an acronym, and instead embodies a philosophy that children—and particularly children in the "developing," or Majority World—matter. That philosophy argues that children, especially those affected by challenges now rarely encountered in Western industrialized countries, deserve a chance for healthy and fully productive lives.

The establishment of UNICEF in 1946 was a result of Cold War politics. When the United States sought to substitute the Marshall Plan (reconstruction support for Allied powers only) for the existing UN Relief and Rehabilitation Administration (which provided support for all countries east or west devastated by World War II), the delegates of Poland and Norway objected that children's fate should not be tied to geopolitical divides. The result of their intervention on behalf of children was the creation of resolution 57(1), establishing the International Children's Emergency Fund. At the time the resolution went through the United Nations' structure on December 11, 1946, the United Nations itself was only a year old. In 1953, UNICEF achieved permanent status as a UN organization. Throughout the 1950s, the primary focus of UNICEF was on children's health and its primary activities were focused on efforts to control or eradicate epidemic diseases. In 1959 the UN General Assembly adopted the Declaration of the Rights of the Child. Those Rights included protection, education, health care, shelter, and good nutrition. In 1961 UNICEF expanded its interests from child health to the "whole child," and child education began to play a much larger role in UNICEF.

Since 1989, with the UN General Assembly's adoption of the Convention on the Rights of the Child, and the 1990 World Summit for Children, UNICEF has become an ever stronger force for children's rights, seeing such rights as the foundation for a broad set of child supportive activities. From an education and child development perspective, UNICEF has, for much of its history, not had a particularly strong early childhood focus. When it has focused on the young child it has tended to be with a health or nutrition emphasis. Commencing in the late 1990s and early 2000s, UNICEF, along with other key international players including the World Bank, greatly increased their focus on the young child. These efforts have been characterized by a holistic appreciation of the child and an emphasis on achieving a higher level of integration across the diversity of services and programs available to children. These emphases are generally being advanced from the perspective of an overall poverty reduction orientation.

It is anticipated that the UN Millennium Development Goals (MDG) for 2015, with their strong emphasis on the eradication of extreme poverty and hunger, will drive much of the global development agenda throughout the first decade of the twenty-first century. While early childhood education is not specifically mentioned in the MDG, effective arguments can be put forward regarding the role of early childhood education in achieving the MDG. Indeed, the degree to which the field of early childhood education is a key player in international development work in the period 2000–2010 is dependent upon those connections being made evident. *See also* United Nations Educational, Scientific and Cultural Organization.

Further Readings: Black, M. (1996). *Children first: The story of UNICEF, past and present.* Oxford: Oxford University Press.

Web Sites: UNICEF Web site, http://www.unicef.org/about/who/index_history.html

Alan Pence

United Nations Educational, Scientific and Cultural Organisation (UNESCO)

Founded on 16 November 1945, the United Nations Educational, Scientific and Cultural Organisation (UNESCO) is a specialized United Nations agency that seeks "to contribute to peace and security by promoting collaboration among the nations through education, science and culture to further universal respect" (UNESCO Constitution, article 1). Based in Paris, France, UNESCO is currently represented by 191 member states and has a global network of fifty-eight field offices and eleven institutes and centres.

The main emphasis of UNESCO's activities in education is the global campaign on Education for All, which seeks to provide basic education for all children, youth, and adults so as to enable them to embark on a path of lifelong learning. The Education for All campaign serves as the cornerstone of UNESCO's education programs by focusing on the expansion and diversification of the provision of basic education to reach the largest number of potential learners. Particular emphasis is given to the issues of quality and access, especially for marginalized and excluded individuals.

With regards to the field of early childhood care and education, UNESCO leads the international policy drive for an integrated early childhood care and education system that encompasses the holistic development of the child. UNESCO's mission to support early childhood policy development is guided by two major international frameworks: the 1990 Jomtien Declaration on Education for All, which states that learning begins at birth and confirms early childhood care and education as an integral component of basic education; and the 2000 Dakar Framework for Action on Education for All. Special importance is placed on Goal One of the Dakar Framework for Action, which aims to expand and improve comprehensive early childhood care and education for all children.

With the aim of building a solid foundation for a child's lifelong learning, the Early Childhood program of UNESCO, part of the Division of Basic Education, actively works with Member States in their efforts to develop and strengthen their national capacity to meet this target of the Dakar Framework. To this end, UNESCO publishes the *Policy Briefs on Early Childhood* and regularly undertakes policy review work in selected countries. To date, this policy review work has included the national early childhood policies of Indonesia, Kenya, Kazakhstan, and Brazil.

In terms of strategy for policy development in the early childhood field, UNESCO focuses on holistic pre-primary education for children who are three to five years of age and on their smooth transition to primary education. This approach fully encompasses all elements of children's emotional, social, physical, and cognitive development, as well as their nutrition and health needs. To address the particular needs of children who are from ages zero to three, countries also are recommended to have a phased plan to be implemented jointly between the national education and social sectors. Through its active collaboration with government officials, UNESCO works toward the goal of expanding and improving early childhood care and education, as well as toward the international development goal of universal primary education. For more information on UNESCO's activities in early childhood education, go to http://www.unesco.org/education/ecf. *See also* United Nations Children's Fund (UNICEF).

Soo-Hyang Choi

V

Video Games. *See* Computer and Video Game Play in Early Childhood

Violence and Young Children

Many kinds of violence occur in the daily lives of children growing up today. They see entertainment violence on the screen—in TV programs, movies, video and computer games. There are highly popular toys connected to violent TV programs and other media that encourage children to imitate in their play the violence that they see on the screen. There is real-world violence that children see in the news—weapons exploding, adults hurting adults, adults hurting children, even children hurting children. And then there is the violence that a growing number of children experience directly in their own homes and beyond, whether from an isolated trauma or as a regular part of their lives in violent communities or in war zones (Feerick and Silverman, 2006). The following are some examples that illustrate this fact:

A child care program is out on a field trip. As the children are about to cross a busy street a police officer offers to stop the traffic so the children may cross safely. One child runs to the teacher, grabs his leg and starts to scream. The teacher finds out later that the police arrested the child's father the previous weekend when the child was present.

A kindergartner walks into her classroom and announces to the other children in the entry area that she wasn't in school the day before because her grandmother died. Another child looks up at her and asks, "Who shot her?"

On September 12, 2001, a teacher notices several children building a structure with large cardboard blocks. Two children get inside and the others aggressively crash it down. They pull out the two children who were inside and report that they are "dead."

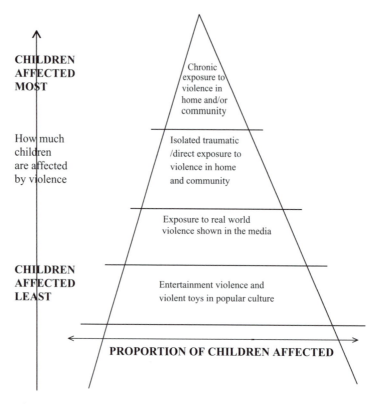

The Continuum of Violence in Children's Lives. Copied with permission from *Teaching Young Children in Violent Times: Building a Peaceable Classroom*, 2nd ed., by Diane E. Levin.

A teacher struggles to deal with the use of toy weapons in her classroom. Several children try to turn anything they can find into one. When she tells them "no weapons in school," they sneak around trying to create and play with symbolic weapons when they think she isn't looking.

The violence in children's lives can be thought of as fitting along a continuum of severity, as shown in the figure. At the bottom is entertainment violence that is most prevalent in American society and touches most children's lives. At the top are the most extreme forms of violence—chronic and direct exposure in the immediate environment, which fewer children experience, at least in most parts of the United States, but which builds onto exposure to the more prevalent forms of violence below it on the pyramid. The degree to which children's development, ideas, and behavior are affected by violence is likely to increase as they move up the continuum, but few children growing up today are likely to avoid experiencing some form of exposure to violence (Levin, 2003).

The Impact of Violence on Young Children

The effects of violence are often most obvious for the most severely involved children, those at the top of the violence continuum. Anna **Freud**'s work during World War II was among the first to direct attention to the devestating effects violence could have on children and how adults could help them cope (Freud and Burlingame, 1943). Since the 1980s, clinicians have recognized that posttraumatic stress disorder (PTSD) can result, a condition whereby children exhibit such symptoms as flashbacks to the traumatic event(s), hypervigilance, regression, sleep troubles, and increased levels of aggression (Garbarino et al., 1999; Groves, 2002). Children with PTSD generally require extended therapeutic help to work through the symptoms.

For early childhood practitioners, it can be helpful to look at the range of ways violence can affect all children to varying degrees (Levin, 2003). First, it is important to keep in mind that children do not experience or understand violence as adults do. Children make their own unique meanings from what they see and hear. They do this based on such things as their age, prior experiences, and individual temperament. For instance, the boy who panicked when he saw a policeman on the street the night after a policeman arrested his father is using his prior negative experience to interpret the new experience negatively as well. So did the child who asked "who shot her" after hearing the grandmother had just died; children who observe regular shootings, whether on television or in their neighborhood, might reasonably assume that if someone dies it is because he or she is shot!

A second concern that educators share is the influence of exposure to violence on how children see the world. Children learn, from both entertainment violence and the violence that they experience directly, that the world is a dangerous place, adults may be unable to protect them, and weapons and fighting are needed to keep people safe. In this situation, one of the most basic human needs—a sense of safety and trust—can be seriously undermined (Erikson, 1950).

Third, the early years is a time when children are working to establish separate male or female identities who can effectively deal with and have an impact on the world. They are developing the confidence and skills they need to get their needs met and solve the problems they encounter, hopefully without violence. And yet, exposure to violence can make children feel that fighting and using weapons are necessary in order to be strong, independent, and competent. Exposure to violence also gives children powerful stereotypes about the relationship of males and females to violence.

Fourth, the period of early childhood is a time when children are learning how to participate in relationships with others and how to rely on and support others in mutually respectful ways as a part of a caring community. As they succeed, children develop a sense of connectedness and belonging that can help them feel secure enough to try new things, experiment, explore, learn, and grow as autonomous individuals. Violence undermines children's ability to develop positive interpersonal skills or a sense of connection with others. The rugged individual who can protect himself or herself is the model held up to be emulated.

Needing others is associated with vulnerability and helplessness. And violence is often seen as the method of choice for solving conflicts with others.

Current theoretical interpretations of the impact of violence on children suggest that they need help understanding the violence they see and overcoming the fears it can create. They often do this through their play, art, storytelling, or writing (as they get older), or by talking to a caring adult. It is through this work that a sense of equilibrium is achieved and learning and development are fostered (Garbarino et al., 1999; Groves, 2002). This may be why teachers, like the one described earlier, so often find young children of today sneaking around with pretend guns more than they did in the past. It also helps us understand Freud and Burlingham's (1947) accounts of children playing out their experiences in World War II England as well as more recent descriptions of children on the West Bank in Palestine playing out scenarios of Israeli soldiers breaking into houses (Levin and Carlsson-Paige, 2006).

Children's ability to engage in the kinds of activities that can help them work through their violent experiences can be seriously undermined by the violence in their lives (Terr, 1990). Their energy and resources are diverted into trying to cope with the violence and the lack of safety that it can bring. The increasing amounts of time they spend with media give them less time to engage in activities that would help them work it out. Then when they do play, it can be taken over by the violence, and at the same time, controlled by highly realistic media-linked toys of violence. When this happens they tend to use imitative, rather than creative, play to meet their needs and be ready to move on. Thus, as the need to work through violence increases, children's ability to work it through can be seriously impaired (Levin and Carlsson-Paige, 2006).

Finally, what children see, hear, and do in their environment becomes the content they use for building ideas about the world. The ideas they build are then used for interpreting new experience and building new ideas. When society provides children with extensive violent content, it is hard for them not to come to see violence as central to how the world works and how they will fit into it. In this way, violence can become a powerful part of the foundation onto which later ideas are built (Levin 2004).

Professional Responses and Responsibilities to Violence in Children's Lives

We now know enough about how seriously violence can threaten the healthy development of young children to conclude that as we work to reduce the violence, we must also consciously work to counteract the harm. Children need the help of adults to process what they have seen, to feel safe in spite of the violence, and to learn alternative lessons to the ones violence teaches. The following table suggests strategies that begin to address the harmful effects. And the more we can infuse them into everything we do with children, rather than seeing them as a series of isolated tasks or lessons, the more successful we will be at meeting children needs in these violent times (Levin, 2003; Rice and Groves, 2005; Silva et al., 2002).

How Violence Undermines Development	What Children Need to Counteract the Harm
• As children feel unsafe and see the world is dangerous and adults can't keep them safe, energy goes to keeping selves safe and violence is one salient way to do it.	• A secure, predictable environment where they feel adults can keep them safe as they learn how to keep themselves and others safe.
• Sense of self as a separate person who can have a positive, meaningful effect on the world is undermined, so many children do not have many skills for feeling powerful and competent, getting their needs met or solving problems without violence.	• To learn how to take responsibility, positively affect what happens in their environment, and feel powerful and important and meet their individual needs without fighting.
• Sense of mutual respect and interdependence is undermined as violence becomes a central part of the behavioral repertoire children learn about how to treat others. Relying on others is associated with vulnerability.	• Many opportunities to experience and contribute to a caring community in which people learn how to help and rely on others and work out their problems in mutually respectful and agreeable ways.
• Narrowly defined and rigid gender division—where boys are violent and powerful and girls are sexy and weak—and racial, ethnic stereotyping often associated with violence undermine human development and relationships.	• Exposure to males, females, and diverse peoples with wide-ranging and overlapping behaviors, interests and skills who all treat each other with respect and work out problems without violence.
• Increased need to tell their stories and construct meaning of violence in their lives through such activities as discussions, creative play, art, and storytelling.	• Wide-ranging opportunities to work through and talk about violence issues, develop rich and meaningful art, stories, and play with open-ended play materials.
• It is harder for children to work through violence as tools for doing so are undermined by time and energy spent trying to cope and keep safe, time spent watching TV, toys that promote imitation of violence.	• Active facilitation of skills necessary to develop meanings, work through violence and feel safe—imagination, creativity, problem-solving ability, play and communication skills, and models for nonviolent behavior.

Adapted with permission from *Teaching Young Children in Violent Times: Building a Peaceable Classroom*, 2nd ed., by Diane E. Levin.

The global community must deal with the root causes of the increasing levels of violence in many children's lives—including rising levels of poverty and inequality, domestic and community violence, global conflict, news violence on TV screens in so many young children's homes, and marketing of entertainment violence to children by media and corporations. But in the meantime, there is much we can and must do in our work with children in group settings and their families to counteract the harmful effects of violence. By creating a safe and respectful environment where children can directly experience the alternatives to the violence in their lives, we will be helping them learn about peace and nonviolence in the way they learn best (Levin, 2006). *See also* Computer and Video Game Play in Early Childhood.

Further Readings: Erikson, E. (1950). *Childhood and society.* New York: W.W. Norton. Feerick, M., and G. Silverman (2006). *Children exposed to violence.* Baltimore: Paul H. Brookes. Freud, A., and D. Burlingham (1943). *War and children.* New York: Ernst Willard. Garbarino, J. N. Dubrow, K. Kostelny, and C. Pardo (1999). *Children in danger: Coping with the effects of community violence.* New York: John Wiley & Sons. Groves, B. (2002). *Children who see too much: Lessons from the child witness to violence project.* Boston: Beacon Press. Levin, D. (2003). *Teaching young children in violent times: Building a peaceable classroom.* 2nd ed. Cambridge, MA: Educators for Social Responsibility and Washington, DC: National Association for the Education of Young Children. Levin, D., and N. Carlsson-Paige (2006). *The war play dilemma: What every parent and teacher needs to know.* 2nd ed. New York: Teachers College Press. Rice, K., and B. Groves (2005). *Hope and healing: A caregiver's guide to helping children affected by trauma.* Washington, DC: Zero to Three. Silva, J., M. Sterne, and M. Anderson (2002). *Act aganst violence training program training manual.* Washington, DC: American Psychological Association and National Association for the Education of Young Children. Terr, L. (1990). *Too scared to cry: Psychic trauma in childhood.* New York: Harper & Row.

Diane E. Levin

Visual Art. *See* Assessment, Visual Art; Child Art; Curriculum, Visual Art

Visual Impairment

A visual impairment is any degree of vision loss that affects a child's ability to complete age-appropriate tasks and is caused by a visual system that was not formed correctly or is not working properly. Visual impairments include low vision and blindness. Low vision refers to a visual impairment that even with correction affects a child's ability to complete tasks, though the child still has the potential to use their vision. Blindness refers to the absence of usable vision, but the term *blind* is often used nontechnically to refer to severe visual impairments, including low vision.

When a child has a visual impairment, there are three primary ways it manifests: visual acuity problems, visual field defects, and visual processing issues. When a child has a visual acuity problem, the images received by the eyes are not crisp and clear. Children with acuity problems resulting from visual impairments have difficulty seeing images at near, intermediate, and far distances, and they may be unable to see clear images at any distance. A person with typical sight has a visual field that allows the person to see approximately 180 degrees left to right and 120 degrees top to bottom. A child with a visual field defect may lack peripheral vision (the vision around the edges), central vision, or may have scotomas (blind spots in any part of the visual field). When children have visual processing problems, there is damage to the posterior portion of the optic nerve and/or the visual cortex. The eye sends a clear image to the optic nerve, but the nerve is unable to transmit the image accurately or the brain is unable to interpret the image correctly. Most children with visual impairments experience a combination of at least two of these manifestations: acuity, field, and processing problems.

Many visual impairments can be treated or controlled through medical intervention. For example, antibiotics can prevent onchocerciasis (river blindness), one of the leading causes of blindness worldwide. Other visual impairments, such as glaucoma, are degenerative but can be treated with medication to slow or halt the progression resulting in the maintenance of some usable vision. Many other visual impairments cannot currently be treated or cured through medical interventions. When medical intervention is possible, it is important to seek treatment as early as possible to increase the chance of successful intervention and to decrease the impact of the visual impairment on development.

In first world countries, many children with visual impairments also have additional disabilities. The concurrent nature of these disabilities is due to the advances in medical technology that increases survival rates for children born prematurely and for children with physical and medical disabilities that carry increased risks for developmental delays. When children are born prematurely, they are at risk for developmental delays and for retinopathy of prematurity, a visual impairment that can result in low vision or total blindness. When children experience brain damage from a physical disability or medical problem, they are at risk for cortical visual impairments in which the portions of the brain that interpret visual images are impaired. Advances in medicine allow for many children born prematurely and with medical or physical problems to survive, and often these children have visual impairments as a result of their other conditions. It is estimated that in the United States approximately 40 percent of children with visual impairments have significant additional disabilities. When additional disabilities exist, they add to the potential for delays in development.

Impact of Visual Impairments on Development

Because vision is a unifying sense, a visual impairment, whether low vision or blindness, impacts a child's overall development. When children with visual impairments receive adequate early intervention services, they develop at rates similar to that of their peers with typical sight. Unfortunately, many children with visual impairments do not receive early intervention services and many developmental delays and mannerisms arise. When children are blind, they have difficulty connecting to the world outside their own body, and when children have low vision, they primarily look and interact with what is within arm's reach, severely limiting their opportunities to learn. Children with visual impairments are at risk for experiencing delays in all areas of development: social–emotional, communication, motor, cognitive, and self-help.

Without intervention, children with visual impairments often develop delays in social–emotional skills, which begin with difficulties bonding with their caregivers owing to lack of eye contact and nonintuitive behaviors. For example, infants who are blind often become still when an adult speaks to them rather than moving their body in excitement as typically sighted children do. This behavior, known as attentive stillness, is an excellent compensatory skill that allows the child to better hear the caregiver, but many caregivers misunderstand the stillness as a sign that the child is uninterested in interacting and stop speaking to the child.

Children with visual impairments often experience differences in their communication development. A child with typical sight is able to learn about a concept (e.g., trucks) by seeing trucks on the street and in books and on TV. Children with visual impairments will learn very little from trucks at a distance or pictures of trucks; they will best learn about trucks by climbing in and on real trucks. Owing to the many visual avenues for learning about trucks, a child with typical sight will likely have opportunities to learn about multiple trucks (pick-up truck, dump truck, fire truck, etc.), while a child with a visual impairment may only be familiar with the pick-up truck driven by the child's family. In addition, many adults engage in atypical communication with children who are blind by labeling everything for them or by asking them many questions. Children imitate what they hear, so many children who are blind ask questions and label objects rather than engaging in meaningful conversations.

Without intervention, children with visual impairments also often experience delays in motor skills. Vision is a strong motivator for children to develop motor skills such as pushing up to see a person or crawling to reach a favorite toy. Children with visual impairments need encouragement and opportunities to explore and develop motor skills that are often delayed without the benefit of typical visual motivators.

Children with visual impairments who have no other disabilities have the cognitive potential of typically sighted children, but their environments often put them at a disadvantage resulting in cognitive delays. All children develop cognitive skills (e.g., object permanence) and concepts (e.g., what is a dog) through experiences and interactions with people and objects in their environments. As discussed above, visual impairments may limit interactions with people, can result in atypical communication patterns, and can inhibit motor exploration. When children with visual impairments have such limited experiences, they have few opportunities to develop cognitive skills and concepts, often resulting in developmental delays.

Many adults feel sorry for children with visual impairments and want to help and protect them. Although all children need protection and help, they also need to learn to care for themselves. Children with visual impairments are unable to observe others taking care of self-help skills such as dressing/undressing, food preparation, eating/drinking, bathing, housecleaning, etc. When children with visual impairments are not actively involved in doing these tasks, they cannot learn how to care for themselves. From a very early age, children with visual impairments should be involved in daily living tasks through partial participation just as their typically sighted peers are.

Interventions

With adequate **early intervention** and **early childhood special education** services, children with visual impairments can develop into healthy, intelligent children and adults who are able to make meaningful contributions to their communities. It is vital that children with visual impairment and their families receive services and supports to encourage appropriate development. Owing to the wide range of visual functioning in children with visual impairments, interventions must be tailored to meet the unique needs of each child; what is appropriate to assist one child with a visual impairment may be detrimental for another. For example, most children with low vision benefit from increased lighting, but some types of visual impairments result in sensitivity to light. Children with these impairments see best with dimmer lighting. Early interventionists and early childhood educators who work with children with visual impairments should be knowledgeable about visual impairments, the impact of visual impairments on development, and interventions appropriate for the child's specific visual impairment. Interventionists and educators must be able to share information with families and assist families in finding culturally appropriate ways of meeting their child's needs. They must also be able to provide direct intervention services to children as needed to teach them disability-specific skills such as braille and orientation and mobility (i.e., moving safely and independently without the use of vision) when appropriate. Educators who specialize in visual impairments and early childhood education are most qualified to meet the needs of children with visual impairments and their families. With appropriate intervention, children with visual impairments can develop and learn at similar rates to children with typical sight.

Further Readings: Web Site: American Foundation for the Blind, www.afb.org. Chen, D., ed. (1999). *Essential elements in early intervention: Visual impairment and multiple disabilities.* New York: AFB Press; Pogrund, R. L., and D. L. Fazzi, eds. (2002). *Early focus: Working with young children who are blind or visually impaired and their families.* 2nd ed. New York: AFB Press.

Wendy Sapp

Vocabulary Development. *See* Read-Alouds and Vocabulary Development

Vygotsky, Lev Semenovich (1896–1934)

Lev Vygotsky is often called the "Mozart of psychology" because, similar to the famous composer, Vygotsky applied his genius early in life and to many different areas. Like Mozart, Vygotsky died young, losing his battle with tuberculosis at the age of 37. Born in 1896 in what was then a part of the Russian empire and is now the Republic of Belarus, Vygotsky had to overcome multiple obstacles during his remarkable life. As a Jew, his admittance to Moscow University depended on his winning a special lottery in spite of having graduated high school with honors. He was also limited in the type of career that would allow him to live outside the Pale, which accounts for his choice to pursue a degree in medicine, switching to law during his freshman year. While attending law classes, Vygotsky did not give up his studies in humanities and he simultaneously enrolled in Shanyavsky University to take classes in philosophy, literature, and linguistics.

After graduating from both Universities, Vygotsky returned to his native Gomel, where he taught literature, language, and psychology to schoolchildren, night school students, and to teachers in pre-service and in-service programs. During this period, Vygotsky developed many innovative ideas that later formed the foundation of his Cultural Historical Approach. In 1924, Vygotsky presented some of these ideas at the All-Russian Congress on Study of Behavior in St. Petersburg. His presentation made such an impression that, although he was an unknown instructor from a small provincial city, he was given a prestigious research position in the Moscow Psychological Institute.

After moving to Moscow in 1924, Vygotsky set forth to create what he hoped would become a new theory for understanding and solving the social and educational problems of his time. In addition to his theoretical work, Vygotsky pioneered new practical applications of his ideas such as "defectology"—a discipline that combined child abnormal psychology and special education. As the head of an experimental laboratory that later became the Institute of Defectology, Vygotsky advocated a new approach to educating children with special needs that focused on helping them acquire special cultural tools that would allow them to fully integrate into the society. Working feverishly as if in a race with his debilitating disease, Vygotsky immersed himself in research, writing, and teaching in child development, educational and clinical psychology, special education, and psychology of art. At the same time, he was expanding the circle of his colleagues and students, which later became the "Vygotsky School." Vygotsky's hopes for the creation of new theory, however, were not fully realized either during his lifetime or even during the lifetime of most of his closest colleagues and students. When the academic openness of the first postrevolutionary years ended, Vygotsky's ideas and the educational practices he initiated were suppressed by the communist government. These ideas and practices reemerged in the 1960s and 1970s, kept alive by Vygotsky's students, who were not only able to preserve the scientific legacy of their leader and mentor, but to enrich the Vygotskian approach to education and to broaden its practical applications.

At the core of Vygotsky's Cultural–Historical Theory is Vygotsky's belief that human development—an individual child's development as well as the development of all of humankind—is shaped by one's acquisition of cultural tools (written languages, number systems, various signs, and symbols) through the process of social interactions. These cultural tools not only make it possible for children to grow into the culture they are being raised in but they also transform the very way the child's mind is being formed, leading to the emergence of higher mental functions—intentional, self-regulated, and sign-mediated mental behaviors. An important characteristic of higher mental functions is their gradual transformation from external and socially distributed (intersubjective) to internal and individual (intrasubjective) through the process of internalization. For Vygotsky, interactions and cooperation with others is more than a favorable condition of child development—it is one of its driving forces.

Vygotsky's views on the development of higher mental functions can be illustrated by his model of the development of private or self-directed speech. Vygotsky saw private speech as a transitional step from social speech directed to other people to inner speech and eventually to verbal thinking. Noticing that children tend to increase the amount of self-talk when facing more challenging tasks, Vygotsky hypothesized that at some point, they start using private speech to organize (plan, direct, or evaluate) their actions, thus transforming spontaneous and unintentional behaviors into thoughtful and intentional ones. This function of private speech makes it an indicator of children's growing mastery of their behaviors, which contrasts with its explanation by Jean **Piaget,** who considered self-talk a manifestation of young children's egocentric, hence immature, thinking.

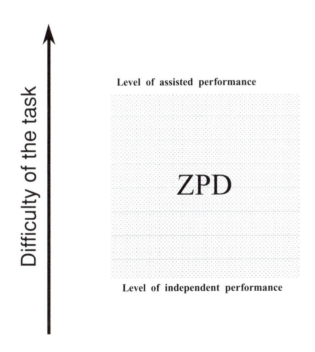

Vygotsky's position on the relationship between education, learning, and development is an extension of his view of child development as a complex interplay of natural and cultural processes. Seeing instruction (both formal and informal) as one of the important sources of child development, Vygotsky disagreed with theorists who believed that child development occurs spontaneously, is driven by the processes of maturation, and cannot be affected by education. He also rejected the view that instruction could alter development at any time regardless of a child's age or capacities. Instead, he proposed a more complex and dynamic relationship between learning and development represented by the concept of

Zone of Proximal Development (ZPD). The ZPD is the area between a child's level of independent performance (what he/she can do alone) and this child's level of assisted performance (what he/she can do with support). Skills and understandings contained within a child's ZPD are the ones that have not emerged yet and could emerge only if the child engages in interactions with knowledgeable others (peers and adults) or in other supportive contexts (such as make-believe **play** for preschool children). According to Vygotsky, the most effective instruction is the kind that is aimed not at child's level of independent performance but is instead aimed at this child's ZPD. This instruction does more than increase the repertoire of skills and understandings; it actually produces gains in child development. In Vygotsky's words, "instruction leads development instead of lagging behind it." Vygotsky's legacy can be found in contemporary interpretations of social **constructivism** and sociocultural theory.

Further Readings: Vygotsky, L. (1987). *Thinking and speech*. Translated by N. Minick. Vol. 1. New York: Plenum Press. Vygotsky, L. (1997). *The history of the development of higher mental functions*. Translated by Marie J. Hall. Vol. 4. New York: Plenum Press. Vygotsky, L. (1998). *Child psychology*. Translated by M.J. Hall. New York: Plenum Press.

Elena Bodrova and Deborah Leong

W

Waldorf Education

Waldorf education is one of the largest international independent school movements in the world and is based on the work of Austrian scientist, philosopher, and researcher Rudolf **Steiner.** In 1919, as Germany faced the task of rebuilding its economic, political, and social systems, Steiner was asked to create a school for children of the workers at the Waldorf-Astoria cigarette factory. He envisioned a school based on an integrated view of human development and curriculum. Steiner framed three stages of development on the way to adulthood: early childhood, middle childhood, and adolescence. Each stage of development was to be met with an integrated curriculum that allows for the nurturing of new capacities.

Rudolf Steiner proposed that teaching must be viewed as an art rather than a science, and thus the teacher needs a wide array of artistic abilities from which to draw. The teacher must become a master of pedagogy, artistic skills and developmental knowledge. There are training centers within the United States and in many other countries. The training is rooted in Anthroposophy, a comprehensive view of the human being as a spiritual as well as a physical being. This plays out in the classroom through activities that appeal to the head (thinking), heart (feeling), and feet (willing). Lessons and activities are composed so as to allow all three components of the young child to be active. Each stage of development offers an opportunity for one or another of these components to be predominant. In early childhood it is the will that is the initial focus, in middle childhood it is the heart, and during adolescence teachers appeal to the thinking of their students. This is not to say that in each stage the others are ignored, but rather that each stage has its own point of engagement.

Contemporary interpretations of a Waldorf education adhere to most of these early principles. Waldorf educators generally receive intensive training in Waldorf pedagogy as well as in child development, painting, music, handwork, and movement. In the Waldorf kindergarten and preschool, the teacher is a specialist in early childhood education. It is through the will, through activity and imitation, that the child is educated at this age. The Waldorf kindergarten is a carefully constructed environment where children play creatively, in surroundings filled with objects from nature and toys that encourage imagination and fantasy. For example, natural construction materials such as wood and stone are preferred over commercially produced building blocks. Children are taught to use natural dyes for the creation of fabrics that are then used to make costumes for their imaginative play. Often these kindergartens are composed of children of mixed ages, ranging from three-and-a-half to five years old. Thus some children may be a part of one class for more than one year.

Rhythm is an essential component of the kindergarten classroom in a Waldorf school. The day is structured in such a way that children have the opportunity to engage in expansive, energetic activities like free play followed by more concentrated activities like morning circle, where songs, poems, circle games, and stories are shared. Alternating active and receptive activities allows the children to engage in tasks with greater attention. Children internalize this daily rhythm and develop a sense of certainty and freedom as they move within the structure of the day in the kindergarten.

Just as the day has a rhythm that helps the children to feel secure as they move through their daily activities, the Waldorf kindergarten also establishes a weekly rhythm. Each day of the week will be marked by a focal activity such as baking, painting, movement, cooking, or modeling. Seasonal festivals that help instill in the children a sense of participation in the workings of the natural world mark the rhythms of the year. Upon entering a Waldorf kindergarten, one is quickly struck by the materials that are provided for the children's play and exploration. Cotton, silk, wool, beeswax, wood, and acorns are found displayed in inviting ways. Most of the materials come from natural sources. Toys are often very simple, suggestive ones, allowing the children to play creatively with them. There may be a large basket of small pieces of branches from a birch tree, for example. These may be used by the children as building blocks or for any number of imaginative uses. Often there will be cloaks, crowns, sashes or simply a basket of cloths that can be used by the children as they enter into imaginative play.

Play is a fundamental activity in a Waldorf kindergarten. It is through play that the children learn about themselves, each other, and the world that they live in. Teachers attempt to create an environment and activities that provide inspiration for the children's play. Stories, puppet shows, and carefully created toys allow the children to fully live into their play.

As movements toward academic standards continue to press children to learn reading and writing at ever-earlier ages, Waldorf kindergartens resist this direction. Feeling that the academic work is more appropriate for middle childhood, these kindergartens focus on developing other foundational skills for school and lifelong success. Although many of the activities may be viewed as part of a pre-reading curriculum, the Waldorf kindergartens prefer to frame such activities as storytelling, dramatics, and poetry as ways for children to learn about their own inner and outer worlds.

Recognizing that imitation is a fundamental way that young children learn about the world around them, the Waldorf kindergarten teacher attempts to fill the day with a conscious use of physical gesture. Poems are recited using the body expressively. Movement games also allow for simple gestures that allow the children to be fully active. The new developments in the neurosciences have demonstrated a connection between movement, memory, and the continuing growth of the neural pathways in the brain. Waldorf kindergartens have based their approach on this premise for the better part of a century.

As children progress into the early grades, they leave the kindergarten teacher behind and forge a new bond with a Waldorf elementary school teacher who, ideally, will be their teacher for the next eight years. This "class teacher" will need to grow along with the children, as he/she will teach all of the academic subjects throughout the eight years of elementary school. Special subject teachers teaching handwork, music, movement, and foreign languages may also work with the class primarily in the afternoons. The mornings are reserved for academic work.

In the Waldorf elementary grades (grades 1 through 8), academic subjects are taught in what is called a "main lesson." This lesson lasts for two hours or more every morning. During the lesson there will be a variety of activities (e.g., recitation, movement, story, an artistic rendering of the lesson), but the focus is on one subject at a time. There may be a four-week-long "block" of math followed by a six-week block of history, for example.

In first grade, the children slowly learn their letters. They are presented through stories, poetry, and song. Many children may have already learned the letter names, but they are reintroduced in such a way as to connect them with pictures and stories that will bring them to life. The teacher may prepare the room with an elaborate chalk drawing of a bear, for example, and tell the story of Goldilocks and the Three Bears. Over the course of the next day or two the bear may slowly be transformed into the letter "B" by way of drawing. The children may use their bodies to make the letter, walk the form of the letter, draw or paint the letter with vivid colors, learn rhymes that reinforce the qualities of the letter, etc.

A quality that is consistent throughout the early years of a Waldorf education is that of "wonder." Throughout kindergarten and the elementary grades an attempt is made at each step to imbue the children with a sense of wonder as they learn about the natural world, the social world, and the world of academics. Subjects are presented in such a way that the child's imagination and body are engaged in the learning. The world is presented as a beautiful place and it is unfolded before them like a vast mystery.

Today there are more than 800 Waldorf schools worldwide, with more than 150 in the United States. The movement has a central organization known as the Association of Waldorf Schools in North America (AWSNA), but each school retains its independent identity. In addition, the kindergartens are served by the Waldorf Early Childhood Association of North America (WECAN), which provides a central source for continuing training and resources for early childhood educators.

Further Readings: Clouder, Christopher, and Rawson, Martyn (2003). *Waldorf education*. Edinburgh: Floris Books; Wilkinson, Roy (1982). *Commonsense schooling*. Surrey, England: Henry Goulden. Association of Waldorf Schools in North America, http://www.awsna.org

Eric Gidseg

War Play

"War play," play with violent content and themes, is a form of play that has seemingly engaged children for centuries and across many cultures. Artifacts of what look like war toys have been found from ancient Egypt and the Middle Ages. It has always been a controversial form of play, with some adults seeing it as part of the normal repertoire of content children (especially boys) bring into their play and others arguing that merely letting children play this way can teach them harmful lessons about violence. But during some periods in history the differing points of view have led to more controversy than other periods. For instance, during the Viet Nam War in the United States, many parents and teachers who opposed the war worked hard to limit children's involvement in this type of play. Theories of child development also provide different perspectives on the meanings and consequences of this type of play on children's development.

Finding Value in War Play

Beginning with Anna **Freud** in England during World War II, researchers have identified a number of developmental issues that may be addressed through war play. Some argue that war play, perhaps more than any other form of dramatic play, can help children feel powerful as they play (Freud and Burlingham, 1943; Jones, 2002). Children can experience a sense of competence. As they pretend to be strong characters and superheroes with super powers, for instance, their self-images as strong people who can take care of themselves may be enhanced. This can help them with separation from home as well. As they assume the role of powerful characters and "pretend to fight," they can learn to gain control over their impulses to stay within acceptable boundaries. War play also can be a special vehicle for learning about the difference between fantasy and reality. And as children take on contrasting roles (e.g., "good guy" and "bad guy"), they learn about how their actions affect one another and begin to understand other points of view. Finally, war play can help children make sense of the violence they see and hear about in the world around them—in their homes and communities and in the media. A child who sees soldiers fighting on television news might bring this image into "war play" in an effort to understand it or make it less frightening (Levin and Carlsson-Paige, 2006; Jones, 2002).

A new phase in war play history began in 1984 when the United States Federal Communications Commission deregulated children's television. Deregulation opened the floodgates for marketing TV-linked toys and products to children, a practice previously prohibited. An abundance of shows, products, and toys linked together around a single theme, usually a violent one, began to saturate the childhood culture. Both the quantity and quality of entertainment violence children saw increased dramatically. And increasingly over the years, videos, video games, movies, and fast-food outlets have joined in these marketing campaigns.

Adults in the United States began to see children's war play begin to change during this same period in the mid-1980s, soon after television was deregulated. Teachers, especially, voiced concerns about the war play they were seeing in early childhood and elementary settings. They described how children were imitating TV "scripts" in their war play and acting out the violence they had seen on television and movie screens instead of inventing and evolving their own stories.

> I visited a kindergarten classroom recently at recess time. The teacher came up to me (Carlsson-Paige) and the first thing she said was, "I hate *Star Wars*. It has taken over the classroom. It's all the kids can think about—they're obsessed with it, mostly the boys. They turn everything into a light saber and start fighting. But they're clever and tell me it's something else, not a weapon. It's all they talk about and all they play."
>
> Later, I went into the classroom and sat at a table with three boys. They were drawing and talking about *Star Wars*. One of them said, "I love *Star Wars*!" He pointed to his head and he said, "I can never stop thinking about it!"

Children's war play began to look more like what Jean **Piaget** (1951/1945) called *imitation* than play. Many children seemed unable to use their war play as a means of actively transforming their own experience, especially the violence they had seen, and thus meeting their developmental needs. The deep meanings that young children construct when their play flows from their own needs and experience were being replaced at least in part by content seen on the screen. And this undermining of creative play continues to be of serious concern to parents and early childhood professionals today, especially in relation to war play.

In Great Britain, similar concerns began to be voiced when violent TV programs and toys from the United States started to arrive in 1986. By the early nineties, at a time when the Teenage Mutant Ninja Turtles program was being aired in over 100 countries, concerns about media-linked war play and toys were raised in such other industrialized countries as Canada, Germany, Greece, and New Zealand.

Finding an Approach to War Play Today

In a society where children are exposed to large amounts of pretend and real violence, it is not easy to find an effective approach to war play in the classroom. There are no simple or perfect solutions for approaching children's war play that fully address both the needs of children and the concerns of adults. Teachers who ban, allow, or facilitate children's war play can all find difficulties with the approach they have chosen.

Banning war play altogether can alleviate many problems for teachers but it also denies children the opportunity to work on the violence they have been exposed to through their play. It can leave children to work out these issues on their own without adult guidance; they can learn lessons that glorify violence that are unmediated by adults. They are also left to feel guilty about their interest in the play. And even when teachers try to ban war play, many say that this approach does not work very well. Children have a hard time accepting limits or controlling their intense need to engage in this kind of play. They find ways to circumvent the ban—by denying the play is really war play (i.e., learning to lie) or sneaking behind the teacher's back to play (i.e., learning to deceive). So while banning war play can be the approach of choice for teachers, it can have a worrisome negative impact on children.

Some teachers who try to allow war play often find that the play, especially media-driven, imitative war play, is so unproductive and out of control that banning seems to be the only choice, at least for periods of time. When this happens, teachers can still provide alternative activities such as drawing, storytelling, writing, and building. This will allow children to work out their ideas about violence and war play–related themes and connect with adults about their needs regarding them. And at the same time, teachers can provide alternative themes to those offered by media that address the same developmental needs that are met in war play. They can encourage dramatic play based on children's books, for example, that touch the deep developmental themes such as mastery, power, and separation that are expressed in war play.

Teachers who decide that they want to allow children's war play almost all find that, in order for children to use their play to meet their needs in a meaningful way in this play, they require direct help from adults (Hoffman, 2004; Katch, 2001). How teachers decide to help will depend on the *quality* of the play children are engaged in. Taking time to watch the play and learn what children are working on and how they are working on it can give teachers the information they need to facilitate war play in ways that will help children get beyond narrowly scripted play that is focused on violent actions. Often children will need help reducing their dependence on highly realistic, media-linked "fighting" toys and learning how to use open-ended toys. Some children will need help bringing new and interesting content into their play that expands the focus of the play beyond violent themes and actions. And many children will need help keeping the play safe and from getting out of control. Teachers can work with children to develop rules for this play that ensure the safety of all of the children in the classroom. Facilitating war play in these ways can provide children with skills to work out the violent content they bring to their play, work on important developmental issues, learn valuable lessons, and move on to new issues rather than stay obsessed with their war play.

Whether teachers partially ban war play or actively facilitate it, talking with children about their war play and the related themes in their drawings, stories or buildings is one of the most important ways adults can help them work out the violence children see and even learn alternatives to that violence. It often helps to begin with an open-ended question. If a child draws what looks like a bomb or an explosion, a teacher can point to it and ask, "Can you tell me about this part of your picture?" Then the teacher can respond based on what is learned about that particular child's ideas, questions, and needs. In all of these instances, it is essential that teachers keep in mind that children do not understand violence as adults do. They may need help clearing up confusions ("The planes that go over our school do not carry bombs"), sorting out fantasy and reality ("In real life people don't carry light sabers"), and getting reassurance about their safety ("I can't let you play like that because it's my job to make sure everyone is safe").

Reducing children's exposure to violence, to inappropriate media, to excessive time-consuming media, and to media-linked war toys is one of the most important ways teachers can foster healthy war play. The less violent content children have, the less violence they will need to try to work out in their play. Through parent workshops and family newsletters that include resource materials, teachers can help families learn more about how to protect children from exposure to violent entertainment and news media and too much time in front of the screen.

At the same time, while parents and educators can do a lot to reduce the violence to which children are exposed, some violence will continue to get in— and it is the job of adults to help children make sense of what they see. It is by connecting with children in their play and in their drawings—as described earlier when the adult begins a conversation with a child about her drawing—that we can convey to children that adults are there to help them deal with the violence they see. For as children grow up in the violent world of today, they need help to work out what they hear, clear up misconceptions and reassure them of their safety to the extent that we can, and provide lessons that teach alternatives to violence (Levin, 1998).

Teachers can reach out to community after-school programs and family day care providers to share materials on creating safer, more violence-free, less media-saturated situations for children. Working to minimize the influence of violent entertainment culture on children will help them restore their war play to its rightful place as a valuable resource for making sense of the violence they see in the world around and working on important developmental issues.

Further Readings: Cantor, J. (1998). *'Mommy, I'm Scared!' How TV and movies frighten children and what we can do to protect them.* New York: Harcourt Brace; Freud, A., and D. Burlingham (1943). *War and children.* New York: Ernst Willard; Hoffman, E. (2004). *Magic capes, amazing powers: Transforming superhero play in the classroom*; St. Paul, MN: Redleaf Press. Jones, J. (2002). *Killing monsters: Why children need fantasy, super heroes, and make-believe violence.* New York: Basic Books. Katch, J. (2001); *Under dead man's skin: Discovering the meaning of children's violent play.* Boston: Beacon Press. Levin, D. E. (1998). *Remote control childhood? Combating the hazards of media culture*; Washington, DC: NAEYC. Levin, D. E., and N. Carlsson-Paige (2006). *The war play dilemma: Everything parents and teachers need to know.* 2nd ed. New York: Teachers College Press. Piaget, J. (1951/1945). *Play, dreams, and imitation in childhood.* New York: W.W. Norton.

Nancy Carlsson-Paige and Diane E. Levin

Watson, John B. (1878–1958)

John Broadus Watson, an American psychologist, developed a new branch of psychology that he termed "**behaviorism**." Drawing on the work of Ivan **Pavlov**, Watson provided experimental evidence that human behavior, although far more complicated than that of other animals, was influenced by the same principles, specifically, learning through association. Watson's behaviorism was the dominant psychological viewpoint in the United States between 1920 and 1930. His work is known to have significantly influenced that of B.F. Skinner.

John Watson was born in Travelers Rest, South Carolina, on January 9, 1878, and he spent his childhood years on a farm. He entered Furman University in Greenville, South Carolina in 1894 at age sixteen. After five years of study, he was awarded a master's degree, and then continued on to the University of Chicago to undertake doctoral study in philosophy and psychology. He subsequently dropped philosophy and in 1903, was awarded a PhD in psychology. In

1908, Watson joined the faculty at Johns Hopkins University in experimental and comparative psychology, where he remained until 1920.

Watson's ideas, first presented between 1908 and 1912, challenged the existing views of psychology, particularly those held by Sigmund **Freud**. Watson questioned the relevance of heredity and internal mental states to behavior, and promoted the concept that behaviorism as a branch of psychology was an objective and rigorous scientific study of human behavior, the goal of which was to predict and mold such behavior. His article "Psychology as the Behaviorist Views It," published in 1913 in *Psychological Review*, is generally considered the seminal statement of his new branch of psychology, behaviorism.

In his research, Watson's comparisons between animal behavior and human behavior initially were based on observations of human infants. However, after his service as a psychologist in World War I, he began conducting experiments. His most significant experiment and the one for which he is best known was conducted in the winter of 1919 and 1920 and involved Albert B. Watson, or Baby Albert, a young infant, and a small white lab rat. The experimenters first established that Baby Albert was not afraid of the lab rat (he had shown an interest in it and reached out to touch it) but was afraid when the experimenters clanged metal with a hammer right behind his head (he cried). Then when Baby Albert was around 11 months old, the experimenters again presented him with the lab rat, but as soon as he touched it, they clanged the metal with the hammer right behind his head, making him cry. They repeated this for several weeks. As a result, Baby Albert cried and tried to crawl away at the mere sight of the lab rat, and in fact showed fear and cried at the sight of anything furry.

This experiment demonstrated that humans (as well as other animals such as dogs) can be conditioned through association of stimuli, a phenomenon called "classical conditioning." This experiment also demonstrated the need for ethical standards in research with humans, especially with infants. Such standards did not exist during Watson's time. In fact, even after the experiment was completed, no attempt was made to "decondition" Baby Albert.

During his illustrious academic career, Watson founded the *Journal of Experimental Psychology*, edited the *Psychological Review*, and served as president of the American Psychological Association. However, in 1920, Johns Hopkins University asked Watson to resign amidst personal turmoil. He did so and later entered the field of advertising. He died in 1958.

Further Readings: Buckley, Kerry W. (1989). *Mechanical man: John B. Watson and the beginnings of behaviorism.* New York: The Guilford Press; Todd, James T., and Edwin K. Morris (1994). *Modern perspectives on John B. Watson and classical behaviorism.* Portsmouth, NH: Greenwood-Heinemann Publishing; Watson, John B. (1998). *Behaviorism.* New York: Transaction Publishers.

Stephanie F. Leeds

Wheelock, Lucy (1857–1946)

Lucy Wheelock was a pioneer in the kindergarten and Sunday school movements in the United States, as well as founder of Wheelock College in Boston,

Massachusetts. A disciple of Friedrich **Froebel,** she was mentored by Elizabeth **Peabody**, founder of many of the first English-speaking kindergartens. When the city of Boston added kindergartens to its public schools, Wheelock was asked to provide the training program for the new teachers. This program, originally named Miss Wheelock's Kindergarten Training School, ultimately became Wheelock College and was directed by Wheelock for fifty years.

While she helped make Froebel's ideas popular in the early childhood community, she was also willing to modify his approach to suit a new time and setting. In 1885 she began a four-year term as president of the **International Kindergarten Union** (IKU), and for that group chaired the Committee of Nineteen. This committee was charged with investigating kindergarten methodology and moderating differences between the orthodox Froebelians such as Susan **Blow** and the progressives such as Patty Smith **Hill**. In 1913, Wheelock authored the committee's report, *The Kindergarten*; however, her committee was not able to unite the two wings of the kindergarten movement.

During her career she led delegations of educators to original Froebel schools in Germany. As the daughter of a congregational minister, she was also active in the Sunday school movement, and applied Froebelian techniques to the religious education of young children. She edited *The Child's Hour,* a Sunday school journal in Boston, and conducted training programs for Sunday school teachers nationwide. One of her most quoted sayings, "Great oaks grow from little acorns" ("Wheelock College Beginnings," np), summarizes her vision of quality early childhood education.

Further Readings: Tharp, Louise H. (1988). *The Peabody sisters of Salem.* Boston: Little, Brown. Wheelock College Beginnings (February 2005). Available online at http://www. wheelock.edu/lucy/lucyhome.htm. Lucy Wheelock (February 2005). Women in American history by *Encyclopedia Britannica.* Available online at http://britannica. com/women/articles/Wheelock_Lucy.html

Mary Ruth Moore

White, Edna Noble (1879–1954)

Edna Noble White was one of a number of nineteenth-century American women who led in developing helping professions in health and nutrition, education, including early childhood; social work; psychology, and home economics. White, an Illinois-born graduate of the University of Illinois, left a legacy for today's early childhood professionals.

After teaching high school for a short time, White became professor and department chair for home economics at Ohio State University. In 1919, Lizzie Merrill Palmer, a wealthy widow, invited her to become the founding director of the Merrill-Palmer School in Detroit, Michigan. Later it became the Merrill-Palmer Institute and today is a department of Wayne State University. The original purpose of the school was "to train young women in homemaking and motherhood."

At a time in American history when some women seemingly defied the female norm of marriage and motherhood by attending universities and building emerging fields of study, White exemplified the group by transforming family education and child development activities into research opportunities. She brought a diversified faculty to Merrill-Palmer to address the interrelated subjects involved.

When White became interested in preschool education in the 1920s, she traveled to England to study with Rachel and Margaret **McMillan**, pioneers in the British innovation of nursery school. While the McMillan sisters emphasized programs for low-income, at-risk children, White's American ideals recognized nursery education's values for all children and promoted the positive impact that early education could have on society.

Merrill-Palmer under White's leadership became prominent among academically related early childhood institutions. In 1927, White was named to the board of directors of the original National Committee on Nursery Schools established by Patty Smith **Hill**. The Committee evolved into the National Association for Nursery Education (NANE) and, in 1964, became today's **National Association for the Education of Young Children** (NAEYC).

White's legacy strengthened the concept of the "whole child," whose learning was to be comprehensive and include physical, emotional, and cognitive aspects. She implemented this belief by bringing together a multidisciplinary faculty at Merrill-Palmer. She recognized that children are not only individuals, but are also ecological beings living in families and communities. In addition, all children would benefit from early education programs, regardless of socioeconomic status and physical or mental abilities. An early proponent of education across the lifespan, White also promoted educational experiences for infants and older children. After retiring, White established a geriatric organization in Detroit, as well as helping to establish the Visiting Housekeepers and youth programs.

To round out a cross-sectional career dedicated to children, families, and communities, Edna Noble White maintained a life-long effort to influence public policies for children. She advised President Franklin Delano Roosevelt during the Great Depression, and served the same role with the Rockefeller Institute.

Further Readings: Braun, Samuel J., and Esther P. Edwards (1972). *History and theory of early childhood education.* Belmont, CA: Wadsworth Publishing Company, Inc.; Lascarides, V. Celia, and Blythe H. Hinitz (2000). *History of early childhood education.* New York: Falmer Press. National Association for the Education of Young Children (2001). *NAEYC at 75: Reflections on the past, challenges for the future.* Washington, DC: NAEYC. White, Edna Noble. The Merrill-Palmer Institute collections in the Walter P. Reuther Library of Labor and Urban Affairs, Wayne State University, Detroit, Michigan. Available online at http://www.reuther.wayne.edu/collections/hefa_1066-mpi-white.htm and http://www.hall.michiganwomenshalloffame.org/honoree.php?C=199&A=20~114~96~172~79~

Edna Ranck

Whiting, Beatrice (1914–2004)

Beatrice Blyth Whiting influenced the social scientific study of culture, child development, and the socialization process. Through her lifelong commitment to comparative studies of children, families, and communities throughout the world, she taught and influenced several generations of anthropologists, child development researchers, and educators. She pioneered the use of comparative ethnographic and quantitative methods that integrated the anthropologist's knowledge of local communities and families with the psychologist's systematic assessments of child behavior and development (Weisner and Edwards, 2002). Her research projects modeled the strength of interdisciplinary, international teams and led to a deeper infusion of cultural understanding into contemporary studies of child development and education.

Whiting graduated from Bryn Mawr College in 1935 and was one of the first women to study anthropology at Yale University, where she received her PhD in 1943. She joined Harvard University as a research associate in 1952, and in 1970 became one of the first women to receive tenure there. With her husband, John W.M. Whiting, she directed three major international comparative studies of human development: The Six Culture Study of the Socialization of the Child (Whiting, 1963; Whiting and Whiting, 1975); the Child Development Research Project at the University of Nairobi (Whiting and Edwards, 1988; Edwards and Whiting, 2004); and the Harvard Comparative Adolescence Project (Whiting and Whiting, 1991).

Whiting's work helped establish the use of intensive, observational studies to investigate the dimensions of children's cultural learning environments. Whiting concluded that the drama of child development necessarily takes place on a stage surrounded by a theater, the cultural community, with characteristic geography, settlement pattern, household living arrangements, and age and gender division of labor and economic routines. The drama on the stage (shaped by those outside forces) involves scenes and characters provided by the child's typical caregivers and social companions, family work responsibilities, and access to the wider community. Together, all these cultural dimensions comprise the cultural learning environment and predict age and gender variations in child social behavior and interaction as the drama unfolds. For example, children who contribute more actively to family subsistence and survival (through child care, food preparation, gardening, and herding) demonstrate significantly more nurturant and prosocial behavior and less dependency. Children in school (and preschool) have more frequent opportunity to interact with large groups of same-age, same-sex peers, where they are relatively competitive, egoistically dominant, and rough-and-tumble (or sociably aggressive) in their play, suggesting that the introduction of age-graded schools (and preschools) historically leads to far-reaching changes in children's normative social behavior (Whiting and Edwards, 1988).

Whiting, a pioneering woman herself, was as concerned with the role of women and families in the transformation of culture as with the socialization of children. Her final publication on the Kenyan village of Ngecha, during the years 1968 to 1973, documented how rural women coped and adapted, while taking into account the needs of their husbands, numerous children, aging parents, and others for whom they were responsible (Edwards and Whiting, 2004). To prepare their children for wage-earning jobs requiring schooling, the mothers modified their parenting goals and behavior and took upon themselves increased workloads and reduced kin support. The children, in turn, experienced evolving educational practices and individualistic achievement expectations that challenged traditional family-based morals and obligations. Whiting's work has made major contributions to the field of early childhood education by illustrating the variety of ways in which child development can be supported in diverse cultural and ecological contexts.

Further Readings: Edwards, C. P., and B. B. Whiting, eds. (2004). *Ngecha: A Kenyan village in a time of rapid social change.* Lincoln: University of Nebraska Press; Weisner, T. S., and C. P. Edwards (2002). Introduction to the theme issue honoring the contributions of Beatrice B. Whiting. *Ethos: Journal of the Society for Psychological Anthropology* 29(3), 239–246; Whiting, B. B., ed. (1963). *Six cultures: Studies of child rearing.* New York: John Wiley; Whiting, B. B., and C. P. Edwards (1988). *Children of different worlds: The formation of social behavior.* Cambridge, MA: Harvard University Press; Whiting, B. B., and J. W. M. Whiting (1975). *Children of six cultures: A psycho-cultural analysis.* Cambridge, MA: Harvard University Press; Whiting, B. B., and J. W. M. Whiting (1991). Adolescence in the preindustrial world. In R. M. Lerner, A. C. Peterson, and J. Brooks-Gunn, eds., *The encyclopedia of adolescence.* New York: Garland Press, pp. 814–829.

Carolyn Pope Edwards

Whiting, John W. M. (1908–1999)

John Wesley Mayhew Whiting, a founder of contemporary psychological anthropology, was a major figure in the field of child development. He was born in Chilmark, Massachusetts, on Martha's Vineyard, where he died one month before his 91st birthday. John Whiting was the revered teacher of many anthropologists for more than thirty years and was unique in his level of engagement in both psychology and anthropology. Inspired by the early work of Margaret Mead, and with his wife of sixty years and research collaborator, Beatrice B. **Whiting**, he built and maintained the comparative study of child rearing and development during the second half of the twentieth century.

John Whiting grew up on a farm on Martha's Vineyard. He attended Phillips Academy, Andover; and Yale University, graduating in 1931. He then joined the anthropology graduate program at Yale, where he worked with George Peter Murdock, Edward Sapir, and John Dollard. He earned his PhD in 1938, returning to Yale as a postdoctoral fellow in the Yale Institute of Human Relations. He turned his dissertation into a monograph, *Becoming a Kwoma* (1941), in which he used learning theory as well as functional anthropology to interpret childhood in New Guinea.

After joining the U.S. Navy during World War II, Whiting returned to the research staff at Yale, where he stayed until 1947, leaving to join Robert R. Sears at the Iowa Child Welfare Research Station, only to leave two years later with Sears to found the Laboratory of Human Development at the Harvard Graduate School of Education. Whiting became Director of the lab in 1953 and remained on the Harvard faculty until his retirement in 1978.

Whiting's first major contribution to the field of cross-cultural studies in child development was with Irvin Child, published in 1953 in *Child Training and Personality.* Subsequently, Whiting organized and supervised field studies of children, adolescents, and parents for the rest of his career. One such study was part of the Harvard Values Study, conducted during the early 1950s with fieldwork in New Mexico. In 1954, together with Irvin Child at Yale and William Lambert at Cornell, Whiting secured funding from the Ford Foundation for a study of socialization in five societies—Mexico, India, Okinawa, the Philippines, and New England. An African community was later added. Beatrice Whiting coordinated the field studies, the data analyses, and the publications on what became known as the Six Cultures Study. This study has been recognized as a classic in early childhood education for its portrayal of cultural variations in child rearing and child development.

The Whitings always took an anthropological perspective on childhood, but their research and their writings were often addressed to developmental psychology and child psychiatry, challenging the ethnocentricism in those fields. Their aim was to provide the empirical evidence, quantitative as well as qualitative, on cultural variations to replace presumptions and prejudices about human nature and its development. These works were also important to anthropology in arguing and illustrating the impact of culture on parenting and childhood experience.

In John Whiting's view, a central problem in the study of human development was how the child internalizes the values of his cultural environment, and he was particularly concerned with the acquisition of defense mechanisms and with the process of identification through which children acquire gender and other identities. He saw Freudian theory as raising questions that required answers from empirical research in diverse cultures. In his influential studies of male initiation ceremonies, he tried to identify the processes that make the ceremonies psychologically salient for the individuals who undergo them, permitting them to resolve unconscious conflicts created by their early experience. He anticipated the recent emphasis on internalization in the Vygotskian mode in child development and the interest in male and female **gender** identities in anthropology.

John Whiting was recognized, by himself and with his wife, for his scholarly contributions. He received the American Psychological Association's G. Stanley **Hall** Award for Distinguished Contributions to Developmental Psychology (1973), was elected to the National Academy of Sciences (1979), and, with Beatrice Whiting, received the Distinguished Contribution Award of the American Anthropological Association (1982). He was the first President of the Society for Psychological Anthropology (in 1978). Whiting continued writing scholarly studies into his late eighties and then wrote an article for a county historical journal about the pond on Martha's Vineyard that provided the setting for much of his long life. That was his last publication.

John Whiting dreamt of an international organization of researchers on child rearing and development from all over the world gathering data on their own cultures and exchanging data to achieve a basis for generalizing to all humans. This would not only be of value for anthropology in scientific terms; it would also achieve equality among the participants in the data exchange and an end to the dominance of Westerners in the field. Although this project remained unfinished, John Whiting built a place for the comparative study of child rearing and development in the social sciences and inspired students to conduct theoretically motivated and systematic research on human development in diverse cultures. See also Freud, Sigmund; Vygotsky, Lev.

Further Readings: Chasdi, Eleanor Hollenberg. (1994). *Culture and human development: The selected papers of John Whiting.* New York: Cambridge University Press. LeVine, Robert A. (2000). John Whiting: Obituary. *American Anthropologist,* 102(1), 3-6. Whiting, John W. M. (1941). *Becoming a Kwoma.* New Haven, CT: Yale University Press. Whiting, John W. M., and Irvin L. Child (1953). *Child training and personality: A cross-cultural study.* New Haven, CT: Yale University Press.

Robert A. LeVine

WIC. *See* Women, Infants and Children

Wiggin, Kate Douglas (1855–1923)

Kate Douglas Wiggin was an educational reformer and novelist, an activist in the nineteenth-century Kindergarten Movement, and the author of the children's classic *Rebecca of Sunnybrook Farm*. In 1878, she became the head teacher at the first free kindergarten in San Francisco and in 1879 founded the California Teacher Training School. During the 1880s, Wiggin wrote articles on early childhood curricula and pedagogy, lectured on children's rights and welfare, and published collections of stories, songs, and games for children. In the 1890s she traveled the Chautauqua lecture circuit, participated in the kindergarten demonstrations at the World Columbian Exposition in Chicago, and spoke before the National Education Association. By the turn of the century, she was part of intellectual and social circles that included most of the notable educators, authors, and artists of her day.

Kate Douglas Wiggin, the daughter of Helen Elizabeth Dyer Smith and Robert Noah Smith, was born Katharine D. Smith. She spent her early childhood in Philadelphia, where her father was attempting to establish a career in law. When his efforts proved unsuccessful, and the family returned to their native state of Maine in the late 1850s. Robert deserted the family in 1860. In 1862, Kate's mother married Dr. Albion K.P. Bradbury. During the remainder of her childhood, the Bradburys lived a comfortable life in the village of Hollis, in southern Maine. In 1873 they moved to California. Two years later Albion Bradbury died, leaving the family in debt. Wiggin's career in education began when she decided to enter teaching in order to help support her family.

Wiggin studied kindergarten methods in Los Angeles with Emma Marwedel, a leading disciple of Friedrich **Froebel** and a protégé of Elizabeth Palmer **Peabody**. When she completed her training in 1878 she became head teacher of the newly founded Silver Street Kindergarten in the impoverished Tar Flats district of San Francisco. To meet the needs of her students, Wiggin extended her activities within the community, offering classes, counseling, and social services to the families of Tar Flats. As a result, Silver Street became an early version of the neighborhood settlement house that was popularized by Jane **Addams** a decade later. Wiggin's kindergarten training and work at Silver Street connected her to an educational reform network that extended from Elizabeth Peabody's office of *The Kindergarten Messenger* in Boston to the flamboyant Sarah Cooper's International Kindergarten Association in Los Angeles. She became committed to the cause, taught, lectured, and—unusual for a woman in the 1870s—took part in public debates advocating for child welfare. During the summer months she traveled across the country visiting schools, attending teachers' institutes, and giving demonstration lessons. In 1881, she married Samuel Bradley Wiggin and gave up classroom teaching. However, she continued to give lectures and direct teacher training at Silver Street until 1893.

In the late1880s the Wiggins moved to New York City and Kate Douglas Wiggin began to write novels depicting the natural wisdom and social plight of children. Her first novel, *The Birds Christmas Carol*, came out in 1888 and was an instant success. Her success was tempered, however, by the sudden unexpected death of Samuel Wiggin in 1889. For the next six years, Wiggin supported herself through writing, lecturing on kindergarten, and giving public readings. During this time, she published a collection of her lectures, *The Rights of Children: A Book of Nursery Logic* (1892), with her sister Nora Archibald Smith as well as two novels that had a significant impact within the national kindergarten network: *Timothy's Quest* (1890), which dealt with the hardships of homeless children, and *The Story of Patsy* (1891), about a child with special needs. By 1894, Wiggin had become a well-known author and was able to purchase a summerhouse in her hometown of Hollis, Maine.

Kate Douglas Wiggin married George Christopher Riggs in 1895 and retired from active involvement in the Kindergarten Movement. However, she retained Wiggin as her professional name and continued her writing career. In 1903, *Rebecca of Sunnybrook Farm* made her an international celebrity. In its first three months, *Rebecca* sold 125,000 copies. It became a national bestseller, was adapted for the theater in both New York and London, and was translated into fourteen languages. Until her death in England in 1923, Kate Douglas Wiggin continued to write collections for children, humorous travelogues, and novels and short stories based on her childhood in Maine.

Further Readings: Benner, Helen Frances (1956). *Kate Douglas Wiggin's country of childhood*. Orono, ME: University of Maine Press; Wiggin, Kate Douglas (1888). *The birds Christmas carol*. Boston: Houghton Mifflin and Company; Wiggin, Kate Douglas (1892). *Children's rights: A book of nursery logic*. Boston: Houghton Mifflin and Company; Wiggin, Kate Douglas (1903). *Rebecca of Sunnybrook Farm*. Boston: Houghton Mifflin and Company; Wiggin, Kate Douglas (1924). *My garden of memory*. Boston: Houghton Mifflin and Company.

Susan Douglas Franzosa

Wollstonecraft, Mary (1759–1797)

An early modern philosophical "mother" of English **feminism** and coeducation, Mary Wollstonecraft survived her alcoholic father's **violence** and resisted his opposition to girls' education by educating herself from an early age. She developed her own remarkable way with children, evident throughout her life and written work. Her thought about children's education critically engaged both taken-for-granted popular assumptions about gender and others' writings on education, extending concern to girls' preparation for moral life, to mothers' preparation for intelligent child-rearing, and to the character of ideal educational partnerships.

As eldest daughter, Wollstonecraft helped her battered mother raise her five younger siblings. A marriage resister among religious Dissenters in the 1780s, she taught young children in a school she established with her two sisters and beloved friend Fanny Blood, and also worked as a governess for Irish aristocrats. Becoming a single mother during the French Revolution, she traveled unescorted with her infant daughter throughout Scandinavia and survived two suicide attempts. Resettling in England, where single mothers and fatherless children were outlaws, she befriended, loved, and married political philosopher William Godwin. He adopted her first daughter, fathered her second daughter (Mary Shelley), and wrote after her death in childbed, "No one was ever better formed for the business of education."

Wollstonecraft's earliest and latest writings most closely detail the maternal educational practices her husband had witnessed. Her *Thoughts on the Education of Daughters* (1787) asserted the educational value of the nursery that avoids what she regarded as needless restraint and silly affected speech, provides rationally consistent discipline, exemplifies good manners, and fosters strong morals. Her *Original Stories from Real Life* (1788) presented a conversational, **narrative** approach to children's moral education, selling so well that William Blake illustrated a later edition (1796). Godwin posthumously published her *Lessons* (1798), fragments narrating her affectionate teaching of a toddler daughter—to talk, to befriend animals, to love a newborn brother, to take safety precautions with dangerous household objects. These early and late works also reflect John Locke's emphasis upon "laying the foundation of a good constitution" in young children, but correct his general neglect of girls' education.

Wollstonecraft wanted mothers educated about human anatomy and health care, and counseled them to breast-feed their own children. *A Vindication of the Rights of Woman* (1791–1792) reiterated those **child care** concerns while also advocating children's (especially girls') freedom to "run wild" as integral to their education in reason. Explicitly critiquing Jean-Jacques **Rousseau**'s *Emile* while commending Catherine Macaulay's *Letters on Education*, this feminist classic also proposed a revolutionary national scheme of coeducational secular day schooling in which girls and boys, both rich and poor, learn to befriend one another from early childhood onward, simultaneously educated in loving homes by parents who are mutual friends. No less than men, argued Wollstonecraft, women might thus develop physical, mental, and moral strength needed to claim eternal life for their God-loving souls, in this life becoming independent, productive citizens and intelligent, virtuous mothers who comprehend their child-rearing duties' patriotic significance for a republic free from slavery and other monarchist tyrannies. *See also* Gender and Gender Stereotyping in Early Childhood Education; Parents and Parent Involvement.

Further Readings: Gordon, Lyndall (2005). *Vindication: A life of Mary Wollstonecraft.* New York: HarperCollins; Jump, Harriet Devine (1994). *Mary Wollstonecraft: Writer.* London: Harvester Wheatsheaf. Martin, Jane Roland (1985); Wollstonecraft's daughters. In *Reclaiming a conversation: The ideal of the educated woman.* New Haven, CT: Yale University Press, pp. 70–102; Todd, Janet (2000). *Mary Wollstonecraft: A revolutionary life.* New York: Columbia University Press; Todd, Janet, ed. (2003). *The collected letters of Mary Wollstonecraft.* New York: Columbia University Press; Todd, Janet, and Marilyn Butler, eds. (1989). *The works of Mary Wollstonecraft.* 7 vols. New York: New York University Press.

Susan Laird

Women, Infants and Children (WIC)

The Special Supplemental Nutrition Program for Women, Infants and Children (WIC) is a federal grant program first established by Congress in 1972. Congress created WIC during the 1969 White House Conference on Food, Nutrition, and Health by amending the Child Nutrition Act of 1966, which was part of President Lyndon Johnson's "War on Poverty" initiative. WIC is administered by the Food and Nutrition Service (FNS), a subdivision of the USDA. Grants are awarded to state health agencies or comparable departments in all 50 states, as well as territories and protectorates. The 88 WIC State agencies administer the program through 2,200 local agencies and 9,000 locations. Congress reauthorized it in 2004.

The primary purpose of WIC is to provide nutritious foods and nutritional counseling, plus health and social services referrals to eligible participants, including pregnant, postpartum, and breast-feeding women, plus infants and preschool children up to age five who are at nutrition risk. Participants must meet income guidelines (at or below 185% of the U.S. Poverty Income Guidelines) to be eligible for nutritious food supplements (Food and Nutrition Services, http://www.fns.usda.gov/wic/).

WIC began as a pilot program in 1972, as a result of the 1969 White House Conference on Food, Nutrition, and Health, and became permanently established in 1974. WIC has improved birth outcomes as well as the health of infants and small children. Mothers' participation in WIC during pregnancy and after birth reduces risk of infant death, lowers the prevalence of small-for-gestational-age deliveries, and decreases low-birth-weight births by up to 25 percent. Participation has grown steadily since the inception of the program. For fiscal year 2005, the average monthly participation was just over eight million people, of which children and infants made up over six million of the participants. WIC is the largest and most successful food supplement program in the United States.

In 2002, almost 47 percent of all infants born in the United States were eligible to receive one or more of the benefits. According to one multisite study in five states and Washington, DC, over a two-year period, about 91 percent of eligible women and children received benefits (Black et al., 2004). Numerous studies have found positive outcomes for WIC participants related to birth, diet, infant-feeding practices, immunization rates, savings on health care costs, cognitive development, birth weights, and improved growth rates for children.

The success of the program and the increasing awareness of the value of early intervention, as well as other challenges that this population faces have led to the expansion of services. Currently, client screening includes dental; lead poisoning; verbal, sexual or physical abuse; immunizations; drug, alcohol, and tobacco use; voter registration; and family reading practices. This merger of health, education, and social services places the WIC program in a unique and important position in the field of early childhood, promoting the health and nutrition of young children and their mothers.

Further Readings: Ahluwalia, I. B., V. K. Hogan, L. Grummer-Strawn, W. R. Colville, and A. Peterson (1991). The effect of WIC participation on small-for-gestational-age births: Michigan. *American Journal of Public Health* 88(9), 1374–1377. Child Nutrition and WIC Reauthorization Act of 2004. Special Supplemental Nutrition Program for Women, Infants, and Children (WIC). Available online at http://www.gop.gov/Committeecentral/bills/s2507.asp. Black, M. M., D. B. Cutts, D. A. Frank, J. Geppert, A. Skalicky, S. Levenson, et al. (2004). Special supplemental nutrition program for women, infants, and children participation and infants' growth and health: A multisite surveillance study. *Pediatrics* 114(1), 169–177. Food and Nutrition Services (n.d.). About WIC: How WIC helps. Available online at http://www.fns.usda.gov/wic/aboutwic/howwichelps.htm. Internet FAQ Archives: Online education. Available online at http://www.faqs.org/nutrition/Smi-Z/WIC-Program.html. Lazariu-Bauer, V., M. L. Woelfel, H. Stratton, and R. A. Pruzek (2004). Comparative analysis of effects of early versus late prenatal WIC participation on birth weight: NYS, 1995. *Maternal and Child Health Journal* 8(2), 77–87; Moss, N. E., and K. Carver (1998). The effect of WIC and Medicaid on infant mortality in the United States. *American Journal of Public Health* 88(9), 1354–1361; Schramm, W. F. (1985). WIC prenatal participation and its relationship to newborn Medicaid costs in Missouri: A cost/benefit analysis. *American Journal of Public Health* 75(8), 851–858; The Research Findings on WIC. Center on Budget and Policy Priorities, Washington, DC, March 1994. U.S. Congress (1966). Child Nutrition Act of 1966, Section 17, as amended through PL 92-433, September 26, 1972 and through PL108-323, October 6, 2004. *U.S. Congressional Record*, Washington, DC. Women, Infants and Children Program (WIC). (n.d.). See Prevention Institute, Oakland, CA. Available online at www.preventioninstitute.org.

John P. Manning

The World Forum on Early Care and Education

The World Forum on Early Care and Education is a biennial conference designed to promote an on-going global exchange of ideas on the delivery of quality services for children in diverse settings. The World Forum has two goals for delegates: first, that they acquire a wealth of new ideas and new perspectives to enrich their work; and second, that they develop meaningful relationships that continue into the future with their peers from other nations. The first five World Forums have attracted an average of 500 delegates from eighty nations. The primary audience of the World Forum is early childhood professionals working in organizations or settings where services are delivered to young children. Early childhood trainers, consultants, advocates, researchers, and public officials also have benefited from attending the World Forum. The World Forum is organized by the World Forum Foundation, a non-profit 501(c)3 corporation. For details, go to www.worldforumfoundation.org.

Bonnie Neugebauer and Roger Neugebauer

World Health Organisation (WHO)

The World Health Organisation (WHO) is the international agency within the United Nations system responsible for health. WHO experts produce health guidelines and standards, and help countries address public health issues. WHO also supports and promotes health research. Through WHO, governments can jointly tackle global health problems and improve people's well-being. WHO's member comprises 192 countries and 2 associate members. They meet every year at the World Health Assembly in Geneva to set policy for the Organisation, approve the Organisation's budget, and every five years, to appoint the Director-General. Their work is supported by the thirty-four-member Executive Board, which is elected by the Health Assembly. Six regional committees focus on health matters of a regional nature. WHO and its Member States work with many partners, including UN agencies, donors, nongovernmental organizations, WHO collaborating centers and the private sector. Only through new ways of working and innovative partnerships can we make a difference and achieve our goals. Last but not least, WHO is people. Almost 8,000 public health experts, including doctors, epidemiologists, scientists, managers, administrators, and other people from all over the world work for WHO in 147 country offices, six regional offices and at the headquarters in Geneva, Switzerland.

The work of WHO affects the lives of every person on this planet, every day, from the food we eat and the water we drink, to the safety of the medications we take and the prevention and control of the diseases that threaten. No single country can solve the growing list of health challenges the world faces today. Infectious diseases such as SARS can circle the globe within weeks, moving at the speed of air travel. Health crises in distant countries become everyone's concern as they contribute to poverty and conflict. At the same time, globalization is contributing to the huge gaps between people who have access to health care, and those who don't. All countries must work together if we are to find solutions to these challenges. This is where WHO comes in.

WHO Priorities

Ensuring global health. One priority is to help ensure global health security by detecting emerging threats to health and managing them quickly. This is done by building a global network that helps to find a disease outbreak wherever it strikes, and rallying top experts to stop it fast. This is crucial in times of peace, and when people's lives are thrown into the turmoil of conflict or natural disaster. People in more than forty countries are currently experiencing emergencies as a result of natural disasters, economic crises, or conflict—whether they are highly publicized, such as the Tsunami in South Asia, or hidden and forgotten, such as the ongoing conflict in the Democratic Republic of Congo. WHO works in countries to help national authorities and communities to prepare by strengthening overall capacity to manage all types of crises; to respond by ensuring effective and timely action to address public health priorities; to recover by ensuring that local health systems are functioning; and to mitigate against the effects of crises on public health.

Reducing tobacco use and promoting healthy diet. Another priority is to reduce tobacco use and promote healthy diets and physical activity to speed up progress in the battle against chronic diseases such as cancer, stroke, heart disease and diabetes. Chronic disease cuts lives short, takes mothers and fathers away from their children, and costs economies billions of dollars. The good news is that people can largely prevent and control chronic disease by reducing three risks. WHO—together with countries, the private sector, civil society and others—is working on several key initiatives to stop the growing chronic disease epidemic.

Achieving millennium goals. A third priority is to build up efforts to achieve the Millennium Development Goals through programs to support countries in the fight against HIV/AIDS, TB, and malaria; to improve the health and nutrition of children and women; and to increase people's access to essential medicines. WHO works with countries to dramatically reduce the appalling rates of maternal and child deaths with technical advice and policy support. WHO is working to achieve global water and sanitation targets to ensure environmental sustainability, which is essential for improving people's health. By developing a global partnership, WHO is working to ensure people have universal access to life-saving drugs including anti-retroviral therapy. Eradicating extreme poverty means addressing diseases that cripple workers, ravage families, and kill children before they can contribute to a better future.

Improving access to better health care. Finally, WHO strives for improvements in health care and fairer access in a world where life expectancy ranges from eighty-five years in Japan to just thirty-six years in Sierra Leone. Wherever they live, people need health services. In many countries, there is little money available to spend on health. This results in inadequate hospitals and clinics, a short supply of essential medicines and equipment, and a critical shortage of health workers. Worse, in some parts of the world, large numbers of health workers are dying from the very diseases that they are trying to prevent and treat. WHO works with countries to help them plan, educate and manage the health workforce, for example, by advising on policies to recruit and retain people working in health.

Throughout the world, poor and vulnerable people have less access to health care, and get sicker and die earlier than people who are more privileged. To address these concerns, WHO set up the Commission on the Social Determinants of Health, which brings together leading thinkers on health care and social policy. Their aim is to analyze the social causes of ill health—such as poverty, social exclusion, poor housing and health systems—and actively promote new policies to address them.

WHO's Constitution states that the "enjoyment of the highest attainable standard of health is one of the fundamental rights of every human being." The Organisation is working to make this human right a reality, and to make people everywhere healthier.

For further information, please contact the following: Meena Cabral de Mello, Senior Scientist, Department of Child and Adolescent Health and Development

(CAH), World Health Organisation, 20 Avenue Appia, 1211 Geneva 27, Switzerland, tel +41-22 791 3616 or +41-22 791 3281, fax +41-22 791 4853, emails: cabraldemellomho.int; cah@who.int. *Web site:* http: //www.who.int/about/en

See also United Nations Children's Fund (UNICEF); United Nations Educational, Scientific, and Cultural Organisation (UNESCO).

Meena Cabral de Mello

World Organisation for Early Childhood Education (OMEP)

The World Organisation for Early Childhood Education (OMEP) (known in French as the Organisation Mondiale pour l'Education Prescolaire and in Spanish as the Organización Mundial para la Educación Preescolar) is an international nongovernmental and nonprofit organization dedicated to advancing the interests and overall well-being of children in all parts of the world, regardless of race, sex, religion, national or social origin. Known by the acronym OMEP in all languages, it was founded as a result of concerns about young children in the post–World War II era. Lady Marjory Allen from Great Britain learned that the **United Nations Educational Scientific and Cultural Organisation (UNESCO)**, newly formed to take over the UN's cooperation activities concerning education, science and culture, did not intend to include the preschool age in its field of activity. Lady Allen had the idea that a new international organization was needed to press UNESCO to address the preschool-age group. She connected with Alva Myrdal of Sweden, and after several international meetings with representatives from many nations, OMEP was established at the 1948 meeting in Prague. Alva Myrdal served as the first Chairman with Lady Allen as Vice-Chairman. The organization was highly influential on the activities of UNESCO in its early years.

By the fiftieth anniversary of its founding, OMEP had over sixty member nations from all over the globe. The official languages of the Organisation remain English, French and Spanish, although other languages may be used. The stated Aims and Objectives of the organization include: to defend and promote the rights of the child, with special emphasis on the child's right of education and care worldwide; to encourage the training of personnel for early childhood education and care; and to collect and disseminate information and to facilitate the understanding of the needs of young children worldwide.

All OMEP members belong through National Committees. National Committees gain full membership after a period as a Preparatory Committee and are required to present an annual report of their activities and pay an annual membership fee. Individual memberships are only for those who are forming a Preparatory Committee in a nation when none exists. Members may be professionals from any discipline with an interest in the well-being of children and their families.

The decision-making body is the World Assembly, composed of the Executive Committee and the Presidents of National Committees. The World Assembly is held once a year, rotating to different nations around the world. The Executive Committee is the administrative body and meets twice a year. Regional or National Committee meetings and conferences may also be held. The OMEP journal, *The International Journal of Early Childhood* (*IJEC*), is published twice a year.

During the years of OMEP's existence, progress has been made on behalf of children in such areas as education, nutrition, and jurisprudence; many more nongovernmental organizations are entirely or primarily devoted to children's issues. OMEP retains its close ties with UNESCO and the UNICEF and remains an international network of professionals interested in all the world's children as guided by the **Convention on the Rights of the Child**.

Further Readings: Goutard, Madeleine (1998). *OMEP 1948-1998: Serving children's needs for 50 years.* Quebec: OMEP Secretariat. OMEP Constitution (2004). Revised at World Assembly, Melbourne, Australia, July 2004. Available online at http://omep.vrserver2.cl/. Roberts, Margaret, ed. (1988). *OMEP: The first ten years 1948-1958.* Herts, UK: OMEP Publications Committee and UNESCO.

Leah Adams

Worthy Wage Campaign

The Worthy Wage Campaign is a national grassroots effort, initiated in 1991 by the **Center for the Child Care Workforce** (CCW), to empower early childhood education practitioners to press for solutions to the poor compensation and low status characteristic of the profession. The campaign was instrumental in raising public awareness of the need to improve job conditions in early childhood education; and in promoting activism, policy initiatives, and legislative activity at the federal, state, and local levels.

The campaign combined leadership and empowerment training for teachers and providers in the early childhood education field with media outreach, public policy work, and community organizing. From its inception, the annual focal point was *Worthy Wage Day*, usually celebrated on May 1, a day of locally based outreach and activism on early childhood education workforce concerns. The campaign created a national network of organizations, practitioners, parents, and other advocates. The CCW provided resources and technical support, offered leadership training opportunities, and organized an annual *Summer Institute*.

Originally conceived as a five-year effort, the Worthy Wage Campaign was coordinated by CCW from 1991 to 1999, and has continued since that time on a more informal basis in a variety of U.S. communities, with Worthy Wage Day observances as well as year-round activism on early childhood education workforce issues.

Further Readings: Center for the Child Care Workforce, A Project of the American Federation of Teachers Educational Foundation. See http://www.ccw.org/about_wage.html. Whitebook, Marcy (2002). *Working for worthy wages: The child care compensation movement, 1970-2001.* Berkeley: Center for the Study of Child Care Employment, University of California. Available online at http://www.iir.berkeley.edu/cscce/pdf/worthywages.pdf.

Dori Mornan and Marci Young

Y

Yale University Child Study Center (1911–2005)

The history of child development as a scientific field of study is a story of the twentieth century. Although a few notable pioneers made isolated contributions to the beginnings of this field as early as the mid–nineteenth century, it did not really coalesce as an investigative science until well after the turn of the century. And the Yale Child Study Center stands as one of the few institutions—and the only one in a major university and school of medicine—that has been a major source of leadership in the field from the outset to the present. This achievement has several important roots—the position of the Center in a research university, the support of many Presidents and Deans, the devotion of faculty, and the prescience of the senior leadership. An important component has been the capacity for long-term planning and program development that has resulted from the dedication of senior faculty, who have devoted their careers to the Center, and the continuity of senior leadership. In the ninety-four years of its existence, from 1911 to 2005 the Center has had only five directors, each of whom has helped guide the Center during distinctive epochs in the fields of child development and child and adolescent psychiatry.

Founded in 1911 by Arnold **Gesell**, M.D., the Yale Child Study Center was the first academic department of its kind in the world to be devoted exclusively to the scientific study of children's development. Dr. Gesell pioneered the field of child development at the Yale University Clinic of Child Development. Dr. Gesell devoted his career to the study and documentation of normal and deviant behavior and the application of principles from developmental psychology to the field of pediatrics. In 1948, the Child Study Center was established as an autonomous department within Yale University and the School of Medicine, and under the leadership of Dr. Milton Senn, expanded its role as a center of excellence in research and clinical care. Dr. Albert J. Solnit became the director of the Center in 1967, and was instrumental in further broadening the scope of clinical and research programs. An emphasis continued on early development in infants and young children, serious developmental and neuropsychiatric disorders, and on psychosocial influences affecting the process of development. Programs for disadvantaged children, early educational intervention, crisis intervention, child psychoanalysis, and neuroscience were developed and expanded. Programs of collaboration with other university departments and with state and social service agencies were established. In 1983, Dr. Donald J. Cohen was appointed director and continued the tradition of leadership by researchers and clinicians grounded in child psychiatry, developmental psychology, and developmental pediatrics. In 2002, Dr. Alan Kazdin, as director and building on the well-established research tradition, facilitated an active scholarship on evidence-based treatments and developing innovative psychiatric treatment models for children and adolescents and rigorous empirical evaluation of those models.

The Center continues to maintain major commitments to clinical research in the fields of child development, early childhood education, social policy, child psychiatry, psychoanalysis, and developmental neurobiology. The range of clinical investigative approaches within the Center includes developmental psychology, neurochemistry and neurobiology, genetics, clinical pharmacology, and neuroimaging. In addition, the Center continues its commitment to developing innovative psychiatric treatments for young children and families from infancy through adolescence. The breadth of interest and number of disciplines represented makes for a multidisciplinary scholarly environment well suited to training young investigators and for enhancing collaborative research among midcareer and senior investigators within the department and with faculty in other departments.

Linda C. Mayes

Young Children

Young Children is a bimonthly publication of the **National Association for the Education of Young Children** (NAEYC). This peer-reviewed journal offers early childhood educators and other concerned readers practical and research-based articles on timely topics of interest. NAEYC members receive the journal six times per year as a member benefit and it is also available on a subscription basis.

The journal's readership—more than 100,000 members and subscribers worldwide—work with or on behalf of young children from birth through age eight. Articles might describe research-based teaching strategies, present theories and research, or discuss current policies affecting young children. Each issue includes a cluster of articles that consider different aspects of the same topic. Cluster themes are decided upon many months in advance.

Guidelines for submitting articles and photographs to *Young Children* appear at http://www.journal.naeyc.org/. This Web site also includes information about advertising in the journal, subscriptions, and a search tool.

Young Children sponsors a web-based resource, "Beyond the Journal" (www.journal.naeyc.org/btj). At this site, journal authors can share items such as book lists, planning formats, samples of children's work, or handouts suitable for staff or family workshops. "Beyond the Journal" also includes full-text articles—some reprinted from *Young Children* and some that appear only on the Web—and "Voices of Practitioners," a feature devoted to teacher research.

Derry Koralek

Z

Zero to Three

ZERO TO THREE is a national nonprofit whose mission is to support the healthy development and well-being of babies, toddlers and families. Founded in 1977 by experts from the fields of pediatrics, research science, mental health, child development and other disciplines, ZERO TO THREE is governed by a multidisciplinary, internationally renowned Board of Directors. Its founding members include T. Berry Brazelton, Selma Fraiberg, Stanley Greenspan, J. Ronald Lally, Bernard Levy, Reginald Lourie, Peter Neubauer, Robert Nover, Sally Provence, Julius Richmond, Albert Solnit, and Leon Yarrow.

ZERO TO THREE has built a reputation for translating and disseminating cutting-edge knowledge on how to promote the healthy development of infants, toddlers, and their families. The organization's work strengthens and supports all those working to support families of young children in our society.

ZERO TO THREE helps parents better understand their child's social, emotional, and intellectual development. The organization communicates with parents directly through our parent publications, our award-winning Web site: www.zerotothree.org, and extensive outreach to news media. On average, ZERO TO THREE staff and board are quoted several hundred times per year in news reports.

ZERO TO THREE works with infant/family programs to achieve quality and excellence by focusing on the "behind the scenes" issues of staff training, management, and leadership that directly affect the quality of services provided to children and their families. ZERO TO THREE is also the designated provider of training and consultation for **Early Head Start**.

For professionals, ZERO TO THREE unites passion and knowledge, presenting the latest findings from clinical research, providing forums for the exchange of ideas across academic disciplines, and promoting national leadership on behalf of young children. This is done through such venues as the annual National Training Institute, the Leadership Development Initiative, the Task Force on Culture and Development, the professional Journal: *Zero to Three*, and landmark publications such as *Diagnostic Classification of Mental Health and Developmental Disorders of Infancy and Early Childhood*.

ZERO TO THREE also guides policy makers as they make important decisions regarding what babies and toddlers need for healthy development as well as on successful strategies, components of quality services, and the needed investments on behalf of young children. Projects include the ZERO TO THREE Policy Center, State Early Childhood Policy Leadership Forum, National Infant and Toddler Child Care Initiative, and the Child Welfare Work Group.

In addition, the ZERO TO THREE Press is the publishing arm of the organization. The Press contributes to the definition and advancement of the infant/family field by providing authoritative information, new ideas, and practical resources to promote the healthy development of babies, toddlers, and their families.

For more information, contact ZERO TO THREE at the following addresses: ZERO TO THREE, 2000 M Street, NW, Suite 200, Washington, DC 20036; www.zerotothree.org.

See also Infant Care; Parents and Parent Involvement.

Tom Salyers